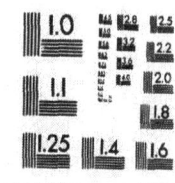

**IMAGE EVALUATION
TEST TARGET (MT-3)**

Photographic
Sciences
Corporation

23 WEST MAIN STREET
WEBSTER, N.Y. 14580
(716) 872-4503

**CIHM
Microfiche
Series
(Monographs)**

**ICMH
Collection de
microfiches
(monographies)**

Canadian Institute for Historical Microreproductions / Institut canadien de microreproductions historiques

© 1993

Technical and Bibliographic Notes / Notes techniques et bibliographiques

The Institute has attempted to obtain the best original copy available for filming. Features of this copy which may be bibliographically unique, which may alter any of the images in the reproduction, or which may significantly change the usual method of filming, are checked below.

L'Institut a microfilmé le meilleur exemplaire qu'il lui a été possible de se procurer. Les détails de cet exemplaire qui sont peut-être uniques du point de vue bibliographique, qui peuvent modifier une image reproduite, ou qui peuvent exiger une modification dans la méthode normale de filmage sont indiqués ci-dessous.

- [ ] Coloured covers/
      Couverture de couleur

- [ ] Covers damaged/
      Couverture endommagée

- [ ] Covers restored and/or laminated/
      Couverture restaurée et/ou pelliculée

- [ ] Cover title missing/
      Le titre de couverture manque

- [ ] Coloured maps/
      Cartes géographiques en couleur

- [ ] Coloured ink (i.e. other than blue or black)/
      Encre de couleur (i.e. autre que bleue ou noire)

- [ ] Coloured plates and/or illustrations/
      Planches et/ou illustrations en couleur

- [ ] Bound with other material/
      Relié avec d'autres documents

- [x] Tight binding may cause shadows or distortion along interior margin/
      La reliure serrée peut causer de l'ombre ou de la distorsion le long de la marge intérieure

- [ ] Blank leaves added during restoration may appear within the text. Whenever possible, these have been omitted from filming/
      Il se peut que certaines pages blanches ajoutées lors d'une restauration apparaissent dans le texte, mais, lorsque cela était possible, ces pages n'ont pas été filmées.

- [ ] Coloured pages/
      Pages de couleur

- [ ] Pages damaged/
      Pages endommagées

- [ ] Pages restored and/or laminated/
      Pages restaurées et/ou pelliculées

- [x] Pages discoloured, stained or foxed/
      Pages décolorées, tachetées ou piquées

- [ ] Pages detached/
      Pages détachées

- [x] Showthrough/
      Transparence

- [x] Quality of print varies/
      Qualité inégale de l'impression

- [ ] Continuous pagination/
      Pagination continue

- [x] Includes index(es)/
      Comprend un (des) index

      Title on header taken from:/
      Le titre de l'en-tête provient:

- [ ] Title page of issue/
      Page de titre de la livraison

- [ ] Caption of issue/
      Titre de départ de la livraison

- [ ] Masthead/
      Générique (périodiques) de la livraison

- [x] Additional comments:/
      Commentaires supplémentaires: Pagination is as follows: p. [7]-539.

This item is filmed at the reduction ratio checked below/
Ce document est filmé au taux de réduction indiqué ci-dessous.

10X	14X	18X	22X	26X	30X
12X	16X	20X ✓	24X	28X	32X

The copy filmed here has been reproduced thanks to the generosity of:

National Library of Canada

The images appearing here are the best quality possible considering the condition and legibility of the original copy and in keeping with the filming contract specifications.

Original copies in printed paper covers are filmed beginning with the front cover and ending on the last page with a printed or illustrated impression, or the back cover when appropriate. All other original copies are filmed beginning on the first page with a printed or illustrated impression, and ending on the last page with a printed or illustrated impression.

The last recorded frame on each microfiche shall contain the symbol ⟶ (meaning "CONTINUED"), or the symbol ▽ (meaning "END"), whichever applies.

Maps, plates, charts, etc., may be filmed at different reduction ratios. Those too large to be entirely included in one exposure are filmed beginning in the upper left hand corner, left to right and top to bottom, as many frames as required. The following diagrams illustrate the method:

L'exemplaire filmé fut reproduit grâce à la générosité de:

Bibliothèque nationale du Canada

Les images suivantes ont été reproduites avec le plus grand soin, compte tenu de la condition et de la netteté de l'exemplaire filmé, et en conformité avec les conditions du contrat de filmage.

Les exemplaires originaux dont la couverture en papier est imprimée sont filmés en commençant par le premier plat et en terminant soit par la dernière page qui comporte une empreinte d'impression ou d'illustration, soit par le second plat, selon le cas. Tous les autres exemplaires originaux sont filmés en commençant par la première page qui comporte une empreinte d'impression ou d'illustration et en terminant par la dernière page qui comporte une telle empreinte.

Un des symboles suivants apparaîtra sur la dernière image de chaque microfiche, selon le cas: le symbole ⟶ signifie "A SUIVRE", le symbole ▽ signifie "FIN".

Les cartes, planches, tableaux, etc., peuvent être filmés à des taux de réduction différents. Lorsque le document est trop grand pour être reproduit en un seul cliché, il est filmé à partir de l'angle supérieur gauche, de gauche à droite, et de haut en bas, en prenant le nombre d'images nécessaire. Les diagrammes suivants illustrent la méthode.

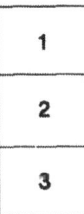

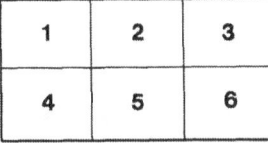

Hou

A PRACT

An I

A C

T

THE

HOUSEHOLD GUIDE

OR

DOMESTIC CYCLOPEDIA.

A PRACTICAL FAMILY PHYSICIAN. HOME REMEDIES
AND HOME TREATMENT ON
ALL DISEASES.

An Instructor on Nursing, Housekeeping and
Home Adornments.

BY
Prof. B. G. JEFFERIS, M. D., Ph. D.,
AND
J. L. NICHOLS, A. M.

ALSO

A COMPLETE COOK BOOK

BY
Mrs. J. L. NICHOLS.

Manufactured and Published by

THE J. L. NICHOLS COMPANY, LIMITED
292 WELLINGTON WEST
TORONTO. - CANADA
AGENTS WANTED

THE GOOD SAMARITAN.

Health and the simplest fare. If thou hast these,
Accompanied with one single steadfast friend—
A conscience which thou dost not fear to bear
To the Great Searcher's eye— and that strong hope
Whose wing ne'er tires, e'en o'er the yawning grave,
Go thou thy way; thou art an emperor,—
Bearing thy crown e'er with thee; go thy way
And thank thy God, who hath bestowed on thee
The gold which monarchs count, but oft in vain.

This Volume will be sent to any address bound in leather on receipt of $1.50

AGENTS WANTED.

Entered according to Act of the Parliament of Canada, in the year one thousand eight hundred and ninety-four, by JOHN A. HERTEL, at the Department of Agriculture.

Entered according to Act of the Parliament of Canada, in the year one thousand eight hundred and ninety-seven, by J. L. NICHOLS & CO. at the Department of Agriculture.

PUBLISHER'S PREFACE.

The object of this volume is, to instruct every housekeeper in economy in household affairs and in the use and application of simple domestic remedies. It may be properly called a book of *Self Instruction* in the art of home doctoring. This work has been especially written to benefit and bless suffering humanity everywhere. The language is simple, and technical terms have been carefully omitted, and the book itself makes up a complete series of Home Lessons in Medicine, which can be read and understood by all classes. There has been rapid progress in the science of medicine in the past few years. Old methods and old receipts have been replaced by new remedies and new methods of application. So it is especially necessary in these times of progress, to have a book which is up to date and abreast of the times.

There are many plants on every farm, in every garden and there are many simple remedies in every home, and other harmless remedies, which can be easily secured, which will relieve pain and cure disease. Simple home remedies and good nursing in ordinary cases, will do more good and give quicker relief than the best practicing physician can with his strong drugs and periodical visits. The most skillful physician can benefit the patient but little without good care and careful nursing in the home. Consequently nursing and caring for the sick is a prominent feature in this work.

This book seems to fill a long-felt want. There have been many books published on medicine, and placed in the hands of the inexperienced homekeepers, but they are not safe guides for anyone to follow, who is unskilled in the art of compounding medicine. Strong drugs are dangerous and their use in the Household Guide is largely discouraged, for they are not safe in the hands of the common people without the direction of a physician. In serious cases of sickness the family physician should always be summoned, but remember that nine-tenths of the ills that afflict mankind can be cured by careful nursing and the application of simple and safe home remedies, and those who secure the Household Guide, will find it ever helpful in giving good counsel in sickness and a safe guide in health.

J. L. NICHOLS.

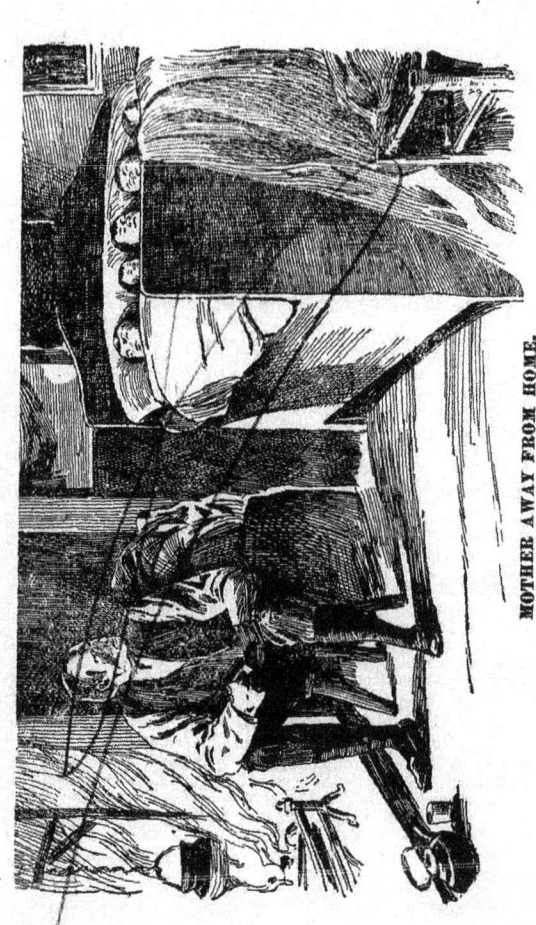
MOTHER AWAY FROM HOME.

TABLE OF CONTENTS.

BOOK I.

Home and Home influences.

Home 22
Woman, Her Power, Qualities.................. 25
The Angel of the Home........................ 25
A Successful Life................................ 26
Mother 26
The Art of Happy Living...................... 27

Health.

Sunshine and Health........................... 29
Healthy Homes.................................... 32
Pure Air... 33
Evils of Window Ventilation.................. 34
How to Keep Well............................... 37
Deep Breathing................................... 38
Evils of Over-eating............................ 40
Time for Digestion.............................. 44
Hints for all Kinds of People................ 44
Tea and Coffee, Why Do We Drink It.... 45
Conditions of Health........................... 46
Occupations 47
Wisdom and Beauty in Rest.................. 49
Laughter, A Great Tonic....................... 50
A Cure for the Blues........................... 51
Charity, Happiness and Length of Days... 52
Sleep 53
Bicycle Exercise 55
Be Good to Yourself............................ 56
As I Grow Old.................................... 56
Why People Die Before Their Time........ 57
Cleanliness 60
Bathing 62
Health in Vegetables and Fruits............ 71
Practical Health Rules......................... 73

Disease... 74

How to Tell Contagious Diseases........... 75
The Wonderful Revelation of the Microscope.. 76
How Microbes or Bacteria Attack the Body... 77

xi

Table of Contents.

How to Destroy Microbes, etc................ 78
Disinfectants 79
Sanitation About the Home.................... 81
Disease Germs in Drinking Water............ 84
Condition of Wells............................... 85
Animals We Drink in Our Water.............. 86
Malaria and Water............................... 87
Accidents and Emergencies, How to Stop
  Bleeding 88
Poisoning, etc..................................... 92
Foreign Bodies in Ear, Nose, and Throat...... 93
Choking, Sunstroke, Coal Gas Suffocation.... 94
Burns 95
Broken Bones 96
Drowning, Snake Bites.......................... 97
Hydrophobia 98
Gas in Well...................................... 99
Poultices, Benefit of, and How to Make Them.. 100
How to Make all Kinds of Bandages.......... 103
Boils, Sprains, Felon........................... 104

Home Remedies and How to Use Them.......... 107
Properties of Salt............................. 108
The Useful Onion............................... 109
Wood Sage, Parsley, Slippery Elm, Red Clover. 110
Gum Arabic, Horehound, American Golden
  Rod, Borax 111
Turpentine, Facts About Eggs.................. 112
How to Gather and Prepare Medical Plants
  and Barks 113
American Poplar, Glycerine.................... 113
Blackberry, Burdock, Garlic, Black Elder, Camphor 114
Cayenne Pepper, Catnip, Cinnamon, Dandelion. 115
Alum, Boneset 116
Dogwood, Ginger, Hops......................... 117
Flax Seed, Horseradish, Juniper, Lemon Juice. 118
Olive Oil, Kerosene............................ 119
Lime, Lobelia, Magnesia, Mustard, Rhubarb.. 120
Pennyroyal, Mandrake, Oakbark, Peach Tree
  Bark 121
Peppermint, Goosegrease, Senna, Sassafras, Sulphur 122
Sweet Flag, Common Baking Soda, Wild
  Cherry, Willow 123
Sage, Saltpetre, Red Pepper 124

Table of Contents.   xiii

Home Remedies and Home Treatment for All Diseases 125
   Colic in Adults 125
   Cramps and Cramp Colic, Colic in Children ... 126
   To Cure Cramps in the Legs, How to Cure Night-Mare 126
   Sleeplessness, Home Remedies 127
   How to Check Vomiting 128
   Neuralgia 129
   Remedies for Neuralgia 130
   Headache, Cause and Cure 131
   Home Treatment for Diarrhea 134
   A Sure Cure for Diarrhea 135
   Pleurisy 135
   Asthma 136
   Lung Fever or Pneumonia 137
   How to Ascertain the State of the Lungs 138
   How to Nurse Typhoid Fever 139
   Typhoid Fever, Malaria 140
   Coughs and Colds 141
   Remedy for Sore Throat 146
   Incontinence of Urine, Diabetes 147
   Gravel, Bright's Disease 148
   Dyspepsia, Egyptian Dyspepsia Cure 149
   Jaundice, Bilious Attacks 151
   A Stomach's Plea 152
   Constipation 152
   Rheumatism 155
   Nervousness 156
   Erysipelas and Cancer, Eczema 157
   Vaccination, Remedy for Small Pox, Heartburn 158
   Saving the Eyes 159
   How to Doctor Sore Eyes 160
   How to Cure the Grippe, Dysentery 161
   Frost Bites and Injuries from Rusty Nails 162
   How to Cure Apoplexy, Bad Breath and Quinsy 163
   How to Cure Piles, Cholera Morbus, Night Sweats 164
   How to Cure the Itch 165
   How to Cure Dyspepsia and Weak Lungs 166
   A Palatable Laxative 167
How to Make all Kinds of Ointments, Liniments, and Salves 168
Uses of Hot Water 173
Brief History of Medicine 176

Chinese Doctors 177
Medicines, Amount for a Dose..................... 178
How to Give Homeopathic Medicines.............. 179
Homeopathic Remedies for More than One Hundred Diseases 180
Effects of Alcohol and Cigarette Smoking........... 186
Massage 192

Sick Room Hints.

    Helps for the Sick Room...................... 201
    An Easy Bed Hammock for the Sick.......... 203
    Rules for Home Nursing...................... 204
    Feeding the Sick............................. 206

Care and Feeding of Infants 210

    A Well Cared-for Baby....................... 211
    Feeding Infants.............................. 213
    Infantile Convulsions........................ 213
    Warning to Mothers.......................... 215
    How to Preserve the Health and Life of Infants During Hot Weather.................. 216
    How to Keep a Baby Well.................... 221
    Developing Healthy Children................. 223
    Bottle Feeding............................... 225
    The Perils of Teething....................... 226
    How to Make Children Healthy, Vigorous and Beautiful 227
    Home Treatment for Diseases of Children...... 229
    An Ailing Child.............................. 230
    Little Mischief.............................. 231
    Nervous Children............................ 232
    Hiccough 232
    Lard and Salt............................... 233
    Colic, Stomach and Bowel Trouble............ 234
    How to Treat Croup......................... 235
    Worms 237
    Constipation, Cheerfulness and Health........ 238
    Diphtheria and Scarlet Fever................ 238
    Scarlet Fever 239
    Home Treatment of Diphtheria............... 240
    Measles and Chicken-pox.................... 241
    Whooping Cough 242
    Mumps 243
    Diarrhea, Summer Complaint, Teething....... 244

BOOK II.

Figure, Form and Beauty 245
    Natural Beauty 246
    Preserving the Figure....................... 247
    A Gymnasium Director's Advice.............. 248
    Cure for Round Shoulders................... 249
    Beauty 250
    To Acquire a Beautiful Form................ 252
    Cosmetics and Cheerfulness.................. 254
    Physical Culture 254
    Take Life as it Comes....................... 256
    Practical Hints on Complexion............... 256
    Skin Troubles 257
    How to Obtain and Preserve a Beautiful Complexion 259
    Cures for Sunburn........................... 260
    How to Remove Freckles, Blackheads, etc..... 261
    How to Remove Pimples and Wrinkles......... 262
    Toilet Hints 263
    How to Take Care of the Teeth.............. 265
    Cleaning the Teeth.......................... 266
    How to Keep the Teeth White, Tooth Powder. 268
    How to Take Care of the Hands, Chapped Hands 269
    Warts, Moles 270
    Cosmetics 271
    How Ladies Should Dress..................... 274
    Hair Dressing............................... 275
    Styles of Wearing the Hair.................. 276
    Structure of the Hair....................... 278
    Falling Out of the Hair..................... 279
    How to Care for the Hair.................... 280
    Glossiness 281
    Dandruff 281
    Hair Oil 281
    Dyeing, Gray Hairs, Waving the Hair, Hair Brushes 282
    Hair Tonics, Shampoos, etc.................. 283
    Hints on Shaving............................ 286
    How to Cure Corns, Chilblains, Ingrowing Nails 289
    How to Cure Bunions......................... 290
    Effects of Wearing Tight Shoes.............. 291
    Pointers About Footwear..................... 292

xvi *Table of Contents.*

Etiquette.
Hints and Helps on Good Behavior............ 293
Practical Rules................................ 296
Etiquette in Speech........................... 299
Etiquette of Dress and Habits................. 300
Etiquette on the Street....................... 301
Etiquette of Calls............................ 302
Practical Rules on Table Manners.............. 303
Social Duties................................. 305
Politeness 309

Invitations.
How to Write Invitations, Forms............... 312

Amusements 318
How to Amuse Children......................... 319
Ring Games and Frolics for Children's Parties. 321
Children's March.............................. 323
Quotation Hunt................................ 324
Distinguished Guests.......................... 324
Cross Questions and Crooked Answers........... 325
Placing Water in a Drinking Glass Upside Down 326
Guessing 326

BOOK III.

The Housekeeper............................... 328
A Model Housewife............................. 329
How to Manage to be Happy..................... 329
Good Rules for the Mistress................... 332
Good Rules for the Servant.................... 333
The Servant Question.......................... 334

Home Adornments................................ 337
Wall Decorations.............................. 338
Furniture, Sitting Room, Bed Room, Kitchen.. 339
Pot-pourri of Roses........................... 341
Rustic Flower Stand........................... 342
Sewing Box.................................... 342
Decorating with Natural Objects............... 343

The Hygiene of the Bed Room 345
Bed and Bedding............................... 346
Airing Sleeping Rooms......................... 347
Home Made Mattresses.......................... 348

Table of Contents. xvii

The **Dining Room** 349
Kitchen Utensils 351
   Household Measures and Weights............. 354
Household Hints 356
   Soda and Charcoal........................ 357
   Lamps and Their Care..................... 358
   Cleaning a Stove......................... 359
   How to Keep Stoves from Rusting........... 359
Family Receipts.............................. 361
   Scientific Method of Removing Stains........ 362
   Removing Stains of all Kinds............... 363
   Uses of Borax............................
   How to Clean Brass, Silver, Copper.......... 368
   How to Polish Nickel-plate................. 369
   How to Remove Rust from Knives........... 369
   How to Remove Stains from Furniture....... 370
   Furniture Polish........................... 371
   Staining a Floor.......................... 372
   Hard Wood Floors........................ 372
   How to Break a String..................... 373
   How to Make Permanent White Wash....... 374
   How to Purify Sinks and Drains............. 374
   How to Make a Perfect Hole in a Piece of Glass 374
   How to Remove a Glass Stopper............ 375
   How to Remove Fly Spots, How to Prepare
      Kalsomine 375
   How to Clean Carpets, Matting, etc.......... 376
   Suggestion for Sweeping Day, Sponging Car-
      pets 377
   Practical Rules for Builders................. 378
   To Prevent Rust on Iron.................... 379
   To Polish Nickel-plate, Zinc, and Clean Rusty
      Steel 379
   Cider Vinegar............................ 380
   Vinegar for Pickles........................ 380
   How to Make Vinegar without Fruit......... 381
   How to Raise Canaries..................... 382
   How to Keep Flowers Fresh................ 383
   How to Enlarge Portraits and Pictures...... 384
   How to Take Measures for Patterns......... 385
   How to Measure for Suit of Clothes.......... 386
   To Clean Neckties, Laces and Ribbons....... 387
   How to Dye all Kinds of Cloth.............. 388

Table of Contents

How to Mix Paints........................... 389
How to Tan Hides with Hair On............ 390
How to Make all Kinds of Glue............. 391
Cheap and Beautiful Ink..................... 392
Inks of all Kinds............................ 393
Blacking, Oil and Dressing for Boots........ 394
Mucilage for Home and Business Use....... 395
How to Improve Leather..................... 396
To Clean Statuary and Marble............... 397
How to Remove Ink Stains.................. 397

Reading the Paper 398

BOOK IV.

Complete Cook Book............................. 399
The Art of Cooking........................... 400
Hints for the Cook............................ 401
Hints on Seasoning........................... 402
Golden Rules for the Kitchen................. 403
Advice to Cooks.............................. 404
Meats, Cooking, Frying, Roasting, Broiling, etc 404
How to Make Meats Tender.................. 407
Stuffed Beef Heart, Ham Cakes............... 408
How to Pickle Beef, Ham and Tongue........ 409
How to Pack Pork............................ 409
Sausages 410
Roasted Turkey............................... 410
Smothered and Fricasseed Chicken........... 411
Deviled Turkey................................ 411
How to Cook all Kinds of Poultry............ 412
How to Carve Turkey, Duck, Chicken........ 413
Stewed Chicken and Dumplings.............. 414
How to Prepare and Cook all Kinds of Fish.. 415
How to Use Canned Salmon.................. 415
Oysters, Soup, Patties, etc.................... 416
How to Make all Kinds of Omelets........... 418
New Egg Dishes.............................. 420
New Dishes of Rice........................... 421
Potatoes 422
Delicious Dishes of Sweet Potatoes........... 424
Vegetable Soup............................... 425
Novel Vegetable Dishes....................... 426
New Ways for Cooking Corn................. 427
How to Make all Kinds of Catsups, Pickles, Salads, etc................................. 429

Table of Contents.

Coffee, a Good Cup of Tea 433
Prize Bread Receipt 434
Breakfast Breads and Cakes 434
How to Make all Kinds of Cakes 437
How to Make all Kinds of Frostings 447
How to Make all Kinds of Cookies 450
Pies and Tarts 453
How to Make all Kinds of Puddings 455
How to Make all Kinds of Pudding Sauces... 464
How to Make Frozen or Other Desserts 465
How to Can all Kinds of Fruit 467
How to Make Jellies 469
How to Make Jams 471
How to Make all Kinds of Preserves 472
How to Make Drinks for the Sick 474
How to Cook all Kinds of Relishes for the Sick 477
Bills of Fare 483
Cold Dinners 485
How to Make Your Own Candies 486

BOOK V.

In the Laundry 491
 How to Make Hard Soap 492
 How to Polish Shirt Bosoms 492
 The Washing of Flannels 493
 How Table Linen Should be Laundered 494
 Silk Handkercheifs, Silk Socks 495
 How to Whiten Clothes 496

How to Destroy House Insects 497
 Fleas 497
 Carpet Bugs 498
 Clothes Moths 499
 Common Moth 500
 To Keep Furs from Moths 501
 To Get Rid of Bed Bugs 502
 Book Moths 503
 Remedies for Destroying Mosquitoes and Flies. 504
 Cure for Wasp Stings 504
 Trapping Ants 505
 Destroying Ants in House and Lawn 506
 How to Get Rid of Rats 507
 Novel but Sure Remedy for Extermination of
  Mice 508

xx   *Table of Contents.*

Yard and Garden.
    Worms on Rose Bushes...................... 509
    Flower-beds and Lawns, Flower Gardens...... 509
    Sweet Peas................................. 510
    Cabbage Worms............................. 511
    Worms on Gooseberry and Currant Bushes ... 512
    Plant Lice 512

Poultry... 513
    Practical Rules for Keeping Poultry.......... 513
    Chicken Cholera, Asthma, Loss of Feathers,
      Gapes 515
    To Destroy Lice............................. 516
    To Pickle Eggs............................. 517
    What to Feed............................... 519
    Poultry Pointers............................. 519

A Complete Medical Dictionary.................... 522

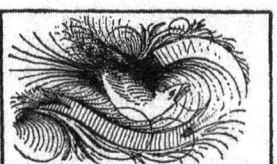

BOOK I.

HOME AND HOME INFLUENCES.

HEALTH AND HAPPINESS.

DISEASE AND DISEASE GERMS.

DISINFECTANTS AND SANITATION.

A THOUSAND HOME REMEDIES FOR DISEASES.

MEDICINES AND MEDICAL TREATMENT.

EFFECTS OF ALCOHOL AND TOBACCO.

MASSAGE.

SICK ROOM HINTS.

TREATMENT OF INFANTS AND CHILDREN.

HOME.

1. The Sublimest Moment in a Young Man's Life.—The sublimest moment in a young man's life is when he can take his newly-wed wife by the hand and lead her under his own roof and say to her, "This is our home." Married life, with the comfort of children, weaves threads of golden joy into the cares and toils of life. No pleasures, no enjoyment can excel the comforts and contentment of a happy home.

2. Home! What a Hallowed Name.—How full of enchantment and how dear to the heart! Home is the magic circle within which the weary spirit finds refuge ; it is the sacred asylum to which the care-worn heart retreats to find rest from the toils and inquietudes of life.

3. **What is Home?**—Ask the lone wanderer as he plods his tedious way, bent with the weight of age, and white with the frost of years, ask him, what is home ? He will tell you, "it is a green spot in memory ; an oasis in the desert ; a center about which the fondest recollections of his grief-oppressed heart cling with all the tenacity of youth's first love. It was once a glorious, a happy reality, but now it rests only as an image of the mind."

4. **Tender Associations.**—Home ! that name touches every fiber of the soul, and strikes every chord of the human heart with its angelic fingers. Nothing but death can break the spell. What tender associations are linked with home! What pleasing images and deep emotions it awakens ! It calls up the fondest memories of life and opens in our nature the purest, deepest, richest gush of consecrated thought and feeling. Next to religion, the deepest and most ineradicable sentiment in the human soul is that of home affections. Every heart vibrates to this theme.

5. **Stronger than Death.**—Home has an influence which is stronger than death. It is a law to our hearts, and binds us with a spell which neither time nor change can break ; the darkest villainies which have disgraced humanity cannot neutralize it. Gray-haired and demon guilt will make his dismal cell the sacred urn of tears wept over the memories of home, and these will soften and melt into tears of penitence even the heart of adamant.

6. **Home of My Childhood!**—What words fall upon the ear with so much music in their cadence as those which recall the scenes of innocent and happy childhood, now numbered with the memories of the past! How fond recollection delights to dwell upon the events which marked our early pathway, when the unbroken home circle presented a scene of loveliness vainly sought but in the bosom of a happy family! Intervening years have not dimmed the vivid coloring with which memory has adorned those joyous hours of youthful innocence.

7. **Peace at Home.**—Peace at home, that is the boon. "He is happiest, be he king or peasant, who finds peace in his home." Home should be made so truly home that the weary tempted heart could turn toward it anywhere on the dusty highway of life and receive light and strength; should be the sacred refuge of our lives, whether rich or poor. The ties that bind the wealthy and the proud to home may

be forged on earth, but those which link the poor man to his humble hearth are of true metal and bear the stamp of heaven.

8. Husband and Wife.—There is nothing in the world which is so venerable as the character of parents; nothing so intimate and endearing as the relation of husband and wife; nothing so tender as that of children; nothing so lovely as those brothers and sisters. The little circle is made one by a singular union of the affections. The only fountain in the wilderness of life, where man drinks of water totally unmixed with bitter ingredients, is that which gushes for him in the calm and shady recess of domestic life.

CLIFF DWELLERS—THE FIRST INHABITANTS OF EARTH.

9. Pleasure.—Pleasure may heat the heart with artificial excitement, ambition may delude it with golden dreams, war may eradicate its fine fibers and diminish its sensitiveness, but it is only domestic love that can render it truly happy!

10. Home.—Let thrones rot and empires wither. Home! Let the world die in earthquake struggles, and be buried amid procession of planets and dirge of spheres. Home! Let everlasting ages roll in irresistible sweep. Home! No sorrow, no crying, no tears, no death; but home! Sweet home! Beautiful home! Glorious home! Everlasting home! Home with each other! Home with angels! Home with God! Home, home! Through the rich grace of our Redeemer, may we all reach it.

WOMAN.

The organization of the home depends, for the most part, upon woman. She is the queen of domestic life. The management of the home necessarily depends upon her. Her character, her temper, her power of organization, her business management is what brings comfort and happiness to the home.

Her Power.— It is generally in woman's power to make home a true home, where comfort and happiness are supreme. True, men whose nobler powers are blunted and whose appetites are in control may be able to defeat much of woman's work. And yet where there is any manhood left, there will be something at least to recognize and encourage the work of the faithful housewife. Men are only apparently leaders. Close scrutiny will generally reveal a woman's power, a woman's encouragement, a woman's love behind them. In her hands rests the power to uplift man from moral degradation.

"They say that man is mighty,
He governs land and sea,
He wields a mighty sceptre,
O'er lesser powers that be;
But a mightier power and stronger
Man from his throne has hurled,
And the hand that rocks the cradle
Is the hand that rules the world."

Qualities.—First among woman's qualities is the intelligent use of her hands and fingers. The tidy, handy, managing woman, at whose fingers' ends are wisdom and virtue, is indispensable to the comfort of a household. Then, again, the successful housewife is a woman of method. Without method in the household, confusion, disorder, and discontent must hold sway. Method and punctuality in the home disperse many clouds of grumblings and put to flight a host of little nuisances that tend to make the home unhappy. Punctuality in preparing breakfast and dinner and in everything that tends to add to the comfort of the home is essential to the happiness of the home. To these qualities add a becoming taste in little things that gives to the humblest home beauty and elegance, and a model home can be found even where poverty exists.

The Angel of the Home.—She does not make any fuss about it, nor ask to have a reporter at her elbow. But her sunny heart of self-forgetting love will not let her hands be at rest while there is any bit of helpful service she can render. If she can, without observation, slip the burnt roll or undercrust on her plate, it is done. If some one must stay at home when there is a day's outing, she tells, with music in every tone, how glad she will be to be left quietly behind and have time all to herself to do ever so many things she has in mind. And none suspect from word or tone how great the sacrifice to give up the pleasure.

Her quick eye detects the oversight or neglect on the part of another, and she quickly hastens to remedy the matter, careful that none shall know her hand has made up another's ilure. Is a harsh round of judgment started by some ill-advised criticism, she deftly and tenderly drops the gentlest, the sweetest possible word for the criticised one, and switches the conversation to other topics.

Do we not all recognize this "angel"? We call her mother, wife, sister. In the glory-land they will call her saint.

A Successful Life is nothing more nor less for man or for woman than living as well as we know how and doing the very best that we can. Success cannot be measured by fame, wealth or station. The life of the humblest woman in the land, if well lived, is as successful as is that of the woman, who, with greater opportunities, is enabled to make the results of her works reach farther. Some of us must live for the few, as others again must live for the many. But both lives are successful. Each of us in this world influences some other being, and it is the quality of our influence, and not the number we influence, which makes our lives successful in the eyes of God. We may believe that we go to our graves unknown and unsung, but not one of us goes out from this world without leaving an impression, either for the good or the bad. And the kind of impression we make while we live, and leave when we die, is the difference between successful and unsuccessful living.

MOTHER.

To her care have been intrusted
All the heroes of all lands;
Still the fate of church and nation
Holds she in her slender hands,
Guiding willful feet and faltering
On through childhood's happy years,
On through youth with its temptations,

With its hopes, its doubts, its fears;
Cultivating all that's noble,
Gently chiding all that's wrong,
Till her children gather round her,
Men and women, pure and strong.
By the quiet ministrations,
In the little realm of home,
For the structure of the ages,
She hath laid the corner-stone.

THIS SWEET LITTLE WOMAN O' MINE.

She ain't any bit of a angel—
  This sweet little woman o' mine;
She's jest a plain woman,
An' purty much human—
  This sweet little woman o' mine.

Fer what would I do with a angel
  When I looked fer the firelight's shine?
When six little sinners
Air wantin' their dinners?
  No! Give me this woman o' mine!

I've hearn lots o' women called "angels,"
  An' lots o' 'em thought it wuz fine;
But give 'em the feathers,
An' me, in all weathers,
  This sweet little woman o' mine!

I jest ain't got nuthin' ag'in em—
  These angels—they're good in their line;
But they're sorter above me!
Thank God that she'll love me—
  This dear little woman o' mine!

THE ART OF HAPPY LIVING.

Yes, and an art it is that deserves the attention and study of all. It includes the art of making the best of everything and should be cultivated and developed by parents and teachers, and perfected by intelligent self-culture. Happiness is not an indescribable something always beyond one's grasp, but is in the reach of all, if we but look for it in the common path of life, in the ordinary routine of every day duty.

Not in Wealth.—It is a serious, but very common error to assume that wealth brings happiness. While abundant means may be convenient, these do not usually or necessarily add to the happiness of the possessor, but on the other hand, sometimes bring care and anxiety, which drive out the last rays of happy living. The humblest lot, although associated with toil, may become a little paradise on earth, when affiliated with it are a seeing eye, a feeling heart, a helping hand, an elevating purpose, and an intelligent effort at self-improvement. Without these essentials even wealth becomes a burden.

Home Atmosphere.—Of all the minor arts and sciences none is more delightful in itself or richer in its compensations than the creation of the home atmosphere; and although the ability to make a home is a natural endowment of some fortunate beings, it is not the less a talent which may be cultivated, and which will continually repay the time and care devoted to its acquirement.

Houses and Homes.—There are houses and there are homes, and it must be a very indifferent or a very selfish woman who cannot evolve a home from the least promising elements, and take pride in improving it to the utmost.

Gift of Arrangement.—The majority of women possess what Hawthorne calls "the gift of practical arrangement," which is, he continues, "a kind of natural magic that enables these favored ones to bring out the hidden capabilities of things around them, and particularly to give a look of habitableness to any place which, for however brief a period, may happen to be their home." Under the skillful touch of these persons, unpromising or incongruous materials are brought into subjection, harmonious arrangements replace stiff outlines, defects are concealed and good points emphasized, so that rooms which have been hard and forbidding assume a genial and inviting aspect. These clever folks not only work their spells upon unlovely surroundings; they accomplish what is even more difficult by giving an air of domesticity and use to the most splendid apartments, effectually dispelling that soulless magnificence which is so depressing to warm-hearted every-day people.

Order.—Order, indeed, must reign in every true home and there must be some regulations for the general good which are gently but firmly enforced. Sometimes mists of discontent or sharp gusts of rebellion darken and disturb the air, but these become fewer as the dear mother way is recognized to be always the best way.

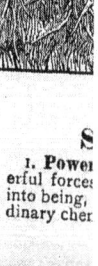

A MORNING WALK.

Sunlight and Health.

1. **Power of Sunlight.**—Sunlight is one of the most powerful forces in nature, kindling the whole vegetable world into being, and making animal life possible by its extraordinary chemical agency. (29)

2. Seclusion from Sunshine.—Seclusion from sunshine is one of the great misfortunes of our civilized life. The same cause which makes the potato vines white and sickly when grown in dark cellars, operates to produce the pale, sickly girls that are reared in our parlors. Expose either to the rays of the sun, and they begin to show color, health and strength.

3. Philosophy of the Influence of Sunlight.—Recent discoveries seem to prove that there is conveyed to animals, by the direct action of the sun's rays, a subtle current of iron. It does not exist in light, or but very slightly, if at all, but it is a part of the sun's rays. Therefore, we must enjoy these rays if we would feel their full effect. This iron it is which is supposed to give color to plants and animals, and to impart strength and beauty. With strength and beauty come health and good spirits, and despondency and fear are banished.

4. Sunlight and Plants.—It is well known that no valuable plant can grow well without being visited by the direct rays of the sun; no plant can bear seed, no fruit can ripen without it. Any vine grown in the dark is white and strengthless. Grass, grain and flowers do not thrive under the shadow of a tree.

5. Sunlight and Domestic Animals.—It is well known that no valuable domestic animals can thrive without being visited often by the sunshine. The fish of the Mammoth Cave are white; their eyes are not opened, because they have never felt the glorious light; they are weak and imperfect, a kind of idiots, if fish are liable to that wretchedness. Swine which are shut under the farmer's barns, and where everything is favorable except the lack of sunshine, do not thrive as well as those which have the ordinary run in the open air. Cows and horses stalled continuously in dark stables become feeble and unhealthy, and become useless in less than half the time of those which run in the open air, or whose stalls permit them to enjoy the influence of the sunlight. The same is true of all other domestic animals.

6. Sunlight and Human Life.—Sir James Wylie says that "the cases of disease on the dark side of an extensive barrack at St. Petersburgh, have been uniformly, for many years, in the proportion of three to one to those on the side exposed to strong light."

7. Sunlight and Miners.—The lack of pure light and pure air in mines tells seriously upon the health of miners. "Fourcault affirms that where life is prolonged to the average term, the evil effects of the want of light are seen in the stunted forms and general deterioration of the human race. It appears that the inhabitants of the arrondissement of Chimay, in Belgium, three thousand in number, are engaged partly as coal miners, and partly as field laborers. The latter are robust, and readily supply their proper number of recruits to the army; while among the miners it is in most years impossible to find a man who is not ineligible from bodily deformity or arrest of physical development.

8. **The Sunlight and Blinds.**—"I wish God had never permitted man to invent green blinds," said a thoughtful and brilliant woman. Why did she say it? Because she saw, wherever she went over our fair and sunshiny land, that green blinds were closely shut upon our comfortable houses, excluding the sun's light, which we may be sure God sends down for some blessed purpose. That blessed purpose is to promote growth, to give strength, to impart color, to gild with beauty, to inspire good thoughts, and to insure light hearts and cheerful faces.

9. **Sunlight and Sleep.**—Sleepless people—and they are many in America—should court the sun. The very worst soporific is laudanum, and the very best sunshine. Therefore, it is very plain that poor sleepers should pass many hours in the day in sunshine, and as few as possible in the shade.

10. **Give the Children Sunshine.**—Children need sunshine quite as much as flowers do. Half an hour is not enough. Several hours are required. The most beautiful flowers that ever studded a meadow could not be made half so beautiful without days and days of the glad light that streams through space. Light for children. Sunshine for the little elves that gladden this otherwise gloomy earth. Deal it out in generous fullness to them. Let the nursery be in the sunshine. Better plant roses on the dark side of an iceberg than rear babies and children in rooms and alleys stinted of the light that makes life.

11. **Scrofula.**—Plants and animals become scrofulous if deprived of light. Get all the light and all the sunshine you can; for all comes from the sun. The sun is the great fountain of light and life.

Healthy Homes.

HEALTHY HOMES.

"Cleanliness is the elegance of the poor."—English Proverb.

"Virtue never dwelt long with filth and nastiness."—Count Rumford.

Health is wealth. Almost all the fevers, cholera, and other plagues result from poisoned air, coming from bad drains, uncleaned streets, and badly kept back yards. House slops and remnants of the table, or decaying vegetables should never be allowed to be thrown in the back yard. Good drains, clean cellars, and general cleanliness about the house, are the only safeguards of health.

Pure air and good ventilation are just as necessary in the house as about the house. Whenever a number of persons live together the atmosphere becomes poisoned, unless means are provided for its constant change and renovation. The death rate is much greater in crowded tenement houses than in the well ventilated and regulated homes of the wealthier classes. Diphtheria, scarlet fever, and other dreaded contagious diseases are more prevalent and fatal in our large cities than in the country or smaller towns.

IMPURE AIR MAKES THE GRAVEYARD RICH.

PURE AIR.

Necessity.—The prime necessity of life is pure air. The body receives its nourishment from food taken into the stomach. This is essential to life, but just as important is the food for the lungs so generously provided in the pure, fresh air all around us. We insist upon it that we must have food for the stomach, but how often do we deprive ourselves of that which is just as important to health and happiness—pure air. A person may live for several weeks without taking food. He may be deprived of drink for some days without serious injury, but deprive him of air but for a few minutes and death will result.

Impure Air.—Those who spend much of the time in the open air are not subjected to the evil effects of impure air as are those who are required to spend most of their time indoors. And yet, all may suffer from the evil effects of a poorly ventilated bedroom, or a cellar where decaying vegetables are sending forth through crevices and cracks into ever apartment of the house poisonous and disease-producing air. The sources of impure air are diverse and manifold.

84 Pure Air.

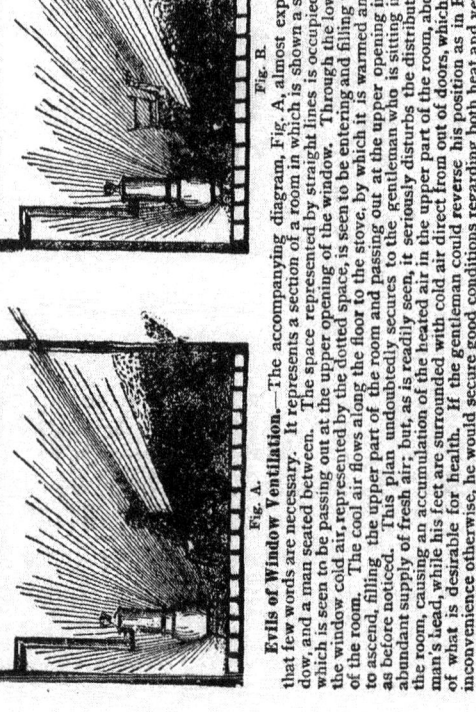

Fig. A.   Fig. B.

Evils of Window Ventilation.—The accompanying diagram, Fig. A, almost explains itself, so that few words are necessary. It represents a section of a room in which is shown a stove, one window, and a man seated between. The space represented by straight lines is occupied by warm air, which is seen to be passing out at the upper opening of the window. Through the lower opening in the window cold air, represented by the dotted space, is seen to be entering and filling the lower part of the room. The cool air flows along the floor to the stove, by which it is warmed and thus caused to ascend, filling the upper part of the room and passing out at the upper opening in the window, as before noticed. This plan undoubtedly secures to the gentleman who is sitting in the chair an abundant supply of fresh air; but, as is readily seen, it seriously disturbs the distribution of heat in the room, causing an accumulation of the heated air in the upper part of the room, about the gentleman's head, while his feet are surrounded with cold air direct from out of doors, which is the reverse of what is desirable for health. If the gentleman could reverse his position as in Fig. B, without inconvenience otherwise, he would secure good conditions regarding both heat and ventilation.

The above illustrations are kindly furnished us by Good Health Publishing Company, Battle Creek, Mich.

Our Duty.—Our duty lies in removing everything from dwelling and yard that may give rise to or produce foul air, and on the other hand in providing for ventilation of every room, especially the bedroom.

Neglecting Ventilation.—That dull feeling in the morning, that headache, that restlessness at night is very frequently the result of bad ventilation or no ventilation at all. No one should occupy a bedroom that does not permit the foul air to escape, and pure air to enter. Many of the diseases to which men are subject are contracted by breathing impure air.

How to Ventilate.—Fresh air can be obtained only from without. Cold air will injure no one, but drafts of cold upon only a part of the body may occasion severe cold. In all attempts to ventilate, drafts should be avoided. A room can frequently be ventilated without causing drafts by lowering a window at the top on one side of a room, and raising another a little at the bottom on the opposite side. There should be two openings, one for the pure air to come in at and another for the bad air to go out at.

Another Method.—A very simple method to ventilate and still avoid drafts is to take a board the length of the window casing and about three or four inches wide. Place this board under the lower sash, thus making an opening between the two sashes where they overlap. In this way the air will enter and be thrown toward the ceiling, and a draft will be avoided. Whatever the method adopted, be sure that ventilation is not neglected. Ventilate your rooms well if you would prolong life.

Night Air.—Some persons have great prejudice against night air. Although night air may be damp and at times not so healthful, yet if we wish to breathe at all at night we must breathe night air, the only kind there is at night. The dangers of night air are largely imaginative, and at the most are nothing to be compared to the dangers and evils of badly ventilated and over-heated rooms.

Plants in a Bed-room.—The theory that plants kept in bedrooms are injurious is contradicted by the best authorities. It is found that taking the whole twenty-four hours through, they do not surcharge the air with carbonic acid gas. Plants purify the air during the night as well as during the day. Strongly scented plants may, by the odors which they emit, be unpleasant to the senses of a nervous person, but aside from this, plants with the cheerful aspect which they give to a room, with the pleasant recreation which their care affords, and with their tendency to remove impurities from the air, are a blessing rather than an injury.

Quantity of Air.—Every person above fourteen years of age requires about six hundred cubic feet of shut-up space to breathe in during the twenty-four hours. If he sleeps in a room of smaller dimensions, he will suffer more or less the serious results of poisoned air. Shut up a mouse in a glass bottle and it will gradually die, by re-breathing its own breath. About half the children born in some manufacturing towns die before they are five years old, principally because they want pure air. Every sleeping room, winter and summer, should have an open window during the night, and the room and the bedding should be thoroughly aired every morning. Remember that pure air in and about the home will do more to preserve health than all medicines.

Cold Air.—Don't be afraid to go out of doors because it is a little colder than usual. The cold air will not hurt you if you are properly protected, and take exercise enough to keep the circulation active. On the contrary, it will do you good. It will purify your blood, it will strengthen your lungs, it will improve your digestion, it will afford a healthy, natural stimulus to your torpid circulation, and strengthen and energize your whole system. The injury which often results from going into a cold atmosphere is occasioned by a lack of protection to some part of the body, exposure to strong drafts, or from breathing through the mouth. Avoid these, and you are safe. Don't be afraid to sleep in a cold room at night with the window a little open. Cold air, if pure, will not hurt you at night any more than in the day, if you are protected by sufficient clothing, and by breathing through the nostrils. If you do not breathe thus, acquire the habit as soon as possible.

Colds and Fevers.—If you wish to be subject to colds, coughs, and fevers, shut yourself in close, hot rooms day and night. If you wish to be free from their companionship, always have plenty of pure air to breathe night and day, take daily outdoor exercise, regardless of the weather, except as to clothing protection.

Providence Blamed.—It is frequently the case that children and infants suffer from bad air and bad air often does its part toward diseasing an infant. The loss of children in this way is generally attributed to "a special dispensation of Providence," and the mother does not stop to think that bad air, improper food and management all had their part in bringing on the disease and making it fatal.

HOW TO KEEP WELL.

The greatest treasure of all—health.

All the gold in the world can not pay for the loss of it.

The secret of how to remain in good health, and, with reasonable care, live to be a hundred, is worth more than the richest gold mine that has been discovered.

Health is a comparative term.

Many persons enjoy excellent health, but through ignorance or carelessness, or both, bring upon themselves diseases that result in much suffering and even premature death. Every person in justice to himself, his family, and the public in general, should devote some time to a careful study of the laws of health. The errors most commonly committed are those most commonly borne in mind. He who assumes habits of moderation, in regular exercise and diet will be able to do much toward lengthening his life. Lack of regular exercise, excesses in eating or drinking, and exclusive devotion to exacting cares, will undermine the strongest constitution. Take good care of yourself while in health. Prize it above millions of gold. When health is gone money can not buy it back again.

Definition of Health.—Sir Andrew Clarke declares that one-half of the population of London is permanently ill. His definition of health is: That state in which the body is not consciously present to us; that state in which work is easy and duty not a hard trial; that state in which it is a joy to see, to think, to feel, and to be. A most excellent definition, and a most cogent argument why we should heed the teachings of hygiene.

Health Hints.—Give your brain sufficient food and an abundant supply of oxygen, and then give it a fair amount of good, hard work every day, if you wish to maintain it in a high state of healthy activity. Attorneys and clergymen who use their brains much are the longest-lived men, showing plainly that regular brain work is good for the general health as well as for the efficiency of the nervous system in particular. The muscular system must be treated in a similar manner, if you do not wish to become subject to fatty degeneration.

Pause and Consider.—If you have worked night and day, overtaxed your brain, and worried yourself generally, then pause and consider if it is worth while to spend your health and strength in gaining that which frequently takes to itself wings, while you are every day becoming more and more a victim of exhaustion and irritability. Reduce life to the simplest terms. Eat and drink simply, live out of doors as much as you can, and when you are inclined to worry and to give your mind up to despondency and despair, then summon philosophy to your aid. In that direction health lies.

DEEP BREATHING.

Cultivate the habit of breathing through the nose and taking deep breaths. If this habit was universal, there is little doubt that pulmonary affections would be decreased one-half. An English physician calls attention to this fact, that deep and forced respiration will keep the entire body in a glow in the coldest weather, no matter how thinly o. may be clad. He was himself half frozen to death one night, and began taking deep breaths and keeping the air in his lungs as long as possible. The result was that he was thoroughly comfortable in a few minutes. The deep respirations, he says, stimulate the blood currents by direct muscular action, and cause the entire system to become pervaded with the rapidly-generated heat.

When to Begin.— Mothers should see that their little ones learn to breathe correctly—that is, through the nose, and to take long breaths. A long breath will expand and exercise the lungs to their fullest capacity, while a short breath only affects the upper part. For people with catarrhal tendencies or weak lungs there is nothing better than deep breathing. It puts the blood in circulation, thus benefiting the entire body. In cold weather deep breathing generates considerable heat and the one who can breathe well never feels the cold as does one who takes short breaths.

Lung Strengthener.—Long breaths are lung strengtheners, and such exercise has cured severe colds in the lungs, and has been known to do more good than medicine in the early stages, or rather, at the appearance, of consumption. Such precaution and prevention cost nothing and it would be well to adopt the method.

Art of Breathing—It is perhaps one of the signs of the times, to those alert for indications, that the art of breathing has become more and more a subject of atttention. Oculists, as well as physiologists, go deeply into its study in a way hardly to be touched upon here. Physicians have cured aggravated cases of insomnia by long-drawn regular breaths, fever-stricken patients have been quieted, stubborn forms of indigestion made to disappear. A tendency to consumption may be entirely overcome, as some authority has within the last few years clearly demonstrated, by exercises in breathing. Seasickness, too, may be surmounted, and the victim of hypnotic influence taught to withstand the force of any energy directed against him.

Systematic Breathing.— Dr. Oertel, of Munich, has written an extensive work on breathing. We cannot enter into the philosophy of his system, but the simple rules laid down, without entering into an understanding of the principles underlying them, have been so helpful to many asthmatic patients and of inestimable value to all who practice them that we cannot pass this subject before calling attention to them. No one need ever "get out of breath" who follows the system, no matter how long the walk or how steep the climb.

Rule for Ascent.— In making any ascent, either by stairway or path, the rule is to use one breath for every step. One should breathe through the nostrils, not talk, and go systematically to work. The fuller the breath the better.

On the Level.— In walking along a level stretch take two steps to every breath. Always begin to exhale or inhale as the same foot touches the ground.

Ridding the Lungs.— The third exercise is for ridding the lungs of the air accumulated there. It is practiced with the mouth open. Inhale as you put the right foot to the ground. Then, as the left touches the ground, exhale naturally, and as the right touches the ground exhale again with an effort, so expelling all the air from the lungs. Then inhale again, now on the left foot, exhale naturally on the right, and with an effort expel the air as the left foot falls. This exercise is kept up for some time, always in this way: Left foot, inhale; right foot, exhale; left foot, expel with effort. Again, right foot, inhale; left foot, exhale; right foot, expel with effort. The process of inhaling, therefore, begins with alternate footsteps.

It must not be supposed that the gait of the individual is badly affected, made unduly awkward by the effort to breathe in this way. On the contrary, when once the idea is grasped, the whole movement of the individual becomes rhythmic and graceful.

These rules, although simple, have been very beneficial to many.

THE EVIL OF OVER-EATING.

Excesses.—The excesses in the use of food and drink of some men are almost beyond belief, and yet, in a few instances, the facts are well authenticated. Brillat-Savarin, himself a famous epicure, relates the following anecdote: A friend expressed the despair of his life that he could never get his "fill of oysters." "Come, dine with me and you shall have enough," said the epicure. The friend did, and ate thirty-one dozen oysters as a prelude to the excellent dinner which was served. Downright gluttony is not given frequent exhibition at the table of gentle people these days. It is considered rather nearer correct to affect a small appetite, such as requires the temptation of dainty dishes. This is, however, very frequently a small bit of deception, but it has merit, even though it leads those who resort to it to supplement meals taken in public, in the privacy of their own pantries.

Duty of Housewife.—In regard to this whole matter of gluttony it is the duty of the good housewife to keep down the appetite of her husband. Particularly is this necessary in the cases of well-to-do professional and business men. In the families of mechanics earning low wages such a warning is almost wholly unnecessary, but it may be said of most men in good circumstances that they eat too freely of rich food. If men would begin careful and systematic physical culture in early youth and continue the practice through life, good health would be the result.

Exercise.—Beyond the age of forty—at a period when so many are physically lazy—the superior value of exercise is apparent; but ordinarily, this is just the time when the hygiene of athletics is neglected. There is no reason why a punching-bag, rowing-machine, pulley-weights and other apparatus should be relegated to college boys and clerks. But having done a good deal of work in his time it is almost impossible to persuade a business or professional man, turning forty, to give any sort of attention to physical culture if such training has been previously neglected. Hence, it is the duty of a woman to keep from her husband all rich compounds that will ultimately ruin his digestion.

High Feeding.—High feeding is occasionally neutralized by hard exercise; but in the absence of the latter it is mischievous in the extreme. If your husband will stand the treatment, begin by switching off from the heavy breakfast of steak, hot rolls, potatoes, etc., and set before him eggs-on-toast, oatmeal, or any other of the many excellent breakfast foods now.

Effects.—The effects of over-eating—or what is equally bad, injudicious eating—are clearly perceived in the case of a man who trains for some athletic event. In really fine condition indigestion is great loss of power. A strong member of a college crew, "hard as nails," was utterly unfit to pull his oarblade through the water on the four-mile journey down the Thames River, at New London, simply because of indiscretion in eating a few nights before. This shows the importance of diet. Napoleon is said to have lost the battle of Leipsic because of a fit of indigestion brought on by unusual indulgence. It is conceivable that a business man may lose a tempting contract, or a professional man an important cause for the same reason. Nor is this all.

Financial Aspect.—The financial aspect of the case is worthy of our consideration. By taking off a little here and a little there; by reducing condiments and sauces, expensive desserts and creamy compounds to a minimum, the grocer's account will be a complete surprise at the end of the month, while the husband's health as well as his pocketbook will show gratifying results. I know of a family whose members almost unconsciously fitted into this simpler way of living, until eventually the butcher and the baker received barely two-thirds of their former dividends. And each inmate of the household could almost have taken an oath that nothing had been subtracted from the menu, so gradual had been the shrinkage.

Advice to Weary Women.—Let some of the women who are brainweary with devising tempting dishes for the good man of the house take this matter to heart, and if they are able to change their husbands from gourmands to athletes a ripe old age is not unlikely.

On the other hand, those of full habit who give unchecked and hearty indulgence to their appetites, should always keep in mind the words Shakespeare puts into the mouth of sweet "Portia's" wise maid: "They are as sick that surfeit with too much, as they that starve with nothing."

Two Meals a Day.—Many have an erroneous idea that if they eat often and a little at a time their body is better nourished and their strength better kept up by so doing. There never was a greater mistake made than this constant lunching, the advice of many doctors to do so notwithstanding. We have known some of the worst cases of dyspepsia brought on by this very habit. We knew a young man, a clerk in a fancy grocery store, who was constantly nibbling from this and that, first candy, then cheese, crackers, fruits and other edibles, indulged in until he never wanted a square meal, and in a few months became a chronic dyspeptic. He was thoroughly cured, however, in a few weeks by a rigid adherence to two meals a day and not even taking the least thing between meals. We have now in mind many cases of greatly improved health and those who have regained perfect health by strict conformity to the two-meal system.

For the Aged.—Especially for people over fifty years old and for those of sedentary habits would we recommend this system of eating, as it gives the digestive organs the needed rest they must have in order to properly and thoroughly digest and assimilate the food which goes to make a healthy body and give us strength to live. Nature intended that we should eat to live, not, as is too often the practice, live to eat.

A Vegetable Diet.—Many noted physicians have in recent years recommended a strictly vegetable diet. It is held that a vegetable diet is far better suited to sustain man in health, and enable him to be fully what he was intended to be, than animal food or a mixed diet. This view may be contradicted, but experience has taught us that many persons would have better health if they were to subsist upon a vegetable diet rather than to partake so largely of flesh.

Life Prolonged.—Dr. Lambe, a noted English physician, says that life is prolonged in incurable diseases about one-tenth by vegetable diet. He has observed no ill consequences from the relinquishment of animal food. The apprehended danger of the change is only a scare, the danger being all the other way. While many may not agree with this opinion, a practical application will demonstrate its worth to all who are sufficiently interested. Errors in diet are the great sources of disease. Amendment of diet is the great basis of recovery. Medicines may relieve or suspend the majority of diseases, but medicines can never cure without the aid of regimen.

Eating When Tired.—Some very severe attacks of indigestion people bring on themselves by eating heartily when in an exhausted condition. A hearty meal stimulates the tired heart momentarily, and so tempts one to fill the stomach inordinately full. Often the hunger of depleted nerves and brain is confused with hunger for more than a moderate amount of food. Self-control is at its ebb, anyhow, when one is very tired. Hence, we need to establish ourselves in a clear idea on this matter, and have it ready for application on occasion.

Rest Before Eating.—A very short period of rest puts the system into much better condition for grappling with food. Take a glass of hot milk and sit down for five or ten minutes, no matter how tired and hungry. Then begin to eat slowly, masticating thoroughly. In a little while the vigor of the stomach will return, and if one leaves off at a reasonable point, all will be well. If very tired it is better to make a very simple, light meal, and take some sleep, before attempting to digest all the food required for building up the waste.

Will Power.—It requires a good deal of will power to control the appetite at such times, when it seems almost a sort of duty to indulge in anything that relieves the sense of goneness. If one has missed a meal and been long without food, it is even then risky to take suddenly all the food one can hold. The over-hungry stomach cannot do as much as the stomach that is just fairly hungry. It is much better in such a case to take a little, give it time to be dissolved, and then take more. A good deal depends on the sort of work that has been done and the physical vigor of the individual.

Brain Work.—Where severe brain work has been done to bring one to the "tired-and-hungry" condition more care is required in eating, especially with a person of delicate organization. Prof. Draper used to emphasize the fact that any highly organized animal or man was liable to injury by abuses which an animal or man of coarser organization could suffer with apparent impunity. He instanced the well-known cases in which halfwitted or stupid men are known to indulge in practices that would promptly wreck a man of high nervous organization, and yet without seeming to suffer.

TIME REQUIRED FOR DIGESTION.

	H. M.		H. M.
Apples, sweet	1 30	Mutton, roast	3 15
" sour	2 00	" broiled	3 00
Beans, pod, boiled	2 30	" boiled	3 00
Beef, fresh, rare, roasted	3 00	Oysters, raw	2 55
" " dried	3 30	" roast	3 15
" " fried	4 00	" stewed	3 30
Beets, boiled	3 45	Pork, fat and lean, roast	5 15
Bread, wheat, fresh	3 30	" " " boiled	3 10
" corn	3 15	" " " raw	3 00
Butter (melted)	3 30	Potatoes, boiled	3 30
Cabbage, with vinegar, raw	2 00	" baked	2 30
" boiled	4 30	Rice, boiled	1 00
Cheese (old, strong)	3 30	Sago	1 45
Codfish	2 00	Salmon, salted, boiled	4 00
Custard, baked	2 45	Soup, beef, vegetable	4 00
Ducks, domestic, roasted	4 00	" chicken boiled	3 00
" wild, "	4 30	" oyster "	3 30
Eggs, fresh, hard boiled	3 30	Tapioca, boiled	2 00
" " soft "	3 00	Tripe, soused, boiled	1 00
" " fried	3 30	Trout, fresh, boiled or fried	1 30
Goose, roast	2 00	Turkey, domestic, roast	2 00
Lamb, fresh, boiled	2 30	" wild, roast	2 18
Liver, beef, boiled	2 00	Turnips, boiled	3 30
Milk, boiled	2 00	Veal, fresh, broiled	4 00
" raw	2 15	" " fried	4 30
Parsnips, boiled	2 30	Venison steak, broiled	1 35

HINTS FOR ALL KINDS OF PEOPLE.

Hints for the Thin.

Eat slowly and masticate thoroughly.
Do not over-eat.
Eat at regular intervals.
Do not eat heartily when fatigued or over-heated.
Rest whenever possible twenty minutes before and twenty minutes after dinner.
Exercise regularly.
Do not bathe after eating, for at least two hours.
Do not exercise physically or mentally for at least a half-hour after eating.
Live outdoors as much as possible, sleep and rest as much as you require.
Avoid worry and cultivate a cheerful disposition.

Hints for the Stout.

Vary your occupations as much as possible.
Sleep in well-ventilated rooms.
Avoid crowds and close atmosphere.
Bathe freely.
Cultivate mental as well as physical activity.
Do not over-eat.

Drink liquids sparingly with meals, freely one hour before or two hours after meals.

Avoid fatigue.

Avoid sugar and starchy foods.

Hint to All.

Eat only what agrees with you.

TEA AND COFFEE.
WHY DO WE DRINK IT?

That fragrant cup of tea, the still more alluring cup of coffee, or the delicious and enticing cocoa or chocolate—what is it makes them each and all so indispensable to their votaries?

One says, "I drink tea because it is so refreshing, it rests me when I am tired." "I take coffee for the reason that I can't do without it," another honestly confesses; and "I drink chocolate because it is so soothing," explains a third.

Not Essential to Health.—These beverages, physiologists declare, are in no sense to be considered as food or as essential to health. They partake of the nature and effects of alcohol, that is, they are stimulating, exhilarating, sometimes sedative, but never nourishing, and they are taken for a similar reason that the whisky drinker takes the still more stimulating liquor. All are unnatural props and false supports seeming to afford strength and in reality giving none.

Disease Producing.—One of the most common causes of dyspepsia and nervousness is the immoderate use of tea and coffee. These drinks contain a poison which, although not fatal in small doses, nevertheless produces a decidedly injurious effect. While chocolate and cocoa are less powerful, they produce the same effects.

The tea and coffee drinkers say "Oh, it doesn't hurt me. I've taken it for years." But the end is not yet, and when the reckoning is suddenly summed up, there is a painful and fatal deficit, and when it is too late to change the habits of a lifetime, the sad fact becomes apparent that these indulgences in strong tea and coffee are not conducive to the best results.

Water the Best Drink.—Many have found a cure for dyspepsia, nervousness, sick headache and other diseases in discarding tea, coffee and all their substitutes. After all has been said that can be said in favor of these drinks it remains true that nature's drink, pure water, is best.

CONDITIONS OF HEALTH.

The organs which are the great sources of health—the organs of purification and invigoration, are to a great extent, within our reach and control. These are the skin, the lungs and the stomach. We can keep the skin clean, warm, and active. We can breathe, plentifully, of pure air, night and day. We can live on simple, natural, healthful food, enough and not too much. We can drink the purest water we can get. These are the chief necessaries of life, and conditions of health.

Value of Health.—No man can enjoy life, or perform its duties worthily, without health; nor can a man give what he does not possess to his posterity. Health is above gold and rubies. Better give a child a good constitution than all other wealth.

Ignorance.—Great masses of people are ignorant of the laws and conditions of health. Multitudes are suffering from diseases that could easily be prevented. The remedy for ignorance is useful knowledge, the remedy for poverty is industry and economy, the remedy for disease is a knowledge of the laws of health.

Economics of Health.—Think of the vast number of physicians, surgeons, medical men, chemists, hospitals and dispensaries, all living on disease—disease that in many cases occurs through the evil habits and vices of the people. Good, simple, natural habits of living give health and long life, so that many persons may pass through life from the cradle to the grave without sickness or pain, without doctors or drugs. All disease is unnatural and preventable.

Wealth and Position are not necessary to a high degree of health and a low death rate. Health is in the reach of all if poisonous narcotics, spiritous drinks, heating condiments and spices, and other poisonous matter are barred out of the system and the great purifying organ of the body—the skin—is kept free, clean, and its pores open by frequent bathing.

Health-Purity.—Purity of birth is the source of health. There have been many holy souls in very sickly bodies who are martyrs, killed by ignorance, or by generations of unwise or wicked ancestors. Again, no one can maintain or regain health without purity of thought, and consequent purity of life. To have a sound mind in a sound body, both must be pure and chaste. Chastity is a condition of health.

State of Society.—It is a sad reflection upon civilization to assert, that the more cultivated and refined man has become, the more sickly and diseased he is found to be. The Creator never designed that any of the powers of the human constitution should suffer from use. It is man's privilege to improve not only his moral and intellectual powers, but his bodily also.

Savage Nations.—When we witness the health and the greater power of endurance that exist among many of the savage nations, and when we consider that even they violate many physiological laws, we are led to reflect upon what might and what will yet be, in that age when enlightened man shall learn how to live in obedience to the Creator's laws. As certainly as the world stands, such a time will yet come, distant although it may yet be.

OCCUPATIONS.

It is generally acknowledged that occupation exerts an important influence on bodily health. Some occupations tend to build up the system and to maintain for many years robust and enduring health, while others are in their very nature unhealthful. Let us notice the advantages, and disadvantages as well, of the leading occupations.

The Farmer.—The farmer has the most healthful employment. He has an abundance of pure air and is usually not necessitated to expose himself to storm and rain. His regular habits and labor in the open air give him a good appetite, digestion, and capacity for sleep. His brain is not worried or overtaxed. Some of the disadvantages of farmer life are small and illy ventilated bedrooms, over-heated and unventilated rooms in winter, and abuse in the way of diet in eating too much and in the use of tea, coffee, and tobacco. Aside from these abuses, the farmer's life, more than any other, tends to longevity. Don't be in a hurry, young man, to leave the farm, you may live to rue the day of your leaving it.

Machinists, and all whose occupation exposes them to an atmosphere loaded with dust, are liable to irritation and inflammation of the respiratory organs, resulting in asthma or consumption.

Blacksmiths are exposed to dust and the intense light of the fire which often injures the eyes.

Masons and Plasterers are liable to injury from dust and from the caustic quality of lime.

Conditions of Health.

Painters suffer from the action of lead and from the fumes of the spirits of turpentine which they constantly inhale. Painters are rarely advanced in years. They should be paid double ordinary wages, if health is to be measured by money.

Miners are injured by want of light, dampness, foul air, and the particles of dust to which they are exposed.

Soldiers have some advantages over other occupations, but in time of peace they suffer from a lack of something to do, and become dyspeptic and in time they are often subjected to exposures and irregular habits. The life of the soldier does not tend to longevity.

Tailors suffer much from dyspepsia and from constipation. Plenty of exercise in the open air would greatly improve their condition.

Seamstresses, on account of small pay, close hours, and entire neglect of exercise, are to be pitied much more than tailors.

Clerks, Accountants, and Copyists are often suffering from want of light, bad air, and a too close application to their work. A frequent changing of position is desirable, the standing position is much more favorable to health than the sitting position, provided only one position can be chosen.

Convicts are as a class free from disease and are often cured of dyspepsia by the plain food and regular habits required of them. Epidemics very seldom scale prison walls, although they may prevail in prison localities. This fact ought not to create a longing to be within prison walls, but is a powerful argument in favor of simplicity of food, regularity of habits and employment, and temperance in all things.

Idlers.—Idleness is not conducive to health, happiness, or longevity. He who has no regular employment is inclined to despondency and dyspepsia. Man in his healthiest and happiest state has regular employment. The retired farmer who enjoys life most and lives longest is the one who regularly keeps himself engaged at something that gives exercise to his mental and bodily powers. Both extremes of idleness and of overwork should be avoided, but the more baneful results are the products of idleness. Richter says, "I have fire-proof, perennial enjoyments called employments."

WISDOM AND BEAUTY IN REST.

Good Health.—In these days of ten-minute-a-day reading, or half-hour studying societies for improving the mind, how many women make it a point to spend certain "minutes" in rest to improve their nerves and their beauty? Good health is of vastly more importance than intellectuality, for of what comfort to its possessor, or to any one else, is the most brilliant mind which lives in a weary or nervous body? Sheer weariness causes more trouble in the world than it ever gets blamed for. A rested person, other things being right, is a pleasant one; while a tired person, under whatever other advantageous circumstances, is almost sure to be cross. Many a family wrangle has started from a few sharp words caused by overstrained nerves.

Personal Appearance.—It is natural—and perfectly right—for a woman always to consider her personal appearance of great importance. That fact should cause the subject of rest to find favor, as those who are always a little overtired never look well. Their faces assume a worried, frowning expression, and wrinkles, gray hairs, dull eyes and sallow complexion follow in natural succession.

The Best Rest.—Would you keep your fresh complexion, and plumpness, and bright eyes? Then rest! Rest often, and rest in the right way. Do not insist that change of occupation is rest. There is no greater delusion. It is nothing of the kind. It simply varies the kind of fatigue—adds another different in location. The best rest, the only real rest, is found in a recumbent position. No one can stand or sit without holding comparatively taut some muscles, and the tension tires them and the nerves by sympathy. To rest, lie down on something entirely comfortable, and relax every nerve and muscle as much as possible. This is not altogether easy to do at first, but "practice makes perfect." The rest of it is wonderful—in fact, the whole secret of rest lies in the one word: relaxation. Notice a baby's or an animal's complete relaxation while it sleeps. Five minutes at a time several times a day—and more if possible—of such rest will certainly add to length of life and happiness.

False Economy.—Many people think that they cannot afford to lie down in the daytime, or if they do that they must improve the time by reading. It is a false idea of an economy of time. Neither the reading nor the resting is well done; and so the time spent is practically wasted. But to take little rests—lying down—does not waste time; it is time invested in a way that pays big dividends.

LAUGHTER A GREAT TONIC.

Keeps the Spirit Buoyant, the Heart and Face Young.

"I presume if we laughed more we should all be happier and healthier," writes Edward W. Bok in the Ladies' Home Journal. "True, we are a busy and a very practical people. And most of us probably find more in this life to bring the frown than the smile. But, nevertheless, it is a pity that we do not laugh more; that we do not bring ourselves to the laugh, if need be.

Best Medicine.—We all agree that a good laugh is the best medicine in the world. Physicians have said that no other feeling works so much good to the entire human body as that of merriment. As a digestive, it is unexcelled; as a means of expanding the lungs, there is nothing better. It keeps the heart and face young. It is the best of all tonics to the spirits. It is, too, the most enjoyable of all sensations.

Better Friends.—A good laugh makes better friends with ourselves and everybody around us, and puts us into closer touch with what is best and brightest in our lot in life. It is to be regretted, then, that such a potent agency for our personal good is not more often used.

Not Expensive.—It costs nothing. All other medicines are more or less expensive. 'Why,' said an old doctor not long ago, 'if people fully realized what it means to themselves to laugh, and laughed as they should, ninety per cent. of the doctors would have to go out of business.' Probably when we get a little less busy we shall laugh more. For, after all, the difference between gloom and laughter is but a step. And if more of us simply took a step aside oftener than we do, and rested more, we would laugh more.

Laughter, not Giggling.—By laughing I do not mean the silly giggle indulged in by some women and so many girls and boys, too. There is no outward mark which demonstrates the woman of shallow mind so unmistakably as that of giggling. There is no sense in the giggle; no benefit to be derived from it. It makes a fool of the person, and renders every one about uncomfortable.

A Healthful Nature.—But just as the giggle is the outcome of a small mind, the hearty laugh is the reflection of a healthful nature. What we want is more good laughers in the world—not more gigglers."

WHY DON'T YOU LAUGH?

Why don't you laugh, young man, when troubles come,
Instead of sitting 'round so sour and glum?
    You cannot have all play,
    And sunshine every day;
When troubles come, I say, why don't you laugh?

Why don't you laugh? 'Twill ever help and soothe
The aches and pains. No road in life is smooth;
    There's many an unseen bump,
    And many a hidden stump
O'er which you'll have to jump. Why don't you laugh?

Why don't you laugh? Don't let your spirits wilt,
Don't sit and cry because the milk you've spilt;
    If you would mend it now,
    Pray let me tell you how:
Just milk another cow! Why don't you laugh?

Why don't you laugh, and make us all laugh, too,
And keep us mortals all from getting blue?
    A laugh will aways win;
    If you can't laugh, just grin—
Come on, let's all join in! Why don't you laugh?

A CURE FOR THE BLUES.

Few women, and men as well, can honestly say that they have never had the "blues." One sometimes sees a cheery soul who will deny all knowledge of "doldrums," but she is usually a woman possessed of remarkable health and full of business interests, or one who literally has no time for moping. Such a woman is proof against any foolishness of the sort.

But foolishness or not, if things go wrong, and if one feels tired and worried and discouraged, one is prone to become despondent and imaginative and out of sorts with the world, and it is then we have to look for that silver lining. Usually a good, brisk walk will bring it to our notice. The physical exercise and mental distraction one finds in the open air will sweep away the cobwebs of the brain as nothing else can. As a race, we Americans are not fond of walking. We exercise too little. We worry too much. We take life too hard. We wear ourselves out in the pursuit of rest. A long, vigorous walk every day is the best tonic for mind and body, and, an almost invariable panacea for the "blues."

Charity.

FEEDING THE UNFORTUNATE POOR.

CHARITY, HAPPINESS, AND LENGTH OF DAYS.

Gently to hear, kindly to judge.—Shakespere.
He hath a tear for pity, and a hand
Open as day for melting Charity.
—Shakespere.

Then gently scan your brother man,
Still gentler, sister woman;
Though they may gang a kennin' wrang,
To step aside is human. —Burns.

1. Charity is a golden chain that reaches from heaven to earth. It is the brightest star in the Christian's character. Without it our religion is like a body without a soul; our friendship a shadow of a shadow.

2. The rich should have charity for the poor and the poor should have charity for the rich, for to-morrow the poor may be rich and the rich poor. It has been so in all ages and will continue to be so as long as man lives.

3. Those who cultivate benevolence and charity in their heart will always find enjoyment in the prosperity of others.

They will find more to cheer and more to enjoy, for a miserly soul is the most miserable of all of God's created beings. In the home of charity there is happiness, and happiness is conducive to health.

4. How sweet are the hands that are reached out to relieve distress; how balmy the influence and virtue of those who try to alleviate the suffering of the poor! Cultivate benevolence, for it is a home virtue and a household beauty. Beware of those people who never remember the needy or have nothing to offer for charity. And let all remember who have been blessed with abundance, that it is not at all uncertain but their children or their children's children will beg for bread. Therefore deal generously with the poor, and you will be happier and healthier and live longer for it.

5. Every good hearty laugh in which a man indulges tends to prolong his life, as it makes the blood move more rapidly and gives a new and different stimulus to all the organs of the body from what it does at other times. So let us have all the joy we can.

SLEEP.

Sleep, in order to be beneficial, must be healthful and profound. Sleep produced by artificial means relieves the mind of its activities, but it is neither invigorating nor refreshing, and is of very little value.

Conditions.—Great care should be taken to have the room and bedding comfortable and clean. Sleep on an elastic mattress rather than a feather bed, and make sure of warm feet. If exercise and rubbing will not warm them, try the hot and cold foot-bath, alternately. A hot water bottle is better than cold feet. A window let down an inch from the top insures a change of air with no draft. A cool room is best. Take the position that gives most comfort, and sleep with the mouth shut. Avoid overheating any part, but especially the lower portion of the spine. If a stomach-cough comes on after going to bed, drink a glass of cold water. To allay a cough from bronchitis, wring half a towel out of cold water, and spread it two thicknesses over the chest, covering with the dry part. In most cases, it will arrest the cough at once, and give quiet sleep. As a rule no invalid should eat within four hours of bedtime.

Not Disturbed.—The sleeper should not be disturbed until he wakes of his own accord. This, of course, will not apply to lazy persons, and those in danger of contracting bad habits in this respect.

Growing Children should, if possible, be permitted to sleep at will. Retiring at an early hour will generally break the tendency to bad habits in respect to rising.

The Need of Sleep.—Why can some men sleep at will, and some "nervous" men, too, while others, sometimes very "heavy" men, with apparently immovable nerves, are tortured by insomnia? Why, too, do some men seem to obtain sufficient rest with five hours' sleep, while others require nine? Do some men "sleep slow," as Mr. Smedley jocularly argued in one of his amusing stories, or do they actually require more sleep? We cannot answer the question any more than the doctors can, but we agree on one side of the subject most heartily with the "British Medical Journal."

Popular Prejudice.—The popular prejudice against sleep works infinity of mischief. There are plenty of sluggards even among the cultivated class, but the sleep sluggard is in that class a very rare specimen.

The Educated.—The tendency of the educated is to wakefulness, and the man who does intellectual work and exhibits what his friends think a disposition to oversleep, is obeying a healthy instinct. Sleep recuperates him, and he knows it. The popular notion that a young man who works with his head, yet sleeps for nine hours, is a sluggard, is popular nonsense. No man whose brain is active and who does not drink ever sleeps more than is good for him.

Early Sleep.—One hour's sleep gotten before midnight is worth two after the midnight hour is past. If those troubled with nervous prostration would try the experiment and thus avoid late suppers their nerves would soon relax and the system would soon regain its normal condition. No one can have perfect health without the necessary sleep of from seven to ten hours every day, and from three to five of these should be put in before twelve o'clock at night.

Unaired Sleeping-Rooms.—Headache, nervousness, and a long list of evils follow in the wake of unaired sleeping-rooms. Drafts cause equally undesirable complications. Beds should not be placed in the direct line between windows and doors. Some prudent housewives have four small screws placed on the window sashes, two at the top on each side and two below them, about five inches. When the window is lowered to this depth every night, a sort of screen made of veiling is fastened by means of strings to the screws. This permits fresh air to enter freely, but prevents a strong wind from blowing against the sleepers.

How to Induce Sleep.—Lengthen the respiration—in other words, breathe slower by taking deeper breaths and expiring the air slowly—and think of the slow rise of the chest, etc. These two things will bring sleep, but why? Slower breathing, of course, means lessened bodily activity, so that is simple. But how does thinking of the chest induce sleep?

Thinking of a thing implies that our bodily as well as mental gaze is fixed on it; to gaze on one's chest the eye-balls must be directed downwards. Those who suffer from insomnia and continually go over the events of the past day (as such do), will find on personal examination that their eye-balls are directed upwards; "to think" it is almost imperative such should be the case; direct the eyes downwards, and keep them so, and "thinking" is not so easy.

It has been recommended that the imagination should conceive the breath issuing from the nostrils; this breath has no shape or form, and hence is, perhaps, a better "object" than the chest. Years ago I learnt to do this, though I did not then know the explanation. Practice no longer necessitates my conceiving such objects as the breath or chest, or feet, or bed-foot, or anything below the level of the eyes. I can compel my eye-balls to turn down at will. It was not easy to get into at first—far from it; but I was determined to drop the bromide, and chanced to hear of this suggestion.

I am now the envy of friends; though over fifty, I sleep for eight hours and sometimes ten, and a most refreshing sleep, too. Dreams do not—they cannot—trouble one who sleeps; only "out-of-sortedness" will cause dreams or broken sleep. I know the plan is a good one.

BICYCLE EXERCISE.

Bicycle Exercise.—To get the real benefit a bicycle can give, don't race, or attempt phenomenal distances. Walk up the severe hills, i. e., those (depending on the person), which cause the slightest inconvenience in breathing. Avoid going with riders who are stronger than you, as you are then about certain to overdo. Sit erect. Wear loose woolen clothing. Go, if possible, into an interesting country, so as to have occasion for little detours afoot, off the road, and so vary the exercise. Go alone if you can not with some one who will stop and rest when you feel like it.

BE GOOD TO YOURSELF.

Think deliberately of the house you live in—your body.
Make up your mind firmly not to abuse it.
Eat nothing that will hurt it; wear nothing that distorts or pains it.
Do not overload it with victuals or drink or work.
Give yourself regular and abundant sleep.
Keep your body warmly clad.
At the first signal of danger from the thousand enemies that surround you, defend yourself.
Do not take cold; guard yourself against it; if you feel the first symptoms, give yourself heroic treatment.
Get into a fine glow of heat by exercise.
Take a vigorous walk or run, then guard against a sudden attack of perspiration.
This is the only body you will ever have in this world.
A large share of the pleasure and pain of life will come through the use you make of it.
Study deeply and diligently the structure of it, the laws that should govern it, and the pains and penalties that will surely follow a violation of every law of life or health.

AS I GROW OLD.

If need be, take my friends, my dole of wealth,
Take faith, and love, and hope, take youth and health;
But while I live, dear God, blight not the flower
Of reason in my brain! Leave me the power
To string together, on fine threads of gold,
My fairest thoughts, as I grow gray and old.

RIPE OLD AGE.

WHY SO MANY PEOPLE DIE BEFORE THEIR TIME.

1. According to the sacred writings of King Solomon, human life has been limited to three score and ten.

2. It is a fact easily ascertained by observation that those people who live to be seventy, eighty, ninety or one hundred years of age have not been of the wealthier classes. People who live what is called high life, eat late and highly stimulating suppers, with irregular hours of rest and sleep, seldom reach that era of life known as old age. Highly seasoned food, champagne, and midnight banquets are not the invigorating influences that preserve the health.

3. The persons who live to old age have never sown many wild oats in youth, they have lived a steady and

Causes of Premature Deaths.

regular life, eating plain food and retired without allowing the cares of the day to interrupt their rest or sleep.

4. Highly seasoned food, and luxuries of any kind always tend to excesses which produce premature decay. For some years past, reported deaths from "Heart Failure" have become frequent and fashionable among practicing physicians, and perhaps the report may have been true, but not the whole truth, for it is probable that in nine cases out of ten the heart failure was secondary and brought on by an ineffectual effort of the stomach or alimentary tract to cast off indigestible matter clogging the way, caused by excesses of over-eating or over-nervous strains.

5. Bright's disease, that most miserable misnamed disease. If statistics could be kept showing the real cause of all deaths occurring between the ages of forty-five and seventy-five, the result in all probability would prove that more than half fall victims to disease engendered by stomach difficulties, brought on by too high living, excesses in both eating and drinking.

6. The habit of constipation is another serious obstacle in the way of long life. Its progress is slow and so insidious as to beguile the sufferer into the belief that it is not pernicious or worthy of attention; and so apprehension is lulled, while the foundation of some fatal chronic disease involving important organs is being laid.

7. When troubled with constipation it is usual to resort to purgatives, which afford temporary relief, but usually have a tendency to confirm the disease. Injections are sometimes used, with no better results, for besides being a bungling remedy they have no permanent influence in overcoming the habit. Bread made of unbolted rye or wheat meal is an excellent remedy, but, not being in common use, few patients can be sure of getting it regularly, especially if engaged in active pursuit, as many are. Before the habit is firmly established, eating fruit desserts at dinner every day is apt to afford some relief, and if there is no habit of constipation it may act as a preventive. Baked apples are excellent for constipation. Eating a fair-sized baked apple (warm or cold) at the beginning of each meal three times a day, has cured many very obstinate cases of constipation. It is a very palatable and cheap remedy, and much more certain and effective than strong drugs.

8. To suggest the methodical use of cold water as a beverage in the absence of thirst, as a means of augmenting the chances of longevity, might seem to render one liable to be called a crank, if not a lunatic; nevertheless the idea

Gladstone, a
at the

Causes of Premature Deaths. 09

claims a physiological origin, and is well supported by experience. Solid and dry as the human body appears, water constitutes more than three-fourths of its bulk, and all the functions of life are carried on in a water-bath. And although the sense of thirst may be trusted to call for a draught of cold water when required, that offers no reason why we may not be benefited by it in the absence of thirst.

9. Drinking cold water as a beverage between meals is surely very conducive to health and increases the chances of long life. People rarely drink anything between meals, and all the liquid is taken with the meals; this surely without question is very injurious to the digestive organs. It is not natural for animals to drink while eating. Man is the only exception. Food should be thoroughly masticated and not washed down with tea and coffee or water.

10. If people would take a good drink of water just before retiring and a good cool glass the first thing in the morning on rising, drink once or twice between meals during the day, the present rate of mortality would be greatly reduced, and there would be much less sickness. The habit of self-indulgence and exposure, the result of swilling beer and other alcoholic stimulants at irregular hours, are productive of more disease than any other agency.

11. Don't be afraid to work; few people are injured by hard work if they take but proper care of their body. More people die from want of exercise than from overexercise.

"Pure water, temperate habits and hard work are the best friends of man."
"Better hunt in fields for health unbought,
Than fee the doctor for a nauseous draught."
—Dryden.

Gladstone, a man hale and vigorous at the age of 86 years.

CLEANLINESS.

Cleanliness.—The Dutch are the cleanliest people in the world, and the latest published statistics show that Holland, in proportion to its population, is the most moral nation on the globe. It is very easy to find a direct connection between the cleanliness of a people and their moral standard.

Tidiness.—Of all the external aids to a moral life none is so potent as tidiness. An untidy man or woman soon becomes a moral sloven. Let a man be careless of his surroundings, of his companionships, of his dress, his general appearance and of his bodily habits, and it is not long before the same carelessness extends into the realm of his morals.

Our Surroundings.—We are all creatures of our surroundings, and we work and act as we feel. If a man lives in a home where carelessness or untidiness in his dress is overlooked, he very soon goes from one inexactitude to another. He very quickly loses himself. The moral fiber of a man, fine of itself, can soon become coarse if the influence of his external surroundings is coarse. I believe thoroughly in the effect of a man's dress and habits of person upon his moral character. I do not say that neatness of appearance and cleanliness of person constitute the gentleman or the man of honor. But I do say that they are potent helps. And I would like to emphasize the importance of this belief upon the women of our homes. For it is given them to be an important factor in these helps to the betterment of the world's morality.

Business Men.—The average American man is a busy creature, and amid the larger business affairs which absorb him he is apt to be neglectful of smaller things. And these smaller things generally take the form of a neglect of personal habits.

Woman's Influence.—Here is where the wife, mother or sister comes in. The American woman is very largely responsible for the appearance of our men. The better the appearance of our men the higher will be the standard of morality, the more potent our influence as a nation. I have often looked at men in business and wondered where their wives were when they left home. Unshaved, practically unwashed, save for a few splashes of water in the face, with either frayed or soiled linen, with clothes unbrushed or shoes unblacked, they appear at their places of business.

Developed or Neglected.—Now a man rarely works better than he looks; certainly never better than he feels. And if a man feels unkempt, the work he does will probably be of the same grade. If, on the other hand, he feels clean, he works clean. The feeling of the worker inevitably communicates itself to his work. It is not that the majority of men are, by nature, unclean. The desire for cleanliness is born in every human being. It is simply a question whether it is developed or neglected.

Late Rising.—But, rising late, some men devote fifteen or twenty minutes to dressing, gulp down what passes for a breakfast, and rush off to their business. Now, no man, I care not how dexterous he may be, nor how simple his dress, can make himself look decent in fifteen minutes. I have heard of men who boasted that they could, and did it every morning. But I have yet to see one who did not show the results of the achievement (?) on his person. Either he is unshaved, or, if the razor is not one of his implements of necessity, the bath is neglected, his shoes lack polish, or his clothes look as if they had been thrown on instead of put on.

Small Things.—Many men laugh at what they call these "small things." They will tell you that "in business such things are not noticed," that "they cut no figure," or that "it is only the fop who regards these things." But cleanliness of body and neatness of appearance are noticed in business. More than that, they are a distinct factor in a man's success. There is a great difference between the neatly-dressed man and the fop. We are too apt to go to extremes in this belief.

Tidy Appearance.—The man of tidy appearance is an important factor in the atmosphere of his office; the fop passes for what he is—nothing. Because a man is neat in his dress he is not necessarily a fop. There is a happy and sensible medium. A man is not to be dubbed a "crank," a "feminine man" or a "fop" who is careful of his appearance at all times. Neatness is a current coin in business, and the man who refuses to believe it or is regardless of it makes a fatal mistake.

A Better Business Man.—The man who makes a point of keeping himself clean, and whose clothes look neat, no matter how moderate of cost they may be, works better, feels better, and is in every sense a better business man than his fellow-worker who is disregardful of both his body and dress, or either. He works at a distinct advantage. The external man unquestionably influences the internal man.

The Morning Bath.—I would give far more for the work done by a man who has the invigorating moral tonic of a morning bath and the feeling of clean linen than I would for the work done by a man who scarcely washes, and rushes into his clothes. Where the bathtub has as yet not made its appearance, the vigorous morning "rub-down" is a substitute within the reach of every man.

A Hasty Beginning.—A man begins his day badly when he hurries and rushes at the beginning of it. The men who have tried both ways know best how potent a factor in their lives is a reasonable time of leisure between their rising and their departure for business. The time spent upon our bodies is never wasted; on the contrary, it is time well invested. A machine of metal and steel must be clean before it can do good work. So, too, the human machine. A disregard of the body and disorder in dress soon grow into moral slovenliness. The temper which governs our care of ourselves and our appearance soon becomes the temper where moral things are concerned.

A Bad Habit.—Inexactitude grows easily and rapidly. It soon becomes a habit in all things. Life travels more quickly on the downward grade than it does on the upward path. It is so much easier to be neglectful of small things than it is to be regardful of them. But, all the same, it is a wise woman who, careful of the small things about the life of the men of her home, keeps her husband, son or brother up to his highest standard. Her labor will come back to her tenfold.

Task Not Easy.—Such a policy is not easy of accomplishment in some cases. There are men who resent what they choose to call the "interference" of their wives in matters purely personal. But the things of best results in this world are always the most difficult ones to acquire. Slovenliness is a hard habit to cure. But it can be cured. And the most arduous campaign where a man's cleanliness and neatness are concerned is worth the results once they are attained. Many men grow careless simply from forgetfulness or habit. A mere reminder of their duty to themselves is often all-sufficient.

Bathing.

BATHING.

Bathing.—More and more the Americans are becoming known as a bathing people. The most moderate house of the working-man now has its bathing room. In homes of more liberal outlay the bathroom connects with the sleeping-room. Servants in such homes are also given their own bathroom. Old-fashioned houses are having a bath put in. New hotels are built with bathrooms attached to the majority of their bedrooms. On every hand, the bath is becoming a national institution. Greater strides have been made in sanitary plumbing than in any part of the domestic machinery. The influence with us has been for good, and it is extending to other nations.

England's Advance.—While the English still use the "hip-baths" in their rooms they are gradually beginning to adopt the bathrooms. All the new houses and hotels in England have private bathrooms, an unheard-of thing until recently. All over Europe the innovation is being accepted just as surely even though more slowly. And the thousands of traveling Americans who insist upon their bath in the morning have brought about this change. Even in France, where the bath is considered more of a luxury than a necessity, the adoption of the bathroom is becoming apparent.

When and How.—Dr. Cyrus Edson, ex-President of the New York Board of Health, writes concerning bathing: "A cold douche or any form of shower bath should not be used when a person is tired or exhausted from any cause, as the reaction on which the shock depends for its beneficial effect does not follow effectually when the system is tired. The result of the shower in such a case is apt to be internal congestion, which may be disastrous. It does not follow, however, that a perspiring person should not bathe until cooled off. As a matter of fact, if the person is not exhausted, the fact that the pores are open is rather advantageous than otherwise, as the reaction is enhanced and will probably follow more energetically.

Not Near Meal Time.—A bath should never be taken within two hours of a hearty meal. The first effect of immersion in warm or in cold water is to derange seriously the digestive process if that is progressing at the time, and by a physiological effect that naturally follows, to unbalance or derange the whole nervous system. The result of this is extremely dangerous to the bather. There are numerous instances of severe illness and even of death caused by bathing while the stomach was full."

Danger After Meals.—Sudden immersion of the body in cold water after a meal and while the process of digestion is going on may be attended with danger; at such a time the abdominal system is the seat of intense physiological congestion and the accumulation of blood in it is suddenly thrown back toward the nervous centers, and the consequence may be a disorder resulting in death.

Beauty in the Bath.—For a beautiful bath, which is very luxurious, the temperature of the water should be from 70 to 75 degrees, and the bath should be of daily occurrence. With this should be used the bran and almond-meal bags, which can be had from any druggist. One for much less expense can make them at home by mixing well one and one-half pounds of clean, new bran, and one-half pound of pulverized orris root, three-quarters of a pound of almond meal, and five ounces of grated white Castile soap. Make seven-inch cheesecloth bags, and put about four ounces into each one, sewing them firmly at the edges, using one for each bath, just as you would a sponge, without soap. The bran and almond-meal bags are luxuries, not necessities, in the bath, and while they add softness and fragrance, will not do away with the necessity of scrubbing in order to produce cleanliness.

Beautiful Women.—The world's most beautiful women

from Greek and Roman days down to the modern Turkish seraglio, have always been of those countries where bathing and anointing have been brought to the perfection of a fine art.

Patting (not rubbing) with soft cloths wet in "April Snow-water or June rain-water," combined with Pears' soap or some of the best "buttermilk" brands, then softly patting again with a dry cloth, ought not to injure the texture or bloom of the loveliest wild-rose complexion. But it must not be forgotten that the whole body needs daily treatment, also, since good circulation is one of the secrets of good coloring.

No Fixed Rule.—It is impossible to give any rule about bathing which will apply to all persons. Each in this must be a law unto himself. In nothing does the desire, so common among mankind, to have others conform to the rule of life adopted by one's self, so often show itself as in the advice given on the subject of baths. You hear some strong man, who delights in the bracing shock of cold water when he rises from his warm bed, not only dilate on the value of the bath taken as he takes it, but seriously advise others to adopt his rule—those others, be it understood, being persons who could not possibly stand the shock of a cold bath. Again, you will hear a man who resorts to the Turkish bath three or four times a week, and derives great benefit therefrom, urge his friend to follow his example, when such a system of bathing would probably prostrate the friend.

Personal Feelings.—The number and temperature of the baths, when they are taken merely for the purpose of cleanliness, must be regulated by the personal feelings of the bather. It may, however, be said that every one can take baths in some form, and emphatically every one should.

Cannot Bathe Too Often.—As long as the result of bathing is not to weaken the bather we can practically say a person cannot, when in health, bathe too much.

Physical Culture.—I have spoken of the hygienic value of the bath, but I have said nothing of the physical pleasure to be derived from it. Every one knows the delicious feeling of cleanliness, the glow of the skin, and the general sense of robust health which follow a good bath. What is more delightful than the exhilaration of a swim in salt water? These results are a part of the experience of all, but it must not be forgotten that in these very physical pleasures there is a distinct hygienic effect.

Bathing.

To Our Girls.—Your skin and your eyes, my dear girl, constitute the thermometer that tells whether you are well, physically, or not. If the first has little spots upon it, is dull to look at, and feels dry, and the second has a glazed appearance, with yellowish whites, then be sure it is time to think whether you are living rightly from the physical standpoint. Now, what does your morning bath amount to? Do you dab over your face, whirl the cloth around your neck, carefully bathe your hands, and then go out of the bathroom fully satisfied that you are quite clean? There are thousands of girls who consider this all that is necessary, and yet, as the old darky mammy would say, "That's nothing more than a lick and a promise."

The Morning Bath.—I do not recommend for any girl in this country a perfectly cold bath. American women are inclined to be nervous and are not over-strong, consequently the wisest thing to do is to plunge into water that is tepid, and which, when one gives one's self a thorough rubbing, will not cause the much-to-be-dreaded cold. This morning bath is taken for cleanliness, and it is the only way, unless, indeed, one stands up and is carefully sponged, by which one can be sure of perfect physical sweetness? Use soap? Plenty of it. But this soap does not need to be of an expensive kind, and the wise girl is that one who chooses the simplest quality and one that is not scented.

Hot Bath.—A hot bath, which is desirable at least once a week, should be taken at night, and the tired girl will be surprised to find, not only how restful it is, but how perfectly delicious her own body feels when she lies down and her eyelids gradually fall over the eyes weary of looking all the day long

Wash Cloth.—The cheap napery that is sold makes a good wash cloth, for you must remember that, while the sponge is desirable in the bath, something more than a sponge is required to make one absolutely clean. By-the-bye, a light quality of flannel, one combining cotton with wool, is also desirable for a cloth. It is only after one has grown accustomed to the morning bath that one realizes all that it means, how, in the best way, it wakens one up, mentally and physically, and starts one out ready to begin the work of another day.

A Hot Bath Brings Sleep.—Suppose a person be tired out by overwork of any kind, to feel nervous, irritable, and worn, to be absolutely certain that bed means only tossing for hours in an unhappy wakefulness. We all know this condition of the body and mind. Turn on the hot water in the bathroom and soak in the hot bath until the drowsy feeling comes, which will be within three minutes; rub yourself briskly with a coarse Turkish towel until the body is perfectly dry, and then go to bed. You will sleep the sleep of the just, and rise in the morning wondering how you could have felt so badly the night before. The bath has saved many a one from a sleepless night, if not from a severe headache the next day.

A Healthful Practice.—As a rule, every person should take a daily bath—some kind of a wash all over the body. After the teeth, face, neck and hands have been cleansed it is a good practice to take a sponge or towel bath, followed by a vigorous rubbing with a rough towel. It is a good rule to first wet the head.

Systematic Bathing is undoubtedly the best of all preventives against all ordinary diseases and equally so against epidemics, as the following facts from official authority clearly show: During the fatal visitation of the cholera in Paris and Lyons in 1832, out of 16,218 subscribers to the public baths only two deaths among them could be traced to cholera. Comment is unnecessary.

The Skin.—The entire skin with its immense network of nerves and myriads of pores, should be made and kept clean by daily bathing and friction. A hot rubbing bath, with soap, may be followed by a pouring or sponging with cold water; then dry with towels and plenty of rubbing.

Patients.—All patients need some kind of bath daily—a washing of the whole body with sponge, towel, the hands or in any convenient manner. Persons who chill may be first washed with warm water and then quickly sponged over with cold. A brisk rubbing will not fail to bring on a reaction and a toning up of the nerves.

The Cleansing Bath.—This should be taken at least once a week. With sponge or towel or the hand apply warm water over the body. Then soap until there is a perfect lather. Then water and soap and finish with a sponge or towel bath of cold water, followed by a good rubbing with dry towels.

The Towel Bath.—This can be taken when one can get a pint of water and two towels. Fold one towel and dip it into the water. Squeeze out some so that you do not wet the floor. Wash face and head as far as you can reach, and the two arms, then more water and wash the front of the body and the thighs. Now open the length of the towel wet all the middle portion, and, taking it by the two ends, pass it over the neck and saw all down the back, fold it four and have another dash down in front and finish with legs and feet. Now wipe dry, and rub briskly all over with a dry towel, the rougher the better.

Prevention Against Colds.—A daily towel bath, which can be taken in any carpeted room, without spilling a drop of water, is an excellent prevention against cold, helps the appetite and digestion, and is a good means of preventing constipation.

Reaction.—Within a reasonable time after a bath the body in all its parts should become naturally warm. If this is not the case the bath has done no good.

Exercise.—Exercise should be taken after the bath until circulation is fully restored. Where this cannot be done friction by rubbing should take its place.

PRACTICAL RULES FOR BATHING.

1. Bathe at least once a week all over, thoroughly. No one can preserve his health by neglecting personal cleanliness. Remember, "Cleanliness is akin to Godliness."

2. Only mild soap should be used in bathing the body.

3. Wipe quickly and dry the body thoroughly with a moderately coarse towel. Rub the skin vigorously.

4. Many people have contracted severe and fatal diseases by neglecting to take proper care of the body after bathing.

5. If you get a good reaction by thoroughly rubbing in a mild temperature, the effect is always good.

6. Never go into a cold room, or allow cold air to enter the room until you are dressed.

7. Bathing in cold rooms and in cold water is positively injurious, unless the person possesses a very strong and vigorous constitution, and then there is great danger of laying the foundation of some serious disease.

8. Never bathe within two hours after eating. It injures digestion.

9. Never bathe when the body or mind is much exhausted. It is liable to check the healthful circulation.

10. A good time for bathing is just before retiring. The morning hour is a good time also, if a warm room and warm water can be secured.

11. Never bathe a fresh wound or broken skin with cold water; the wound absorbs water, and causes swelling and irritation.

12. A person not robust should be very careful in bathing; great care should be exercised to avoid any chilling effects.

ALL THE DIFFERENT KINDS OF BATHS, AND HOW TO PREPARE THEM.

THE SULPHUR BATH.

For the itch, ringworm, itching, and for other slight skin irritations, bathe in water containing a little sulphur.

THE SALT BATH.

To open the pores of the skin, put a little common salt into the water. Borax, baking soda or lime used in the same way are excellent for cooling and cleansing the skin. A very small quantity in a bowl of water is sufficient.

THE VAPOR BATH.

1. For catarrh, bronchitis, pleurisy, inflammation of the lungs, rheumatism, fever, affections of the bowels and kidneys, and skin diseases, the vapor bath is an excellent remedy.

2. **Apparatus.**—Use a small alcohol lamp and place over it a small dish containing water. Light the lamp and allow the water to boil. Place a cane-bottom chair over the lamp, and seat the patient on it. Wrap blankets or quilts around the chair and around the patient, closing it tightly about the neck. After free perspiration is produced the patient should be wrapped in warm blankets and placed in bed, so as to continue the perspiration for some time.

3. A convenient alcohol lamp may be made by taking a tin box, placing a tube in it, and putting in a common lamp wick. Any tinner can make one in a few minutes at a trifling cost.

THE HOT-AIR BATH.

1. Place the alcohol lamp under the chair, without the dish of water. Then place the patient on the chair, as in the vapor bath, and let him remain until a gentle and free perspiration is produced. This bath may be taken from time to time, as may be deemed necessary.

2. While remaining in the hot-air bath the patient may drink freely of cold or tepid water.

3. As soon as the bath is over the patient should be washed with hot water and soap.

4. The hot-air bath is excellent for colds, skin diseases, and the gout.

THE SPONGE BATH.

1. Have a large basin of water of the temperature of 88 or 95 degrees. As soon as the patient rises rub the body over with a soft, dry towel until it becomes warm.

2. Now sponge the body with water and a little soap, at the same time keeping the body well covered, except such portions as are necessarily exposed. Then dry the skin carefully with a soft, warm towel. Rub the skin well for two or three minutes, until every part becomes red and perfectly dry.

3. Sulphur, lime or salt, and sometimes mustard, may be used in any of the sponge-baths, according to the disease.

THE FOOT BATH.

1. The foot-bath, in coughs, colds, asthma, headaches and fevers, is excellent. One or two table-spoon fuls of ground mustard added to a gallon of hot water, is very beneficial.

2. Heat the water as hot as the patient can endure it, and gradually increase the temperature by pouring in additional quantities of hot water during the bath.

THE SITZ BATH.

A tub is arranged so that the patient can sit down in it while bathing. Fill the tub about one-half full of water. This is an excellent remedy for piles, constipation, headache, gravel, and for acute and inflammatory affections generally.

THE ACID BATH.

Place a little vinegar in water, and heat to the usual temperature. This is an excellent remedy for the disorders of the liver.

A SURE CURE FOR PRICKLY HEAT.

1. Prickly heat is caused by hot weather, by excess of flesh, by rough flannels, by sudden changes of temperature, or by over-fatigue.

2. **Treatment.**—Bathe two or three times a day with warm water, in which a moderate quantity of bran and common soda has been stirred. After wiping the skin dry, dust the affected parts with common corn starch.

Vegetables and Fruits.

HEALTH IN VEGETABLES AND FRUITS.

Water cress is a remedy for scurvy.

Carrots for those suffering with asthma.

Asparagus is used to induce perspiration and purges the blood.

Turnips for nervous disorders and scurvy.

Spinach is useful to those suffering with gravel.

Lettuce is useful for those suffering from insomnia.

Blackberries as a tonic. Useful in all forms of diarrhea.

Cranberries for erysipelas are used externally as well as internally.

Bananas are useful as a food for those suffering from chronic diarrhea

Walnuts give nerve or brain food, muscle, heat and waste.

Pine kernels give heat and stay. They serve as a substitute for bread.

Apples supply the higher nerve and muscle food, but do not give stay.

Oranges are refreshing and feeding, but are not good if the liver is out of order.

Dried figs contain nerve and muscle food, heat and waste; but are bad for the liver.

Green water-grapes are purifying (but of little food value); reject pips and skin.

Blanched almonds give the higher nerve or brain and muscle food; no heat or waste.

Blue grapes are feeding and blood purifying; too rich for those who suffer from the liver.

Juicy fruits give more or less the higher nerve or brain, and some few, muscle food and waste; no heat.

Prunes afford the highest nerve or brain food; supply heat and waste, but are not muscle-feeding. They should be avoided by those who suffer from the liver.

Honey is wholesome, strengthening, cleansing, healing and nourishing.

Pieplant is wholesome and aperient; is excellent for rheumatic sufferers and useful for purifying the blood.

Lemons for feverish thirst in sickness, biliousness, low fevers, rheumatism, colds, coughs, liver complaints, etc.

Celery is invaluable as a food for those suffering from any form of rheumatism; for disease of the nerves and nervous dyspepsia.

Figs are aperient and wholesome. They are said to

Vegetables and Fruits.

be invaluable as a food for those suffering from cancer. They are used externally as well as internally.

Salt to check bleeding of the lungs, and as a nervine and tonic for weak, thin-blooded invalids. Combined with hot water is useful for certain forms of dyspepsia, liver complaints, etc.

Fresh ripe fruits are excellent for purifying the blood and toning up the system. As specific remedies, oranges are aperient. Sour oranges are highly recommended for rheumatism.

Tomatoes are a powerful aperient for the liver, a sovereign remedy for dyspepsia and indigestion. Tomatoes are invaluable in all conditions of the system in which the use of calomel is indicated.

Raw beef proves of great benefit to persons suffering from consumption. It is chopped fine, seasoned with salt and heated by placing in a dish in hot water. It assimilates rapidly and affords the best of nourishment.

Peanuts for indigestion; they are especially recommended for corpulent diabetes. Peanuts are made into a wholesome and nutritious soup, are browned and used as coffee, are eaten as a relish, simply baked, or are prepared and served as salted almonds.

Eggs contain a large amount of nutriment in a compact, quickly available form. Eggs, especially the yolks of eggs are useful in jaundice. Beaten up raw with sugar are used to clear and strengthen the voice. With sugar and lemon juice, the beaten white of egg is used to relieve hoarseness.

Onions are almost the best nervine known. No medicine is so useful in cases of nervous prostration, and there is nothing else that will so quickly relieve and tone up a worn-out system. Onions are useful in all cases of coughs, colds and influenza; in consumption, insomnia, hydrophobia, scurvy, gravel and kindred liver complaints. Eaten every other day they soon have a clearing whitening effect on the complexion.

Apples are useful in nervous dyspepsia; they are nutritious, medicinal, and vitalizing; they aid digestion, clear the voice, correct the acidity of the stomach, are valuable in rheumatism, insomnia, and liver troubles. An apple contains as much nutriment as a potato in a pleasanter and more wholesome form.

PRACTICAL HEALTH RULES.

1. It is no doubt a fact that health is at the command of most people. If people are sick, it is generally their fault, and not their misfortune. It is the violation of the laws of health that produces disease.

2. The average life in America would be about eighty years if proper care were taken of the mind and body; at present it is only thirty-four years.

3. To avert cold feet, wear two pairs of stockings, one pair of cotton or silk, the other of wool, and the natural heat of the feet will be preserved if they are kept clean.

4. Late hours and anxious pursuits exhaust the system, and produce disease and premature death. Therefore the hours of labor and hard study combined should be short.

5. Be moderate in eating and drinking; eat simple and plain food, avoid strong drink, tobacco, snuff, opium, and every excess, and your life will be lengthened many years.

6. A mild temper, and a serene and placid disposition will preserve health and lengthen life.

7. Never eat at irregular intervals. Regularity of meals is a necessity if dyspepsia and other forms of indigestion are to be avoided. Some persons are continually munching cakes, apples, nuts, candies, etc. This practice cannot be too severely condemned.

8. Never overload the stomach. Eating too much is about as bad as swallowing the food whole. The stomach is unable to digest the food, and it consequently ferments and produces disease.

9. Late suppers should always be avoided. Persons who indulge in hearty suppers never secure as sound sleep as those who eat lightly early in the evening.

10. Food should always be of good quality. Stale vegetables, which have lain in the market and withered for a long time, or fruit that is not perfect, is very injurious to the health.

11. One of the most essential things to health is a regular and vigorous system of bathing. Remember that "Cleanliness is next to Godliness."

DISEASE.

Disease is a departure from health and is not a natural condition. If all the causes of disease could be avoided man might expect to live on healthfully from youthful vigor to a good old age. Although we may not be able to live free from bodily ailments, yet the voluntary habits of the individual affect the health conditions more than all other agencies combined, and in this respect we manufacture our own diseases or preserve our existing state of health.

Kinds.—Disease is either acute or chronic. An acute disease lasts but a short time and then terminates in health or death. A chronic disease comes on more slowly and lasts for a long time. Some diseases are acute in the beginning and develop into a chronic nature. Acute diseases are much more easily cured than chronic.

Epidemic.—An epidemic disease attacks a number of persons at the same time, such as fever, smallpox, cholera, when they prevail to a considerable extent in any locality.

Contagious.—A contagious disease is one that is communicated, directly or indirectly, from one patient to another.

Infectious.—A disease is infectious when it requires positive contact to cause it to spread from one person to another. The itch is an infectious disease.

Hereditary.—An hereditary disease is one transmitted from parent to child, from ancestor to descendant.

Malignant.—This is applied to a disease that takes on a severe, obstinate, and unfavorable form, while a mild disease yields readily to curative powers.

Extermination.—Dr. Abernethy, of London—a man of scientific ability—says, "Simplicity and abstemiousness in our dietetic habits will exterminate a growing disease, but to exterminate both the disease and the doctor we must first exterminate the purveyor and the cook." It is manifest that all of our diseases, all pains and aches, all forms of sickness are produced by violations of the laws of our being, directly and indirectly, most of these being connected with dietetic abuses, with such as are produced by the use of intoxicants, tobacco and opium.

BENEATH THE FINGER NAILS.

Beauty and attractiveness demand that great care be bestowed upon the finger nails. But besides this, danger may be lurking beneath the nails in the form of bacteria.

How to Tell Infectious Diseases.

The idea that there is danger in being scratched by another person has no significance as far as the nail itself is concerned. The danger lies not in the nail, but in possible bacteria under the nail, so that a self-inflicted scratch may be as bad as any other.

Biting the finger nails is a bad habit, for there is the risk of swallowing the germs of some infectious disease. The nails have a tendency to gather particles of dust and dirt that may be full of germs. The best method of cleansing the nails is with a brush and plenty of soap and water. A slight scratch with a pin or needle under the nail has often resulted in introducing germs that have brought on the painful felon or whitelow.

How to Tell Contagious Diseases and How Long They are Infectious.

The following points will help to determine the nature of a suspicious illness:

Disease.	Rash or Eruption.	Appearance.	Durat'n in days.	Remarks.
Chicken-pox.	Small rose pimples changing to vesicles	2d day of fever or after 24h'r's illness	6-7	Scabs from about 4th day of fever.
Erysipelas.	Diffuse redness and swelling	2d or 3d day of illness		
Measles.	Small red dots like flea bites	4th day of fever or after 72 hours' illness.	6-10	Rash fades on 7th day.
Scarlet Fever.	Bright scarlet, diffused	2d day of fever or after 24 hours' illness.	8-10	Rash fades on 5th day.
Small-pox.	Small red pimples changing to vesicles, then pustules	3d day of fever or after 48 hours' illness.	14-21	Scabs form 9th or 10th d'y, fall off about 14th.
Typhoid Fever.	Rose-colored spots scattered	11th to 14th day	22-30	Accompanied by diarrhœa.

Disease.	Symptoms appear.	Period ranges from	Patient is Infectious.
Chicken-pox	On 14th day	10-18 days	Until all scabs have fallen off.
Diphtheria	" 2d day	2-5 days	14d's after dis'pear'ce of membr'ne
Measles*	" 14th day	10-14 days	Until scalt'g and co'gh have ceas'd
Mumps	" 19th day	16-24 days	14 days from commencement.
Rotheln	" 14th day	12-20 days	10-14 days from commencement.
Scarlet Fever.	" 4th day	1-7 days	Until a scaling has ceased.
Small-pox	" 12th day	1-14 days	Until all scabs have fallen off.
Typhoid Fever	" 21st day	1-28 days	Until diarrhœa ceases.
Wh'op'g-co'gh†.	" 14th day	7-14 days	Six wks. from beginning to wh'op

*In measels the patient is infectious three days before the eruption appears.

†In whooping-cough the patient is infectious during the primary cough, which may be three weeks before the whooping begins.

The Wonderful Revelations of the Microscope. The Discovery of the Invisible Assailants of Health.

The microscope has revealed a new kingdom of invisible life. The air we breathe, the water we drink, the air above us and the earth beneath us, are filled with countless myriads of little bodies, known as "microbes," "bacteria," "bacilli," etc. They are the most insidious, relentless and powerful enemies to human life, and destroy more lives than war, famine, fire, murder, shipwreck, and all other casualties combined. There is scarcely a disease known to mankind which is not due to the entrance of these "microbes" into the body. Disease is simply the manifestation of their presence. They feed upon the blood and tissue until destroyed, or death destroys their victim.

All acute contagious diseases, such as small-pox, chicken pox, scarlet fever, typhus fever, measles, influenza, whooping cough, hydrophobia, etc., are the results of living microbes, which have gained access to the blood or tissue.

Another class of microbes, says Dr. Samuel Hart, are called miasmatic contagions. The germs are propagated in diseased persons, but, as a law of their further development, they must undergo one change outside of the body, in some decomposing organic body, before they can again produce their peculiar disease in healthy persons except by inoculation. Typhoid fever, yellow fever, cholera, diphtheria, acute consumption, erysipelas, etc., belong to this class of disease.

When the microbes originate entirely in decomposing matter, continues Dr. Hart, the diseases caused are intermittent fever, remittent fever, continued malarial fever, etc.

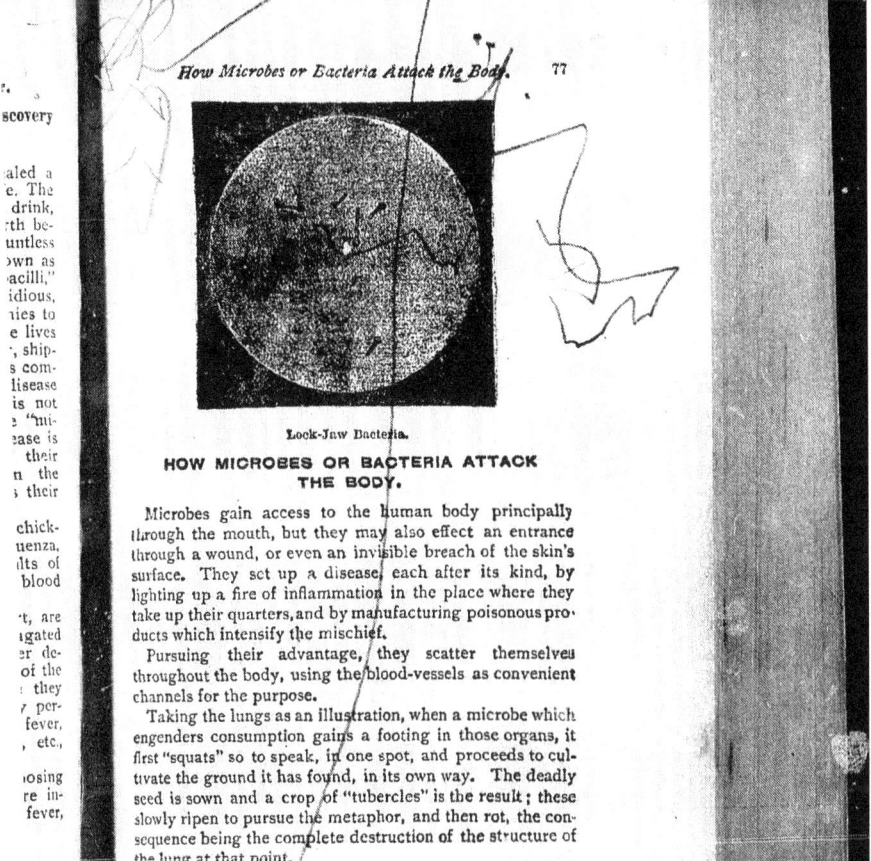

Lock-Jaw Bacteria.

HOW MICROBES OR BACTERIA ATTACK THE BODY.

Microbes gain access to the human body principally through the mouth, but they may also effect an entrance through a wound, or even an invisible breach of the skin's surface. They set up a disease, each after its kind, by lighting up a fire of inflammation in the place where they take up their quarters, and by manufacturing poisonous products which intensify the mischief.

Pursuing their advantage, they scatter themselves throughout the body, using the blood-vessels as convenient channels for the purpose.

Taking the lungs as an illustration, when a microbe which engenders consumption gains a footing in those organs, it first "squats" so to speak, in one spot, and proceeds to cultivate the ground it has found, in its own way. The deadly seed is sown and a crop of "tubercles" is the result; these slowly ripen to pursue the metaphor, and then rot, the consequence being the complete destruction of the structure of the lung at that point.

HOW TO DESTROY MICROBES.

The person, as well as the house and yard, must be kept clean. Cold water is, of course, most useful; but every man, woman and child ought to take a hot bath about once a week, and frequent changes of underclothing should be made. Still more important, perhaps, is the character of the drinking-water we consume, for ninety-nine cases out of a hundred of typhoid fever are due to contaminated drinking-water. Boiling for half an hour will make water sufficiently pure for practical safety, which can not be said of filtering alone. Indeed, if a filter can not be cleaned, instead of being a blessing it is a curse, and a serious source of danger. There appears to be but one satisfactory filter in the market, and it is not altogether adapted for use in private houses.

If there has been sickness in the house, additional precautions ought to be taken. The paper on the walls of the sick-room should be removed and burnt; the walls and ceiling should then be washed with a solution consisting of one part of bichloride of mercury to 1,000 parts of water. This germ-destroyer, often called corrosive sublimate, is a deadly poison, and must be handled with great care. All bed-linen and other clothing from the room occupied by the sick person should be boiled for no less than three hours, and to every four gallons of water used for this purpose one pound of sulphate of zinc may be added.

Cats and dogs are a serious source of danger if they have been permitted to roam around promiscuously at their own sweet will, as they carry the germs of disease with them, and quite frequently convey most serious disorders not only to children, but to grown persons. As there is no satisfactory method of sterilizing these animals, it is best to have none of them about the house unless they can be kept within bounds.

Fresh air, pure water, and sunshine are the deadly microbe's worst enemies, and attention to a few simple hygienic rules will enormously lessen the chances of disease, while, if a few simple precautions, such as those already mentioned, are neglected, the probability of some microbic disorder attacking some member of the household is considerably increased.

HOW TO DISINFECT A ROOM.

We present our readers with an abstract of a recent lecture by J. H. Kellogg, M. D.

The best means to disinfect a room which has been occupied by a consumptive or a person suffering from any other infectious disease is to burn sulphur in it. To do this, take a dishpan and place a flat plate in the bottom of it, and on this set a kettle containing the proper quantity of sulphur mixture—equal quantities of sulphur and charcoal. Fill the pan with water so that it comes half way up on the kettle. Then turn alcohol or benzine on the mixture, ignite and get out of the room as speedily as possible. Alcohol is much the best to use, and two or three ounces will be sufficient for several pounds of sulphur. Let the room remain closed for twenty-four hours.

Previous Preparation.—The room should be prepared previously by having every crack about doors and windows tightly pasted or stopped up. The object of using water is that the heat of the kettle will cause evaporation and send moisture out into the room, for the spores being very tenacious of life, dry sulphur fumes are not sufficient to kill them all. In the dry state the product is simply oxide of sulphur, but when water is added we have sulphuric acid, which is powerful enough to kill the spores as well as the germs.

Sufficient Quantity.—It is of the utmost importance that a sufficient quantity of the sulphur be used to make the work effective. I have seen people attempt to disinfect a large room with a handful of sulphur barely sufficient to disinfect a dry-goods box. It amounts to nothing whatever. Ascertain the size of the room, and burn three pounds of sulphur for every 1,000 cubic feet of air. Take, for instance, a room which is 12 by 15 feet floor measurement, and 10 feet high, which gives a cubical contents of 1,800 feet. This is so nearly 2,000 that it would be best to take six pounds of sulphur to disinfect it.

Chloride of Lime.—Some people distribute a handful of chloride of lime about, which gives a sanitary smell, but is really of no value. Many strange notions as to disinfection prevail, and all sorts of valueless recommendations are going the rounds of the papers. For instance, I called upon a patient once and found a tub of water under the bed, and it was explained to me that it was for the purpose of absorbing germs. Others will set powdered charcoal around on trays, or a little chloride of lime on a saucer. Some people seem to imagine that the germs are going to hunt up the disinfectant and destroy themselves. A strong solution of copperas will kill all the germs it touches, but not the spores or seeds of the germs.

Half a pound of chloride of lime to a gallon of water makes a good disinfectant to destroy germs in excreta, provided the chloride of lime is good, but the most of it is poor, having lost its disinfectant properties.

Corrosive Sublimate.—Another excellent disinfectant is corrosive sublimate, but it is too dangerous for common use, unless kept under lock and key. It is best used in connection with permanganate of potash, one drachm of each to a gallon of water. This will make a reddish or purplish solution, and if marked poison, and handled with care, will be dangerous chiefly to germs. This solution is equal to about one part in a thousand of each, and the corrosive sublimate will destroy the germs, and the permanganate of potash will destroy the odors as well as furnish coloring matter. A solution of corrosive sublimate alone is colorless, odorless, and nearly tasteless, which facts greatly increase the risks of using it. About one part in 20,000 is sufficient to kill germs, but to disinfect excreta it is necessary to use a strong solution, the bulk of the disinfectant equaling that of the excreta.

Clothing.—For disinfecting the clothing from the bed and the patient, soak for four hours, either in a solution of corrosive sublimate and water or the same length of time in a two per cent. solution of carbolic acid. The latter is to be preferred for general purposes, for it will not affect the texture, while corrosive sublimate will shrink flannel clothing and make it harsh.

Walls and Floor.—A solution of corrosive sublimate may be used to disinfect a room by washing the walls and floor in it, but the permanganate of potash must be left out from this as well as from the solution for disinfecting clothing, for it will stain. To set any of these things in a room does no good; a disinfectant must be distributed to be available.

A Good Disinfectant.—Dr Stone says: "All authorities, I believe, are agreed in giving the preference to chlorine, which may be evolved by mixing in a bottle two tablespoonfuls of common salt, two tablespoonfuls red lead and one-half a wineglassful of strong oil of vitriol in a quart of water. The bottle should be kept cool, tightly stopped and in a dark place. A little of this fluid exposed in a saucer, sprinkled on the floor, or soaked in sheets of old linen and hung about the rooms, rapidly destroys effluvia. Green copperas (sulphate of iron) one pound, dissolved in a gallon of water, is another very excellent agent, and the same may be said of the fumes of sulphur (sulphurous acid) for unoccupied rooms. Chloride of lead solution is another potent fluid; it is cheap, involves very little trouble, is instantaneous in its effect and perfectly safe. Indeed, any of the above will be found to destroy the rankest compound or villainous smell that ever offended the nostril."

Copperas.—The very best disinfectant and deodorizer known is copperas. A double handful dissolved in a bucket of water and used to wash drain pipes and receptacles of waste material will keep such places above suspicion. The water in pitchers and flower-holders should be changed every day. On attention to such seemingly trivial details may hang a human life.

Carbolic Acid.—When it is required to use carbolic acid as a disinfectant, it should be mixed with boiling water. This promptly overcomes the usual antagonism between the acid and the water, and converts them into a permanent solution which will keep for weeks.

SANITATION ABOUT THE HOME.

Cleanliness.—The maxim "Health is wealth" is not appreciated as a truism; more frequently health is only prized as a blessing when it is wanting. The health of the household depends upon the scrupulous cleanliness of the premises more than upon any other one thing. The responsibility for this must largely rest with the house mother, she being the one usually more sensible of any needed change, and so the plainest and simplest expositions of sanitary science should be familiar to her.

Drains and Sinks.—The location of drains and sinks should be carefully considered and their condition frequently inspected. The drain pipe from a kitchen sink should lead for rods away from the house and let the outlet reach the roots of trees or shrubs which specially delight in moisture, as the willow or the quince. Never use an open box to convey any form of slops. Wood is often used as a conductor pipe, but in a short time it becomes thoroughly saturated with filth, and thus a breeder of disease and a menace to health. Tile is better than wood, and being porous, much of the moisture oozes out as it passes along.

Iron Pipes are good as long as they last, but will rust

82　　　　　　　　Sanitation

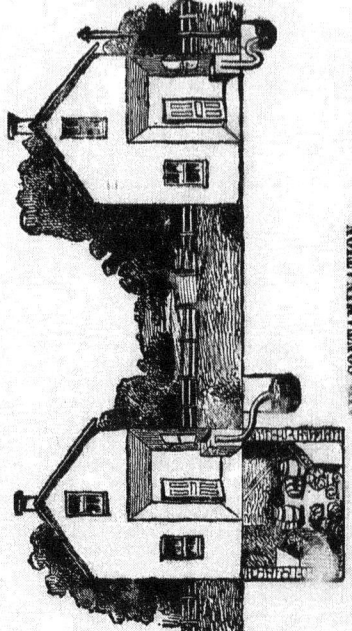

AIR CONTAMINATION.

The above cut is an illustration of a very common source of disease. At the left hand is shown a house, the inmates of which are being poisoned by destructive gases laden with disease germs which emanate from the cesspool, in which may be seen bits and barrels of decomposing vegetables, as of the cesspool filled with the accumulations of years. The foul gases and germs from the cellar find ready access to the rooms above through the open cellar door and from the seething cesspool they ascend to the house through the untrapped drain pipe which communicates with the sink. At the right hand may be seen a house which is protected from cess-pool contamination by means of a trap in the drain pipe. As will be seen, the foul gases pass up through the ventilating pipe into the open air, instead of being drawn up into the house through the kitchen sink.

This cut is taken from *The Monitor of Health*, by permission of the publishers, Good Health Publishing Co., Battle Creek, Mich.

in the course of time. Lead is the best and most durable of all, but is also the most expensive. However, if the expense of a lead drainage pipe is set over against a doctor's bill and other expenses incident to sickness, it will be cheap in comparison, and who would consider it for a moment when weighed against the precious life of some member of the family.

Disinfectant.—Whatever material is used as a conductor, the drain should be flushed with some good disinfectant solution as often as once a week in warm weather. Copperas is as good as anything for ordinary use and has the advantage of being cheap. It can be procured of a druggist for about three or five cents a pound. Dissolve in the proportion of one-fourth of a pound to a gallon of water and use very freely. Plug the outlet and pour enough into the sink to fill the pipe its full length. Use the solution as near the boiling point as convenient, for the reason that a hot fluid is more penetrating than a cold one, an advantage if tile or wood is used. A hot solution is further advantageous as a solvent of whatever waste particles may have lodged at various points or gathered the length of the pipe. Dishwater usually contains more or less grease, and this will be melted and washed out if the disinfectant is poured in hot. Potash, sal-soda and lye may be used instead of copperas.

Refrigerators in which food is kept should be kept scrupulously clean and the pipe conveying the drippings from it should be entirely disconnected from the drainage system of the house. Milk and butter should not be placed near vegetables, especially those having a strong smell. Place a piece of charcoal in your refrigerator.

A Home Made Filter.—An eminent sanitarian, Dr. Parkes, has given directions for a home-made filter for drinking water. A large common flower-pot is covered over at the bottom, the opening and all, with a piece of clean flannel or of zinc gauze. Over this put a layer of coarse gravel about three inches deep, and over the gravel a layer of white sand of the same depth. Above the sand put four inches of charcoal, broken in fragments. If possible use animal charcoal. Lay over the top a clean, fine sponge that covers it, or if you have not a sponge, a layer of clean flannel. The top layer, whether of flannel or sponge, is to be made sterile by frequent washing and boiling. Set the filter in a wooden frame, and under it put a clean vessel to receive the water as it comes through the filter.

DISEASE GERMS IN DRINKING WATER, AND HOW TO COMBAT THEM.

1. Taking a little filtered beef bouillon, clear as crystal to the eye, and showing under the microscope not a trace of life, let us place it in a glass flask and, boiling it repeatedly to destroy any germs it may contain, set it aside in a warm place with the mouth of the flask open. In a few days the liquid previously so limpid becomes very turbid. If we take a drop and magnify it 1,000 diameters we shall see that the liquid is crowded with life, and the few ounces of bouillon contain a vaster population than our greatest cities can boast of.

2. Cohn has seen bacillus in infusions at blood heat divide every twenty minutes. We have calculated this rate for twenty-four hours, and have found that at the end of the first day there would be as the descendants of a single bacillus 4,722,366,482,869,645,213,696 individuals; and though we can pack a trillion (1,000,000,000,000) in a cubic inch, this number would fill about 2,500,000 cubic feet. This is clearly not what they do, but simply what they are capable of doing for a short time when temperature and food supply are favorable.

3. Since the multiplication of bacteria is so favored by the warmth of Summer, it requires special sanitary precaution, in order to keep free from disease.

4. **Vegetable Refuse or Slop.**—If garbage and slops are thrown about the house, you can readily see what millions and myriads of bacteria will form, and how the whole ground will soon swarm with them. They will more or less work their way among the things that must be eaten, or if a heavy rain should come, will easily find their way into the well and contaminate the water. Malaria, typhoid fever, etc., will soon be the result.

5. **Sink Holes.**—There should be a sink hole for garbage, slops and other refuse matter of the house, and this sink hole should be sufficiently far from the well, so as not to contaminate the water.

6. That sunshine is a germicide as well as a tonic has but recently been proved: if we take two flasks containing the bacillus with spores, and keep one in the direct sunshine for a long time, while the other, exposed to the same heat, is kept from the sun, we find the sun-exposed spores have lost their virulence, while the others remain. Is there need to further press so patent a lesson? As bacteria grow best in the presence of considerable moisture, we may ex-

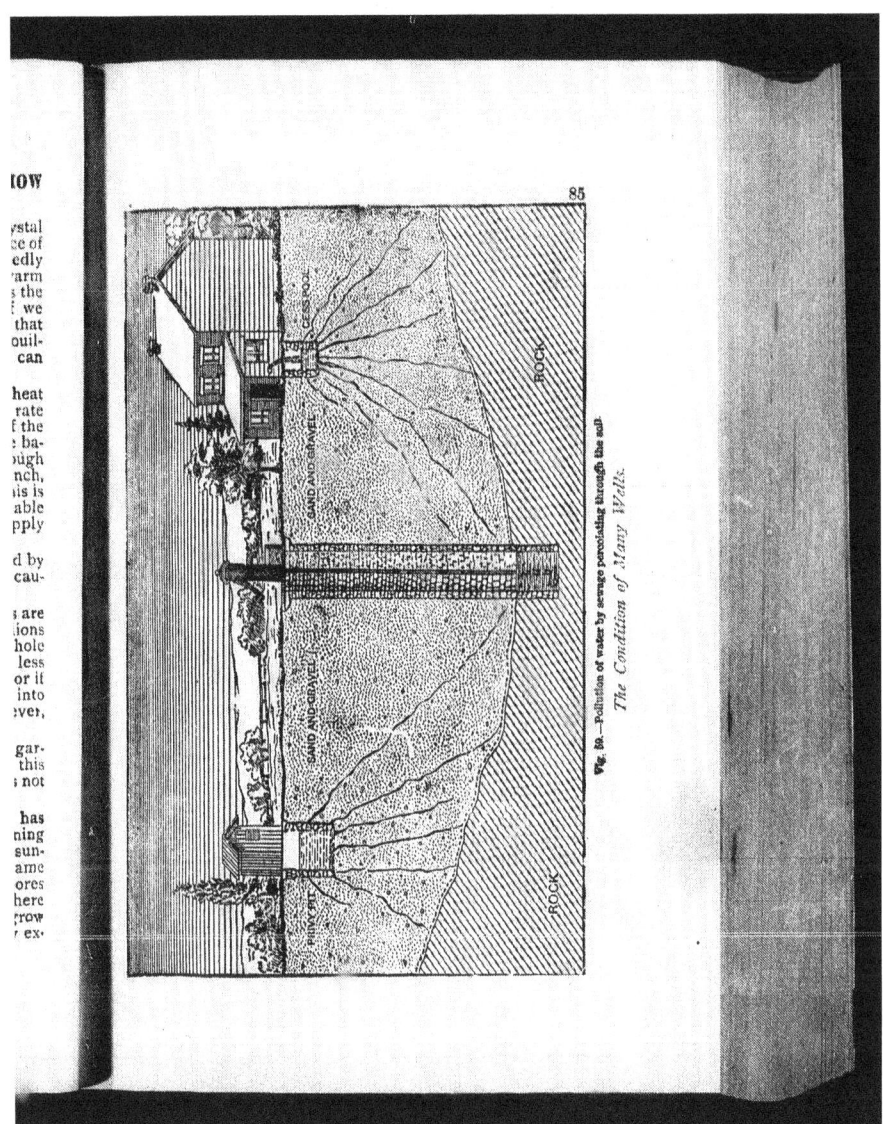

Fig. 20.—Pollution of water by sewage percolating through the soil.
The Condition of Many Wells.

Impure Water.

pect to encounter them in greater abundance in water than in air. Rain water contains 60,000 to a quart, the Vanin four times as many, while the polluted Seine from 5,000,000 to 12,000,000.

7. Remedy for Impure Water.—The minute size of bacteria renders it very difficult to use any system of filtration and have pure water. If the water is impure there is but one absolutely safe method, and that is boiling.

8. Boiling Water.—No disease germs producing bacteria can stand boiling for an hour or so. It destroys all vegetable and animal impurities. All doubtful water should be thoroughly boiled.

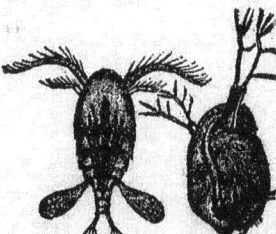

Animals that dwell in our drinking water.

THE ANIMALS WE DRINK IN OUR WATER.

The above illustration shows some of the animals we drink in impure water, which is a very prolific source of many diseases.

Thousands of wells are so situated that they receive a drainage from filthy and decomposing matter, or are polluted by slop holes' imperfect drains, that are too closely adjacent to the well.

Water from many of the wells is unfit for the human stomach, and some of them are as poisonous as Paris green. Impure water may be used for a time without any perceptible injury, but it is only a matter of time when it will develop into typhoid fever, diphtheria and many other diseases.

In either case, when well water is used, people should look the location over carefully, to see if the lay of the land is such as to allow decomposing matter from the surface of the ground or any other place to soak into the well. If this is the case, it should be abandoned at once if you value life, for it is positively known that thousands have lost their lives by using such water.

Every well should be laid up with brick or lime-stone and cemented about four feet from the surface. That will make a safe protection.

Heavy rains will often cause water to flow into wells, which has a very bad effect, and often develops disease germs.

MALARIA AND WATER.

The most recent scientific authorities are of the opinion that malaria is a water-born disease. In vast malarial districts, it is not the air which the inhabitants breathe, but the water they drink, which brings on the much-dreaded malarial fever. That this is the case in some sections of the land, has been clearly proved by the immunity from fever of such families as depended on filtered rain-water, and not on the wells of the country.

It has also been noted that horses and other animals, brought into certain sections of the country, thrived well so long as they were housed and drank from the cistern supply of the barns, but sickened and died when left to wander in the fields, and drink from brooks and pools. If this should be clearly proven, it might be possible to stamp out one of the greatest evils of life in some sections of the country.

It is not a difficult matter to collect the rain-water in a clean cistern. It should be passed through a filtering medium that is frequently renewed, as it is now known that a filter too long in use becomes one of the most effective means of contaminating the water it is intended to purify. The filter that is clogged up with impurities is far worse than none at all, and this is the condition of a great many cistern filters.

As an extra precaution, even the cistern-water ought to be boiled, poured in a clean earthen jar, and cooled in a pure atmosphere. The ice formed from contaminated water is almost as objectionable as the unclean water itself, as a large number of bacteria are undisturbed by frost. Such a jar of boiled water should be daily renewed, as if it is left standing any length of time it will soon take on the same objectionable features as the water of the country.

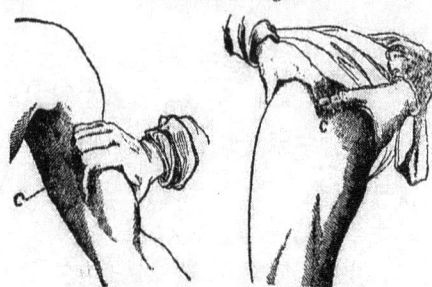

Accidents and Emergencies.

HOW TO STOP BLEEDING.

1. **Cause.** — Bleeding is the result of the rupture of an artery, vein, or other small blood vessel, and may be caused by a cut, bruise, or may take place spontaneously.

2. **Fainting.** — If a person is fainting on account of loss of blood, do but little to rally him, as fainting tends to stop the bleeding.

3. **Arterial Bleeding.** — If the blood is a bright scarlet color and comes out in throbbing jerks, it comes from an

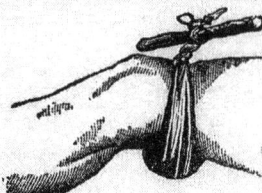

artery, and the fingers must be placed on the wound with considerable pressure till bandages can be applied, or tie a handkerchief tightly around the limb or member above the injury and place a stick in it and turn it until the pressure is sufficient to stop the flow of blood.

Arterial bleeding is the most dangerous and a physician should at once be sent for.

4. **Venous Bleeding.** — Venous blood is dark colored and flows continually. It can usually be stopped by pressure

Accidents and Emergencies.

with the fingers or a piece of linen. The injured parts may be drawn together, and sticking plaster used as soon as the flow of blood ceases.

5. **Tight Bandages.**—If the limb should become purple, loosen the bandages a little, and if the flow of blood begins again it can be tightened up so as to control it until the physician arrives.

6. **Precaution.**—If an artery is cut, compress above the wound, and if a vein is cut, compress below.

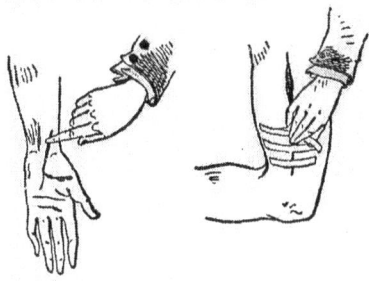

7. **Accidents.**—When an accident happens there is usually not much time to decide what is best to be done. Help, to be effectual, must be prompt, and often delay implies further injury or loss of life.

It is well to fix in the mind a few general principles of treatment in the more common accidents. When the emergency arises these are recalled instinctively and form the basis of action. The means by which they are to be carried into effect follow naturally and the necessity is met.

For simple, superficial cuts nothing more than cold water and lint will be required, the patient remaining quiet.

In a lacerated wound, with small streams of blood issuing from several points, lint, cold water and ice dripped into the wound, together with a slight pressure over the region from which the blood issues, will be sufficient.

Binding a bunch of cobwebs or a handful of flour on the wound, or bathing it in strong vinegar, is sometimes effectual.

8. **Hemorrhage** from the lungs is always alarming, but unless it is very violent, seldom threatens life immediately. Raise the head and shoulders slightly with pillows. Fill a pitcher with boiling water, pour in a teaspoonful of spirits of turpentine, and let the fumes be inhaled. Give small pieces of ice and enforce perfect quiet. Blood from the lungs is bright red and frothy, and is coughed or spit up.

9. **The Stomach.**—Blood from the stomach is dark, mixed with particles of food, and comes in the act of vomiting. The person should be kept perfectly quiet, lying down, and ice wrapped in a cloth or ice bag placed over the stomach.

10. **Nose Bleeding.**—Epistaxis, or bleeding from the nose, is sometimes very troublesome. Keep the head thrown back, holding a wet cloth or sponge to receive the blood, at the same time raising the arms above the head. Press the fingers firmly on each side of the nose where it joins the upper lip. Place some cold substance, as a lump of ice, at the back of the neck or on the forehead at the bridge of the nose. If these remedies are ineffectual, have a little fine salt or alum sniffed into the nostrils.

11. **Ordinary Nose Bleeding** may be stopped by snuffing cold water up the bleeding nostril. If this fails after a few trials, place a little salt into the water. Filling the nose with a corner of the handkerchief for a few moments is a good remedy; or grasping the nose with the thumb and forefinger, and holding it firmly closed for a few moments, will generally cure the severest cases in a very short time.

CUTS AND WOUNDS.

1. **Clean the Wound.**—In case of a wound first clean it and wash it thoroughly with warm water, and when the bleeding ceases, bring the edges together, either fastening them with a bandage or court plaster.

2. **Sewing a Wound.** — If the wound is very wide a few stitches may be necessary. Take a needle and silk thread and oil both needle and thread thoroughly with vaseline or pure lard. Each stitch should be tied into a knot, and should be left at least twenty-four hours before removing.

3. **Pieces Cut Out.**—If a patch or portion is cut completely away, quickly clean the portion cut away and replace it and keep it in the exact position by court plaster or

bandages. No time must be lost in the treatment of a case of this kind.

4. Stabs. — Stabs are more dangerous than common wounds, and the wound must be kept open and never be closed up until it heals naturally. All persons suffering from stabs should remain quietly in bed until all serious symptoms have disappeared.

5. Gun Shot Wounds. — All wounds of this character are serious and a physician should be promptly summoned.

6. Sprains.—Sprains are the straining of the tendons and ligaments, and require great care and caution in their treatment. The injured member should be kept very quiet and bandaged with warm water. Then apply freely Arnica, Pond's Extract or the like.

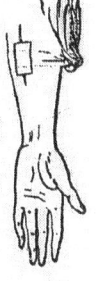

UNUSUAL EMERGENCIES.

1. **Poisoning.**—When poison is swallowed, an excellent remedy is to mix one heaped tea-spoonful of salt and one heaped tea-spoonful of mustard in a glass of water and drink immediately. Then give the whites of two eggs in a cup of coffee. Give the eggs alone if the coffee cannot be readily secured.

2. **Treatment of Poisoned Wounds.** — Suck poisoned wounds, unless the mouth is sore; enlarge the wound, or if very serious cut out the part without delay, or cauterize with a hot iron.

OTHER REMEDIES FOR POISONING.

In poisoning by opium strong coffee should be given, the victim being kept roused and awake, if possible, until medical aid be obtained.

The antidotes to arsenic are tablespoonful doses of dialyzed iron, magnesia and castor oil.

Carbolic acid: Give a tablespoonful of Epsom salts stirred in water, and repeat.

Ammonia: Oil of any kind.

Oxalic acid: Give chalk, lime, lime-water or magnesia freely.

Corrosive Sublimate: White of egg and milk in quantities.

In poisoning by an acid the use of alkalis is indicated, as soda, magnesia, chalk, lime and soapsuds. When the mischief has been wrought by strong alkalis acid must be used, as vinegar, lemon juice or hard cider.

When the mucous membrane of the mouth is much inflamed or destroyed give raw eggs, flour stirred in water, flaxseed tea, arrowroot, or any soothing drink. Stimulation can be applied by means of hot water bottles or bags to the feet and over heart, and by rubbing the extremities. Alcoholic stimulant should be administered very cautiously

Fainting is caused by an interruption of the supply of blood to the brain. The head should be lowered immediately. Often laying the person down will revive her without other measures. The head may be allowed to hang over the side of the couch for a few moments. Smelling-salts may be held to the nose and heat applied over the heart to stimulate its action. Open a window or outer door to admit plenty of fresh air, unfasten the clothing to permit free circulation. In severe cases when unconsciousness is prolonged, a mustard paste must be placed over the heart; if the breathing stops artificial respiration can be begun. It is useless to try to give stimulants by mouth unless the person is sufficiently conscious to be able to swallow. The attack usually passes off in a few minutes, but the invalid should be made to lie still and be kept quiet for some time after it.

Convulsions in a grown person are always alarming. In children they proceed from a variety of causes, some of which are comparatively unimportant. A fit of indigestion or the irritation from cutting teeth may produce them. They may indicate the commencement of disease, but they are seldom fatal, and while the doctor should be sent for, there is no cause for immediate alarm.

FOREIGN BODIES IN EAR, NOSE OR THROAT.

There are few accidents more alarming to a mother than when a child swallows a foreign body.

If it has gone beyond reach of the finger no special effort should be made to dislodge it. Nature will probably take care of it if she is not interfered with. Emetics or cathartics may produce disastrous results. The only thing that can be done is to give a plentiful meal of soft food.

Foreign Bodies in the Ear.—These do not usually occasion much discomfort for a time, and as the passage of the outer ear is closed at the end by a membrane they cannot penetrate farther, and may safely be left until they can be removed by a competent person. When an insect has entered turn the head on one side with the affected ear uppermost and gently pour in a little warm water. When this runs out the drowned intruder comes with it.

Water should not be used when a pea or bean has been introduced, because they swell when moist.

Foreign Bodies in the Nose.—These may sometimes be drawn out with a bent hairpin. If not easily removed in this way they should not be poked at. A little snuff or pepper may be sniffed in, or the opposite nostril tickled with a straw. The act of sneezing will probably dislodge the substance; if not it should be left for a surgeon to extract.

Foreign Bodies in the Throat.—This may be a very serious accident whether it occurs in the windpipe or the food passage. It demands immediate action or the result may be a fatal one. Send for the doctor at once, as he may have to open the windpipe to save the victim's life. Meantime slap the sufferer on the back between the shoulders. Insert the finger as far down as possible to try to grasp the obstruction and remove it. Turn the person's head downward and slap the back forcibly.

If breathing ceases the patient should be laid on the back, the arms pulled upward, the hands resting on the top of the head, then brought down and pressed on the chest, repeating the movements sixteen times in a minute.

Strangulation.—When a person is strangling, make him swallow the white of an egg, but do not beat it. This will almost certainly dislodge the obstruction, unless lodged in the trachea.

Sunstroke and Gas Suffocation.

3. **Choking.**—If badly choked, get upon all fours and cough.

4. **Fish Bone in the Throat.**—Press the tongue down with a spoon handle so as to be able to look down the throat and with a pair of tweezers remove the bone. If this cannot be done, swallow the whites of several eggs (one at a time), or take a big bite of bread and swallow it; if this fails, send for a good surgeon at once.

5. **Sunstroke.**—Remove the patient in the shade, and apply cold water to the head and neck, and a mustard plaster to the feet. Administer strong stimulants.

6. **Coal Gas Suffocation.**—If the patient does not breathe, produce artificial respiration; place the patient on his face and turn the body gently, but completely, one side and a little beyond; then again on the face and so on alternately. Repeat these movements deliberately and perseveringly, fifteen times only in a minute.

BURNS.

There is no accident more terrible than severe injuries from fire. All well-instructed persons know that when a woman's dress is in flames water is almost useless to extinguish it unless she could be plunged under it. The fire can be put out only by cutting off the supply of air, without which it cannot burn. This can be done by enveloping the person in a rug, blanket or any woolen article of sufficient size.

Baking Soda.—The pain from slight burns is very great.

An excellent application is a thick paste of common baking soda moistened with water, spread on a piece of linen or cotton, and bound on the part. This can be kept wet by squeezing water on it from a sponge or cloth until the smarting is soothed.

Starch.—A thick coating of starch can be used instead of the soda, or wheat-flour if nothing better can be had, but neither should be applied if the skin is broken. In this case it is better to use vaseline, olive or linseed oil or equal parts of raw linseed oil and lime water. The doctor will apply some preparation containing carbolic acid.

If the air can be effectually excluded from a burn the pain is relieved.

Blisters should be pricked and the fluid absorbed with a soft cloth before applying a dressing.

If the cloth adheres to the skin the loose part should be cut away and the patches of material soaked off with oil or warm water.

When the injury is extensive the sufferer will be prostrated and may die from the shock. Heat should be applied to the extremities and over the heart, and hot drinks given until the doctor comes.

Burns From Acid.—In burns from a strong acid the part should be covered with dry baking soda or lime, as the alkali will neutralize the acid. No water should be used, but a dressing of cosmoline or oil applied after the alkali has been brushed off.

When the burn has been caused by an alkali an acid must be used. A person recovering from the effects of a burn requires very nourishing food.

White of Eggs.—A soothing application for burns is to cover them with the white of an egg. This forms a coating over the injured flesh and protects it from the air.

Another Remedy.—Some think there is nothing that can equal lime and lard. Take sifted air-slacked lime and mix with lard. Spread on a cloth. If the burn is deep, another plaster should be made at once to lay on. As soon as the lard gets warm it will begin to burn again. Scrape the plaster on and mix in more fresh lime. After the wound quits burning the plasters should be kept on and will heal the sore. Air-slacked lime is valuable and should be kept in the house at all times, as it affords instant relief for burns.

Magic Cure.—Loose cotton, slightly moistened with linseed oil, has almost a magical effect in relieving the pains of severe burns.

BROKEN BONES.

A Broken Bone need not be set immediately. This knowledge saves much unnecessary anxiety when the doctor cannot be procured at once.

The parts must be put in as comfortable position as possible and most nearly corresponding to the natural one. It is necessary to give support above and below the break.

Handle the injured part very carefully, not to force the rough ends of bone through the skin.

Improvise splints of some kind—two strips of wood, a couple of stout book covers, or pieces of pasteboard. Place on one side when it is a limb that is injured, and bind them in place with handkerchiefs. A long pillow firmly tied will answer the purpose, or in case of injury to a leg it may be fastened to its fellow if nothing better can be done, remembering to tie it above and below the injury.

Shoulder-Bone.—When the shoulder-bone is broken place the arm on the injured side across the chest, the hand touching the opposite shoulder, and fasten it in place by passing a broad bandage around the body.

Fracture of the Ribs.—In fracture of the ribs pin a towel around the body until the doctor comes.

In a simple fracture the bone is broken, it may be, in several places, but there is no deep flesh wound extending to the seat of the injury; when there is such a wound the fracture is said to be compound.

When there is a fracture the part is unnaturally movable unless the ends of the bone have been driven together or impacted.

Dislocation.—In a dislocation the bone is forced out of its socket at the joint. There is more or less deformity, and it is difficult to move the limb. The last point helps to distinguish it from the fracture. Time is of importance, as the swelling which supervenes increases the difficulty of reducing it or returning the bone to its proper place. Hot applications may be made if the surgeon cannot be had immediately.

FOR BARB WIRE CUTS.

Take carbolic acid 1 ounce, water 1 pint; mix. Apply this to the cut three or four times a day until the cavity gets nearly full with new flesh, and then apply mutton tallow.

How to Treat a Drowning Person.

Place the patient with face downward, and wrist under his forehead, so that the water can run out of his mouth and throat. Then restore breathing by turning the patient on his right side, and excite the nostrils with ammonia or snuff. Dash cold water upon the face and chest. If this is not effectual, turn the patient first upon his face and then upon his back gently, at the same time pressing the back between the shoulder blades gently with the hand. This assists forcing the air out of the lungs, and will stimulate respiration. As soon as breathing is established, apply warm flannels and bottles of hot water to the stomach and feet. Hot water bags can be used instead of hot bottles, if it is convenient.

HOW TO CURE A SNAKE BITE.

The part bitten swells to enormous proportions immediately, and assumes various colors, and the person bitten will pass from nausea and vomiting to delirium and unconsciousness. If death does not follow from the first effects, it is likely to follow from the fever and inflammation of the wound.

Treatment:—Suck the wound vigorously to withdraw the poison, and stop the circulation with a handkerchief and stick as shown on page 88. In all instances large and frequent drinks of brandy or whiskey with a free application of kerosene oil to the wound will prove an effectual remedy. Keep the wound tied up with a bandage soaked in kerosene oil. Give the patient all the liquor he can drink. It is always best to consult a physician as soon as possible.

IMAGE EVALUATION
TEST TARGET (MT-3)

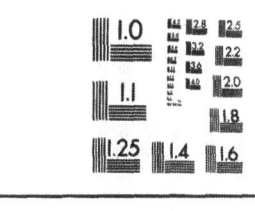

← 6″ →

Photographic
Sciences
Corporation

23 WEST MAIN STREET
WEBSTER, N.Y. 14580
(716) 872-4503

RABIES OR HYDROPHOBIA.

Immediate Treatment for Mad Dog Bite.

If a person has been bitten by an animal suspected to be rabid, he should immediately suck the wound thoroughly. If on an extremity, bind the limb tightly between the heart and wound to encourage bleeding. Cleanse the wound with simple hot water, or a saturated solution in hot water of Boracic Acid, and dress with frequent renewals of the same, or a saturated solution of Boracic Acid in glycerine. When the wound is once thoroughly cleansed, it should be allowed to heal. Persons who have been bitten by suspected animals should understand that not more than 16 per cent. of persons bitten by dogs, *actually rabid*, take the disease. The animal should be confined and watched to determine whether it is suffering from the disease, that the treatment of the victim may be decided thereby. It is best to cauterize the wound after cleansing it.

DEATH GAS IN A WELL.

How to Avoid it and How to Get Rid of it.

1. The gas which produces death in a well is what is called carbonic acid gas. It is much heavier than air, and consequently will always accumulate in the bottom of a well; and if an unsuspecting man goes into it he is at once suffocated, gasps for breath and falls; some one not understanding the cause of the trouble goes down, and he will also become a victim. Many lives are annually lost in this way.

2. To find out whether gas has collected in the well, let down a light, and if it goes out there is a good deal of gas in the well; if it burns dimly when it comes near the bottom, there is sufficient gas to make it dangerous.

3. A very good way for a man who goes down into a well is, to take a candle or a lamp with him, as shown in the above illustration. He must hold the candle considerably below his mouth, or it will do no good. If the light goes out or becomes very dim he should stop at once, for another step might bring him down into the gas, and one breath of this poisonous gas will render him senseless.

4. To get rid of this gas from the bottom of the well, it can be dipped out with buckets, the same as water, because it is heavier than air.

5. Another method is to take a bundle of straw or shavings, and set it on fire. This heats the gas and makes it lighter than air, and it will rise and escape.

6. Another method. Throw slaked lime mixed with water down the sides of the well. This will at once absorb the gas.

THE BENEFIT OF POULTICES.

The chief object of a poultice is to supply and to retain heat and moisture for the relief of pain and internal congestion. The best poultice is made of ground flax seed, but bread, cornmeal or hominy may be substituted.

The greatest benefit of a poultice comes from its heat; therefore great care should be taken to apply it very hot.

In order to render a poultice more effective in relieving and diminishing deep-seated pain, as in the chest or abdomen, mustard may be added to the flax seed. This does not produce any unpleasant irritation of the skin, and is far better for ordinary purposes than a mustard plaster. In this case the mustard should be carefully mixed with a little warm water and then stirred into the flax seed just before it is spread upon the cloth. The amount of mustard depends upon the intensity of the pain and the age of the person. Poultices after being applied to the body should be covered with either oiled silk or flannel, so that the heat may be retained. A fresh hot poultice should be applied as soon as the first one cools.

Poultices should never be made unnecessarily thick or heavy, and they should be frequently repeated. They ought always to be put on warm, and as moist as they can be made, without being so soft as to flow when placed upon the skin. When they become dry and the temperature falls, they can do little if any good, and may possibly do more injury than service.

The common poultices are useful in all cases of inflammation that cannot be cut short, to assist the process of suppuration and the tendency of matter to the surface.

A list of these poultices, and their methods of preparation, should be found in the medicine closet of every home, where, in cases of emergency, they may be ready for hurried reference, when their soothing effects are most needed.

How to Make All Kinds of Poultices. 101

MAKING A PORK AND ONION POULTICE.

How to Make All Kinds of Poultices.

A PORK AND ONION POULTICE, GOOD FOR WOUNDS MADE BY RUSTY TOOLS OR NAILS, BRUISES, AND LACERATED WOUNDS.

Take raw salt pork and about the same bulk in boiled onions, and chop together thoroughly fine in a wooden bowl and apply warm and bind on about half an inch thick on the injured or wounded parts.

BREAD AND MILK POULTICE.

Break up wheat bread into small pieces and pour on boiling milk and stir well until the mass is brought to the thickness of mush. Spread upon a cloth and apply to the surface intended to be poulticed.

FLAXSEED-MEAL POULTICE.

Place the ground flaxseed in a basin and pour on boiling water, mixing it thoroughly, so there will be no lumps. Spread it a quarter of an inch thick upon folded cloth and lay over it a piece of cheese-cloth. Apply as needed.

SLIPPERY-ELM POULTICE.

Moisten the powdered slippery-elm bark with hot water, spread and apply as directed for flaxseed-meal poultice.

YEAST POULTICE.

Take about one pound of oatmeal and add to it one-half pint of yeast and heat the mixture until it swells. Apply to cloth as in other poultices.

CHARCOAL POULTICE.

Powder fresh charcoal and mix it with bread. Pour on warm water and stir it thoroughly and apply in such quantities as may be deemed necessary.

ONION, TURNIP, OR CARROT POULTICES.

Boil the onions, turnips, or carrots, and stir in sufficient cornmeal to make a thick paste. Apply warm to the surface.

MUSTARD POULTICE.

Mix ground mustard with warm water and apply next to the skin, or for milder effects place a thin cheese-cloth between the skin and the poultice.

BRAN POULTICE.

Place the quantity of bran required, according to the size of the poultice, upon the top of boiling water, and when the heat has penetrated the bran, stir it gently in. Pour off the surplus water, and apply the poultice as hot as it can be borne.

BREAD POULTICE.

Boil about one-half pint of water in a small, clean, lined saucepan, into this put two ounces of stale bread, and let it soak for a few minutes, and apply.

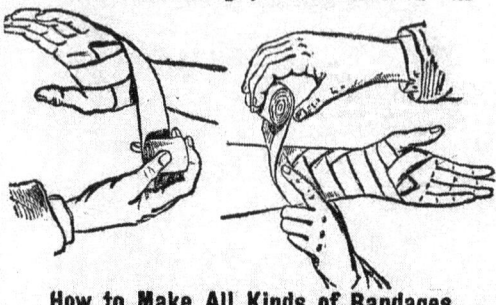

How to Make All Kinds of Bandages
FOR WOUNDS AND SORES.

1. Every wound or bruise should be well bandaged with soft, *linen* rags, and protected from the air.
2. Care should be used not to draw the bandages too tightly, as it will cause much suffering.
3. If a limb is bleeding badly, wrap a handkerchief around it above the wound. Tie a small stick into it, and twist it until the blood stops flowing. — Serious bleeding always results from the cutting of an artery, and demands immediate attention.
4. An artery can always be known by its beating, or by the blood escaping in jets, and if severed in any other parts of the body except the limbs, the flow of blood must be stopped by placing the hand upon the wound and holding the parts together until a physician can be summoned.
5. Sores and ulcers should be cleansed and dried every day, and new and *clean* bandages applied. No wound or sore will heal rapidly unless kept perfectly clean.

A CURE FOR BOILS.

1. Take a good tonic of some kind, to stimulate the system and cleanse the blood. Some preparation of sarsaparilla is a very good remedy.
2. A good tonic will prevent other boils from coming.
3. Eat nourishing food, such as eggs, beefsteak, mutton, poultry, etc.
4. Apply bread and milk or flaxseed poultices, until ready to open, or use the skin of a boiled egg wet.
5. After opening the boil thoroughly, and squeezing out all the pus, apply a warm poultice for a day, and then wash with castile soap or boracic acid, and dress it with soft linen until well.

A SPRAINED HAND.

HOW TO CURE BRUISES AND SPRAINS.

For bruises and sprains there is nothing better than hot water, applied as warm as can be endured without too much pain. Apply the water with several thicknesses of flannel, and change it as soon as it gets cool. Applying cold water to bruises and sprains is an injury instead of a benefit. It should never be done. After a day or two any kind of liniment may be applied. Gentle rubbing after a few days will aid materially.

"ONLY A SPRAIN."

The reason why a sprain is often not more speedily cured is that it is considered "only a sprain," and not sufficient attention is paid to the injury at the time. A sprain may become a very serious matter if not properly treated, but with proper, immediate and thorough treatment a cure will soon be effected.

The first thing to be done is to immerse the part in hot water. The water should be as hot as can be borne, and should be kept up to a constant temperature by frequent additions. It will be necessary to continue this treatment for a long time, it may be for hours, or until every trace of soreness is practically dispelled.

The part is then to be tightly strapped in a bandage in a position just short of absolute fixity. The best article to use in such a case is what is called in medical parlance a "Martin's Bandage." This is a long, narrow strip of sheet rubber, of sufficient strength to withstand considerable strain and fitted at one end with tapes for tying. It is easily seen that by the use of this bandage the desired pressure can be obtained without complete immovability.

Another Remedy for Sprains.—Wormwood boiled in vinegar and applied hot as can be borne on a sprain or bruise is an invaluable remedy. The affected member should afterward be rolled in flannel to retain the heat.

LEMON FOR FELON.

When it is suspected that a felon is coming on the finger, procure a lemon and cut off part of one end. Then with a pair of pointed scissors or small blade of knife cut out the hard core in center of the lemon, removing any seed that may be in the way, and push the finger into a lemon and let it remain there until all symptoms disappear, which will not be longer perhaps than a day and a night. However, if one lemon does not suffice, use another.

Experience With a Punctured Wound.—Last summer I had a painful experience, which threatened serious results, from a punctured wound received on the bottom of my foot by stepping on one of those little brass staples which are used in a piece of cardboard to fasten the prices on goods. It had fallen on the floor at night, while putting away some of the day's purchases, and was unobserved until I stepped on it. The points pierced about half an inch into the ball of the foot. An abscess threatened to form at the bottom of the wound. After trying various remedies to no avail, I thought of lemons, and bound the pulp over the inflamed wound. The remedy proved effectual and the dreaded abscess was prevented from forming.

Bruises.—Mothers will do well to remember this in case of stone bruises which little barefoot boys sometimes suffer so much with. Begin in time with the lemon and prevent these painful afflictions.

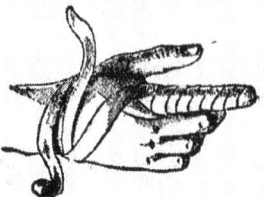

HOW TO CURE FELONS.

Symptoms.—Throbbing pain, which is often felt up the arm; tender to the touch; hand of a dusky red color.

Home Treatment.—Apply poultices wet with laudanum, or wash in a solution of carbolic acid to soften the parts; wipe dry and apply a coat of collodion and give the patient a good dose of physic.

General Treatment.—If the above treatment is not sufficient, go to a physician and have it lanced so as to lay open the flesh to the bone.

CARBUNCLES.

Carbuncles are nothing more or less than large boils accompanied with more or less pain and constitutional disturbances.

Home Treatment.—First look after the general health of the patient and administer an easily digested diet. Give a few stimulants or tonics. Apply large flaxseed poultices to the carbuncle. If the carbuncle is very large and painful, the family physician should be consulted.

HOW TO REMOVE WARTS.

To destroy warts apply a mixture of chromic acid and water, equal parts, or an application of carbolic or nitric acid will have the same effect, or rub the warts night and morning with sal ammoniac moistened in water. This will remove them in a short time.

HOME REMEDIES AND HOW TO USE THEM.

A Green Herb is Worth More than a Latin Phrase.

People have too long been educated to look upon a medical monopoly as the safest means of ensuring their health; they swallow nauseous drugs, but turn with indifference from vegetables as a medicine, while they eat them with complacency at their dinner; that which is thought excellent to sustain them in health loses its power when they are prostrated by disease.

Herbs and vegetable substances have this superiority over mineral medicines, in that they are a food as well as a medicine. Those who use herbs as a medicine will find the sick able to subsist upon these medicines, when the lightest of food is rejected, thus giving nature time to rally her forces. It is too often the case that a patient reads a pompous recommendation of a medicine of which he has no knowledge, and swallows it with avidity, in the hope of obtaining relief, when, if he knew its component parts, he would fly from it as from the fangs of a rattlesnake.

The intelligent reader is here taught how to remove diseases in the quickest and safest manner, and if he closely follows the suggestions made in the following pages he will be as well fitted to cope with diseases as many who have passed through the curriculum of the schools.

Dr. Robinson says, that "amidst all the different branches of knowledge which have engaged the attention of mankind there can be none of equal importance (religion only excepted) to the treatment or cure of the disease to which the human family is subject; for," says he, "the soul in a diseased body is like the martyr in his dungeon; it may retain its value, but it has lost its usefulness."

The Wonderful Curative Properties of Common Salt.

1. Common salt possesses great curative properties, and it is an excellent household remedy, and always at hand.

2. Heated dry and applied to outer surface, over the seat of inflammation or congestion, it will give almost instant relief.

3. Applications of hot solutions of salt and water or vinegar will act like magic upon toothache, neuralgic headache, and other similar diseases.

4. For catarrh and sore throat a spray of warm water and salt, applied often, will cure almost every case, if taken in time. For hay fever and those other slight forms of nasal diseases which produce constant sneezing, there is no remedy more quickly effective, and often curative, than the vapor of heated salt and alcohol. (Heat it very hot, and breathe the vapor for ten minutes at a time, four or five times a day.)

5. For sensitive and bleeding gums, apply salt and cold water once or twice a day. A sure cure.

6. Slight bleeding can be easily checked by the use of salt and water.

7. Tender feet may be cured in a very short time by daily brisk rubbing with cold water and salt.

8. A pinch of salt in hot water, taken either just before or just after eating, greatly aids digestion, and has cured many cases of dyspepsia.

9. A cup of hot water and salt will sometimes quiet the severest vomiting when nothing else will.

10. **Caution.**—Salt eaten with the food in too great quantities is very injurious. Too much salt dries up the blood, and gives the skin a yellow pallor.

11. Neuralgia of the feet and limbs can be cured by bathing night and morning with salt water as hot as can be borne; when taken out, rub the feet with a coarse towel.

12. Severe pains in the bowels and stomach are often speedily relieved by the application of a bag of hot salt.

13. A weak solution of salt and water is recommended by good physicians as a remedy for imperfect digestion, and for a cold in the head it is a complete cure snuffed up from the hollow of the hand. We have known severe chronic cases of catarrh entirely cured by persistent use of this simple remedy every night and morning for several months, when the best efforts of the best physicians failed to do any good. It should be used milk warm.

14. A good handful of rock salt added to the bath is the next best thing after an "ocean dip," and a gargle of a weak solution is a good and ever-ready remedy for a sore throat.

15. One of the most effective remedies known for the sick headache is to place a pinch of salt on the tongue and allow it to dissolve slowly. In about ten minutes it may be followed by a drink of water.

16. There is nothing better for the relief of tired or weak eyes than to bathe them with a strong solution of salt and water, applied as hot as it can be borne.

17. Salt is most excellent for cleansing the teeth. It hardens the gums and sweetens the breath.

THE USEFUL ONION.

The medicinal qualities of the onion are not to be despised. An onion will cure the earache quicker than any other remedy. Take two or three good-sized onions. Peel them and cut in thin slices. Lay the slices on a cloth and heat until hot. Bind this to the head, letting it extend beyond the ear at least one inch all the way round. An onion poultice is most useful in cases of internal inflammation, and onions are an excellent remedy for diphtheria and pneumonia. When the digestive system is apt to become overloaded with rich, greasy or sweet foods, plenty of onions should be eaten as a counterbalance. They are good for the stomach, the complexion, and the nerves when eaten either boiled or raw, but of course the unpleasant odor left on the breath after indulgence in them is a barrier to their use to many people who would otherwise be able to take advantage of the good there is in them. To overcome all this, and give every one a chance, an old remedy is suggested—parsley. To entirely destroy the bad odor of onions eat a small sprig of this pretty green herb either with your meals or immediately after them. There will be nothing in the breath or about the person at all suggestive of the odoriferous bulb five minutes after the parsley is eaten.

WOOD SAGE.

It is an excellent bitter, and removes obstructions from the kidneys and liver; as a diuretic, it acts freely upon the bladder; it likewise cleanses old sores; if taken in a green state and mixed with linseed, or oatmeal, it makes a good poultice, and may be applied to old sores, or inflammations with good effect.

TANSY.

A tea of this herb will relieve gravel, strangury, weakness and pain in the back and kidneys; it is also good for female weakness. The leaves when bruised are used for soothing contusions, etc.

PARSLEY.

The seed, herb and root are all possessed of strong diuretic properties, and have an aromatic taste. This plant is powerfully diuretic, and gently aperient; it is useful in dropsical cases, or in affections of the kidneys.

SLIPPERY ELM.

The inner bark of this tree is a valuable demulcent, possessing very soothing qualities, and is particularly applicable, both as a medicine and injection, in cases of dysentery and other diseases of the bowels. A teaspoonful of the powder mixed in half a pint of hot water, and sweetened, forms an excellent drink in irritation of the mucous membrane of the stomach and bowels. It may be used as a poultice in all cases of local inflammation with great benefit.

RED CLOVER.

The flowers of the common clover, such as is cut for hay, are a valuable article; a salve made of them is good for cancer, old sores and sore lips; it is soft and adhesive, and the flowers contain so great a quantity of honey that it enhances the medicinal properties of the salve. To make this salve take a large brass or tin kettle, or boiler, fill it with clover heads or flowers, cover them with water, let them boil briskly for an hour, then strain and press the flowers well, and then re-fill the same vessel with flowers, putting them in the same liquor; strain again, and simmer down, until it is of the consistency of thick tar. With this salve we once cured a cancer of very long standing, keeping up at the same time, by internal medicines, a lively action in the system; for old sores of every description this salve is equally good. In making it, great care should be taken not to burn it, or its virtue will be much impaired.

Clover tea purifies the blood, clears the complexion and removes pimples; dried clover may be used for tea.

GUM ARABIC.

This gum will not mix with spirits, but it readily dissolves in twice its quantity of water; when in this fluid state it becomes an excellent mucilaginous medicine, useful for coughs, or hoarseness; or also acts as a diuretic.

HOREHOUND.

As a tonic, it possesses great power; it likewise stimulates by acting as an expectorant, having a tendency to loosen the phlegm. Take a strong decoction of this valuable herb on going to bed, the first time you have the misfortune to take cold, and add to each dose half a teaspoonful of cayenne pepper, with a tablespoonful of good vinegar. A syrup made of horehound and ginger-root is excellent for children when attacked with the whooping cough, or for sudden colds; or it may be pulverized and mixed with half its quantity of ginger, a teaspoonful of cayenne, and one of cloves; this, when well sweetened and taken hot on going to bed, will be found to be one of the best medicines that can be obtained.

AMERICAN GOLDEN ROD.

Sweet-scented golden rod. This herb may be used for the headache, as also to produce perspiration; it possesses stimulating and nervine properties, and may be given in the form of tea, in lieu of any of the mints; its taste is sweet and spicy, and on the whole agreeable.

BORAX.

1. Borax is, in the first place, one of the most powerful, if not indeed the most powerful, *antiseptic* known.
2. It is priceless for its convenience on the *toilet table;* used to wash the *head*, as much as one can hold in the hollow of the hand to about a quart of water—it destroys *dandruff*.
3. It allays the heat of *sunburn*, bleaches out tan and redness, helps *freckles* and moth to a great degree, in a weak solution relieves *inflammation of the eyes*, as after crying and in rheumatic affections.
4. It is an invaluable ingredient in almost every *dentifrice*, and cure for canker in the mouth, and for any gumboil.

5. It cleans the brush and comb, and is a whitener and purifier everywhere, used with discretion, as too much of it is too drying.

6. It is good in the *general bath*, after one has been exposed to contagion.

7. It is very efficacious as a *gargle* in mild sore throats.

8. Care, however, must be taken to swallow none of it, as, although a few accidental drops swallowed might do no irreparable harm, large or frequent quantities are capable of ruining the kidneys.

9. If the spot of a mosquito bite is wet and borax plastered upon it, all sting and itching cease very shortly.

TURPENTINE.

Turpentine has almost as many uses as borax. It is good for rheumatism, and mixed with camphorated oil and rubbed on the chest, is one of the best remedies for bronchial colds.

FACTS ABOUT EGGS.

To prevent bed sores, apply with a feather the white of an egg beaten with two teaspoonfuls spirits of wine.

Hoarseness and tickling in the throat are relieved by a gargle of the white of an egg beaten to a froth with a tumblerful of warm sweetened water.

Beat an egg fifteen minutes with a pint of milk and a pint of water, sweeten with granulated sugar, bring to boiling point and when cold use as a drink. It is excellent for a cold.

Put coffee into the pot, add the white of an egg and stir well before pouring on any water. Leave the yolk in the shell to be used in a similar manner another time. This makes a strengthening morning drink.

An old-time but very effective remedy for an obstinate cough is to place three unbroken eggs in very strong cider vinegar (increase the strength by boiling if necessary). In three or four days the acid will eat the shells, then beat the mixture well, and thicken with honey. Take two tablespoonfuls before each meal.

An army nurse gives this remedy for chronic diarrhea, which she said was used successsfully by the soldiers: Drop eggs in water, crush a very small place in the shell to prevent bursting, then wrap in wet paper and roast in the ashes to a fine powder. It will take several hours. Sift, and take a teaspoonful of the powder three times a day.

GLYCERIN.

There is hardly a family medicine-chest that does not contain its bottle of glycerin, and yet the writer has observed that in most cases this reliable remedy is depended on for nothing more than the relief of "chapped" hands and faces.

There are a great variety of ways in which glycerin can be employed to the very best advantage. For "chaps" and reddened and roughened skin, the best results are obtained by diluting the glycerin with an equal part of rosewater.

It is an excellent plan to put a little glycerin in the iodin that is applied to the chest in case of a severe cold.

In cases of severe burns, glycerin applied immediately gives great relief.

A violent attack of coughing may be instantly relieved by a tablespoonful of glycerin in hot milk.

Mixed with sulphuric acid, glycerin is an excellent remedy for throat troubles of all kinds. The mixture is used as a gargle, and should be freshly made at each using.

HOW TO GATHER AND PREPARE MEDICINAL PLANTS AND BARKS.

1. Barks should be gathered as soon as they will peel easily in the spring.
2. Leaves and herbs should be collected just before they begin to fade in autumn.
3. Flowers, when they first begin to blossom.
4. Seeds, just before they are ripe.
5. Roots may be dug at any time, thoroughly washed, cleaned and dried.

THE AMERICAN POPLAR.

This is a good tonic, and is a good remedy for *chronic rheumatism*, *dyspepsia* and general *debility*. Use only the inner part, dried and powdered.

Dose. A heaping teaspoonful three or four times a day.

BLACKBERRY.

1. The root is recommended for diarrhœa, dysentery and summer complaint in children.
2. Boil the small roots in a quart of water and reduce this quantity by boiling it down one-half.
3. One or two tablespoonfuls may be given three or four times a day.

BURDOCK.

1. In Scrofulous or in obstinate skin diseases it is considered as one of the best home remedies.
2. Take a handful of the freshly bruised root to two quarts of water and boil down one-half.

Dose.—Drink about one pint per day.

GARLIC.

1. Garlic is recommended for whooping-cough, coughs, colds, asthma and worms.
2. It may be used by external application, or made into a syrup by adding white sugar, and taken in such quantities as may be deemed necessary.

GARLIC.

BLACK ELDER.

1. The flowers, the berries and the bark all possess medicinal properties.
2. An ointment made by stirring the fresh flowers into clean melted lard, and subsequently straining it, is an excellent remedy for burns, scalds, wounds and old obstinate sores.
3. The berries are laxative and are good in rheumatism, gout, skin diseases and habitual constipation.
4. The berries can be preserved by canning the same as any other fruit, or they may be dried.

CAMPHOR.

Applied externally in rheumatism, enlarged joints, bruises and sprains, spirits of camphor is considered one of the best of domestic remedies. One-half or one-fourth of a teaspoonful taken internally will cure colic, diarrhœa, and, in its first stages, it is considered an excellent remedy for a cold.

CAYENNE PEPPER.

As a condiment, it prevents flatulence from vegetable food and increases the digestive power of weak stomachs. As a medicine it is a powerful and useful stimulant in paralysis, fevers, etc. It is of great efficiency in chronic ophthalmia. In malignant sore throat it is a useful gargle. Doses may be given from three to eight grains.

CATNIP.

Catnip is an excellent domestic remedy, and will produce active perspiration. Good for colds, headache and similar diseases.

DOSE. Make a strong tea and drink before retiring.

CINNAMON.

1. Cinnamon will relieve vomiting, colic and diarrhea.
2. A drop of oil of cinnamon will often relieve very serious toothache. Apply to tooth with a little cotton.

DANDELION ROOT AND PLANT.

DANDELION.

1. The dandelion is recommended for *biliousness, chronic inflammation* of the *liver, constipation* and *coughs.*
2. The root should be collected in July, August or September.

DOSE. A strong infusion may be drank freely two or three times a day, or the fluid extract can be procured at any drug store.

ALUM.

1. Alum should always be kept in the house. It is one of the best remedies known to stop bleeding.
2. A heaping teaspoonful of powdered alum, placed in a common teacup of water, will stop the flow of blood in any ordinary wound where no large artery has been severed.
3. Snuffing a solution will stop bleeding of the nose.
4. A teaspoonful of powdered alum and molasses will cure the croup in children. It will also cure painter's colic.
5. A mild solution of alum will relieve inflamed eyes.
6. A wash made with a teaspoonful of alum and a quart of water will prevent offensive sweating, and will often cure pimples on the face of young persons.
7. Burnt alum will remove proud flesh in wounds and sores.

BONESET OR THOROUGHWORT.

This is a good remedy for malarial diseases, chills and fevers, and is also a tonic.

Dose. Make the leaves and flowers into a strong tea, and take about a wineglassful at a time.

DOGWOOD BLOSSOMS.

DOGWOOD.

1. Dogwood is a familiar tree, the bark of which is good in fever and ague. It is also used as an appetizer.

2. Make a strong tea by boiling a handful of the bark in a quart of water.

Dose. Take a wineglassful three times a day.

GINGER.

1. The medical virtues of ginger tea in relieving colic, diarrhœa and indigestion, cannot be questioned.

2. A cup of strong ginger tea, taken on going to bed, will often cure a cold.

3. Ginger tea may be taken copiously for any bowel trouble.

HOPS.

1. Hops have long been known to possess soothing and sleep-producing properties. A cup of strong hop tea will produce pleasant sleep.

2. A hop poultice will relieve the pain of a bruise, a sprain or other injuries

FLAXSEED.

This is an excellent remedy for coughs, colds, disorders of the bowels, kidneys and bladder, etc.

Preparation. To make the best kind of flaxseed tea, place the seeds in a small linen bag and suspend the bag in a dish of water, four tablespoonfuls for each quart of water. After allowing the seeds to soak for several hours, remove the same and the tea will be ready for use. Add a little lemon juice for flavor.

FLAX.

Dose. Give in quantities as may be necessary.

HORSERADISH.

1. It is an excellent remedy for hoarseness, dropsy, rheumatism and palsy.

2. Make a syrup by boiling the root, and add sufficient sugar to make it palatable.

Dose. Two tea-spoonfuls two or three times a day.

JUNIPER.

The berries of the Juniper tree have always been considered as excellent home remedies in dropsy, skin diseases and scrofula; they may be eaten fresh or dry.

Dose. Two tea-spoonfuls of berries two or three times a day. It is better to bruise them thoroughly with a hammer, breaking all the seeds before taking.

LEMON-JUICE.

1. Hot lemonade taken on retiring, will break up a cold in its first stages.

2. Some very serious cases of dropsy can be cured by eating lemons. The patient should commence by eating one lemon a day, and increasing it until ten or fifteen are eaten each day.

3. Very strong lemonade, with but little sugar, will relieve influenza, cold in the head and inflammatory rheumatism if taken often.

4. It will remove ink-stains from white cloth, also iron rust, and freckles from the skin.

Home Remedies, and How to Use Them.

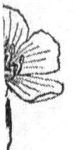

OLIVE OIL.

1. A wineglassful every few minutes will relieve cramp colic.

2. A teaspoonful rubbed along the spine of a very young infant will loosen the bowels better than giving internal remedies.

3. Applications externally will soothe and relieve most all kinds of skin diseases.

KEROSENE OIL.

1. Kerosene Oil will relieve rheumatic pains, sciatica and neuralgia.

2. Apply it with thorough and repeated rubbing of the affected parts.

3. It is also recommended for burns, scalds, sprains, bruises and sores. Apply in mild quantities.

LIME.

1. Allowing children to breathe the vapor from slaking lime is good for croup and diphtheria.

2. Take about one-half pound of unslaked lime, and pour upon it a quart of hot water. Let it stand for a few hours, and draw off the clear liquid. This makes an excellent gargle in croup and diphtheria. It is also an excellent remedy for itching eruptions on the skin, such as hives, if applied externally. Taken inwardly, it will relieve immediately heartburn and many forms of dyspepsia. It will also relieve bowel complaints of children, when the child has wind in the stomach and is restless and fretful.

LOBELIA.

1. Lobelia is a common plant and is given as a remedy for asthma, lockjaw and coughs.

2. It is violent in its action and a fatal poison in overdoses. Care should be taken in reference to the quantity used. It is better and safer to allow the physician to prescribe it.

MAGNESIA.

Magnesia will relieve sour stomach, acidity of the stomach, heartburn, colic, dyspepsia and similar diseases. It is a mild laxative, suitable to children.

Dose. Take a tea-spoonful as many times as may be required.

MUSTARD.

1. Mustard is an excellent household remedy. In cases of poisoning, when taken in large quantities, it will produce vomiting.

2. A tablespoonful of white mustard seed mingled with syrup, and taken once a day, will act gently on the bowels and is a beneficial remedy in dyspepsia and constipation.

RHUBARB.

Rhubarb will cure wind on the stomach, measles, and will act mildly upon the bowels. The aromatic syrup may be procured at the drug stores.

Dose. A tablespoonful for an adult.

PENNYROYAL.

1. Pennyroyal will promote perspiration and is good for coughs and colds.

2. Make a strong tea and take at going to bed.

3. A warm foot-bath may accompany the medicine with good effects.

MANDRAKE OR MAY-APPLE.

This is a stimulant, a tonic and a laxative. It is excellent for liver complaint, especially when it is in a torpid and inactive condition.

Dose. Dry and powder the root, and take about one teaspoonful. This dose may be repeated two or three times a day. Some persons are more or less affected by it. The dose should be according to effects.

OAK-BARK.

1. Oak-Bark may be given with advantage in fever and ague, diarrhœa and bleeding from the lungs. It is also good as an external application.

2. The acorns, when roasted, are believed to be a remedy for scrofula and other skin diseases. A strong tea of the bark has also been recommended as a wash for old sores and foul ulcers.

3. A poultice made of powdered bark will relieve pain, and is also considered a good remedy for sores and ulcers.

Dose. Make a tea of the bark and take in such quantities as may be deemed necessary. No serious effects of an overdose.

PEACH-TREE BARK.

The bark of the peach-tree is sedative, and will control nausea and vomiting. It also possesses mild tonic properties.

Dose. Make a strong tea of the bark and drink a wineglassful three times a day.

PEPPERMINT.

Externally applied it is an efficient remedy in neuralgia. It is good for sickness of the stomach, colic and cholera of children.

DOSE. Essence of peppermint may be given in doses of from ten to twenty-five drops in water, or on a lump of sugar.

GOOSE GREASE.

Goose oil applied externally and internally is an excellent remedy for sore throat, hoarseness, coughs, etc.

SENNA LEAVES.

SNAKEROOT.

1. The Virginia Snakeroot, when made into a strong tea, is useful as a gargle in sore throat, and will bring out the eruptions in scarlet fever and measles.
2. When the tea is taken internally, it will produce perspiration and will often cure a cold and rheumatism in the first stages.

SENNA.

Senna is the leaves of a small tree which grows in northern Africa. It is a sure and safe purgative of moderate power. It will cure costiveness and other similar troubles.

SASSAFRAS.

The bark made into a tea makes a pleasant drink, and will relieve dysentery and inflammation of the bladder. It will also relieve inflammation of the eyes when applied externally.

SULPHUR.

Old cases of rheumatism are often improved by sulphur baths and sulphur tea. It will also cure the itch and loosen the bowels.

DOSE. Powder sulphur and mix with molasses. A teaspoonful three times a day.

SWEET FLAG.

Sweet Flag is recommended for pain in the stomach or bowels. It can be taken in the form of a tea, sweetened with a little sugar, or the root may be eaten without any preparation.

COMMON BAKING SODA.

1. This is good for sour stomach, heartburn, water-brash, and will often relieve distress in the stomach, sudden diarrhœa, etc. An even teaspoonful should be stirred into a wineglassful of water and taken in one dose; children according to age.

2. If children are wakeful, restless and cross, throwing up curdled milk from the stomach, nothing is better than a little soda and cold water. Soda will often relieve rheumatism, and soda-baths are very efficacious in curing various skin diseases.

3. Caution. The daily use of soda should not be carried too far, as it is liable to weaken the stomach, and thin the blood too much.

SWEET FLAG.

WILD CHERRY.

1. This is good for general weakness, poor digestion, lack of appetite, nervousness and coughs. It is also considered an excellent remedy for the first stages of consumption or palpitation of the heart.

2. The parts used in medicine, are the berries and inner bark of the roots and branches.

Dose. A heaping teaspoonful of the dried and powdered bark, soaked twenty-four hours in one quart of cold water. Take a wineglassful four or five times a day.

WILLOW.

1. The inner bark is a good remedy in fever and ague and similar diseases.

2. Make a strong tea of the inner bark, and take in quantities to suit the patient.

SAGE.

This is an excellent remedy for wind, colds, or night sweats.

Dose. Make the same into a strong tea and drink a teacupful several times a day, or as emergency may demand.

SALTPETRE (NITRATE OF POTASH).

An excellent domestic remedy for inflammatory rheumatism, sore throat, asthma, dysentery, gravel, and skin diseases.

Dose. Of a tablespoonful of powdered saltpetre stirred in a pint of cold water, take two or three tablespoonfuls every two hours. For gravel boil the same quantity in new milk and give three or four tablespoonfuls of the liquid to a dose. For sore throat it is used as a gargle. For asthma soak paper in a strong liquid of saltpetre water, then dry. Burn the paper and inhale the smoke and it will give speedy relief. For dysentery take a teaspoonful of powdered saltpetre and stir into a tumbler of water. Take a teaspoonful of this every hour.

RED PEPPER.

A teaspoonful of red pepper mixed with molasses and taken in one dose, is considered one of the best remedies for delirium tremens and sea-sickness.

HOME REMEDIES AND HOME TREATMENT FOR ALL DISEASES.

In the following pages we give the symptoms, causes and treatments of diseases from which mankind suffers.

We are free to say that in all cases we prefer the Home Treatment to any other, as under proper care it is the most simple, reliable, efficacious, and at the same time the most economical method, and never leaves any evil after effects.

For the benefit of those who prefer Homeopathic or the Regular Treatment, including drugs, we have in most cases given these treatments also.

COLIC IN ADULTS.

SYMPTOMS.—Colic is a griping pain in the bowels, chiefly about the navel, relieved by pressure, and often accompanied with a painful distension of the whole of the lower region of the bowels, with vomiting, costiveness, and spasmodic contraction of the muscles of the abdomen.

CAUSES.—The complaint is produced by various causes, such as indigestible fruits, long continued costiveness, cold, or it may be due, as in painter's colic, to poisoning by lead.

HOME TREATMENT.—Hot fomentations applied to the abdomen to relieve the pain, and a strong physic. One of the best is blue mass in 5 or 10 grains. Tepid water injection in the bowels, a few drops of peppermint in hot water, or strong catnip tea, will often give speedy relief. Keep the feet dry and avoid food, that disagrees with the patient.

HOMEOPATHIC TREATMENT. — Colocynth when cramps in region of the navel with diarrhœa. Nux vomica when from constipation and indigestible food. Chamomilla when in children. Ipecac, if vomiting is an accompanying symptom.

REGULAR TREATMENT. — If caused by some indigestible article of food, a dose of castor oil had better be given, say a tablespoonful for an adult, to which from ten to fifteen drops of laudanum may be added. If the pain is very severe a turpentine stupe may be applied over the abdomen. The following mixture will be found very useful in such cases: Solution of the muriate of morphia, 2 drachms; spirit of chloroform, ½ ounce; water to make 2 ounces. A teaspoonful to be given every two hours until the pain is relieved.

CRAMPS AND CRAMP COLIC.

Home Treatment.—For cramp colic give a wineglassful of olive oil. For cramps, rubbing the parts thoroughly with the hands or a piece of flannel will generally produce relief. The application of turpentine or spirits of hartshorn, rubbed on with the hand, is highly recommended.

COLIC IN CHILDREN.

A good remedy is nothing more nor less than glycerin, as much as the child will take. It is best to begin with a teaspoonful, but there is no fear of giving too much. The first effect is the quieting of the cry of pain; the second, the belching of the gas; later the gas passes away downward, and finally, after an easy movement of the bowels, the child falls into a sweet, restful sleep. Try it, its efficacy will surprise you, as will also the readiness with which the little one will suck it from the spoon.

CRAMPS IN THE LEGS.

Many persons of either sex are troubled with cramp in one or both of the legs. It usually comes on during night and while it lasts the pain is acute. Most people jump out of bed—the cramp nearly always comes on just after going to bed or while undressing—and either rub their legs or get some one to do it for them. There is something easier than to overcome the spasm, and the method suggested is as follows: Provide a good strong cord—a garter will do if nothing else is handy. When the cramp comes on, take the cord, wind it around the leg over the place in which the pain is felt and take one end in each hand, and give it a sharp pull, one that will hurt a little. The cramp will cease instantly, and the sufferer can go to bed assured that it will not come again that night.

HOW TO CURE NIGHTMARE.

Cause.—Nightmares are probably the result of indigestion, late suppers, too much excitement or hard thinking, cold feet, costiveness, flatulence, etc.

Home Treattmen.—Avoid the causes and eat light suppers. Sleep with another person. A little cayenne pepper or baking soda, taken just before retiring, will be found efficacious.

HEALTHY POSITION FOR THE HEAD AND BACK.

HOME REMEDIES FOR SLEEPLESSNESS.

Many suffer from nervousness and want of sleep. Many remedies have been given, but few have proven successful. The following are some of the best household remedies known.

1. A bath, taken just before retiring, is highly recommended. If this is not satisfactory wash the face, neck and hands in cold water, and then retire and keep the mind quiet.

2. If the trouble is a want of sleep after the first nap, get up and walk around the room two or three times. With some this is a sure remedy.

3. Lie with the head to the North, for there is no doubt something in the electrical effects of the earth upon the body when in that position.

4. Bad sleepers should always rise early and retire early, and they should never take a nap during the day.

5. Sleepless persons should avoid exciting conversation or reading, hard study, or any kind of mental excitement during the evening.

6. Tea and coffee should never be drank for supper.

7. When lying in bed, first draw in the breath slowly, letting it out suddenly, then draw it in suddenly and let it pass slowly out a number of times alternately. This is highly recommended.

8. A cup of hot water taken just before retiring will often produce the desired results.

How to Sleep.

UNHEALTHY POSITION FOR THE HEAD AND BACK.

Many diseases have their beginning in sleeping on high pillows.

9. Nervous and sleepless persons are often benefited by sleeping on a pillow of hops.
10. In case of nervous irritability a warm foot-bath will often produce sleep.
11. If the above home treatments are not sufficient, take from 5 to 10 grains of bromide of potassium just before retiring.
12. A brisk walk in the open air just before retiring will often effect a perfect cure.

HOW TO CHECK VOMITING.

Home Treatment.—A teaspoonful or two of hot water sometimes acts like a charm; a pinch of salt will often relieve vomiting; ice dissolved in the mouth, will often accomplish what other medicines will not; a mustard paste over the stomach is highly recommended. Much, however, depends upon the diet. If the stomach is in a restless condition, only the lightest kind of food should be taken, and it can be easily determined in a few days what food the stomach will or will not retain. Perfect rest is generally more necessary than food or medicine. For chronic vomiting lime water is one of the best remedies.

General Treatment.—Subnitrate of bismuth in 2 to 5 grain doses, or oxalate of cerium in 1-grain doses, or one drop of the tincture of ipecac, taken in a wineglassful of water.

Homeopathic Remedies.—Nux vomica and arsenicum.

NEURALGIA.

Cause.—The cause is obscure in many cases. It may result from an impoverished condition of the blood. It may be caused by violent passions, strong emotions, excessive exercise, mental depression, malaria, or lead poisoning.

Symptoms.—Sudden, sharp and darting pains feeling like hot wires piercing the parts. The parts more commonly affected are the face, the muscles between the ribs, and the hip and leg. When it is in the hip and leg, it is generally called sciatica. It sometimes attacks the heart.

Home Treatment.—Bathe the affected parts in salt water, Use nourishing diet. Neuralgia in the face is often relieved by taking a good active cathartic. An external application of peppermint is highly recommended. Eat plenty of fat meat, and avoid tea, but drink plenty of milk. Avoid exposure to dampness. For sciatica wear chamois leather drawers.

General Treatment.—Fifteen grains of carbonate of iron three times a day, taken in a little syrup. This treatment for a month or more will have beneficial effects. A seidlitz powder taken every morning, or a small quantity of cream of tartar or citrate of magnesia, will produce excellent results. Three grains of quinine three times a day may produce the desired results. For neuralgic headache take 15 grains bromide of potash three times a day.

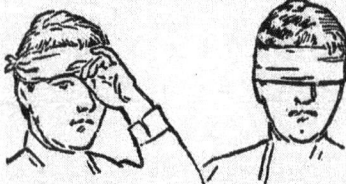

REMEDY FOR NEURALGIA.

Hypophosphite of soda, taken in 1 drachm doses three times per day in beef tea, is a good remedy for this painful affection. So is the application of bruised horse-radish, or the application of oil of peppermint applied lightly with a camel-hair pencil.

Neuralgia.

Sure Cure.—The most stubborn cases of neuralgia are apt to yield to a hot water treatment. Wherever the pain is located, there a hot water bag should be applied. The suffering part should be wrapped in a blanket, and the unfortunate patient should be put to bed and covered with more blankets and induced to drink at least three cups of water as hot as the palate can stand. This treatment may seem severe, but it is sure to bring relief.

A Hot Bath, a stroll in the fresh air, shampooing the head in weak soda-water, or a timely nap in a cool, quiet room will sometimes stop a nervous headache. When overfatigued from shopping or sightseeing a sponge dipped in very hot water and pressed repeatedly over the back of the neck between the ears will be found exceedingly refreshing, especially if the face and temples are afterward subjected to the same treatment. Neuralgia is caused not only by cold air, but by acidity of the stomach, starved nerves, imperfect teeth, or by indolence combined with a too generous diet.

Heat is the best and quickest cure for this distressing pain. A hot flat-iron, passed rapidly and deftly over several folds of flannel laid on the affected spot, will often give relief in less than ten minutes, without the aid of medicine. Hot fomentations are of equal value; though when the skin is very tender it is more advisable to use dry heat, nothing being better for the purpose than bags of heated salt, flour or sand, which retain warmth for a long time.

Cold Water, applied by the finger tips to the nerves in front of the ear, has been known to dispel neuralgic pains like magic.

Charcoal.—When caused by acidity a dose of charcoal or soda will usually act as a corrective. Sick headache is accompanied by bilious symptoms, and attacks usually come on when the person is overtired or below par physically. This is a disease of the first half of life, and often stops of its own accord after middle age. A careful diet is imperative in every case, sweetmeats and pastry being especially pernicious.

Reflex Action.—Eating heartily when very tired, late dinners, eating irregularly, insufficient mastication or too much animal food, especially in the spring or during hot weather, are frequent causes of indigestion, causing headaches by reflex action.

HEADACHES.

In considering the subject of headache we should never lose sight of the fact that we are studying merely a symptom and not a disease. Pain, and especially the pain under consideration, is a danger signal set by nature to warn the sufferer that a deep-seated malady threatens the body. A celebrated physician once called pain "the prayer of a nerve for healthy blood." No truer saying was ever uttered.

Digestion.—By far the most common form of headache is that due to a disordered condition of the organs of digestion. Such headaches are the results of indigestion and constipation, as well as of over-indulgence in eating or drinking. A disordered stomach or a sluggish condition of the bowels, combined with overwork and too little exercise in the open air, are frequent causes of headache in persons who pursue sedentary and indoor occupations.

Remedy.—The remedy for this kind of headache is the exercise of regularity and moderation in eating, with an avoidance of food which is innutritious and difficult of digestion, and attention to the regularity of the bowels. The last point is of especial importance.

Eye Strain.—One variety of headache, the cause of which is sometimes overlooked, results from eye-strain. The provision of proper glasses, and treatment calculated to improve the tone of the muscles of the eyes, have been followed by prompt relief in numberless instances.

Sick Headache.—The following cure for sick headache I have used with perfect success, and it is much to be preferred to powerful drugs, which injure the system, and if taken repeatedly are soon found to lose their efficacy. At the same time it is well to remember that pain is nature's danger signal, and a warning to rest. After driving off a headache, lie down for an hour or two, and keep as quiet as possible during the rest of the day. Neither the brain nor the stomach should be taxed for twenty-four hours.

Cayenne Pepper.—Mix a tablespoonful of cayenne pepper to a thick paste with vinegar, spread it on a strip of thin cloth, which may be folded together, and bind on the forehead from temple to temple. Then swallow a "pinch" of the pepper—say a quarter of a teaspoonful—in a teaspoonful of vinegar or lemon juice. The plaster will burn, but not blister, and in the course of ten minutes the headache will disappear under the stimulating effect of this treatment.

Hot Water.—Sick headache can usually be cured by soaking the feet and the hands above the wrists in water hot as can be borne; it may have a little salt or mustard in it, to keep from taking cold after it. Sip slowly boiling hot water, and go to bed in a darkened room. Eat nothing until you feel a need or desire for food, then take a little milk or a cracker, or some other very simple food.

Walking Backward.—The *Medical Record* is authority for the statement that nervous headache may be cured by the simple act of walking backward ten minutes. "It is well," says the writer; "to get in a long, narrow room where the windows are high, and walk very slowly, placing first the ball of the foot on the floor, and then the heel. Besides curing the headache, this exercise promotes a graceful carriage.

Dangerous Practice.—I know of no more dangerous practice than to treat headache pain blindly with drugs, unless it be to treat insomnia with sedatives. Both lines of treatment lead to the abuse of anodynes and hypnotics, and as a usual thing result in a continued condition of invalidism.

Constipation.—One very common cause of headache which, if not the only cause, is, at least, a great factor in it, and amenable to home treatment with medicine, is constipation. Of course, outdoor exercise is the best possible thing for permanent cure. It is very easy to relieve most forms of headache by means of the coal-tar derivatives, of which so many are in the drug market. These form the basis of the many headache cures found on the druggists' shelves. Their use is not entirely without danger, for they are powerful heart depressants if taken in doses of any considerable size.

Preventive.—After all, the best treatment for headache is preventive, and if we would all follow Kant's golden rule in disposing of each day, allotting eight hours for work, eight hours for play and eight hours for sleep, we would soon leave headaches and the ills attending them behind.

HOW TO CURE THE HEADACHE.

Definition.—Megrim, hemicrania or sick-headache is a pain in the head coming on periodically and usually located in the left side of the head, accompanied by nausea and vomiting. Simple nervous headache may occur in any part of head, and comes on irregularly from many causes.

Causes.—The causes of headache are legion. Many diseases produce headache. Some of the most common causes are fever, colds, derangement of stomach or bowels (especially constipation), bad nutrition, and general debility. Rheumatic and gouty people are much subject to sick headache, and it is often hereditary. Insufficient sleep and mental worry are frequent exciting causes.

Home Treatment.—Look for cause, and remove it if possible. Regulate the diet and keep the bowels in good condition. Plenty of out-door exercise with freedom from care, will prevent the attacks. For a throbbing headache, with flushed face, apply cold water or ice bag to the head. Hot foot bath and inhalation of camphor, or mustard plaster on back of neck. For headache with pallor of face, and faintness on standing, apply hot water to the head freely, and inhalations of ammonia will often relieve.

General Treatment.—For throbbing headache with flushed face, ten to fifteen grains of the bromide of potassium will often relieve. For headache with pale countenance the inhalation of the nitrite of amyl will, if employed early, often cut short an attack of sick headache. The following may be used occasionally:

   2 scruples of phenacetine,
   10 grains of citrate of caffeine.

Mix and make into twenty capsules.

Take one when necessary.

Cannabis Indica taken in gradually increasing doses for many months will sometimes cure the headache permanently. Begin with quarter of a grain taken morning and evening, and gradually increase, until two grains or more are taken at a dose.

SICK HEADACHE.

Cause.—Eating indigestible food, a lack of sufficient sleep, constipation, anxiety, want of out-door exercise, etc.

Symptoms.—Dizziness, pain in the forehead and temples, blurred sight, nausea and vomiting.

Home Treatment.—Moderate diet, avoiding all rich gravies, late suppers, or stimulating drinks. Take a Seidlitz powder every morning and evening, or drink a cup of strong catnip tea just before retiring, or take two teaspoonfuls of finely powdered charcoal in half a glass of milk. Cover up warmly and perspire freely.

HOME TREATMENT FOR DIARRHŒA.

Great care should be taken not to check the difficulty too soon. Look first carefully to the food and eat only moderately and very nutritious and very easily digested food. Rest and quiet is always necessary to promote a cure. If this is not sufficient, take half a teaspoonful of common soda three times a day, or take a few doses of rhubarb syrup, or blackberry cordial or blackberry wine.

"Dr. Daniel's Diarrhœa Remedy."
  Tinct. Rhubarb, 1 ounce,
  Tinct. Catechu, 2 ounces,
  Tinct. Jam. Ginger, 1 ounce,
  Paregoric, 2 ounces,
  Lime Water, 2 ounces. Mix.

One teaspoonful in a little cold water, every time the bowels move.

Dr. Daniels has used this remedy in his extensive practice for over thirty years, and it always effects a cure.

A SURE CURE FOR DIARRHEA.

The plant called "White everlasting," botanical name *Gnaphalium Polycephalum*, is one of the best remedies for diarrhea. The plant is found in some parts of the United States and Canada. The following is the prescription:

Take a handful of the herb, flowers and leaves included, and boil in one pint of water. Strain the decoction and boil down to one-half pint. Add an equal quantity of milk and bring to a boil so as to scald the milk. Dose: For adults, one-half teacupful; for children, accordingly. If desired, it may be sweetened with white sugar.

PLEURISY.

Cause.—Violent strain or injury. It may be caused by other diseases, such as erysipelas, rheumatism, measles, etc., but it is generally caused by sudden cold or exposure to dampness.

Symptoms.—It generally begins with a chill and a stitching pain in the side.

Home Treatment.—In the first stages of the disease home treatment will generally be sufficient. A spirit vapor bath; hot fomentations applied to the chest; or hot plates wrapped in a flannel and applied to the chest are excellent.

General Treatment.—Give two or three drops of the tincture of aconite every three hours. If the patient is weak this remedy should not be persisted in.

ASTHMA.

The following is Dr. Coffin's celebrated method of treating asthma: To moderate the severity of the paroxysm inhale warm steam from an inhaler or the spout of a teapot. The treatment consists in giving a strong decoction of valerian root with cayenne, made very fine and well sweetened; immerse the feet of the patient in warm water, into which you may put a little mustard. Let him drink freely of a strong tea of yarrow; after which give him half a teaspoonful of lobelia with a small quantity of cayenne pepper and half a teaspoonful of valerian; let this be repeated till the patient vomits freely, which seldom fails to give relief.

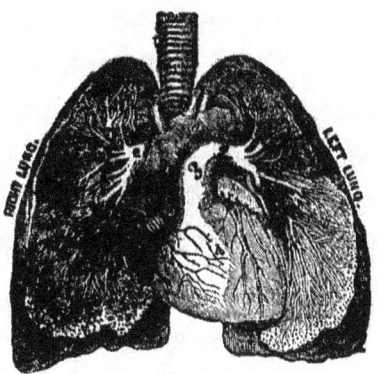

ASTHMA.

Cause.—It is hereditary in many people. It may be caused by fog, smoke, fumes of various things, as new hay, etc., indigestion, heart disease, nervous condition, exposure, or bronchitis.

Symptoms.—The symptoms are so well known that very little description is necessary. Loud and frequent coughing, wheezing, shortness of breath, and sometimes nausea and vomiting.

Home Treatment.—Those suffering from asthma should eat only easily digested food. Eat light suppers and avoid catching cold. Shower baths every morning are highly recommended if the patient is sufficiently strong. Drinking strong coffee is sometimes a great relief in a fit of asthma. Burning nitre-paper and inhaling the fumes is very effective. Smoking jimson-weed (thorn-apple) is an excellent remedy in some cases. Keep the bowels open.

General Treatment.—One-half ounce of the tincture of lobelia; one-half ounce of the wine of ipecac. Take a half teaspoonful every half hour until expectoration begins, or, take five grains of iodide of potassium in syrup and water three times a day.

LUNG FEVER OR PNEUMONIA.

Causes.—Overexertion, exposure to cold, heart disease, wounds, foreign substance in the lungs, bronchitis, etc.

Symptoms.—Cold in the chest, loss of appetite, restlessness and chills, high fever, quick pulse, and rapid breathing, a patch of red on one or both cheeks, the expectorations of a rusty color or streaked with blood. Pain in the chest is always a prominent symptom.

Home Treatment.—Cloths rung out of cold water laid over the chest and renewed every ten minutes, or hot fomentations applied to the chest, well regulated diet, and some good active stimulant. A good dose of castor oil or citrate of magnesia is very beneficial. A flaxseed poultice half an inch thick placed entirely around the chest is highly recommended. Keep the room at an even temperature.

General Treatment.—
    Bi-carbonate of potash, 2 drachms,
    Syrup of gum arabic, 3 fluid ounces.
Mix and give a dessertspoonful in water six times every twenty-four hours.

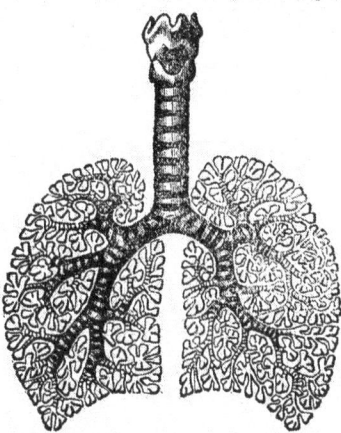

HOW TO ASCERTAIN THE STATE OF THE LUNGS.

Draw in as much breath as you can conveniently, then count as long as possible in a slow and audible voice without drawing in more breath. The number of seconds must be carefully noted. In a consumptive the time does not exceed, 10, and is frequently less than 6 seconds; in pleurisy and pneumonia it ranges from 9 to 4 seconds. When the lungs are sound, the time will range as high as from 20 to 35 seconds. To expand the lungs, go into the air, stand erect, throw back the head and shoulders, and draw in the air through the nostrils as much as possible.

After having then filled the lungs, raise your arms, still extended, and suck in the air. When you have thus forced the arms backward, with the chest open, change the process by which you draw in your breath, till the lungs are emptied. Go through the process several times a day, and it will enlarge the chest, give the lungs better play, and serve very much to ward off consumption.

How to Nurse Typhoid Fever.

Physicians say that in many diseases nursing is of more importance than medicine. This is especially true of typhoid fever. It has to run a certain course, which cannot be cut short by medicine. The vital question is whether the strength of the patient can be so husbanded as to keep him alive until the poison has spent itself. The seat of the disease is in the small intestine, which is ulcerated. The danger is that these ulcers may perforate the coat of the intestine and cause death. There is an unreasoning fear of typhoid fever as a contagious disease. It is not infectious if it is properly nursed. It can only be communicated from the discharges, and if these are thoroughly disinfected there is no danger. A plentiful supply of pure air is the first requisite. The room should be ventilated, and the temperature kept at 65°. If possible the carpet should be taken up and the floor about the bed wiped up each day with a cloth, wrung out of a solution of bichloride of mercury, fifteen grains to a quart of water. A druggist will weigh powders of sixty grains each. One of these can be added to a gallon of water and the liquid used for disinfectant purposes. It is a deadly poison.

The clothing should be changed whenever it is necessary. It is inexcusable to permit soiled clothing to remain near the patient because he is supposed to be too weak to bear having it replaced with fresh. If properly done it will not even tire or distress him.

Water Cure.—Of all diseases the water cure has probably accomplished the greatest achievements in fevers. A fever asks for water—its natural remedy. One deep draught may cure a mild attack. The hot air bath, the Turkish bath, the wet sheet pack, the blanket sweating pack have accomplished remarkable cures in fevers.

TYPHOID FEVER.

Definition.—An acute self-limited disease, due to a special poison; characterized by dull headache, fever, followed by stupor and delirium, diarrhœa, tenderness of abdomen, which may show a peculiar eruption, rapid prostration and slow convalescence.

Cause.—Special typhoid germ called the bacillus typhosus, which gains entrance to the system through infected water, milk, ice, meat or other food. The atmosphere is never impregnated with the fever germs.

Symptoms.—Feeling of lassitude, headache, disturbed digestion and sleeplessness, coated tongue, chill or chilliness followed by fever, which is higher in the evening and gradually increases. Diarrhœa usually, and on the seventh day an eruption resembling flea-bites on abdomen. At the end of the third week the disease reaches its highest stage and the fever gradually abates.

Home Treatment.—Keep the patient quiet, and give plenty of fresh air and a nourishing liquid diet. Milk is the best; never give solid food, and give the milk in small quantities every two or three hours. Turpentine stupes applied over the abdomen to relieve the pain, and cool drink or pellets of ice slowly dissolved in the mouth to quench the thirst. Good nursing is of great importance. The urine and stools should be promptly disinfected to prevent the spread of the disease, and a physician should be consulted.

MALARIA.

(Ague Chills and Fever—Intermittent Fever.)

Definition.—Disease characterized by a cold, a hot and a sweating stage, followed by an interval of complete intermission; varying in length from a few hours to several days.

Cause.—A special germ called bacillus malaria, aided by exposure to sudden cold, over-exertion, excess in eating and drinking, etc.

Symptoms.—Chill, nausea and great thirst, followed by fever and headache, which gradually subsides as perspiration begins, after which the person feels quite well, till the next chill comes on.

Treatment.—During the intermission, give a brisk purgative followed by ten or twenty grains of quinine given three to five hours before the chill is expected. Repeat once or twice, and the paroxysms will be broken up.

The fever is most frequent in swampy districts, and to insure a permanent cure, the patient must remove to a dry, healthful locality.

HOW TO CURE A COLD.

The first thing necessary is to get up a free and copious sweating. The object is to get the blood in active circulation and open the pores so that the poisonous matter can be thrown out through the skin.

REMEDIES.

1. A hot foot-bath and a good dose of strong ginger tea just before going to bed. Retire and cover warmly.
2. A hot foot-bath and a pint of hot lemonade taken just before going to bed will produce good results.
3. Flaxseed tea or a mild cathartic will often break up a cold.
4. If the cold is accompanied by a cough, give the following prescription:

    1 ounce of Compound Syrup of Squills.
    1 ounce of Syrup of Wild Cherry.

Mix, and take a teaspoonful every two hours.
Also see Home Remedies.

AN EXCELLENT COUGH SYRUP.

    Syrup of Rhubarb, 4 ounces.
    Syrup of Ipecac, 4 ounces.
    Syrup of Senega, 4 ounces.
    Syrup of Morphia, 12 ounces.

Mix them thoroughly.
Take a half teaspoonful every three or four hours for an adult, children in proportion to age.
Shake well before using.

GERMAN COUGH SYRUP.

    Syrup of Morphia, 3 ounces.
    Comp. Syrup of Tar, 3½ ounces.
    Chloroform, ¼ Troy ounce.
    Syrup of Wild Cherry, 2 ounces.
    Glycerine, 1 ounce.

Mix thoroughly.
Always shake the bottle before using.
One teaspoonful three or four times a day.

CATARRH CURE.

    Carbolic Acid, pure, 1 drachm.
    Glycerine, 4 drachms.
    Distilled Water, 1 drachm.
    Fluid Extract of Stramonium, 2 drachms.

Mix them.
Dilute 1 drachm of the mixture with 4 ounces of water, and use with a nasal douche.

COUGHS AND COLDS.

These are of so frequent occurrence that we treat them more at length, giving many excellent and valuable suggestions. The best remedy may fail where other means, diet, bathing, pure air, etc., are neglected.

Colds and What to Do with Them.—It would be well if we could begin by changing the name. The fact is that colds, so-called, are all poisonings, but are brought on in quite different ways. The nerves of the skin are shocked, and its excretory functions are arrested. The retained poison then causes the inflammation or "cold." Very commonly the skin has been put into an over-sensitive and inactive condition already by overheated rooms, overdressing, neglect of bathing, or bad air; and then exposure too slight to be recognized as such at the time does the rest.

Indigestion.—With many persons a "cold" comes on when they get digestion out of order, in certain ways. Here the acrid fluids, produced in the alimentary canal by fermentation, are themselves the poison which throws the mucous membrane of nose or throat into inflammation. Many colds, and especially that form accompanied by fever-sores on the lips, are due to infection.

Cold Air, if pure, does the most of anything to limit the inflammation, and check the growth of germs in the inflamed tissues. A Turkish bath or other sweat bath often helps immensely, by restored skin action.

Diet.—The diet should be simple; any indigestible food or eating food rapidly makes the matters worse. Some do better on a limited allowance of food, even on fasting; others need a generous diet, though plain.

Remedy.—Doses of oil, cod-liver oil, skunk's oil, goose grease, and many other sorts, have been found to help certain persons when suffering from colds; but not all. It is probably a question of digesting them or not. But whatever further medication one may elect, do not let it divert attention from the one greatest remedy—cold, pure air.

Best Remedy.—There are many good remedies for a cold, but the best remedy is not to take cold at all.

The best way to do that, I find, is to have so good a supply of natural warmth within that outside temperature cannot easily lower it, and this I achieve by keeping my blood always full of the oxygen in fresh air, and flowing swiftly by reason of plenty of exercise. Then, to let my skin do its natural work of being warm, elastic water-tight covering for my flesh, keeping it so by the free use of cold water—instead of the warm water which opens the pores and relaxes the skin's elasticity and by clothing it in such a way that its exudations are soaked up and carried off quickly.

First Stage.—To treat a cold successfully no time should be wasted at its incipient stage. The herald of approach is usually noticed in heaviness of the eyes and a dull, peculiarly "big" feeling of the head similar to the effect of quinine. Physicians say that one in perfect health does not contract a cold; it is only when some of the bodily organs fail to perform their regular duties that the cold makes attack upon the system.

Quinine.—Two-grain doses of quinine administered every two hours during the day are often all that is necessary to keep the enemy at bay—by toning up the system and making it impregnable. These doses may be taken in capsules or in cold liquid coffee; the latter covers up the bitter taste almost entirely and prevents it from lingering in the mouth. Soaking the feet in hot mustard water just before retiring, quickly followed by a hot lemonade, is efficacious.

Cubeb.—If the nostrils are stopped so as to prevent easy respiration, crush cubeb berries in a cloth and smoke them in a new clay pipe, forcing the smoke through the head and nostrils. The head will be as clear as a bell in five minutes, so that you can breathe naturally and all night. Use this remedy only before retiring, or when you can remain within doors, as it is said to open the pores to the extent of placing the system in great danger if exposed to the air very soon after using. Cubeb smoke disinfects and heals and will cure catarrh if used every night regularly.

Hoarseness.—For hoarseness, vaseline is good; take as much as will adhere to the finger; allow it to slowly creep down the throat several times a day and at bed time. This is excellent for croupy children, and it is not difficult to induce them to take it, for it is nearly tasteless. A fresh egg beaten and thickened with sugar, freely eaten, will relieve hoarseness, or take a lemon or sour orange, open one end, dig out the inside, sweeten and eat.

Ginger.—Ginger in hot or cold milk, sweetened a little, is a good night drink; the milk covers the smarting taste of the ginger to a great extent.

Coughs and Colds.

Bad Effects of Steam.—Avoid being over steam as much as possible, or if it cannot be avoided, do not go into the open air for at least an hour after leaving the steamy kitchen. If one had the facilities for a Turkish bath at night just before bed time, a cold could be broken up in a short time, but the trouble of exposure to steam is the almost unavoidable exposure to cold air soon afterward.

Peach Tree Bark.—A tea steeped from peach tree bark and made thick with strained honey is also very healing in inflamed throat and lungs. Nitro-hydro-chloric acid (diluted) is one of the finest remedies for a cough that can be found, and is highly recommended at the University of Michigan. Ten drops of acid to half a glass of water, sweetened to taste; take a teaspoonful every half hour until relieved. Do not leave the spoon in the liquid. Small drug stores seldom keep this acid, but were it generally known and more easily procured, many a hard cough might be prevented.

Mustard Plaster.—When the cold seems to have made the lungs its special point of attack, apply a mustard plaster mixed with the white of an egg, to draw the irritation to the surface as quickly as possible; then follow with a poultice of cooked linseed oil meal. If this does not afford relief, call the doctor, for the case is a serious one.

Liquid Tar.—For coughs, an excellent home preparation is made as follows: Boil a tablespoonful of liquid tar in a quart of rain water; strain through a cheese-cloth; place again over the fire; add a pound of horehound candy, a cup of granulated sugar and a half a spoonful of pulverized alum.

Cold Sores.—A German prescription for preventing cold sores from coming to a head is to paint them five or six times daily with equal parts of boracic acid and water.

Coughs and Sore Throats may be much alleviated by glycerin and lemon juice diluted with water, taken at night. Hot flaxseed tea with lemon juice sweetened with rock candy, is excellent also.

Hot Water.—A sudden and wearing attack of coughing often needs immediate attention, especially in consumptives and those chronically ill. In an emergency, that ever-useful remedy, hot water, will often prove very effective. It is much better than the ordinary cough mixtures, which disorder the digestion and spoil the appetite. Water almost boiling should be sipped when the paroxysms come on. A cough resulting from irritation is relieved by hot water through the promotion of secretion, which moistens the irritated surfaces. Hot water also promotes expectoration, and thus relieves the dry cough.

An Acute Cold is very disagreeable and if neglected may prove very serious. In its early stage it may be avoided by use of camphor. If the chest seems "tight," rub it thoroughly with equal parts of sweet oil and camphor, and wear a compress during the night, of flannel saturated with the mixture, heated and covered with dry flannel. Three or four drops of camphor in a glass of hot water, taken at night, is excellent. If the throat is a little sore, use a gargle of ten drops of camphor to a tablespoonful of water, being careful not to swallow this. Rubbing the nose with sweet oil and camphor and inhaling the fumes of the latter will help matters when the head feels full with a fresh cold.

COLD IN THE HEAD.

Camphor.—Five drops of spirits of camphor may be given on sugar for cold in the head and repeated twice in half an hour. It is usually very effective if its use is begun early, when the first symptoms are developing.

Lemon.—Dr. Willing says: "A simple remedy for cold in the head is the juice of a ripe lemon. This is squeezed into the hand and sniffed well up the nose. Two or three applications may be necessary.

Air and Diet.—Almost instant relief may be had in the case of a cold in the head, by a rigid and systematic practice of open air exercise and inhaling long breaths of fresh air four or five times a day. This practice, in conjunction with a spare diet and occasionally skipping a meal altogether, will cure almost any cold in the head if taken in the first stage of the disease.

TO PREVENT NIGHT COUGH.

When coughing at night is particularly troublesome, the thorough warming of the bed, previous to its being occupied, will often avert an attack. The taking of a warm drink, preferably a glass of hot milk, before retiring, or better after going to bed, is equally as good. The opportunity to warm a bed is not always possible, but it is generally very easy to secure a hot drink of some kind, no matter where one happens to be. One of the nicest ways to warm a bed is by ironing the lower sheet, and as much of the upper one as is thrown back when the bed is opened. After this is done quickly draw up the bed clothing and place bottles of hot water or the old-fashioned warmed log or bricks in between the ironed sheets.

REMEDY FOR A SORE THROAT.

A thin slice of raw fat pork dusted with cayenne pepper is by good authority considered the best remedy for a sore throat, and this is the way to apply it, so the greasy strip shall be securely held in place, poulticing the throat from ear to ear and not slipping down on the collar bone, where it can do little good to swollen tonsils, or rolling away from the throat altogether.

Cut a strip of flannel three and one-half inches wide and long enough to pass under the chin and tie on top of the head. Halve this strip lengthwise, leaving an uncut five or six inch length in the center on which to baste the pork. When this has been sprinkled with cayenne and applied to the throat, tie the upper strings snugly on top of the head and the lower ones at the back of the neck.

Another Remedy.—For sore throat, use an ointment made of equal parts of melted mutton tallow and kerosene oil, stirred until cold, to successfully incorporate the oil; apply outwardly and wrap the throat with a soft cotton cloth; woolen cloth heats, and is liable to blister.

Home-Made Gargle.—For local treatment of the throat, the simple home-made gargle of vinegar, salt and water is good for a slight attack, but for one more severe, dissolve chlorate of potash in water in the proportion of a teaspoonful of chlorate to a pint of water. Gargle the throat every half hour, using caution about swallowing much of it, as the chlorate is poisonous if taken in large quantities. Physicians recommend this in case of diphtheria.

For Ordinary Sore Throat.—Nothing surpasses a wet bandage passed around the throat at night, covered by numerous folds of dry woolen goods. A shawl will serve for this. Rub the throat well with tepid water, followed by lanoline ointment, when the compress is taken off.

Benefits of Gargling.—If people would wash out their mouths twice or three times a day with an antiseptic solution, there would not be near so much sickness. There are any number of proprietary antiseptics that are excellent for this purpose, but many more simple agents that are as good or better. One of the best of the latter is carbolic acid. A very weak solution of this, gargled and held in the mouth two or three times a day, will work wonders. Immediately after using, one will find that the mouth feels cleaner. A great majority of the common throat and lung troubles come from the lodgment of disease microbes within the mucous membranes of the mouth. The free use of antiseptics will kill these germs.

HOW TO CURE A SORE THROAT.

Home Treatment.—Sage tea as a gargle and also as a drink. Make a gargle of the following prescription:
  Chloride of potash, 1 drachm,
  Tincture of iron, 20 drops,
  Water, 1 glass.
Mix, and gargle the throat every hour.

A DOMESTIC REMEDY.
  2 tablespoonfuls of common salt,
  2 tablespoonfuls of strained honey,
  3 tablespoonfuls of vinegar,
  ¼ teaspoonful of camphor.
Mix and gargle the throat a dozen times a day.

EXTERNAL APPLICATION FOR SORE THROAT.

Wring a cloth out of salt and cold water and, keeping it quite wet, bind tightly about the neck and cover with a dry cloth. It is best to use this at night.

INCONTINENCE OF THE URINE.

Definition.—When a person cannot retain urine, and also has a frequent desire to urinate. It is a troublesome and annoying disease. One may be passing urine unconsciously during sleep, or may dribble away, which generally causes chafing and soreness.

Causes.—In children it may be caused by worms, or drinking too much water before retiring, or injuries or weakness of the organ. In adults, paralysis of the bladder or weakness.

Home Treatment.—Avoid all acid or salty food, tea, coffee and alcoholic liquors. The patient should take a cold bath every day, rubbing the skin thoroughly with a rough towel after each bath; have out-door exercise; sleep on a hard mattress, and avoid hot drinks toward evening.

Regular Treatment.—If the difficulty is worms, that should be remedied at once; if caused by paralysis or weakness of the bladder, take one drop of tincture of cantharides three times a day and keep the bowels open.

DIABETES (Excessive Quantities of Urine.)

Causes.—It is difficult to say what causes this disease, but it is generally conceded to be exposure, intemperance, injuries and certain fevers. It is as common to men as to women.

Symptoms.—Excessive quantities of urine of a very pale yellowish hue or quite colorless, which contains sugar in large quantities; thirst, lassitude, and great dryness and harshness of the skin, also loss of flesh.

Home Treatment.—Avoid all food containing starch and sugar, such as bread, vegetables, pie and cake. Eat meats of all kinds, eggs and bran bread, drink skim-milk and butter-milk; coffee may be taken without sugar. Avoid severe exercise, and bathe the skin thoroughly and frequently. A competent physician should be consulted.

GRAVEL.

Definition.—Gravel is caused by small stony substances which form in the kidneys or the bladder, and are often passed with the water. Some are subject to gravel every few months, but where the stone becomes large an operation is necessary.

Symptoms.—Pain in the end of the penis, constant desire to make water, pain in the bladder just before urinating, bloody urine. The only way to determine the existence of a gravel in the bladder is by the use of a surgical instrument. If the patient suffers from any of the above symptoms, the family physician should be consulted at once.

Home Treatment.—Avoid intoxicating liquors and drink only soft water, lemonade, milk, cider, alkaline, mineral and soda waters; avoid eating sugar, butter, fat meat, and exercise freely out of doors. The patient should take a tumbler of cold water an hour before dinner and at bed time; frequent baths and warm clothing are necessary. When suffering from pain, drink a copious quantity of flax-seed tea.

BRIGHT'S DISEASE.

Definition.—Bright's disease is a disease of the kidneys known by the presence of a substance called albumen in the urine. It is more frequently caused by the use of alcoholic liquors, exposure to cold, wet, etc.

Symptoms.—A pale and puffy appearance of the face; general pains and weakness; headache and lassitude.

Home Treatment.—A good test for Bright's Disease is the following: Take a wineglassful of urine and put into it a few drops of nitric acid; if the patient is suffering from Bright's disease, the urine will have a white cloudy appearance. Hard work and severe exercise must be avoided. Wear good warm flannel next to the skin; keep the bowels open and take a warm bath every day. Take cod liver oil, drink skim-milk and eat nourishing food. If dropsy makes an appearance, it may be checked by drinking freely of cream of tartar lemonade.

DYSPEPSIA.

Dyspepsia is not only a very common disease, but it is a cause or complication of almost all other diseases. It makes the lives of thousands poor and painful, weak and miserable. As we cannot live without food, we cannot live well unless our food is properly digested.

Any disease may come with, or proceed from dyspepsia. The hypochondriac or monomaniac is first of all a dyspeptic. Nervous exhaustion is a consequence as well as cause. Most cases of lung disease begin with dyspepsia. Nine cases out of ten of what are called diseases of the heart are really dyspepsia. The heart may have no organic disease, but it sympathizes with the wretched stomach, and when the disease of the heart happens to be the fashionable malady, doctors tell you that you have it.

Always in a Hurry.—We Americans are always in a hurry. If we were to carry our hurry and bustle only into business matters and circles, this characteristic might be a commendable one, but when our foreign friends notice that this same spirit is carried into our restaurants and public eating resorts as well as into the dining room of the home, they are no longer surprised at the large number of American dyspeptics.

Health Sacrificed.—An observer noticed that in city restaurants the average length of time occupied at the meal was less than twelve minutes. Health is sacrificed for the sake of a few more minutes to business. Such haste is exceedingly detrimental to the health of the digestive organs. Unmasticated food is injurious and produces inflammation of the walls of the stomach.

Obstinacy of Disease.—No disease is more obstinate or more hopeless than certain forms of dyspepsia. The first condition of cure for a worn-out, disordered stomach is rest, the small quantity of food on which a dyspeptic can live, and gain in strength and in weight is surprising.

Chief Cause.—Eating too much food is a more frequent cause of dyspepsia than eating bad food. Irregular eating is as frequent a cause of stomach disease as over-eating.

Chief Cure.—The chief cure must then be abstinence—rest to the wearied and exhausted stomach and a very pure and moderate diet. No stimulants, no condiments, no over-work, no over-worry. Remove all cause of disease. Observe all conditions of health. Eat, drink, breathe and bathe as you ought and nature will effect a cure more speedily than art.

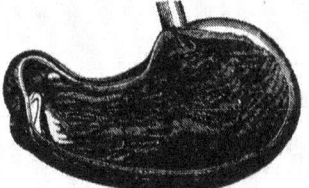

THE HUMAN STOMACH.

HOW TO CURE DYSPEPSIA.

Cause.—Excessive and fast eating, irregular time for meals, eating too much, sedentary habits, improper use of purgative drugs, hard study, or hard work just before or after meals, tight lacing, etc.

Symptoms.—Irregular appetite, pain in the stomach, furred tongue, offensive breath, nausea, bad taste in the mouth in the morning, an irritable feeling in the stomach after each meal, sour or bitter fluids arising from the stomach, heart-burn, etc.

Home Treatment.—Regular rest and regular exercise. Retire early and arise moderately early. Avoid eating pie, cake, pork, sausage, hard dried meats, cheese, lobsters, crabs, pastry of all kinds, canned salmon, soups, and newly baked bread; also all kinds of beer and liquors. Eat oatmeal, cracked wheat, graham bread and all kinds of fruits that will agree with the patient. Masticate the food thoroughly and eat slowly. Drink a glass of hot milk before each meal. A little pepsin taken immediately after each meal will often give great relief. Drink nothing while eating.

Common Treatment.—The following prescription is one of the best that is known and no doubt has cured as many people as any one prescription given by a physician:

"Dyspepsia Cure."

2 drachms hyposulphite of soda,
2 drachms sub. nit. bismuth.

Mix. Make into twelve powders.

Take one powder every three hours in little water or milk.

"EGYPTIAN DYSPEPSIA CURE."

Powdered rhubarb, 2 drachms.
Bicarbonate of soda, 6 drachms.
Fluid extract of gentian, 3 drachms.
Peppermint water, 7½ ounces.
Mix them.

One teaspoonful in a little cold water half an hour before meals.

JAUNDICE.

Cause.—Excesses in eating and drinking; a debauch; dyspepsia, or the use of alcoholic drinks; some obstruction in the bile duct, as a gall stone or currant seed; malaria; climate, as cool nights succeeding warm days.

Symptoms.—Derangement of the stomach and bowels, constipation, diarrhœa, or bitter taste in the mouth, thirst, indigestion, skin has a peculiar yellow color and itches, slight feverishness, whites of eyes yellow, stools become clay colored, and spirits depressed.

Home Treatment.—Give a warm bath night and morning, adding to the water an ounce of carbonate of potassium, and give a good laxative, as a tablespoonful of epsom salts. Allow the patient to drink a glass of lemonade once in four hours made with bitartrate of potassium. Restrict the diet to milk if possible, avoiding all starchy, fatty or sweet articles of food.

BILIOUS ATTACKS.

Symptoms.—Dizziness, loss of appetite, coated tongue, drowsiness, tired feeling, vomiting of bile, etc.

Home Treatment.—Take a dessertspoonful of cream of tartar and stir it into a pint of boiling water, and when cool drink it on an empty stomach. Repeat this about twice a day. Then drink a good strong tea made from the root of dandelion two or three times a day, one good dose just before retiring. Or a little common soda taken two or three times a day will often give the desired results. A few doses of quinine will often be all that is necessary.

A STOMACH'S PLEA.

"Give me only plain food, and not too much, and I will ensure a speedy digestion and excellent health; but how am I to dispose of the mass of costly rubbish that I am daily compelled to receive? Soup, beef, venison, vegetables, puddings, jellies, fruits, wine and many superfluous delicacies. How can any sensible stomach digest such a mass of amalgamated matter? The stomach of a plowman, having only plain food to digest, has little labor compared with mine. He assists his stomach in its digestive operations by taking plenty of good, refreshing exercise, while my owner, after arresting my power of digestion, adds thereto by taking no exercise. Is it strange that my owner is sick? Give me proper treatment and doctors and doctor bills can be dispensed with."

CONSTIPATION.

Dr. W. C. Lyman Truly Says:—There is one remarkable remedy that can be published here or anywhere. It may meet the "How?" of some despairing sufferer, who has endured many things in the way of taking of advertised remedies, and has been regularly and irregularly prescribed for more times than he can remember. It is this: Simply to chew the food finer.

Hot Biscuits.—The worst thing to be said against hot biscuit, pancakes, and fresh bread is that they tempt us to swallow them hastily. This ends in undissolved lumps of dough rolled together in the stomach, in which lumped-up condition they remain to the end.

Laxatives.—The drugs that act as laxatives all have a deplorable drawback in common. They leave the bowel torpid and insensitive to the stimulus of its ordinary contents. In other words, they must be taken continuously, once their use is started, as a habit, or constipation sets in worse than ever as the true and legitimate result of their employment. The more irritating and "active" the drug, the more profound the exhaustion of sensibility and vital activity that comes on after the drug has had its first effect. Among these drugs I do not class the ox-bile, now sold in capsules and in powder form. That is a physiological substitute for a deficiency of human bile, having considerable merit.

Good Advice.—Let us address a word to those who either find the taking of a laxative tiresome, or know it to be absolutely pernicious, that is, leading afterward to still more obstinate inaction of the bowels than before. First of all, before beginning that expensive makeshift, the laxative, give the matter long and careful study. To swallow a laxative is the beginning of defeat.

Two Simple Remedies.—Two simple procedures will usually restore normal action to the bowels. Drink a pint of cold water before breakfast, a half a spoonful or less at a time, that is, in little sips, the whole sipping exercise taking at least twenty minutes. Chew the food to a cream; so thoroughly, that is, that it can not very well go into solid form again, but will blend with the digestive juices, particularly the bile, and remain fluid.

Diet.—Coffee and tea, sugar spices, pastry, and hot biscuit are to be avoided. Dry toast, or some other equivalent of the German zwieback (which must be chewed to be swallowed), fruit, vegetables of the succulent varieties, and rare-done meats are the best foods. Some are helped by graham bread; some by figs (the seeds acting as exciters of peristalsis); sedentary persons by regular exercise.

Glycerine.—Injections of a little glycerine for temporary relief are better policy than an irritant taken by the mouth —which must disturb and exhaust the sensibility of the whole alimentary tract, as it passes along. Ox-gall in capsules is an internal remedy which has not this objection, and which is a fair temporary measure where the liver is at fault.

Great Abuse.—Let no remedy, however, divert attention from the great abuse, an abuse from which constipation must be expected and considered due—that of swallowing food without masticating it well. The writer has known constipation that has resisted all the supposed remedies to disappear at once and permanently, when the sufferer began chewing her food to the consistence of cream.

Old Age.—In old age a daily drive or gently massage of the bowels are often advisable. Horseback exercise will benefit a good many. Some cases, where constipation is due to a nervous or dynamic cause, yield to high grade homeopathy. More fats, such as butter, in the dietary help others. But however hard the problem may be, more study is what is called for, not a laxative medicine.

CONSTIPATION.

Definition.—Inactivity of the intestines or bowels, due to weak condition of the muscular walls of the bowels—or the lack of proper amount of fluid—from deficient secretions of bile, intestinal fluid, or often from a lack of fluid diet.

Causes.—Dyspepsia, sedentary habits, disease of the liver, character of food, irregular habits, malaria, and lead poisoning.

Symptoms.—In healthy condition the majority of persons have one stool each day. In constipation, the bowels are moved every three or four days, with great straining and distress.

Home Treatment.—

1. Beware of harsh purgatives, they make matters worse.

2. A regular hour each day must be established for going to stool.

3. Sufficient time must be taken to permit the bowels to become thoroughly evacuated.

4. Careful regulation of the diet; not too much nor too little food should be taken. Avoid tea, cheese, crackers, all highly seasoned food, and eat plenty of fruit with coarse bread, such as graham, and cornmeal, ginger-bread made with molasses, and oatmeal porridge. Plenty of water should be taken between meals.

These rules should be rigidly enforced before any permanent cure can be hoped for.

An orange eaten before breakfast, or at night before retiring, often acts well.

A glass of hot water taken half an hour before breakfast with a pinch of salt is beneficent.

Regular Treatment.—If the above rules are complied with, the following may be used with benefit:

    Fluid extract of cascara sagrada, 4 drachms,
    Glycerine, 1 1-3 drachms,
    Syrup sarsaparilla, 2 2-3 drachms.

Take one teaspoonful an hour after meals, or once a day as needed.

A glycerine suppository or a teaspoonful of glycerine, used as an enema, may act well.

In acute cases a dose of epsom salts or castor oil should be used, or an injection of warm soap suds.

"DR.

Home Remedies and Home Treatment. 155

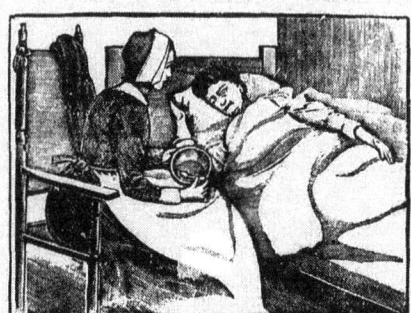

"DR. DANIELS' CELEBRATED EXTERNAL RHEUMATIC REMEDY."

Fluid ext. of belladonna, 1 ounce,
Fluid ext. of aconite root, ½ ounce,
Fluid ext. of colchicum seed, 1 ounce,
Fluid ext. of arnica, 1 ounce,
Chloroform, 1 ounce.

Mix the fluid extracts together first, then add the chloroform, and shake all together thoroughly. Always shake well before using.

To be applied externally only, and thoroughly rubbed in.

RHEUMATISM.

Rheumatism is divided into acute, chronic and muscular.

Acute Rheumatism is sometimes called rheumatic fever. This is generally brought on by exposure to cold, and affects the joints, which become painful and swollen.

Chronic Rheumatism is similar to acute rheumatism, with the exception that there is an absence of increased heat and redness. It is supposed to be the same as the acute form, only it is milder, but more persistent.

Muscular Rheumatism is a disease which affects the muscles, and often shifts from one place to another, but usually remains fixed in the muscles first attacked. The muscles in the back part of the neck and shoulders are very frequently attacked, also the muscles of the back.

CAUSE.—Usually an inherited tendency; exciting causes or exposure to cold, excessive meat diet and insufficient exercise.

SYMPTOMS.—Pain in the joints, tenderness, swelling or redness of the skin, swelling of the joints, and soreness of the muscles

HOME TREATMENT.—Wrap the red or swollen parts in flannel soaked in hot water or in a hot solution of common baking soda and water. Small mustard plasters placed over the affected joints or parts are highly recommended. Two or three tablespoonfuls of lemon juice in a glass of water three or four times a day often produce excellent results. For muscular rheumatism keep the affected parts warm and bathe two or three times a day with arnica. Rub it in with a coarse flannel, stimulating the muscles by thorough rubbing. A hot bath at bed time to induce free perspiration.

A rheumatic person should wear woolen garments next the skin and also sleep in warm blankets during the cold season of the year. Take a good dose of rhubarb at bedtime.

NERVOUSNESS.

It is not a disease, but it is a derangement of the nervous system, and may be produced by various causes; mental work, fatigue, anxiety etc.

HOME TREATMENT.—Rest; a cloth wet with cold water tied upon the head at night; a good bath every day. Diet of graham bread, milk, with plenty of cream and the fat of beef and mutton. Seek for the cause and remove it if possible.

Fat for the Nervous.—Nervous people should eat fat food. Every irritable and exhaustive nerve should, if possible, be coated with fat. Fat is to a tender nerve what an air cushion is to a tired invalid—it eases jolts wonderfully. With the fat should be combined grain foods and vegetables for strength, and fruits to keep up a healthful consistency of the blood.

OPIATES INCREASE NERVOUSNESS.

The longer you take opiates the less you will sleep, as they will tend to make you nervous and restless. Bravely give them up and depend upon alkalies which are mild sedatives and upon tincture of hyoscyamus, which is soothing to the nerves.

Take bromide of potash, borax, salt and phosphate of sodium, one drachm of each, dissolved in half a pint of water, which contains sixteen large spoonfuls of water, roughly estimated. Dose, a large spoonful four times a day. Drink Dutch cocoa, milk, or water, or any effervescing drink, but no tea or coffee.

In the evening, fifteen or thirty drops of tincture of hyoscyamus in a little water.

If your spine is hot apply a towel wrung out in hot water to the small of the back or nape of the neck for ten or twenty minutes, taking care not to wet your night clothes or to take cold.

All these measures will quiet your nerves and when time is given to overcome the force of the opium habit, if it has been formed, you will get sweeter rest than you ever got from opium. As soon as you begin to sleep enough drop the hyoscyamus.

ERYSIPELAS.

Erysipelas is accompanied with drowsiness and sometimes delirium when it affects the face and head. It is produced by exposure to sudden changes of heat and cold, which close up the excretory vessels and prevent perspiration. It is preceded by cold shiverings, with alternate flushings and fever.

Treatment.—Wash the affected parts and the surrounding skin with soap, and then apply a solution consisting of one part carbolic acid to twenty parts of alcohol. Instead of the alcohol some take common mucilage; others vaseline.

Another method is to apply compresses wet with a solution of salicylate of soda, one part to twenty of water, covering the compresses with rubber gutta-percha tissue.

CANCER.

The following treatment has completely cured several persons of cancer, and is vouched for: Take sheep sorrel, the variety with yellow flower, bruise the whole stalk, flower and all, and press out the juice. Boil it down one-half and bottle. Apply with a quill three or four times a day. Wash the sore with castile soap between applications. Drink red clover blossom tea.

One individual well known to the writer, finding no relief after submitting to a surgical operation, used the above simple remedy, and was cured. Many years have passed, but there are no symptoms of the disease left.

ECZEMA.

An ointment of equal parts of zinc and tar is good. A solution of two teaspoonfuls of soda to a pint of water is another good application.

HOW TO VACCINATE.

Vaccination was for a long time considered a perfect specific against small-pox, and the blood once influenced by the lymph of cow-pox would, it was supposed, ever afterward repel the disease of small-pox, however the patient might be exposed to its infection. Experience, however, has proved this to be a fallacy, and that persons, although twice vaccinated, may be attacked by the dreaded disease. It is, however, satisfactory to know that after vaccination, small-pox, if it should occur, is always mild, seldom pits the skin, and is never dangerous.

REMEDY FOR SMALL-POX.

1 grain sulphate of zinc; 1 grain foxglove (digitalis).
½ teaspoonful sugar.

Mix with 2 teaspoonfuls of water, add 4 oz. of water. Dose, 1 spoonful every hour, child in proportion. From experience it is known that nothing will break up this frightful disease sooner than continued and persevering bathing, with the water at a comfortable temperature.

HEARTBURN (Acidity of the Stomach.)

There is no such thing as heartburn. What is commonly called heartburn, is nothing more nor less than acidity of the stomach, or a derangement of the digestive organs, and can be easily remedied by taking half a tablespoonful of powdered magnesia, or half a teaspoonful of saleratus, or by drinking a little lime water, or by dropping a few burning coals of hardwood to a tumbler of water, and drinking the water.

SAVING THE EYES.

When the eyes are sore or inflamed, what shall be done for their relief? Rest is the first essential, and in a severe case, let this mean darkness obtained by a bandage of black cloth, for a day or two. Rest of the body and mind, if the eye trouble is the result of overwork, is the next essential. Go where the air is pure. It is said that hundreds of cases of loss or impairment of sight among workingmen in large cities could be prevented every year if oculists could send these sufferers for three months to a country home. Avoid wind, dust, and smoke.

Diet.—The diet should be limited and readily digestible. Very little should be taken at supper. The food should be masticated very thoroughly.

Dr. Agnew.—The late Dr. Agnew used to relate to his classes a case where an elderly man came many miles to New York to be operated on for an ulcerous malady of the eyeball. The surgeons in the hospital declined to operate, considering the process to be too far advanced. Dr. Agnew chanced to see him at table, and stepped in. He sat down beside him and showed him how to eat. Two weeks later he went home well, without operation or other treatment.

First Offense.—The first offense against the eyes is reading or writing in a poor light. Clerks who work by gaslight in poorly lighted buildings in cities, especially during the short, clouded days of winter, furnish many cases of sore and tired eyes. If gaslight must be used to any extent for close work, the eyes should be shaded, and care must be taken not to have more light in one eye than in the other.

Second Offense.—The second offense is reading with the head bent over. This favors congestion of the eyeball.

Third Offense.—The third is reading on trains. Here the stream of objects flying past at the window strains an eye that is also engaged with the printed page. Too many changes of focus, and too many uses of the muscles of fixation, strain the powers of the eyes.

All abuses of the sight bring their retribution as old age comes on, if not sooner.

Eye Glasses.—An experienced oculist says that a great many people injure their eyesight by not keeping their glasses bright and highly polished. They allow dust or moisture to accumulate upon them; then they are dim and semi-opaque, and the eyes are strained by trying to look through them. For properly cleaning eyeglasses a Japanese paper napkin is said to be excellent.

HOW TO DOCTOR SORE EYES.

Cause.—Exposure to cold, dust, injuries, catarrh, scarlet fever, measles, etc. When the eye feels as if there were fire sand in it, a competent physician should be at once consulted, because it is a symptom of inflammation which demands special attention.

Home Treatment.—Bathe the eyes every two or three hours in warm water. Place a few grains of alum in the water before using. Cleanliness is very necessary. The application of a cloth moistened with a solution of aconite in the proportion of one part of aconite to twenty of water will prove soothing and beneficial. Never apply hot fomentations to the eye without consulting a physician. A rubber bag or bladder filled with pounded ice and held to the eye is a good and safe remedy.

CAMPHORATED EYE WATER.

15 grains sulphate of copper,
15 grains French bole,
4 grains camphor,
4 ounces boiling water.

Infuse, strain, and dilute with two quarts of cold water and apply three times a day.

HOW TO CURE EARACHE.

Home Treatment.—Apply hot fomentations, or drop into the ear equal parts of laudanum and sweet oil. A pillow of hops or salt heated and applied to the ear will often furnish relief. If an insect gets into the ear, drop into the ear a few drops of sweet oil. If there is a discharge in the ear, it should be syringed out every day with warm water and the family physician consulted.

Home Remedies and Home Treatment.

HOW TO CURE THE GRIPPE.

Definition.—This wide-spread distemper, socalled La Grippe, is not yet fully understood. It probably is due to some kind of bacteria. The Grippe has characteristics similar to those of a severe cold.

Symptoms.—General debility, decided soreness and boneache all over the body, especially in the back and lower limbs. Much pain back of the head or over the eyes.

Home Treatment.—Live on a pure milk diet for several days. If milk does not agree add a large tablespoonful of lime water for each teacupful. Boil the milk before giving it to the patient and let him sip it with a teaspoon, instead of drinking it.

General Treatment.—In connection with the above treatment give the patient 3 grains of quinine, and 1½ hours after 4 grains of "Antifebrin," a recently discovered valuable preparation, which can be purchased at any drug store. Repeat the dose of quinine and Antifebrin every three hours, making them alternate every 1½ hours. Continue until the attack is broken up.

DYSENTERY OR BLOODY FLUX.

Causes.—Exposure to wet and cold in the chilliness of the evening, sleeping on damp ground, or between damp sheets, malaria, errors in diet, bad air, excessive fatigue, etc.

Symptoms.—Begins with diarrhœa, loss of appetite, nausea and very slight fever for two or three days; then the true dysenteric symptoms begin, to-wit: pain or pressure over the abdomen, colicky pains about umbilicus, burning pain in rectum, with constant desire to go to stool; stools contain blood, mucus and pus, and are evacuated with straining and pain; bloody and offensive discharges from the bowels.

Home Treatment.—Keep the patient quiet. It is best for the patient to remain in bed, though the attack be mild. Eat chicken broth, or other soups, and very light food, such as milk, cream, rice, etc. A little ice kept in the mouth is very soothing and will often relieve vomiting. Apply woolen cloths wrung out of hot water to which a few drops of turpentine have been added. Washing out the rectum with tepid or hot water adds much to the comfort of the patient and has a curative effect. A teaspoonful of charcoal every morning and evening will produce good results. Blackberry tea made from the

Blackberry root is very beneficial. If these remedies are not sufficient, a competent physician should be consulted at once.

Homœopathic Treatment.—Bryonia alternately with aconite every three hours. If there is severe headache give belladonna.

A CURE FOR FROST BITES.

If any portion of the body has been frozen, keep the person away from all heat until you can apply snow or cold water. Rub the parts carefully, but thoroughly, until the frozen flesh becomes soft and assumes a natural color. It is best to rub the frozen part an hour or more while thawing. Apply olive oil or lard after the rubbing has been completed.

INJURY FROM A RUSTY NAIL OR WIRE.

When anyone is injured by running a nail or wire into the flesh, hold the wound over burning sugar as soon as possible, and it will prevent the poisonous effect, and little, if any, soreness will be the result.

HOW TO CURE

Apoplexy, Bad Breath and Quinsy.

---

1. **Apoplexy.**—Apoplexy occurs only in the corpulent or obese, and those of gross or high living.

Treatment.—Raise the head to a nearly upright position, loosen all tight clothes, strings, etc., and apply cold water to the head and warm water and warm cloths to the feet. Have the apartment cool and well ventilated. Give nothing by the mouth until the breathing is relieved, and then only draughts of cold water.

2. **Bad Breath.**—Bad or foul breath will be removed by taking a teaspoonful of the following mixture after each meal: One ounce chloride of soda, one ounce liquor of potassa, one and one-half ounces phosphate of soda, and three ounces of water.

3. **Quinsy.**—This is an inflammation of the tonsils, or common inflammatory sore throat; commences with a slight feverish attack, with considerable pain and swelling of the tonsils, causing some difficulty in swallowing; as the attack advances, these symptoms become more intense; there is headache, thirst, a painful sense of tension, and acute darting pains in the ears. The attack is generally brought on by exposure to cold, and lasts from five to seven days, when it subsides naturally, or an abscess may form in tonsils and burst, or the tonsils may remain enlarged, the inflammation subsiding.

Home Treatment.—The patient should remain in a warm room, the diet chiefly milk and good broths, some cooling laxative and diaphoretic medicine may be given; but the greatest relief will be found in the frequent inhalation of the steam of hot water through an inhaler, or in the old-fashioned way through the spout of a teapot.

Home Remedies and Home Treatment.

HOW TO CURE PILES.

Definition.—Piles are divided into two kinds, internal and external, according to the location.

Cause.—Habitual constipation, violent horseback riding, indigestion, the use of strong cathartics, dysentery, wearing corsets, eating highly seasoned food, etc.

Home Treatment.—Use an injection of a pint of cold water every morning and take a few grains of rhubarb daily; this will often cure cases of long standing, or take an injection of alum and water of the strength of one or two teaspoonfuls of alum to a pint of water, or take two grains of sulphate of iron to an ounce of water. An injection of this will stop the bleeding.

Where there is much pain a hip-bath of fifteen to twenty minutes, if the pain is very severe it will produce relief. Apply a bread and milk poultice four or five times a day is also a good remedy.

CHOLERA MORBUS.

Cause.—It is more prevalent in warm than in cold climates. It is usually the result of eating excessively of indigestible articles, such as unripe fruits, uncooked vegetables, melons, or intoxicating drinks.

Symptoms.—Nausea, vomiting and purging, cramps and pains, sometimes intense thirst and quick pulse.

Home Treatment.—Let the patient remain quiet and lie in bed. Take a teaspoonful of saleratus every two or three hours, or make a good strong tea of rhubarb root and drink freely. Drop a few live hardwood coals in a tumbler of water and drink the water; repeat this every two hours. Or make a strong tea of the leaves or bark of the peach tree and drink freely every few minutes. Avoid drinking cold water.

Any of the above domestic remedies will be found efficient and helpful.

NIGHT SWEATS.

Night sweats are generally a symptom of weakness, and can easily be remedied by toning up the system by eating nourishing food, such as beefsteak, oatmeal, cracked wheat, baked potatoes, fruits, etc. A good tonic may be taken. Bathe the body in salt water every other day. A good dose of sage tea before retiring will prove very beneficial.

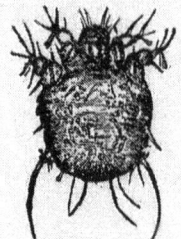

THE ITCH INSECT.

How to Cure the Itch.

The itch is an infectious skin disease caused by little animals called animalculæ, which burrow in the skin and cause intense itching.

2. CAUSE.—Bad air, unwholesome food, unventilated houses, dirty beds and clothing. It can only be communicated by contact.

3. SYMPTOMS.—It begins with slight eruptions between the fingers, on the finger joints, on the wrist, under the arms, on the thighs, etc.

4. REMEDY.—Keep the bowels open and regular. Take flower of sulphur and lard or fresh butter enough to make a good ointment and anoint the body all over every night before retiring. Wash thoroughly with warm water every morning.

5. Take internally a teaspoonful of flower of sulphur and molasses once a day.

6. After cure burn clothes or bake them several hours in a hot oven.

ITCH OINTMENT.

Unsalted butter,	1 pound.
Burgundy pitch,	2 ounces.
Powdered saltpetre,	1 drachm.
Powdered sulphur,	1 pint.

Melt, and mix thoroughly together and apply every evening.

166   *How to Cure Dyspepsia and Weak Lungs*

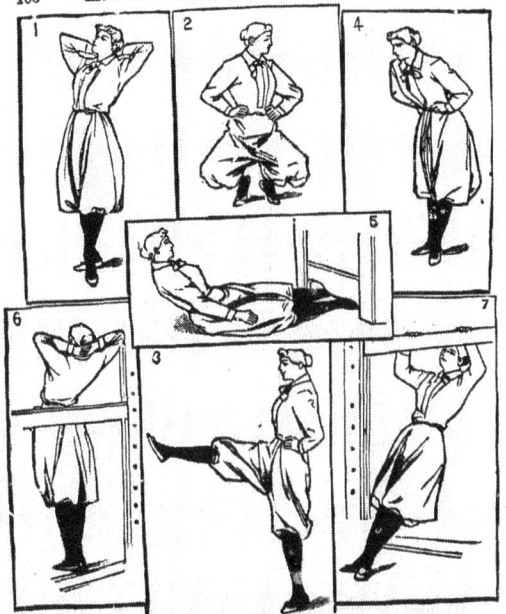

HOW TO CURE DYSPEPSIA AND WEAK LUNGS BY MORNING EXERCISE.

Make a frame that will fit in the door, that can be easily taken apart and put together, and then go through the following exercise:

Stand in a walking position, one foot in advance of the other, your hands on your hips, and twist the trunk to the side of the rear foot as far as possible; then change feet and twist to the opposite side. Repeat fifteen times to each side. Do the same twisting with your hands clasped behind your neck, your shoulders well held back.

Stride standing. Rise on your toes and bend your knees outward and downward. Repeat ten times slowly.

Stand on one foot, your hips firm, and slowly raise your other leg, extended in front; keep a steady balance. Change feet and repeat.

Stand with your heels together, your hands on your hips. Bend your body forward, to the side, backward and to the opposite side, then forward to complete the circle. Repeat and rotate your body in opposite directions.

Lie on your face, with your hips firm and your feet held under a bureau; try to raise your head and shoulders as far as possible, with deep inspiration. Repeat, turning your body.

Bend your body over a bar in the doorway, or your stair railing, backward, forward and sideways, with your hands clasped behind your neck.

Place your bar low; hang under it with your body extended stiffly and resting on your heels. Slowly draw your chest up to touch the bar by bending your elbows outward. Repeat.

Combine these movements with deep respiration, opening a window for good, pure air; make each exercise as useful to the muscles as possible; they are corrective exercises—not merely amusing. Rub your stomach with cold water after the exercise. This treatment persevered in, with self-restraint at the table, is the best for dyspepsia and weak lungs.

A PALATABLE LAXATIVE.

Make a strong, concentrated infusion of senna leaves; strain this through a muslin cloth and boil in the strained liquid as many prunes of good quality as can be well boiled in the quantity of infusion. Stew the prunes in the liquor thoroughly, in the same manner as if for the table, properly seasoning. When well cooked put in a glass jar, screw the top down tightly, and set away in a cool place. Two or three or four of these prunes, eaten during the day, will overcome some of the severest cases of constipation. There is no suggestion whatever of the senna in the taste of the prunes, and the effect is most desirable. If taken at bedtime, when a laxative is desired, the bowels will move nicely in the morning.

HOW TO MAKE ALL KINDS OF OINTMENT.

FOOT OINTMENT FOR ALL DOMESTIC ANIMALS.

Equal parts of tar, lard and resin, melted together.

GOLDEN OINTMENT.

One drachm of orpiment mixed with 2 ounces of lard to the consistency of an ointment.

PILE OINTMENT.

2 drachms powdered nutgall,
1 drachm powdered opium.
1 ounce lard,
2 drachms melted wax.

Mix, and apply three times a day.

MAGNETIC OINTMENT FOR MAN AND BEAST.

1 pound elder bark,
1 pound spikenard,
1 pound yellow dock root.

Boil in 2 gallons of water down to 1, then press the strength out of the roots and boil the liquid down to ½ gallon; add 8 pounds of the best resin, 1 pound of beeswax, and tallow enough to soften. Roll in rolls, and apply by warming and spreading on linen.

HEALING OINTMENT.

4 ounces resin,
6 ounces lard,
2 ounces yellow wax.

Mix, and strain through a cloth.

FOR CHAFING AND OTHER SKIN IRRITATIONS.

Rice flour, 1 pound,
Rose pink, 5 grains,
Oil of rose, 10 drops,
Oil of sandalwood, 5 drops.

Mix thoroughly.

RECEIPTS FOR ALL KINDS OF LINIMENT.

BARRELL'S INDIAN LINIMENT.

1 qt. alcohol,
1 oz. tincture of capsicum,
½ oz. oil of origanum,
½ oz. oil of sassafras,
½ oz. oil of pennyroyal,
½ oz. oil of hemlock,

Mix.

ARNICA LINIMENT.

Add to 1 pint of sweet oil, 2 tablespoonfuls of tincture of arnica. Good for wounds, stiff joints, rheumatism, and all injuries.

LINIMENT FOR OLD SORES.

(Man or Beast.)

Common salt, 1½ tablespoonfuls,
Opium, 1 ounce,
Camphor gum, 1 ounce,
Oil of origanum, 1 ounce,
Ammonia, 2 ounces,
Alcohol, 1 pint.

Liniments and ointments should always be applied to the patient with the hand; if applied with cotton or a cloth the good effect obtained from the friction would be lost.

Liniments.

A FAMILY LINIMENT FOR ACCIDENTS, BRUISES, LAMENESS AND SWELLING.

Alcohol, 95 per cent., 1 gallon,
Oil of sassafras, 3 ounces,
Oil of origanum, 3 ounces,
Tinct. of arnica, 3 ounces,
Tinct. of camphor, 2 ounces,
Tinct. of opium, 2 ounces,
Tinct. of valerian, 2 ounces,
Tinct. of Guaiaci, 1 ounce,
Aqua ammonia, 1½ ounces,
Chloroform, 2 ounces,
Tinct. cochineal sufficient to color.

Mix them and make a liniment.
Be sure and shake well before using.

SOAP LINIMENT.

Sulphuret of potassium, 3 ounces; soap, 1 pound; sufficient water to melt together; add 1 pound olive oil; 3 fluid drachms oil of thyme; mix well. This is a remedy for skin diseases.

DR. DANIELS' CHLOROFORM LINIMENT.

Sweet oil, 1 ounce,
Oil sassafras, ½ ounce,
Aqua ammonia, 4 F., 4 ounces.

Shake thoroughly, and add:

Laudanum, 1 ounce,
Tinct. arnica, 2 ounces,
Chloroform, ½ ounce. Mix.

Nothing better in the world for rheumatism, bruises, sprains, etc. Rub in thoroughly.

Shake before using.

HOW TO MAKE ALL KINDS OF HEALING SALVES.

A SALVE FOR BURNS, FROSTBITES, CHAPPED HANDS, ETC.

Turpentine, 1 ounce,
Beeswax, 1 ounce,
Sweet oil, 1 ounce.

Melt oil and wax together, and put in the turpentine when sufficiently cooled.

A SALVE FOR BROKEN BREASTS, ABSCESSES, FEVER SORES, ETC.

Lard, ½ ounce,
Resin, ¼ ounce,
Beeswax, ¼ ounce.

Then steep ¼ ounce of tobacco in 2 ounces of salt water; strain and boil down to one-half the original quantity. Then mix with the other ingredients while warm.

AN EXCELLENT HEALING SALVE.

Lard, 6 ounces,
Yellow wax, ½ ounce,
Burgundy pitch, 8 ounces.

Melt, and mix together thoroughly.

A SALVE FOR RHEUMATIC PAINS, ULCERS, BRUISES, ETC.

Resin, 2 ounces,
Mutton tallow, 2 ounces,
Oil of red cedar, ½ ounce,
Oil of wormwood, ¼ ounce.

Melt, and mix thoroughly.

A SALVE FOR ALL KINDS OF SORES, CUTS, BRUISES, ETC., IN MAN OR BEAST.

White wax, 4 drachms,
Lard, 18 drachms,
Crystallized carbolic acid, 3 drachms.

Melt the wax and lard together. Stir until cooled, and then add the carbolic acid previously liquified.

LIP SALVE.

Take of Lard, 1 ounce,
Cacao butter, 1½ ounces,
Spermaceti, ½ ounce,
Yellow wax, 1½ drachms,
Alkannet root, 15 grains.

Melt, and keep liquid over fire for ¼ hour; then strain through cloth and add

Oil of lemon, 5 drops,
Oil of bergamot, 9 drops,
Oil of bitter almonds, 2 drops.

This is an excellent emollient application for abraded or chafed surfaces. Apply at night on linen cloth.

HOW TO USE HOT WATER AS A MEDICINE, AND ITS WONDERFUL CURATIVE AND MEDICINAL PROPERTIES.

To drink water internally it should be used at about 100° Fahr. Hot water possesses more medical properties than almost any other liquid or substance. It is a domestic remedy that is available to all and can easily be applied.

1. There is nothing better for cuts, bruises, congestion of the lungs, sore throat, rheumatism, etc., than hot water.

2. Headache almost always yields to the application of hot water to the feet and to the back of the neck.

3. A towel folded several times and quickly wrung out of hot water and applied over the face will relieve, and many times cure, toothache and neuralgia.

4. A strip of flannel or a napkin folded lengthwise and dipped in hot water and wrung out and then applied around the neck of a child that has the croup, will often bring instant relief. Apply every five minutes.

5. Hot water taken freely half an hour before bedtime is one of the best remedies for constipation.

6. A cup of hot water taken just after rising before breakfast has cured thousands of indigestion.

7. There is no other domestic remedy so widely recommended by physicians for the disease of dyspepsia.

8. Persons suffering with cold hands and feet will often find a great relief by taking a cupful of hot water several times a day.

9. A hot hipbath will often relieve the distressing sensation of dysentery, the itching of piles, etc.

10. The inhaling of steam is often efficient in relieving coughs, colds, sore throat, asthma and croup.

174　　*The Use of Hot Water in Diseases.*

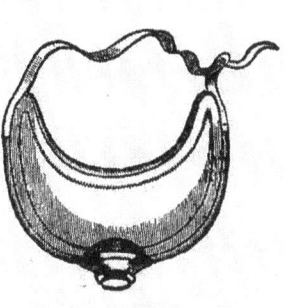 

HOT-WATER THROAT BAG　　　　HOT-WATER BAG.

HOW TO APPLY AND USE HOT WATER IN ALL DISEASES.

1. **The Hot-Water Throat Bag.** The hot-water throat bag is made from fine white rubber fastened to the head by a rubber band (see illustration), and is an unfailing remedy for catarrh, hay fever, cold, toothache, headache, earache, neuralgia, etc.

2. **The Hot-Water Bottle.** No well-regulated house should be without a hot-water bottle. It is excellent in the application of hot water for inflammation, colic, headache, congestion, cold feet, rheumatism, sprains, etc., etc. It is an excellent warming pan and an excellent foot and hand warmer when riding. These hot-water bags in any variety can be purchased at any drug store.

3. Boiling water may be used in the bags and the heat will be retained many hours. They are soft and appliable and pleasant to the touch, and can be adjusted to any part of the body.

4. Hot water is good for constipation, torpid liver, and relieves colic and flatulence, and is of special value.

5. Caution. When hot-water bags or any hot fomentation

is removed, replace dry flannel and bathe parts in tepid water and rub till dry.

6. For inflammations it is best to use hot water and then cold water. It seems to give more immediate relief. Hot water is a much better remedy than drugs, paragoric, Dover's powder or morphine. Always avoid the use of strong poisonous drugs when possible.

7. For those who suffer from cold feet there is no better remedy than to bathe the feet in cold water before retiring and then place a hot water bottle in the bed at the feet. A few weeks of such treatment results in relief if not cure of the most obstinate case.

HOW TO USE COLD WATER.

Use a compress of cold water for acute or chronic inflammation, such as sore throat, bronchitis, croup, inflammation of the lungs, etc. If there is a hot and aching pain in the back apply a compress of cold water on the same, or it may simply be placed across the back or around the body. The most depends upon the condition of the patient.

WHAT HOT WATER WILL DO.

According to a prominent New York physician, it
Will cure dyspepsia, if taken before breakfast;
Ward off chills, when one comes in from the cold;
Stop a cold, if taken early in the stage;
Relieve a nervous headache;
Give instant relief to tired and inflamed eyes;
Prove efficacious for sprains and bruises;
Frequently stop the flow of blood from a wound;
Is a sovereign remedy for sleeplessness;
Causes wrinkles to flee and backaches to vanish.

A BRIEF HISTORY OF MEDICINE.

Ancient Greeks.—The ancient Greeks in their desire to honor the healing art, cherished the myth that the first knowledge of medicine came from gods and demigods. The Romans, though in general more practical than the Greeks, evinced less sense of the importance of the healing art, and for centuries held practices of medicine in small esteem. Foreigners who tried to establish the art at Rome were looked on with contempt and suspicion.

Cato.—The elder Cato said that these doctors came to Rome to put an end to the people. He cautioned his friends to let them alone, and preferred to treat his family and neighbors from an old hand-book of medical recipes which had probably been delivered to him by his father, who in turn had received it from his progenitors.

Romans.—Romans of means had physicians in their own houses. These men were slaves, for, odd as it seems, many Roman slaves were accomplished in literature, art and science. At one time the selling price of a slave doctor was about the equivalent of three hundred dollars in our money.

Julius Cæsar.—After the time of Julius Cæsar, who encouraged physicians, the art began to "lift its head" in Rome, and later men of character and position, though generally foreigners, entered the profession. Some of them accumulated large fortunes, and one made the equivalent of at least five hundred thousand dollars in a few years.

In some countries, where physicians did not thrive, sick people were placed on the road-side, that travelers who had suffered with like maladies might suggest remedies.

Drug Shops.—Such crude efforts were supplanted at Rome by shops, in which various drugs and medicines were sold. Then, as now, quacks abounded, and the government, for the protection of the people, ordered that all remedies should bear a label declaring the character of the medicine, the name of its inventor, the sickness for which it was prepared, with a list of its ingredients and full directions as to the way in which it should be taken.

Disorders of Stomach.—For disorders of the stomach a favorite prescription was to the effect that the sufferer should read aloud in a clear distinct tone some book or speech, and then take moderate exercise.

A Brief History of Medicine.

Physicians were divided, as now, into various classes of specialists—doctors for the eye, for the throat, etc. Even in those old days women practiced medicine, although they did not reach prominence in the profession.

Surgeons used various instruments, resembling in some measure those of today. They had ear-probes, syringes, instruments for cutting bones, and the like. In very early times dentists came into notice, and an ancient author refers to "gold fillings."

Chinese Doctors.—A Chinese doctor is employed by the year to attend the family and keep its members in good health. When one falls ill the doctor's pay is stopped until the patient recovers.

THE CELEBRATED DR. KOCH.

THE GREAT REVOLUTIONS IN THE PRACTICE OF MEDICINE.

The wisdom of today is the ignorance of tomorrow is an old but true maxim. Enlightened chemistry, with the aid of the microscope, has made startling discoveries within the last few years. Old medicines and old remedies in the field of medicine and surgery have been so changed and supplanted by new ideas, that scarcely a vestige of the principles and practice of the old-time methods remain. Prof. Tyndall, of England, Louis Pasteur, of France, Dr. Koch, of Germany, and many other eminent scientists, have made wonderful discoveries with the microscope, and placed new fields of study before the medical profession.

How Much Medicine to Take as a Dose.

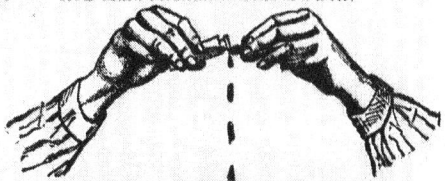

HOLD THE VIAL IN ONE HAND AND THE CORK IN THE OTHER.

How Much Medicine to Take as a Dose.

NAME OF DRUG.	DOSE.	NAME OF DRUG.	DOSE.
Aloes	3 to 15 grains.	Syrup of Sarsaparilla	1 to 4 teasp'fuls.
Anise Oil	5 to 15 drops.	" Seneka	1 to 2 teasp'fuls.
Aqua Ammonia (dilute)	10 to 30 drops.	" Rhubarb	1 to 2 teasp'fuls.
Balsam Copaiba	10 to 40 drops.	Tannic Acid	1 to 5 grains.
Balsam of Fir	3 to 10 drops.	Tinct. of Aconite Root	1 to 5 drops.
Bismuth	5 to 40 grains.	" Aloes	1 to 6 teasp'fuls.
Bromide of Potassium	5 to 40 grains.	" Asafœtida	¼ to 1 teasp'ful.
Buchu Leaves	20 to 40 grains.	" Belladona	10 to 30 drops.
Calomel (as alterative)	1-12 to 1 grain.	" Bloodroot	¼ to ½ teasp'ful.
Castor Oil	1 to 8 teasp'fuls.	" Columbo	1 to 2 teasp'fuls.
Citrate of Iron	2 to 5 grains.	" Camphor	5 to 60 drops.
Citrate Iron & Quinine	3 to 8 grains.	" Cayenne	10 to 60 drops.
Cream of Tartar	½ to 8 teasp'fuls.	" Castor	¼ to 1 teasp'ful.
Dover's Powder	5 to 10 grains.	" Catechu	¼ to 2 teasp'fuls.
Elecampane	20 to 60 grains	" Cinch. Comp.	¼ to 4 teasp'fuls.
Epsom Salts	¼ to 1 ounce.	" Colchicum	10 to 20 drops.
Gallic Acid	5 to 10 grains.	" Digitalis	5 to 20 drops.
Iodide of Potassium	2 to 10 grains.	" Ginger	¼ to 1 teasp'ful.
Kino	10 to 30 grains.	" Gentian Com	¼ to 2 teasp'fuls.
Mandrake	5 to 20 grains.	" Guaiac	¼ to 1 teasp'ful.
Mercury with Chalk	2 to 8 grains.	" Kino	¼ to 2 teasp'fuls.
Morphine	⅛ to ¼ grain.	" Lobelia	¼ to 1 teasp'ful.
Muriate of Ammonia	5 to 20 grains.	" Muriate Iron	10 to 30 drops.
Opium	½ to 2 grains.	" Myrrh	½ to 1 teasp'ful.
Paregoric	1 teaspoonful	" Nux Vomica	5 to 10 drops.
Peppermint Essence	5 to 30 drops.	" Opium (Laudanum)	10 to 25 drops.
Pepsin	1 to 5 grains.	" Rhubarb	1 to 4 teasp'fuls.
Quinine	1 to 10 grains.	" " & Senna	1 to 4 teasp'fuls.
Rochelle Salts	¼ to 1 ounce.	" Tolu	1 to 1 teasp'ful.
Rhubarb	5 to 30 grains.	" Valerian	¼ to 2 teasp'fuls.
Saltpetre	5 to 20 grains.	Turpentine	4 to 10 drops.
Santonin	2 to 5 grains.	Wine Ipecac (Diaph.)	10 to 30 drops.
Syrup of Squills	½ to 1 teasp'ful.	" " (Emetic)	2 to 8 teasp'fuls.
" Iodide of Iron	15 to 30 drops.	" Colchicum Root	10 to 30 drops.
" Senna	1 to 6 teasp'fuls.		

Children should take from ⅛ to ¾ of a dose, according to age. Or divide the age of the child at its next birthday by 24 and take that fractional part of a dose for an adult.

How to Measure Medicines. 179

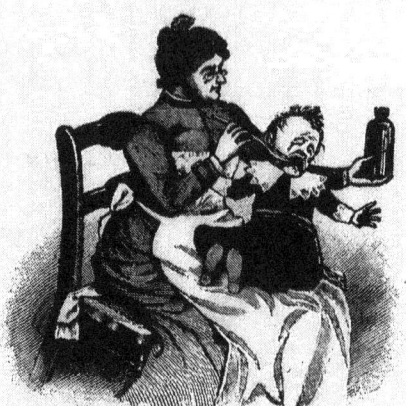

BITTER MEDICINES MAY HAVE GOOD EFFECT.

HOW TO GIVE HOMEOPATHIC MEDICINES.

Time.—The most appropriate times for taking medicines, as a rule, are on rising in the morning, and at bedtime.

The Dose.—The disease, age, habits, etc., must regulate the quantity of medicine. In general, it is safe to adopt the following rule: For an adult, one drop of 3x tincture, or its equivalent in pellets or globules. For children and infants from one-half to one-third the quantity. The repetition of doses must be governed by the disease. Acute diseases may require very frequent doses every ten or twenty minutes. Chronic diseases once a day.

HOW TO USE ALL KINDS OF HOMEOPATHIC REMEDIES.

1. **Ague.**—*In marshy places.*—Arnica, arsenicum, carbo veg., cinchona. *In damp, cold seasons.*—Calcarea, carbo veg., cinchona, lachesis. *In spring and summer.*—Antimonium crudum, arsenicum, belladonna, capsicum. *In autumn.*—Bryonia, cinchona, nux vomica, rhus, veratrum *An attack every day.*—Aconitum, arsenicum, belladonna, bryonia, calcarea. *Every other day.*—Antimonium crudum, arnica, arsenicum, belladonna, bryonia

2. **Alopecia** (*loss of hair.*)—From previous illness, grief, etc.—Phosphorus, aconitum, ignatia, calcarea, silicea, china, cantharis.

3. **Appetite, Loss of.**—Nux vomica and pulsatilla; if there is any constipation with derangement of the stomach, podophyllin; if with debility, china.

4. **Apoplexy.**—Aconitum, opium, belladonna, nux vomica. **Predisposition to.**—Strict temperance in eating and drinking; avoidance of excitement, haste, heated rooms, etc.

5. **Asthma.**—Arsenicum and ipecac; if it is a nervous attack use gelsemium.

6. **Barber's Itch.**—Atimonium tarraricum, arsenicum.

7. **Bed Sores.**—Glycerine-cream or calendula-lotion; also calendula or arnica plaster. **Prevention of.**—Washing the parts exposed to pressure morning and evening with tepid water; after drying with a soft towel, a little glycerine or glycerine-cream should be rubbed evenly over the parts.

8. **Bilious Attacks.**—Chamomilla and nux vomica alternately; if with constipation, podophyllin.

9. **Bladder.**—*Catarrh of*—Antimonium crudum, pulsatilla, cantharis. *Inflammation of*—Cantharis, aconitum

10. **Boils.**—When large looking like carbuncles, arsenicum, belladonna. When there is a disposition towards boils, give lycopodium, sulphur and silicea, twice a week.

11. **Bowels.**—Inflammation of—Aconitum, belladonna, colocynth, arsenicum bryonia; also hot fomentations, poultices, or wet compresses.

12. **Bronchitis.**—Aconite and bryonia alternately for acute bronchitis; for chronic bronchitis, bryonia and phosphorus alternately.

13. **Bruises.**—Arnica (externally).

14. **Buzzing in the Ears.**—Pulsatilla and mercurius; if particularly while eating, with disordered digestion, take nux vomica.

15. **Cancer.**—Arsenicum, hydrastus.

16. **Canker of the Mouth.**—Mercurius, arsenicum (idiopathic); carbo veg. nitric acid (mercurial); sulphuric acid spray, locally.

17. **Catarrh or Cold in the Head.**—Aconite and nux vomica alternately; if there is watery discharge from the nose, arsenicum and bryonia alternately; if with cold in the chest, bryonia and aconite alternately, or chamomilla with hepar sulphur alternately; if with hoarseness, take phosphorus.

18. **Chicken Pox.**—Rhus tox. Sulphur, antimonium tar.

19. **Chorea** (St. Vitus' dance).—Cuprum, veratrum, viride, belladonna, ignatia, cimicifuga, rac. arsenicum.

20. **Cholera Morbus, Cholera.**—Use veratrum, ipecac, colocynth.

21. **Colic, Flatulent.**—Colocynthis and pulsatilla alternately every ten minutes; when better every hour or two.

22. **Cold in Chest.**—If with dry hard cough take aconite and bryonia alternately; if the cough is loose and rattling, take ipecac alternately with tartar emetic; if with hoarseness, phosphorus.

23. **Constipation.**—Nux vomica alternately with bryonia.

24. **Consumption.**—Phosphorus, arsenicum, drosera, lycopodium; also aconitum or bryonia.

25. **Convulsions.**—Belladonna and hyoscyamus alternately, first using hot water bath.

26. **Costiveness.**—Nux vomica and sulphur alternately every night and morning.

27. **Cough.**—Dry, ipecac and bryonia alternately; hoarse, hepar sulphur and phosphorus alternately; loose, pulsatilla and tartar emetic alternately.

28. **Croup.**—Aconite, spongia and hepar sulphur in rotation, fifteen minutes apart; when better every two hours.

29. **Cuts and Lacerated Wounds.**—Should be treated with tincture of calendula. It works magically in healing rapidly and removing inflammation.

30. **Cystitis** (Inflammation of the bladder).—Cantharis, apis mellifica.

31. **Deafness** (from cold).—Aconitum, mercurius, belladonna, pulsatilla, dulcamara.

From Enlargement of Tonsils.—Mercurius, belladonna, calcarea phosphorus, carbo veg.

After Measles.—Pulsatilla, sulphur, belladonna; after scarlatina, belladonna, hepar sulphuris, calcarea; after small-pox, mercurius, sulphur, belladonna; from nervous disease, phophorus, china.

32. **Diarrhea.**—Bilious, chamomilla or mercurius; simple diarrhea, china alternately with mercurius; painful diarrhea, arsenicum and veratrum alternately. A dose after every stool.

33. **Diphtheria.**—Belladonna used alternately with merc. iod. Where there is croup complication, kali bich., and gargle or touch white spots with alcohol dilute.

34. **Diseases of Infants.**—Colic and diarrhea, with vomiting, ipecac; obstruction of the nose, with running from the nose, chamomilla; dry obstructions of the nose, nux vomica; constipation, bryonia and nux vomica alternately; sleeplessness, coffea; fever, with dry skin, aconite; difficult teething, calcarea carb. The pellets may be mashed with the fingers before placing on the child's tongue.

35. **Dysentery.**—Use aconite and mercurius cor. alternately, a dose after every stool.

36. **Dyspepsia.**—Pulsatilla and chamomilla alternately.

37. **Dropsy.**—Arsenicum, apis, bryonia, china.

38. **Earache.**—Pulsatilla, belladonna and mercurius in rotation every fifteen minutes; when better every three hours. Use hot applications.

39. **Eczema** (a non-contagious itching eruption).—Arsenicum, calcarea, mercurius, rhus tox. sulphur.

40. **Epilepsy.**—Belladonna, cuprum, veratrum vir. ignatia, arsenicum, calcarea (chronic).

41. **Epistaxis** (bleeding from the nose).—Hamamelis; (dark blood) ipecacuanha; (bright blood) pulsatilla; (absent or deficient period) bryonia, aconitum.

42. **Erysipelas.**—Belladonna if with red smooth skin; if with blisters or vesicles, rhus tox.

43. **Eye.**—In inflammation use aconite, belladonna and gelseminum, in rotation.

44. **Faceache or Neuralgia.**—Aconite, chamomilla and belladonna in rotation every fifteen minutes; when better

every three hours; if not better in a day or so, take aconite and mercurius in rotation.

45. **Fever.**—Aconite every half hour. Scarlet fever, aconite and belladonna alternately; rheumatic fever, aconite, bryonia and rhus tox. in rotation; fever in infants, aconite and chamomilla; chills and fever, use arsenicum, ipecac and china in rotation.

46. **Flatulence.**—Nux vomica, carbo veg.; (stomach) lycopodium; (bowels) china.

47. **Gall Stones.**—Aconitum, mercurius, podoph, nux vomica, china (preventive).

48. **Giddiness.**—Belladonna, nux vomica, bryonia, aconitum, pulsatilla, gelsemium.

49. **Hay Fever.**—Ipecacuanha, arsenicum.

50. **Headache.**—Nervous headache, belladonna and bryonia alternately every fifteen minutes; sick headache, nux vomica and bryonia alternately every half hour; congestive headache, throbbing, belladonna every fifteen minutes; headache of females, pulsatilla.

51. **Heart Disease.**—Aconite, gelsemium and digitalis.

52. **Hectic Fever.**—China, phosphorus, arsenicum, sulphur, mercurius.

53. **Hiccough.**—Nux vomica, aconitum, ignatia, sulphur veratrum viride.

54. **Hoarseness.**—Aconite alternately with hepar sulphur. If these fail, mercurius.

55. **Hooping Cough.**—Ipecacuanha, drosera, cuprum veratrum gelsemium, veratrum viride, or belladonna (with head symptoms).

56. **Hysteria.**—Ignatia, gelsemium, pulsatilla.

57. **Impure Blood.**—Hepar sulphur and sulphur alternately.

58. **Influenza.**—Camphor (the chill stage); aconite (chills and heats); arsenicum (prostration); kali bichromicum (troublesome cough).

59. **Itch.**—Hepar sulphur; also apply powdered sulphur and lard externally.

60. **Inactive Liver.**—Alternate mercurius sol. and podophyllin.

61. **Jaundice.**—Aconite, bryonia, mercurius, phosphorus (malignant); China, nux.

62. **Kidney Troubles.**—Aconite and bryonia alternately.

63. **Lead Colic.**—Opium, alum, belladonna, sulph. ac. platinum.

64. **Liver.**—Enlargement of, merc. iod. also abdominal compress; inflammation of, aconite, bryonia, mercurius cor.

65. **Lumbago** or pain in small of the back.—Rhus tox., nux vomica and bryonia in rotation.
66. **Leucorrhœa.**—Sepia, cimicifuga and caullophyllum.
67. **Lungs.**—Inflammation of, aconite alt. phosphorus, bryonia.
68. **Measles.**—Aconite and pulsatilla alternately. If the rash disappears, take sulphur; if it hesitates to disappear, use gelsemium and ipecac alternately.
69. **Morning Sickness.**—Macrotin in alternation with nux vomica.
70. **Mumps.**—Mercurius and belladonna alternately, or china and phosphorus alternately.
71. **Neuralgia.**—Aconite, belladonna and bryonia are prominent remedies.
72. **Nervous Debility.**—China and phosphorous alternately, four hours apart.
73. **Nettle Rash.**—Aconitum, if the eruption is preceded by much fever. Dulcamara, when excited by exposure to cold and damp. Pulsatilla, when the eruption has been produced by eating unwholesome food. Belladonna, when the eruption is attended by violent headache and red face.
74. **Obesity.**—Excessive accumulation of fat, china, apis.
75. **Ophthalmia.**—Catarrhal-aconite, mercurius, belladonna, pulsatilla.
76. **Paralysis.**—Nux vomica, rhus, phosphorus, gelsemium, aconite.
77. **Piles.**—Gelsemium and nux vomica alternately, a dose every two hours; in chronic piles, use nux vomica and sulphur alternately, a dose every night and morning.
78. **Pleurisy.**—Give aconite alternately with bryonia; put hot water bags to feet and hands, and drink hot water.
79. **Prurigo.**—Of the anus (a popular eruption with intolerable itching). Nitric acid, sulphur; also glycerine of hydrast, or freshly made chloroform ointment.
80. **Quinsy.**—Belladonna, mercurius, iod.
81. **Rash.**—During teething, cham.; antimonium crudum (with diarrhea); arsenicum (with prostration).
82. **Remittent Fever.**—Gelsemium (specially in children), arsenicum, veratrum, china, ipecacuanha, rhus.
83. **Retention of Urine.**—Nux vomica, opium, aconite, camphor.
84. **Rheumatism.**—Aconite, bryonia, and rhus tox. in rotation.
85. **Ringworm.**—Rhus tox. and sulphur alternately.
86. **Rickets.**—Silicea, calcarea carbonica, sulphur. Also out-door air, cold or tepid salt water baths, and a teaspoonful of cod-liver oil twice a day.

87. **Salivation.**—From mercury—Nitric acid, hepar sulphur.
88. **Scarlatina.**—Simple—Aconite alternately with belladonna; sulphur (convalescence); with throat affection (anginosa), mercurius, apis.
89. **Sciatica.**—Colocynth, rhus, arsenicum, nux vomica.
90. **Sleeplessness.**—Belladonna, gelsemium.
91. **Sore Throat.**—Belladonna alternately with mecurius; for quinsy take the above two in rotation, with hepar sulphuris.
92. **Stings of Insects.**—Apply a piece of raw onion, or saleratus and water.
93. **Sunstroke.** — Camphor, belladonna, gelsemium, veratrum viride.
94. **Toothache.**—Aconite, chamomilla and mercurius in rotation every half hour
95. **Tongue.** — Coated. — Antimonium crudum (milky white); kali bichromicum (yellowish); pulsatilla (roughish white; rhus bapt. (brownish).
96. **Tuberculosis** (the condition of the body in which tubercules are deposited).—Phosphorus, calcarea carbonica.
97. **Typhus Fever.**—Aconite, bryonia or veratum viride, arsenicum, belladonna, phosphorus.
98. **Urinary Difficulties.**—Where discharge is burning and scanty, cantharis; where there is over-secretion and inflammation of bladder, apis mel. alternate with copaiva; where difficult from taking cold or with fever, aconite.
99. **Vomiting.**—From indigestible food, pulsatilla, antimonium crudum, ipecacuanha, iris.
Chronic. Arsenicum, hydras.
Of blood. Ipecacuanha, hamamelis, nitric acid, China.
100. **Warts.**—Rhus tox. or nitric acid, *internal* and *external*; sulphur.
101. **Whitlow.**—Silicea fluor., hepar.
102. **Whooping Cough.**—See "Hooping Cough."
103. **Worms.**—Cina for pin or seat worms and hepar sulphur.

OBJECT LESSONS OF THE EFFECTS OF ALCOHOL AND CIGARETTE SMOKING.

By Prof. George Henkle, who personally made the post-mortem examinations and drew the following illustrations from the diseased organs just as they appeared when first taken from the bodies of the unfortunate victims.

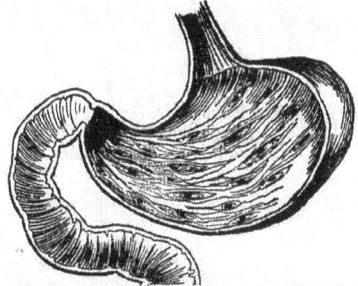

THE STOMACH of an habitual drinker of alcoholic stimulants, showing the ulcerated condition of the mucous membrane, incapacitating this important organ for digestive functions.

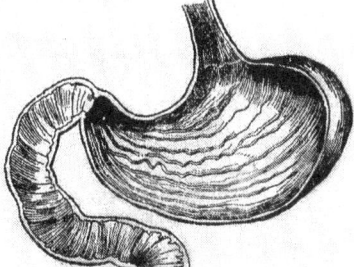

THE STOMACH (interior view) of a healthy person with the first section of the small intestines.

The Liver. 187

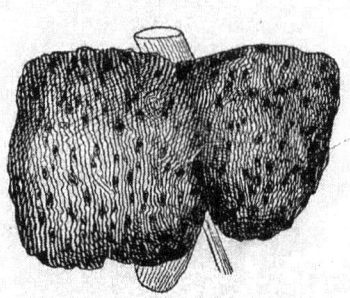

The Liver of a drunkard who died of Cirrhosis of the liver, also called granular liver, or "gin drinker's liver." The organ is much shrunken and presents rough, uneven edges, with carbuncular non-suppurative sores. In this self-inflicted disease the tissues of the liver undergo a cicatrical retraction, which strangulates and partly destroys the parenchyma of the liver.

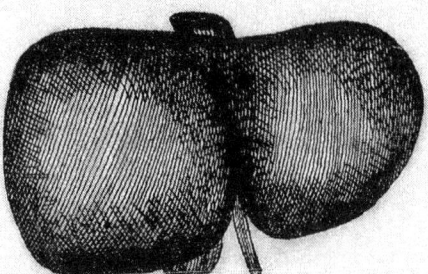

THE LIVER IN HEALTH.

The Kidney.

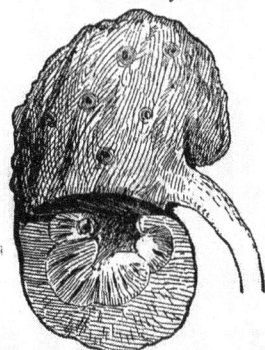

THE KIDNEY of a man who died a drunkard, showing in upper portion the sores so often found on kidneys of hard drinkers, and in the lower portion, the obstruction formed in the internal arrangement of this organ. Alcohol is a great enemy to the kidneys, and after this poison has once set in on its destructive course in these organs no remedial agents are known to exist to stop the already established disease.

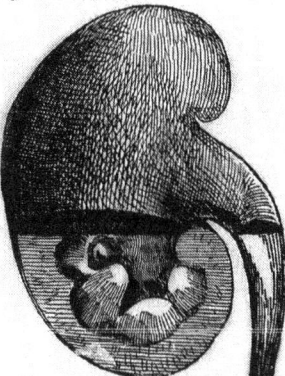

THE KIDNEY in health, with the lower section removed, to show the filtering apparatus (Malphigian pyramids). Natural size.

The Lungs and Heart. 189

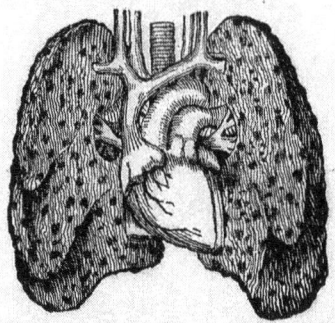

The Lungs and Heart of a boy who died from the effects of cigarette smoking, showing the nicotine sediments in lungs and shrunken condition of the heart.

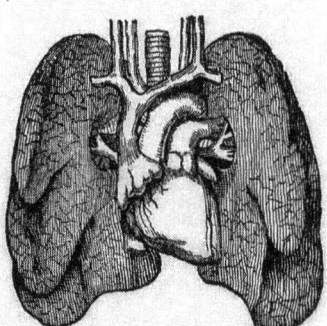

THE LUNGS AND HEART IN HEALTH.

THE DESTRUCTIVE EFFECTS OF CIGARETTE SMOKING.

Cigarettes have been analyzed, and most physicians and chemists were surprised to find how much opium is put into them. A tobacconist himself says that "the extent to which drugs are used in cigarettes is appalling." "Havana flavoring" for this same purpose is sold everywhere by the thousand barrels. This flavoring is made from the tonka-bean, which contains a deadly poison. The wrappers, warranted to be rice paper, are sometimes made of common paper, and sometimes of the filthy scrapings of ragpickers bleached white with arsenic. What a thing for human lungs!

The habit burns up good health, good resolutions, good manners, good memories, good faculties, and often honesty and truthfulness as well.

Cases of epilepsy, insanity and death are frequently reported as the result of smoking cigarettes, while such physicians as Dr. Lewis Sayre, Dr. Hammond, and Sir Morell Mackenzie of England, name heart trouble, blindness, cancer and other diseases as occasioned by it.

Leading physicians of America unanimously condemn cigarette smoking as "one of the vilest and most destructive evils that ever befell the youth of any country," de-

Destructive Effects of Cigarette Smoking. 191

claring that "its direct tendency is a deterioration of the race."

Look at the pale, wilted complexion of a boy who indulges in excessive cigarette smoking. It takes no physician to diagnose his case, and death will surely mark for his own every boy and young man who will follow up the habit. It is no longer a matter of guess. It is a scientific fact which the microscope in every case verifies.

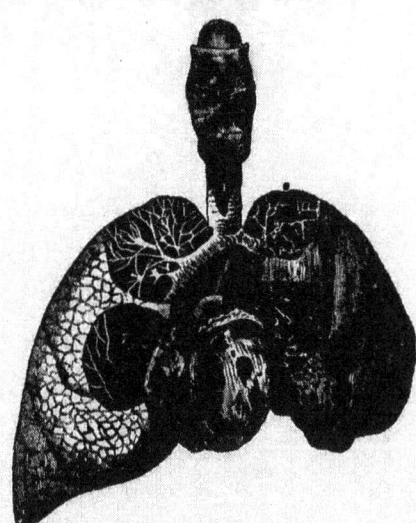

Illustrating the shrunken condition of one of the Lungs of an excessive smoker.

**IMAGE EVALUATION
TEST TARGET (MT-3)**

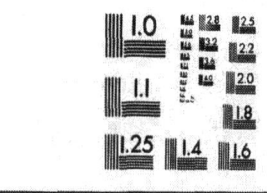

← 6" →

Photographic
Sciences
Corporation

23 WEST MAIN STREET
WEBSTER, N.Y. 14580
(716) 872-4503

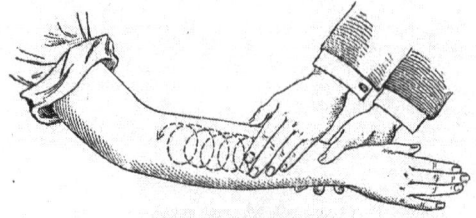

CURING A PARALYZED HAND.

A New Method of Healing.

HOME LESSONS IN MASSAGE.

1. Standard of Qualification.—The standard of qualification for the practice of massage may be thus defined:

First.—Good physique and good health absolutely essential.

Second.—Cleanliness in every particular is of the greatest importance.

Third.—An intelligent interest in the patient's welfare.

Fourth.—Perfect devotion and zeal in carrying out fully and carefully the duties of the work to the minutest detail, so as to ensure the confidence of the patient.

Fifth.—Good temper and forbearance are necessary.

Sixth.—Absence of fuss and undue haste.

Seventh.—Intelligence and even refinement are advantageous.

Eighth.—A happy, cheerful disposition, with vivacity and dexterity, readiness and ability, not forgetting a pleasant, contented face, complete the standard of individuality.

2. The Perfect Hand for Massage Work should be soft, smooth, dry and fleshy, and of good normal, healthy temperature. You will find that every part of the hand must be made available, and there is no position which the hands and fingers can assume which cannot be adapted to some form of massage.

3. The Room Temperature.—The room should be of comfortable temperature, say from 62 to 65 degrees F. The couch or bed upon which the patient is placed should not be too soft or yielding. As little as possible of the body of the patient should be exposed at one time. In general massage one hour should lapse after a meal before the process is commenced, and the process should extend from thirty to forty minutes, twice a day, between 11 and 12 in the morning, and 5 and 6 in the evening; or between 12 and 1 midday, and 8 and 9 at night.

4. **Silence.**—Always demand silence during the time that you are manipulating. Do not talk to your patient, and do not allow your patient to talk to you. After the operation is over, it is imperative that the patient should be made thoroughly warm. I want you particularly to remember this question of warmth after every form of massage, whether local or general.

5. **For Neuralgias.**—For neuralgias of the head and neuralgias in general, apply equal parts of chloroform and castor oil, and for painful joints you can use the same application.

For the abdomen, liquid vaseline is to be preferred, and it should be used freely from the commencement (always.)

You will not forget that in all paralytic, and other muscular affections, you do not use any kind of lubricant whatever at the time of manipulating, but after the operation is over it is frequently advantageous to grease the parts to prevent radiation of heat, and secure warmth.

6 **Masseeing the Head.**—One hand of the operator is carried over the mastoid portion of the temporal and upwards to the vertex of the head, whilst the other hand is carried over the opposite frontal eminence. Both hands are so directed that they meet each other at the top of the head.

7. **How Freqently Applied.**—The weaker the patient is the oftener he ought to have the treatment. The treatment should be applied at least once a day, and sometimes twice, in order to derive the most benefit from it. The effect which is derived from one treatment should not be lost before the next treatment is applied.

8. **Usefulness of the Institution.**—Experience teaches us the usefulness of the institution, as many patients thus treated have recovered their health after having suffered from diseases which could not be cured by other remedies.

9. **Hand Rubbing.**—The virtue of hand rubbing has been known for many years. Persons have been revived and restored to life and health when apparently dying, by an active, brisk and thorough system of rubbing with the hands.

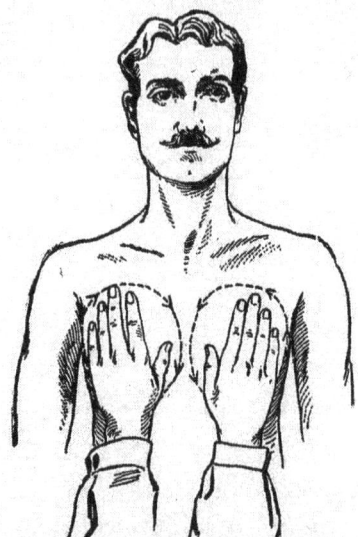

TREATING THE LUNGS IN GENERAL MASSAGE.

10. **What It Will Do.**—Hand rubbing or massage will increase circulation, temperature, respiration, nutrition and improve digestion. It will increase the appetite, produce rest and sleep and relieve pain and remove congestion. The general principles of thorough hand rubbing will always be strengthening and stimulating to the system, and quieting to the nerves.

Home Lessons in Massage.

MASSAGE OF THE BACK FOR RHEUMATISM, BACK-ACHE, PARALYSIS, NERVOUSNESS AND SPINAL TROUBLE.

General Treatment.

1. Stroking with both hands, one on each side of the spinal column, from the base of the skull down to the sacrum. If on a large person the operator had better divide the back into three parts, in such a manner as to first work next to the spinal column, then over the center of the back and finally over the sides, remembering that by the last manipulation he may conveniently reach the liver or spleen, if desirable, in certain cases. In the case of an infant, and especially in infantile paralysis, we often use, in the stroking, only the index and the middle fingers, one on each side of the spinal column.

2. Make a closed hand or fist, and compare the former with the latter, and observe the difference in the effects of each when applied to the body. You will soon discover that the movements of the hand partially closed as described, are of a much lighter character. The annexed figure conveys an idea of this form of manipulation.

The following form of hand is that which might be called the boat or saucer hand. The fingers and thumb are slightly flexed, so that the palm of the hand forms a concavity.

CURING KIDNEY TROUBLE AND BACK-ACHE

3. Kneading with the two thumbs, one on each side of the spine, so as to act upon the spinal nerves. The hands should be spread over the back, supporting the sides if possible. Hacking with one hand on each side of the spine, up and down, from the sacrum to the neck,

CURING NERVOUSNESS AND LUNG TROUBLE.

A CURE FOR CONSTIPATION, DYSPEPSIA AND COLIC.

4. All your movements must be done rhythmically, quiet and regularly at first. When, however, you find that they are unattended with any discomfort to your patient, they may be carried out with considerable rapidity. But under no condition is it justifiable to perform abdominal massage in a hurried and jerking manner.

5. You now effleurage over the abdominal wall, and remember that all your movements should be in the course of the large bowel, from right to left of your patient, upwards on the right and downwards on the left. Pick up the skin, areolar tissue and fat by the usual petrissage movements, beginning in the right inguinal region, and working round to the left inguinal region. If you have to bring about the absorption fat, great rolls of fat, you must grasp it firmly in your hands and knead and squeeze it as though it were dough.

CURING CONSTIPATION.

6. Stroking with both hands from the ankle to the hip, the hand on the outside reaching up to the crest of the ilium, the thumb of the hand on the inside, with moderate pressure, going down towards the groin. (Avoid pressure upon the tibia.)

Friction with the thumb upon the outside of the leg from ankle to knee joint, covering principally the flexors of the foot.

Home Lessons in Massage. 797

7. A Lame Knee Joint.—I would advise you never to meddle with the knee joint, unless under the advise of a surgeon. If you are not careful you might do great harm. No other synovial sac is capable of such extreme distension as that of the knee joint. Under ordinary conditions the amount of synovia in a joint is just sufficient to keep the parts of the joint lubricated; but it sometimes happens that the knee joint contains over a pint of fluid, or even more, and pressure of some kind from without is frequently necessary to bring out its absorption. I have to tell you how you are to manipulate to exercise this pressure to bring about absórption.

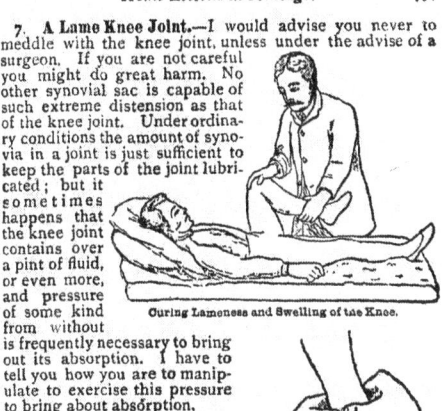

Curing Lameness and Swelling of the Knee.

8. For Bruised or Swelled Leg.— Lubricate your hands well with a mixture of equal

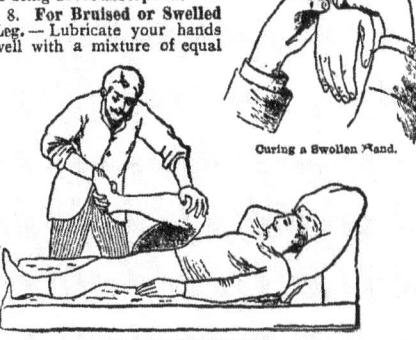

Curing a Swollen Hand.

CURING A BRUISED LEG.

parts castor oil and chloroform ; place one hand firmly six inches above the knee, and the other six inches below it. With a fairly strong grip you advance the one hand downwards, and the other hand upwards to within about four inches of each other, and you will now be exercising pressure upon the outskirts of the swelling. Don't relax your hold of the parts, but carry your hands bilaterally, that is to say, one hand will now be on the outer side of the swelling, whilst the other is upon the inner side. You then press equally upon the swelling with both hands, using pressure and counter-pressure; continue these gliding and pressure movements for ten or fifteen minutes. Of course, you must exercise pressure in direct ratio with the pain and sensibility of the part; if there be little or no pain, such as you find in bursal swellings, then your movements may be active; but if there be pain, then your movements must be slowly, steadily and carefully conducted.

Curing a Leg with an Ulcer.

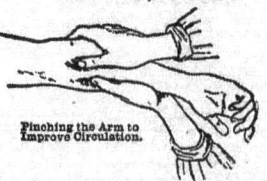

Pinching the Arm to Improve Circulation.

9. **For Cramps and General Lameness.**—Kneading with the thumb and fingers, which manipulation is called pinching, is also used to reach individual muscles, but is preferred on a deep-seated tissue. Kneading with both hands, called squeezing, is used upon the lower extremities and upon the arm proper for adults. The aim of the manipulation kneading is to reach the separate muscles with a firm double pressure and expose them to an action similar to that of friction.

Home Lessons in Massage. 199

TO STIMULATE THE NERVES AND INCREASE THE CIRCULATION OF BLOOD.

10. **Muscle Rolling.**—Grasping the limb with the palm of both hands, and making a quick, alternate pushing-and-pulling motion, and gradually gliding downward from the shoulder, the muscles of the arm will be rolled against each other, whereby the circulation of the blood is very much increased. Repeat three or five times.

11. **Friction.**—Friction is performed with the fingers and palm of the hand from the shoulder and downward, grasping around the limb with both hands, repeated ten to thirty times. This should be done in slow time. This has a quieting effect on the nerves, and by irritating the walls of the blood-vessels the circulation of the blood in the capilaries is stimulated.

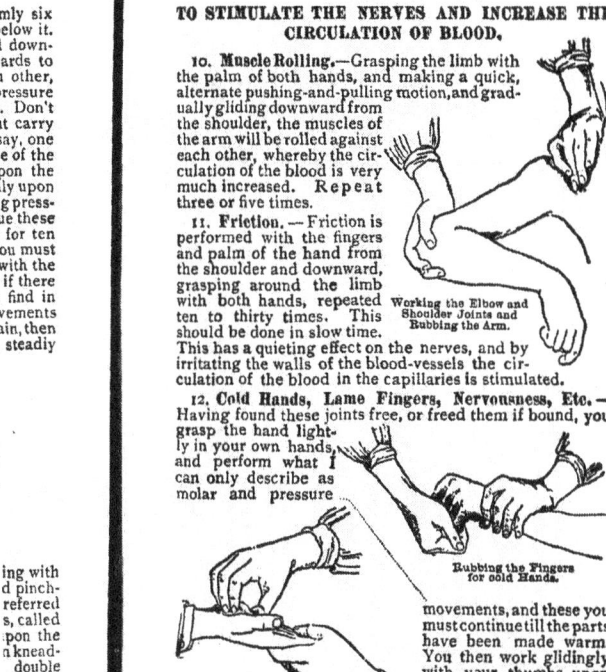

Working the Elbow and Shoulder Joints and Rubbing the Arm.

12. **Cold Hands, Lame Fingers, Nervousness, Etc.**—Having found these joints free, or freed them if bound, you grasp the hand lightly in your own hands, and perform what I can only describe as molar and pressure movements, and these you must continue till the parts have been made warm. You then work glidingly with your thumbs upon the dorsal surface of the hand whilst your fingers are digitating the palmar surface. After this you

Rubbing the Fingers for cold Hands.

Curing a Felon.

lay the back of your patient's hand flat in your own left hand, and with the palmar surface of your right hand exercise brisk friction and percussion movements.

13. **Nervousness, Insomnia and Bone Aching.**—Circular stroking, pressing, kneading, circular friction are all to be given from the tip of the fingers toward the shoulder.

14. Grasp the patient's finger with your thumb and the two first fingers, and make a firm pressing and stroking movement upward toward the hand; at the same time let your finger glide in a circular way round the patient's finger, describing the motions of a screw. Let your fingers glide easily back to the starting point (the tip of the patient's finger), and repeat the motions fifteen to twenty times on each finger.

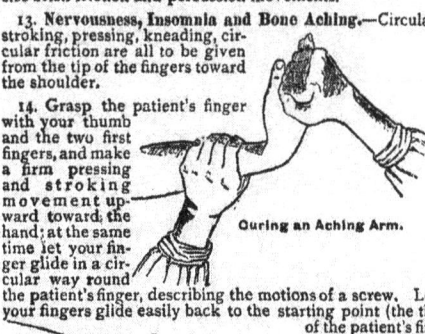
Curing an Aching Arm.

15. The elbow joint can now be manipulated, and we next proceed to work the arm between the elbow and the shoulder, and here the movements are precisely similar to those for the forearm. This part presents a fitting sphere for rolling movements between the hands, as shown in the cut.

Curing Cramps.

16. Just as in the upper extremity you begin by working at the finger joints, you now commence at the lower extremity by working all the toe joints; you then manipulate the foot in the same way that you did the hand, and work the heel of your hand well into the sole of the foot.

Rubbing with the Bottom of the Hand.

HINTS AND HELPS FOR THE SICK ROOM.

1. Keep the room clean and well ventilated, but avoid a draft. Take a board six inches wide, that just fits between the sides of the window at the bottom; raise the window six inches, put this board in, leaving one inch space between it and the window proper. In this way air can enter a room without creating a draft.

2. Never whisper or talk loud. Wear slippers or shoes that do not squeak.

3. Never bring a large quantity of food to a sick person; it will destroy instead of stimulate the appetite of the patient.

4. Always treat your sick as if they were your honored guests, and get out your best and prettiest dishes.

5. Make the sick room as cheerful as you can and keep the house quiet. Have shades on all the lamps.

6. Do not leave medicines where the patient can reach them, for a sick person will often do things which he would not do if well.

7. Humor the sick as much as possible, and avoid finding fault, scolding, or acknowledging that you are tired, etc.

8. Never go outside the door with the doctor. It creates suspicion on the part of the patient.

9. Be careful to avoid visitors as much as possible.

202 *How the Sick May Help Themselves.*

10. Change the pillows, sheets, etc., often, and wash the face and hands of the sick two or three times a day.

11. Be careful not to allow the patient to smell the cooking of food or anything else.

12. Do not take sewing into the room, or fuss around the room. Whatever is to be done, do it promptly.

13. Be kind, be cheerful, be careful and do just as the doctor tells you.

HAND STRAPS FOR THE SICK.

HOW THE SICK MAY HELP THEMSELVES.

Put up iron screen sockets so stoutly that there can be no danger of giving way, and fasten half-inch rope to them and at the end of the rope put hand pieces of soft cloth or webbing. Set the sockets firmly in the wall about three feet apart, so as to give room for all possible movement.

It is wonderful how a very sick person can move himself by taking hold of the hand straps. It is generally much better than could be done by the most skillful nurse, and creates less pain and suffering. The patient has the advantage of lifting himself to any position he may desire.

How the Sick May Help Themselves. 203

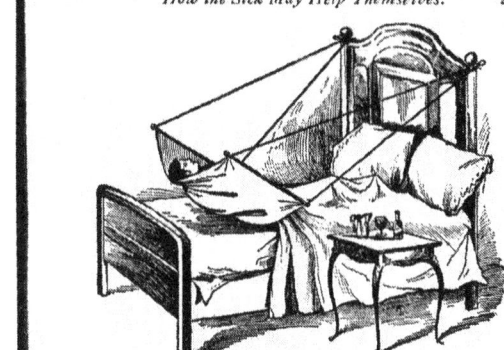

THE NEW BED HAMMOCK.

HOW TO MAKE AN EASY BED HAMMOCK FOR THE SICK.

A bed hammock is a very simple but refreshing change for the sick when pillows refuse obstinately to "lie easy" or have grown hotly wearisome.

Take a bit of very stout cloth a yard deep and four feet long, after a double hem has been turned two inches deep across each end. Sew a long length of webbing stoutly to each of the four corners. Take two light rods, each a yard long; a small broomstick makes excellent ones. Put a stout screw-eye in either end of both rods, slip them into the hems, pass the webbing through the eyes and your hem work is complete. To use this bed hammock all that is required is to fasten the webbing to the bedposts on each side, then the sick person can recline at ease against the cloth. This hammock affords almost infinite variety of position. It can be shifted in almost any form. It may be padded with cushions or left cool and single. A person may sit upright in it and eat dinner, or may recline in any position. It is surely a wonderful change and relief for the sick.

RULES FOR HOME NURSING.

1. The nurse at home need not learn anything which will not be necessary for every woman to know or practice in her family at some time in her life. Remember nursing the sick must be mastered by careful study and attention. It cannot be mastered in a few careless and occasional observations.

2. Good, intelligent nursing has often more to do with the patient's recovery than the medicine. Reading to patients (when they are not too sick) in a low, kind and gentle tone will often withdraw their minds from their own ills and brighten them up wonderfully. It is often worth more than a dose of medicine.

3. Nursing the sick consists of a knowledge of making up beds rapidly and comfortably; washing and cleansing patients; and an ability to study the patient's wants in changing position; the giving of medicines, etc.

4. Learn to make an application of poultices, blisters, etc.

5. The use of baths and a knowledge of rubbing patients with the hands.

Home Nursing.

READING TO THE SICK.

6. How to attend a physician dressing wounds, bandaging and padding of splints.

7. How to make a record of physician's instructions with regard to sleep, taking of medicines, diet, etc.

8. How to observe and record temperature, respiration and pulse.

9. A thorough knowledge of the preparation of food and nourishing drinks for the sick is very necessary.

10. Little things requiring prompt attention are always coming up in a sick room. The doctor cannot be there all the time—and a nurse must not only possess a grain of common sense, but know how to use it.

Reading Aloud in the Sick Room.—"With regard to reading aloud in the sick room," says Florence Nightingale, "my experience is that when the sick are too ill to read to themselves they can seldom bear to be read to. Children, eye patients, and uneducated persons are exceptions, or where there is any mechanical difficulty in reading. People who like to be read to have generally not much the matter with them; while in fevers, or where there is much irritability of brain, the effort of listening to reading aloud has often brought on delirium. I speak with great diffidence, because there is an almost universal impression that it is sparing the sick to read aloud to them."

FEEDING THE SICK.

Trivial Matters.—Matters which might seem trivial to a well person are often of the greatest importance to one who is confined to his bed with sickness. A careless or wilful neglect of such details on the part of the nurse may cause what little appetite the patient has to disappear, while on the other hand, a careful observance of them may encourage a capricious desire for food into becoming a genuine and pleasurable appetite.

Bathing.—Before offering the sick person food his face and hands should be bathed.

Punctuality and regularity should be as strictly observed in serving the invalid's meals as in giving him medicine.

Quantity.—The proper quantity of food to offer the sick and the extent of its dilution are matters requiring nice observation and care. Milk, gruels, beef tea and stimulants should not be diluted to the extent of making the quantity of the fluid so great that the patient tires of swallowing, and stops before he has obtained the required amount of nourishment.

Hot Foods should be served very hot, and cold articles very cold; lukewarm food is unpalatable. In serving hot drinks or foods, the cups or plates should be first well heated.

Untasted Food, dishes after use, or half-emptied cups and glasses should never be left standing about the sick room.

Palatable.—Equally important is it to make all food look inviting by offering it with the most attractive china obtainable, and with only the cleanest of linen.

Too Greasy.—Food is often made unpalatable by being too greasy. This is a common objection to meat broths. Mutton and chicken broths should always be skimmed several times before they are served. The last trace of oily substance can be removed by passing blotting-paper or a bit of bread over the surface.

The Unexpected.—When the appetite flags it is unwise to ask the patient beforehand what he would like to eat. Often it is the unexpected which pleases.

The Smell of Cooking and the noise of the preparation of food should be kept from the sick-room, if possible. The nurse should not taste the food in the patient's presence, or with his spoon, nor should she serve food with unclean hands.

Patients may appear too ill to notice these details,

whereas frequently they are only too ill or too uncomplaining to speak of them.

A Mistake.—Just enough in the most easily digestible form, is the rule to keep in sight. To get the stomach out of order or rebellious, in the hope of increasing strength by extra food, is a serious mistake and one that is nowadays often made.

Jellies.—If fruit is desirable, better give it in the form of orange, pineapple, or grape juice, or baked apple, or stewed peaches. Gelatin is not nutritious.

Gruels, well made and thin, are usually to be recommended for first place. Beef-tea is a starvation diet. Eggs are good if digested well. But be sure they are before repeating. Scraped beef is a good article. Milk kumyss, and cream kumyss suit certain cases admirably. The gluten preparations when made quite fluid are of marked value, and are not as well known as they deserve to be. Hot salted milk is standard in diarrheal troubles.

Use Your Own Judgment.—If a patient expresses a wish for some article, consider the matter. Otherwise do not ask what he would like, but bring at the proper time, what has been made ready, and serve as daintily as may be. Raw eggs whipped up with milk must be taken in small spoonfuls; not at a draught.

Malt.—The preparations of malt have proved disappointing, after some years of use, since they came in recommended then in the last terms of praise.

Wine.—Wine should not be added to foods for sick persons. It only delays ultimate recovery. In slight ailments, or when not feeling quite well, dry buttered toast, with an egg and hot milk, for a meal or two, is the diet which commonly serves best.

Not Much Food.—Only a small quantity of food should be offered to any person with a delicate appetite. It is very much better that such a quantity should be devoured, and the appetite crave more (which can be so easily prepared), rather than that an excessive supply—especially if not attractively presented—should spoil the little appetite, and send the whole away with loathing. No food or drink should be allowed to stand in the sick room. Aside from the danger of unwholesome absorption from the atmosphere, as might very often be the case, the constant presence becomes an offense to the eyes, and often leads to loathing and dislike.

Seasoning.—Another danger comes from excessive seasoning. For the weak stomach it is desirable oftentimes to have just the right degree of spicing to gently stimulate; but it is even more important to avoid an excess, or that which will do injury. Pepper should not be used, and there is danger in being too generous with salt. It is very liable to irritate, causing thirst, and gastric disturbance may be aggravated by it.

A Nutritive Diet.—Following protracted illness, a nutritive and gently stimulative diet should be taken. This may properly include albuminous and nearly all mucilaginous substances, fish, game, beef, mutton, poultry (young), eggs, peas, asparagus, baked potatoes, etc., with a proper proportion of cooked fruits as an offset.

Fruit.—Apples, sweet ones preferred, baked with an unbroken skin, are excellent. Add no more sugar than just enough to make the fruit palatable. Oranges are excellent eaten at the beginning of a meal, especially in the morning.

Hot Milk.—Hot milk is regarded as one of the very best stimulants. It must not be boiled, which renders it constipating, but heated as hot as it can be comfortably taken, and should be sipped with a spoon, not drank; it is more digestible if taken slowly.

Arrowroot.—Arrowroot is a reliable food for the sick room, and many can eat it when little else that is available can be taken. One good way to prepare it is to take a teaspoonful of the powdered arrowroot, moisten it with a tablespoonful of cold water, rub it smooth and add a tablespoonful of warm water, then pour on boiling water and stir till transparent. Sweeten slightly, and add a little nutmeg and other flavoring if desired. Another way, and by some preferred, is to boil half a pint of milk, mix two teaspoonfuls of arrowroot with a little cold milk, and gradually add it to the boiling milk, stirring it carefully so that there may be no lumps. A little sugar or salt should be added, but care must be taken not to overflavor. Use only the best arrowroot, as there are inferior kinds in the market.

Cleansing the Mouth.—One of the first concerns of a nurse should be to see that the patient's mouth is kept clean and sweet. This can be done by having the mouth rinsed with pure water or diluted listerine—two teaspoonfuls to a tumbler of water—after each taking of food. If the patient is unable to do this for himself, the attendant should do it for him, with a swab of fresh absorbent cotton, moistened with the mouth-wash, and fastened to a small, flexible stick.

Sour Mouth.—A foul or sour mouth frequently so interferes with the appetite and the sense of taste that the patient refuses food which otherwise he might gladly take. Milk especially lingers in the mouth, and fermenting there destroys the sense of taste and develops germs which interfere with digestion. It is much easier to keep the mouth clean than to disinfect it after it has been neglected.

Dry Lips.—In case the patient's lips are dry or parched they should be moistened with cold cream or vaseline. Glycerine should never be used for this purpose.

Raising the Head.—When it is necessary to raise the patient's head in order to give him nourishment or medicine, the attendant's hand should be placed beneath the pillow, so as gently to raise the head and pillow together. In this way a better support is obtained, the operation is more comfortable for the patient, and the head is less likely to be bent so far forward as to interfere with swallowing.

Small Glass.—A small tumbler should be used, and should never be more than two-thirds filled. A thirsty patient derives far more satisfaction from draining a small glass than from sipping from a large one which he is not permitted to empty.

Fluids.—When the patient is being fed with fluids, wholly different receptacles should be used for holding his medicines, or the association of ideas may be strong enough to destroy the appetite, or even to produce nausea. This danger of unpleasant association should never be lost sight of by the nurse.

Nourishment should never be offered at inopportune times. In serious cases only need the patient be aroused from sleep to take nourishment or medicine. During the night food of some sort should always be at hand to be given to the patient in case he should need it.

The Care and Feeding of Infants.

1. **The Great Mortality of Infants.**—The great mortality of infants is now no longer attributed so much to hand-feeding as to the injudicious manner in which it is generally conducted. Infants die more on account of ignorance of parents than quality of food.

2. **The Wasting Diseases of Infants and Children.**—One of the highest authorities on the treatment of infants says: "There is another class of cases where nutrition is equally unsatisfactory, although the supply of food is liberal enough. These cases occur where weaning is premature, or where the child has been brought up by hand and the kind of food chosen to replace the natural nourishment is injudiciously selected, so that the limited digestive power of the child is unable to convert it into material necessary for growth and development. Here the diet substituted for the mother's milk, although nutritious enough in itself, yet supplies little nutriment to the infant.

3. **Deficient Degree of Nutrition.**—Weakness in a child otherwise healthy, shows a deficient degree of nutrition, and therefore calls for an increased supply of nourishment, yet at the same time calls for increased care in the selection of the kind of food. There is a difference between food and nourishment. The very fact that the secretion of saliva in the young child does not become established until the third month after birth seems to indicate that before that age starchy foods are unsuited to the infant, as saliva is one of the most important agents in the digestion of starchy foods.

4. **Cow's Milk and Condensed Milk.**—Cow's milk and condensed milk, although diluted, are also improper food for infants when used alone. To quote from Dr. Routh, "Cow's milk, except the animal has been fed exclusively upon grass, is almost always acid in stall-fed cows; human milk is always alkaline; hence, another reason why cow's milk disagrees with many children."

5. **Not Free From Danger.**—Even those children who are fed entirely upon cow's milk are not free from danger. Cow's milk contains a larger quantity of solid matter than a woman's milk, owing principally to an increase in the amount of caseine (cheese,)

Children are, no doubt, frequently found to thrive upon this diet, their digestive power being equal to the demands made upon it. Others, however, and by far the largest pro-

ints.

mortality
and-feed-
generally
orance of

en.—One
ints says:
is equally
il enough,
, or where
id of food
idiciously
e child is
owth and
mother's
plies little

in a child
of nutri-
f nourish-
re in the
between
cretion of
hed until
at before
s saliva is
of starchy

milk and
r food for
h, "Cow's
on grass,
nilk is al-
nilk disa-

dren who
danger,
er than a
in the

ive upon
demands
gest pro-

A WELL CARED-FOR BABY.

portion, are not equal to this daily call upon their powers. They cannot assimilate this mass of curd. Consequently, unless rejected by vomiting, it passes through them undigested; their wants are not supplied and they starve for lack of nourishment, although swallowing every day a quantity of milk which would be ample support for a much stronger and healthier infant. Such children are exceedingly restless and irritable.

6. **Stools Should Be Carefully Examined.**—In all cases where the food of an infant is found to be insufficient or unsatisfactory the stools should be carefully examined, and if, as is so frequently the case, they are found to consist of pale, round, hard lumps, showing a cheesy appearance, the necessary precautions in providing the child with a diet he is capable of digesting should at once be seriously considered.

7. **Difference Between Cow's Milk and Woman's Milk.**—A more important difference is the denseness of the clot formed by the curd of cow's milk. Ample dilution with water does not affect this property. Under the action of the gastric juice the particles of caseine still run together into a solid compact lump. This is not the case with milk from the breast. Human milk forms a light, loose clot, which is readily disintegrated and digested in the stomach. The difficulty which even the strongest children find in digesting cow's milk is shown by the masses of hard curd which a child fed exclusively on this diet passes daily from the bowels. The difference between the milks is answerable for much of the trouble and disappointment experienced in bringing up infants by hand; and unless measures are adopted to hinder the firm clotting of the caseine, serious dangers may arise.

8. **Sugar Must Be Increased.**—In order, then, that cow's milk in chemical composition and physical properties, may therefore be fit for an infant's use, the proportion of sugar must be increased, the proportion of caseine must be reduced and made easily digestible, and it must be rendered alkaline.

9. **Artificial Food.**—Many different kinds of artificial food have been patented, but no doubt Mellin's Food is among the best now in use.

10. **Sterilized Milk.**—In using cows milk it should always be sterilized even if some Mellin's Food or other preparations are mixed into it. See other portions of the book.

FEEDING INFANTS.

1. The best food for infants is mother's milk; next best is cow's milk. Cow's milk contains about three times as much curd and one-half as much sugar, and it should be reduced with two parts of water.

2. In feeding cow's milk there is too little cream and too little sugar, and there is no doubt no better preparation than Mellin's food to mix it with (according to directions).

3. Children being fed on food lacking fat generally have their teeth come late; their muscles will be flabby and bones soft. Children will be too fat when their food contains too much sugar. Sugar always makes their flesh soft and flabby.

4. During the two first months the baby should be fed every two hours during the day, and two or three times during the night, but no more. Ten or eleven feedings for twenty-four hours is all a child will bear and remain healthy. At three months the child may be fed every three hours instead of every two.

5. Children can be taught regular habits by being fed and put to sleep at the same time every day and evening. Nervous diseases are caused by irregular hours of sleep and diet, and the use of soothing medicines.

6. A child five or six months old should not be fed during the night—from nine in the evening until six or seven in the morning, as overfeeding causes most of the wakefulness and nervousness of children during the night.

7. If a child vomits soon after taking the bottle, and there is an appearance of undigested food in the stool, it is a sign of overfeeding. If a large part of the bottle has been vomited, avoid the next bottle at regular time and pass over one bottle. If the child is nursing the same principles apply.

8. If a child empties its bottle and sucks vigorously its fingers after the bottle is emptied, it is very evident that the child is not fed enough, and should have its food gradually increased.

9. Give the baby a little cold water several times a day.

INFANTILE CONVULSIONS.

Definition.—An infantile convulsion corresponds to a chill in an adult, and is the most common brain affection among children.

Causes.—Anything that irritates the nervous system may cause convulsions in the child, as teething, indigestible food, worms, dropsy of the brain, hereditary constitution, or they may be the accompanying symptom in nearly all the

214 *The Care of Infants.*

acute diseases of children, or when the eruption is suppressed in eruptive diseases.

Symptoms.—In case of convulsions of a child parents usually become frightened, and very rarely do the things that should be done in order to afford relief. The child, previous to the fit, is usually irritable, and the twitching of the muscles of the face may be noticed, or it may come on suddenly without warning. The child becomes insensible, clenches its hands tightly, lips turn blue, and the eyes become fixed, usually frothing from the mouth with head turned back. The convulsion generally lasts two or three minutes; sometimes, however, as long as ten or fifteen minutes, but rarely.

Remedy.—Give the child a warm bath and rub gently. Clothes wrung out of cold water and applied to the lower and back part of the head and plenty of fresh air will usually relieve the convulsion. Be sure and loosen the clothing around the child's neck. After the convulsion is over, give the child a few doses of potassic bromide, and an injection of castor oil if the abdomen is swollen. Potassic bromide should be kept in the house, to use in case of necessity.

THE OLD-TIME ROCKING-HORSE.

A Warning to Mothers.

THE DANGERS OF OVERFEEDING.

Many young children suffer from overfeeding. Mothers, eager for their babies to become fat, or fearful that their crying may be from hunger, unwittingly feed them too often.

A child of three months was recently brought to a physician, because it suffered from colic pains, diarrhœa and vomiting, and was poorly nourished. It appeared that the child had been fed as often as it would take food, which was sometimes as frequently as once an hour. A proper lengthening of the intervals between the feedings, under the physician's advice, was productive of good results. Similar cases are not uncommon.

A child of between six weeks and six months of age should not be fed oftener than once in three hours. From six months to ten months it should not be fed more than six times in the twenty-four hours, and at intervals of three hours during the day-time. At ten months, five times in the twenty-four hours is sufficient for healthy children.

The stomachs of most children who are too frequently fed become irritable and incapable of retaining food, while the milk fed in this way by the mother becomes so altered as to afford less nourishment than it should.

Other children too frequently fed will continue to digest and absorb the excess of food given them, and as a consequence will accumulate fat, sometimes showing the result of overfeeding merely in eczematous, or scaly, patches on the cheeks, or even the whole face and head.

When intestinal disorders result, as in the end they surely will, from too frequent feeding, the child will be really hungry; the surplus food acting as an irritant in the intestines is expelled before a sufficient amount for nourishment becomes absorbed. The child will then waste away, and if such treatment be persisted in—and if it survives—will surely become a victim to chronic intestinal disorders.

Mothers cannot be too deeply impressed with the importance of regular feeding at proper intervals.

216 *To Preserve the Health and Life of Infants,*

HOW TO PRESERVE THE HEALTH AND LIFE OF YOUR INFANT DURING HOT WEATHER.

BATHING.

1. Bathe infants daily in tepid water and even twice a day in hot weather.

If delicate they should be sponged instead of immersing them in water, but cleanliness is absolutely necessary for the health of infants.

CLOTHING.

2. Put no bands in their clothing, but make all garments to hang loosely from the shoulders, and have all their clothing scrupulously clean, even the diaper should not be reused without rinsing.

SLEEP ALONE.

3. The child should in all cases sleep by itself on a cot or in a crib and retire at a regular hour. A child always early taught to go to sleep without rocking or nursing is the healthier and happier for it. Begin at birth and this will be easily accomplished.

CORDIALS AND SOOTHING SYRUPS.

4. Never give cordials, soothing syrups, sleeping drops, etc., without the advice of a physician. A child that frets and does not sleep is either hungry or ill. If ill it needs a physician. Never give candy or cake to quiet a small child; they are sure to produce disorders of the stomach, diarrhœa or some other trouble.

FRESH AIR.

5. Children should have plenty of fresh air summer as well as winter. Avoid the severe hot sun and the heated kitchen for infants in summer. Heat is the great destroyer of infants. In excessive hot weather feed them with chips of ice occasionally if you have it.

CLEAN HOUSES.

6. Keep your house clean and cool and well aired night and day. Your cellars cleared of all rubbish and whitewashed every spring, your drains cleaned with strong solution of copperas or chloride of lime, poured down them once a week. Keep your gutters and yards clean and insist upon your neighbors doing the same.

EVACUATIONS OF A CHILD.

7. The healthy motion varies from light orange yellow to greenish yellow, in number, two to four times daily. Smell should never be offensive. Slimy mucous-like jelly passages indicate worms. Pale green, offensive, acrid motions indicate disordered stomach. Dark green indicate acid secretions and a more serious trouble.

Fetid dark brown stools are present in chronic diarrhœa. Putty-like pasty passages are due to acidity curdling the milk or to torpid liver.

218 *How to Preserve the Health and Life of your Infant.*

BREAST MILK.

8. Breast milk is the only proper food for infants, until after the second summer. If the supply is small keep what you have and feed the child in connection with it, for if the babe is ill this breast milk may be all that will save its life.

STERILIZED MILK.

9. Milk is the best food. Goat's milk best, cow's milk next. If the child thrives on this *nothing else* should be given during the hot weather, until the front teeth are cut. Get fresh cow's milk twice a day if the child requires food in the night, pour it into a glass fruit jar with one-third pure water for a child under three months old, afterwards the proportion of water may be less and less, also a trifle of sugar may be added.

Then place the jar in a kettle or pan of cold water, like the bottom of an oatmeal kettle. Leave the cover of the jar loose. Place it on the stove and let the water come to a boil and boil ten minutes, screw down the cover tight and boil ten minutes more, then remove from the fire, and allow it to cool in the water slowly so as not to break the jar. When partly cool put on the ice or in a cool place, and keep tightly covered except when the milk is poured out for use. The glass jar must be kept perfectly clean and washed

To preserve the Health and Life of Infants.

and scalded carefully before use. A tablespoonful of lime water to a bottle of milk will aid in digestion. Discard the bottle as soon as possible and use a cup which you know is clean, whereas a bottle must be kept in water constantly when not in use, or the sour milk will make the child sick. Use no tube for it is exceedingly hard to keep it clean, and if pure milk cannot be had, condensed milk is admirable and does not need to be sterilized as the above.

DIET.

10. Never give babies under two years old such food as grown persons eat. Their chief diet should be milk, wheat bread and milk, oatmeal, possibly a little rare boiled egg, but always and chiefly milk. Germ wheat is also excellent.

EXERCISE.

1. Children should have exercise in the house as well as outdoors, but should not be jolted and jumped and jarred in rough play, not rudely rocked in the cradle, nor carelessly trundled over bumps in their carriages. They should not be held too much in the arms, but allowed to crawl and kick upon the floor and develop their limbs and muscles. A child should not be lifted by its arms, nor dragged along by one hand after it learns to take a few feeble steps, but when they do learn to walk steadily it is the best of all exercise, especially in the open air.

Let the children as they grow older romp and play in the open air all they wish, girls as well as boys. Give the girls an even chance for health, while they are young at least, and don't mind about their complexion.

220

A delicate child should never be put into the bath, but bathed on the lap and kept warmly covered.

HOW TO KEEP A BABY WELL.

1. The mother's milk is the natural food, and nothing can fully take its place.

2. The infant's stomach does not readily accommodate itself to changes in diet; therefore, regularity in quality, quantity and temperature is extremely necessary.

3. Not until a child is a year old should it be allowed any food except that of milk, and possibly a little cracker or bread, thoroughly soaked and softened.

4. Meat should never be given to very young children. The best artificial food is cream, reduced and sweetened with sugar and milk. No rule can be given for its reduction. Observation and experience must teach that, because every child's stomach is governed by a rule of its own.

5. A child can be safely weaned at one year of age, and sometimes less. It depends entirely upon the season, and upon the health of the child.

6. A child should never be weaned during the warm weather, in June, July or August.

7. When a child is weaned it may be given, in connection

with the milk diet, some such nourishment as broth, gruel, egg, or some prepared food.

8. A child should never be allowed to come to the table until two years of age.

9. A child should never eat much starchy food until four years old.

10. A child should have all the water it desires to drink, but it is decidedly the best to boil the water first, and allow it to cool. All the impurities and disease germs are thereby destroyed. This one thing alone will add greatly to the health and vigor of the child.

11. Where there is a tendency to bowel disorder, a little gum arabic, rice, or barley may be boiled with the drinking water.

12. If the child uses a bottle it should be kept absolutely clean. It is best to have two or three bottles, so that one will always be perfectly clean and fresh.

13. The nipple should be of black or pure rubber, and not of the white or vulcanized rubber. It should fit over the top of the bottle, no tubes should ever be used. It is impossible to keep them clean.

14. When the rubber becomes coated, a little coarse salt will clean it.

15. Babies should be fed at regular times. They should also be put to sleep at regular hours. Regularity is one of the best safeguards to health.

16. Milk for babies and children should be from healthy cows. Milk from different cows varies. Some authorities insist that it is better for a child to have milk from the same cow, while others prefer mixed milk from a herd, as less liable to changes.

17. Many of the prepared foods advertised for children are of little benefit. A few may be good, but what is good for one child may not be for another. So it must be simply a matter of experiment if any of the advertised foods are used.

18. It is a physiological fact that an infant is always healthier and better to sleep alone. It gets better air and is not liable to suffocation.

19. A healthy child should never be fed oftener than once in two hours, gradually lengthening the time as it grows older; at 4 months 3½ or 4 hours. At 5 months a healthy child will be better if given nothing in the night.

20. Give an infant a little water several times a day.

21. For colds, coughs, croup, etc., use goose oil externally and give a teaspoonful at bed-time.

"Jackie," our "Home Ruler."

Developing Healthy Children.

Growing Children.—Growing children of both sexes need plenty of good brown bread, puddings of oat and Indian meal, potatoes in various digestible forms—not fried—and milk and light nourishing soups. Nor must these articles take the place of good roast meat. A child's sense of hunger is a sharp reality and he soon becomes faint with it. Children grow more between twelve and seventeen than they do in all the years of life that follow. It is in this time that bone and muscle, nerve and energy are to be manufactured and stored up against middle life, the time when they will begin to need them.

Appetite.—Do I not know how absolutely insatiable a boy's appetite can be? He will devour a hearty dinner of roast beef, mutton or veal, vegetables and pudding at twelve o'clock, and be far gone in the pangs of starvation before five.

Sleep.—But it is not only in regard to food that parents are negligent. Sleep, which gives clearness to the eye and buoyancy to the step, and makes walking in the open air a joy and ever-increasing delight—Sleep is ruined or spoiled in a dozen different ways. Children's parties and evening entertainments are the means used to rob many children of their growth and vitality. While children are in school they have no business with "social life." School work and the necessary daily exercise in the fresh air and sunshine are as much as should be permitted. Between these and their growth they are sufficiently taxed. All children should go to bed early, comfortable, easy in mind, in a well-ventilated room, and should be allowed to sleep until they waken of their own accord. If they sleep at all they will not fail to waken just as soon as it is good for them. And if they don't sleep? Then they are on the sure road to a fit of indigestion or brain disease.

Going to School.—Many children enter the schoolroom at nine o'clock day after day looking wan and heavy-eyed. I shudder at the ill-health they are storing up for the future. It is sad and strange to see how easily mothers, often good mothers too, in other respects, shut their eyes to the beginning of this evil in those dearer to them than their own life —their children.

Cause of Premature Decay.—The children now standing on the threshold of manhood and womanhood sink into premature decay and fall by the wayside at an age when strength and ability should enable them to withstand prolonged effort in the schoolroom—and all for want of proper systematic attention to health. Parents must put a stop to the causes which excite ill-health, and not rush to the doctor to cure their children. All the medicine in the world cannot counteract the effect of foolish, persistent neglect and continued indulgence.

BOTTLE FEEDING.

1. **The First Requisite.**—The first requisite for carrying out bottle feeding with thoroughness is that somebody should take charge of the child who has a special interest in it. Some person ought to be in special charge over the bottle, nipple and rubber tube. If a rubber tube is used, it should be kept thoroughly clean and never allowed to remain empty. Keep it submerged in water, and then carefully clean and cleanse it before using. The health of the child depends upon absolute cleanliness of the bottle and its attachments.

2. **One Bottle of Tainted Milk May be Fatal to an Infant,** and, though a mother, or nurse, may day after day watch with the most zealous care the preparation of the baby's food, the souring of the milk, its mixture with contaminated water, the change of pasture of the cow may bring on an attack of diarrhœa or vomiting which may become uncontrollable.

3. **Fresh Milk.**—The fresher the milk, the more readily it will be digested; indeed, the warm milk just from the cow is far more digestible than that which has been kept with every precaution for a few hours. There must be some change which milk undergoes, as it is noted by all observers that the milk when warm from the cow is but slightly acid, or neutral, but after it has stood for awhile it always shows a very decided acid change. Mother's milk is always alkaline.

4. **Selection and Preservation of Milk.**—Great care should be taken in the selection of milk and in its preservation, even after it has reached the house, until used. If there is the slightest suspicion that the milk is not fresh, or that it has been subjected to much jolting, it should be boiled at once, and then put in a refrigerator to be warmed for each bottle. The boiling will destroy its ferments, and in that way diminish the chances for intestinal disturbances.—See sterilized milk in another portion of this book.

5. **Single Cow.**—The question of obtaining milk from a single cow is one that has been frequently insisted upon, and if one is satisfied that such milk is obtained and is found to have agreed with the child, it may have many advantages; but the ordinary mixed milk from a dairy of common cattle will be less liable to daily changes; it will maintain, as it were, an average of quality and condition. Not only should milk be pure and sweet, but it should be free from all matters that carry with them disease.

6. A Pure Gum Nipple.—Dr. W. Thornton Parker, of Newport, Rhode Island, recommends a pure gum nipple with two holes as far apart as possible, as the best for the nursing bottle, and also says regarding the matter as follows: "When there is only one hole, the infant in nursing compresses the nipple and sends the milk in a stream in such a manner as often to nearly strangle itself. Milk coming through one hole is not as comfortable as when it comes through two, and the effort of nursing becomes disagreeable and wearisome to the little feeder. The best way to nurse an infant is by holding it in the arms, and give it the bottle in the same position and height as if it were really nursed by its mother. When it has finished nursing, the bottle should be removed, emptied and cleansed. Never should the bottle be left in the infant's care to use at will."

7. A Mixture Resembling Mother's Milk.—The milk from an ordinary dairy should be obtained as fresh as possible, mix together half a pint of this milk and half a pint of pure water, and to this should be added about two hundred grains or two heaping teaspoonfuls of milk sugar, with four grains of soda; it should then be brought to a boil, after which two tablespoonfuls of cream should be stirred in, and it is ready for use, to be given by bottle or drinking cup, at about the body temperature.

THE PERILS OF TEETHING.

The period of dentition is not without peril to the infant and often brings great anxiety to the fond mother. As the various organs are in a state of growth and development the infant is peculiarly susceptible of disease. The irritation caused by the process of teething makes the child fretful and peevish upon the slightest provocation. The dangers of this period are largely averted by keeping up a looseness of the bowels, thus protecting the nerve centers and the various important organs of the body from harm. Washing the mouth frequently with cold water repels many an attack of serious illness, caused by the general irritation of the dentition period. Never attempt to hasten matters by cutting the gums.

HOW TO MAKE CHILDREN HEALTHY, VIGOROUS, AND BEAUTIFUL.

1. The physical conditions and developments of the child should be as carefully watched as its health, for the beauty, strength and health of a child depends largely upon the care and instruction of the parents.

2. Hereditary tendencies to disease must be carefully considered. If there is heart disease, consumption, or other constitutional diseases in the family, the children should be taught early to take regular and vigorous exercise every day, and as much of it out doors as the weather and circumstances will permit. There is nothing that overcomes hereditary disease in children so successfully as vigorous exercise and well ventilated sleeping rooms.

3. Give the children nourishing food, and until six years of age they should live mostly upon a milk diet.

4. From the earliest infancy, children must have an ample supply of pure air. Keep the bed-room well ventilated.

5. Never let children younger than fifteen years of age wear stays of any kind. During childhood the bones yield easily to pressure, and very many injuries and deformities have their beginning by bad methods of dress, and all forms of artificial bandages, corsets, garters, waist-strings, or an excess of weight hanging from the hips, should be avoided. All garments made for children should hang from the shoulders.

6. Children who play out-of-doors in cool and damp weather should wear good heavy shoes, with thick soles.

7. It is an excellent practice for families to secure a good text-book on gymnastic or calisthenic exercise, and when children are five years of age to begin and give them a regular systematic training every day. This will develop their muscular strength, give grace to their figures and gestures, develop their lungs, and strengthen the constitution in general. Both girls and boys should be trained by taking regular physical exercise daily, or taught to perform some daily task, which will answer the same purpose.

8. Indulge children in all kinds of out-door games, croquet, lawn tennis, etc., and your children will enjoy happiness and health.

9. Be sure to give children plenty of sleep. They should retire early and not be disturbed in the morning, but be permitted to enjoy their full desire of sleep.

10. Children should never drink coffee, tea, cocoa, or chocolate, for it will make the skin thick and yellow and often produce other serious disorders. Milk and water should be the only drink of children.

11. Little girls playing out-of-doors should have their faces protected, as they are liable to become freckled, and freckles are sometimes very difficult to remove. They should wear good large sun-bonnets or broad-brimmed hats.

12. Don't be afraid if your children scream and shout in their play, and think them boisterous. Let them develop their lungs.

HOME TREATMENT FOR THE DISEASES OF INFANTS AND CHILDREN.

Medicine.—The young mother who is far from a physician may remember for her comfort that a child very seldom really requires medicine. What it needs is what she can give without danger—proper food, pure air, cleanliness and rest.

Infants.—Most of the disorders of children, particularly of infants, arise from some derangement of the digestive tract. The food is not of proper quantity or quality. It is not assimilated; that is, taken up by the blood for the nourishment of the tissues, and the child suffers. It is pale and fretful, throws up its food in undigested masses, and does not thrive as a healthy child should. The first thing to be done is to change the food. Add a tablespoonful of lime-water to each six of food; if this does not succeed, try using one-fourth cream instead of all milk with water. Vary the strength of the food by adding more or less water. If still unsuccessful, try some of the artificial foods until one is found agreeing with the baby.

Older Children.—With older children an error of diet is very apt to be followed by feverishness and restlessness. High temperature does not mean as much with children as with grown persons. A child may have a temperature of one hundred and three or one hundred and four degrees at night and yet be comparatively well in the morning. A simple enema of soap and water given with a syringe such as should be in every household, is the safest way of producing a movement if there is constipation.

Syrup of Rhubarb.—A child two years old may have half a teaspoonful of spiced syrup of rhubarb or a teaspoonful of liquid citrate of magnesia, if there is reason to think that indigestible food is the cause of the attack. When this acts there will be an immediate improvement.

Early Deaths.—Out of the 984,000 persons that died during the year of 1890, 227,264 did not reach one year of age, and 400,647 died under five years of age.

Responsibility.—What a fearful responsibility, therefore, rests upon the parents who permit these hundreds of thousands of children to die annually. This terrible mortality among children is undoubtedly largely the result of ignorance as regarding the proper care and treatment of sick children.

Homeopathic Remedies.—For very small children it is always best to use homeopathic remedies.

AN AILING CHILD.

Fresh Air.—An ailing child should be kept in a pure atmosphere and have fresh air to breathe. This does not mean that the windows must be thrown wide open and the little body chilled with draughts. The temperature of a nursery should never fall below sixty-five degrees, and in illness be kept at from sixty-eight to seventy degrees. Fresh air must be admitted and enough artificial heat supplied to keep the temperature uniform. Of course, in extremely cold weather the window must be closed and the room aired when the child is asleep. At this time it can be covered from head to foot with a blanket, the face protected and the window opened for a few minutes. The extra covering must be left on until the thermometer again registers sixty-eight degrees. In ordinarily mild weather the window can be lowered from the top about two inches and a strip of flannel tacked over the opening to prevent a draught. If the window does not open at the top a piece of board two inches wide and exactly fitting the window frame can be put under the lower sash. The child should be kept away from the window.

Warm Bath.—A warm bath is always grateful to a sick child. The water should fully cover the person and feel pleasantly warm to the hand. As the little patient is lifted out wrap it in a warm blanket and dry it under that with a warm towel. Put on a flannel night-dress, or jacket, over the cotton night-gown. If the attack is the beginning of an eruptive disease, the bath will help to bring the eruption to the surface. An ailing child should not be allowed to sleep in the room with other children.

First Symptoms.—If parents would watch for the first symptoms of illness in their children and take things in time, they might often save themselves from great anxiety, and doctor's bill, and their little ones from pain and suffering. Nearly every ailment proceeds at first from a cold. Sometimes a child droops and seems heavy and languid for days, going to school unwillingly and dropping asleep over lessons. At such times, instead of chiding and spurring the weary one on to exertion, it would be far better to give the child a vacation a few days.

Honor at Expense of Vigor.—Never mind whether your little boy or girl stands first on the roll of honor or not. See to it that no honors or rewards are gained at the expense of vigor and health. Never slight the beginnings of a cold. From six to ten drops of turpentine will gen-

in a pure
is does not
en and the
rature of a
ees, and in
rees. Fresh
at supplied
n extreme-
l the room
an be cov-
protected
The extra
again reg-
veather the
two inches
to prevent
the top a
g the win-
The child

l to a sick
n and feel
nt is lifted
that with
or jacket,
the begin-
) to bring
uld not be
en.
r the first
things in
at anxiety,
n and suf-
om a cold.
d languid
ing asleep
and spur-
far better

ether your
or or not.
at the ex-
eginnings
will gen-

LITTLE MISCHIEF.

erally arrest a cold at the beginning; we have used it for the past twenty-five years and always with good results. The part of wisdom is to look out well for beginnings.

NERVOUS CHILDREN.

The importance of protecting the nervous system in infancy from rude shocks should be kept in mind.

As a rule, the more quiet a baby is kept during the first year of its life, the better chances it has for a life of health and happiness. The fact that so large a proportion of the human family die in infancy is due largely to the folly of nurses and the ignorance of mothers. Overbright babies do not commend themselves to physicians, who know that the first year of a child's life should be spent largely in sleep. All effort to arouse the dormant mind of the child at this period is attended with danger. The foolish practice of tossing a helpless baby in the air, while it screams both with affright and delight, is a most dangerous one. A physician with a large practice tells the story of a precociously bright child which showed evident delight when tossed in this way by a doting grandfather, who was accustomed to play with it in this way every evening. The child trembled with delight when the night's frolic was over, but one evening from this trembling it passed into a spasm, the first indication of one of those fatal brain diseases against which medical science is helpless. Nothing could be done but to wait until the little life had flown to a happier land.

NAUSEOUS REMEDIES.

It is said that the most nauseous physic may be given to children without trouble by previously letting them take a pepperment lozenge, a piece of alum or a bit of orange peel. Many people make the mistake of giving a sweet afterwards to take away the disagreeable taste. It is far better to destroy it in the first instance.

HICCOUGH.

Sips of warm water, kneading the abdomen, percussing the spine, fixing the attention intensely, often relieve hiccough.

Five or six drops of nitrate of amyl, on handkerchief, pressed close to the patient's nose, will prove very beneficial to one suffering with hiccoughs.

LARD AND SALT.

Scarlet Fever.—An eminent physician says that if he were confined to one single remedy in cases of scarlet fever, he should choose lard. Rub the little sufferer with it thoroughly and often. It allays the fever and softens the parched skin. The amount thus absorbed is simply astonishing.

Inflammation of the Bowels.—Of course the safe way is to send for the doctor without delay. But in the country, one is often obliged to wait a long time. Anxiety makes the time seem long anywhere, and simple remedies are often very efficient helps. So, while you are waiting, make a paste of lard and salt, fold a wide pillow-case (as that is always at hand) into a large square, spread on the paste and lay the cloth smoothly, paste side down, over the bowels, stomach, sides, and as far toward the back as you can. When the inflammation is severe, the lard will be absorbed in a very short time. Be prepared to change the paste as often as needed. Never mind wasting the salt. There is no particular rule, only be sure to stir in enough. All that is not needed will remain on the cloth.

One always has this remedy in the house. So it can be made ready in a moment, and the quicker the better is the order in such cases. I have used it where the patient was in a perfect agony of suffering, and the doctor far away. The result was always more than satisfactory, there being a very perceptible decrease of pain in a wonderfully short time. Of course the doctor smiled knowingly when I told him, but then I was quite willing he should smile, for the patient was comfortably sleeping when he arrived.

In another case all other remedies failed, and it was said that the patient must die—but she didn't.

Croup.—Cover the throat and chest with the lard and salt paste, adding to it a sprinkling of mustard.

Pneumonia has yielded to the same treatment as that used for croup. In either case no time should be wasted. Act quickly.

Pleurisy.—Apply flannel cloths wrung out of hot mustard water and change often, or a mustard paste.

Carbuncles.—Tomato poultice, thickened with powdered crackers. Never known to fail.

Coughs.—A bottle of camphorated oil and some absorbent cotton should be kept in the medicine chest of every household. No remedy will more quickly afford relief than absorbent cotton soaked in the oil and laid on the chest of the sufferer.

Diseases of Infants and Children.

COLIC.

1. Babies often suffer severely with colic. It is not considered dangerous, but causes considerable suffering.

2. Severe colic is usually the result of derangement of the liver in the mother, or of her insufficient or improper nourishment, and it occurs more frequently when the child is from two to five months old.

3. Let the mother eat chiefly barley, wheat and bread, rolled wheat, graham bread, fish, milk, eggs and fruit. The latter may be freely eaten, avoiding that which is very sour.

4. A rubber bag or bottle filled with hot water put into a crib will keep the child, once quieted, asleep for hours. If a child is suffering from colic it should be thoroughly warmed and kept warm.

5. Avoid giving opiates of any kind, such as cordials, Mrs. Winslow's Soothing Syrup, "Mothers' Friend," and various other patent medicines. They injure the stomach and health of the child instead of benefiting it.

6. **Remedies.**—A few tablespoonfuls of hot water will often allay a severe attack of the colic. Catnip tea is also a good remedy.

A drop of essence of peppermint in 6 or 7 teaspoonfuls of hot water will give relief.

If the stools are green and the child is very restless, give chamomilla.

If the child is suffering from constipation and undigested curds of milk appear in its fæces, and the child starts suddenly in its sleep, give nux vomica.

An injection of a few spoonfuls of hot water into the rectum with a little asafœtida is an effective remedy and will be good for an adult.

STOMACH AND BOWEL TROUBLE.

A tablespoonful at bedtime of equal parts of castor oil and aromatic syrup of rhubarb is one of the best remedies for children with stomach and bowel trouble now in use.

Prescription:—2 oz. castor oil,
          2 oz. aromatic syrup of rhubarb.

Diseases of Infants and Children. 235

HOW TO TREAT CROUP.

SPASMODIC AND TRUE.

SPASMODIC CROUP.

Definition.—A spasmodic closure of the glottis which interferes with respiration. Comes on suddenly and usually at night, without much warning. It is a purely nervous disease and may be caused by reflex nervous irritation from undigested food in the stomach or bowels, irritation of the gums in dentition, or from brain disorders.

Symptoms.—Child awakens suddenly at night with suspended respiration or very difficult breathing. After a few respirations it cries out and then falls asleep quietly, or the attack may last an hour or so, when the face will become pale, veins in the neck become turgid and feet and hands contract spasmodically. In mild cases the attacks will only occur once during the night, but may recur on the following night.

Home Treatment.—During the paroxysm dashing cold water in the face is a common remedy. To terminate the spasm and prevent its return give teaspoonful doses of powdered alum. The syrup of squills is an old and tried remedy; give in 15 to 30 drop doses and repeat every 10 minutes till vomiting occurs. Seek out the cause, if possible, and remove it. It commonly lies in some derangement of the digestive organs.

TRUE CROUP.

Definition.—This disease consists of an inflammation of the mucous membrane of the upper air passages, particularly of the larynx, with the formation of a false membrane that obstructs the breathing. The disease is most common in children between the ages of two and seven years, but it may occur at any age.

Symptoms.—Usually there are symptoms of a cold for three or four days previous to the attack. Marked hoarseness is observed in the evening, with a ringing metallic cough and some difficulty in breathing, which increases and becomes somewhat paroxysmal till the face, which was at first flushed, becomes pallid and ashy in hue. The efforts at breathing become very great, and unless the child gets speedy relief it will die of suffocation.

Home Treatment.—Patient should be kept in a moist, warm atmosphere, and cold water applied to the neck early in the attack. As soon as the breathing seems difficult give a half to one teaspoonful of powdered alum in honey to produce vomiting and apply the remedies suggested in the treatment of diphtheria, as the two diseases are thought by many to be identical. When the breathing becomes labored and face becomes pallid, the condition is very serious and a physician should be called without delay.

Powdered Alum.—Powdered alum and sugar is an excellent remedy for croup, or for colds when the throat seems to be filled up. But sometimes the attack of croup comes on and there is no powdered alum in the house.

Kerosene.—In such cases take a spoonful of sugar, put a few drops of kerosene on it and give that. Repeat the dose until a teaspoonful of kerosene has been taken internally. Also rub the throat and chest with a little kerosene, then cover it with cotton batting. When there is a troublesome, dry cough, salt taken dry on the tongue, in small quantities, will relieve the majority of cases.

WORMS.

Pin Worms.

Pin worms and round worms are the most common in children. They are generally found in the lower bowels.

Symptoms.—Restlessness, itching about the anus in the fore part of the evening, and worms in the faces.

Treatment.—Give with a syringe an injection of a tablespoonful of linseed oil. Cleanliness is also very necsary.

Round Worms.

A round worm is from six to sixteen inches in length, resembling the common earth worm. It inhabits generally the small intestines, but it sometimes enters the stomach and is thrown up by vomiting.

Symptoms.—Distress, indigestion, swelling of the abdomen, grinding of the teeth, restlessness, and sometimes convulsions.

Treatment.—One teaspoonful of powdered wormseed mixed with a sufficient quantity of molasses, or spread on bread and butter.

Or, one grain of santonine every four hours for two or three days, followed by a brisk cathartic. Wormwood tea is also highly recommended.

Swaim's Vermifuge.

2 ounces wormseed.
1½ ounces valerian.
1½ ounces rhubarb.
1½ ounces pink-root.
1½ ounces white agaric.

Boil in sufficient water to yield 3 quarts of decoction, and add to it 30 drops of oil of tansy and 45 drops of oil of cloves, dissolved in a quart of rectified spirits. Dose, 1 teaspoonful at night.

Another Excellent Vermifuge.

Oil of wormseed, 1 ounce.
Oil of anise, 1 ounce.
Castor Oil, 1 ounce.
Tinct. of myrrh, 2 drops.
Oil of turpentine, 10 drops.

Mix thoroughly.
Always shake well before using.
Give 10 to 15 drops in cold coffee once or twice a day.

CONSTIPATION.

1. This is a very frequent ailment of infants. The thing necessary is for the mother to regulate her diet.

2. If the child is nursed regularly and held out at the same time of each day, it will seldom be troubled with this complaint. Give plenty of *water*. Regularity of habit is the best remedy. If this method fails, use a soap suppository. Make it by paring a piece of white castile soap round. It should be made about the size of a lead pencil, pointed at the end.

3. Avoid giving a baby drugs. Let the physician administer them if necessary.

4. An unsuitable diet quickly causes irregularity of the bowels in children.

5. Cream and butter are to be recommended on porridge and cornmeal. Oatmeal gruels should be used by older children, who should also be encouraged to drink as much water as they crave. For children three years and older, stewed prunes, orange juice, honey and bread, olive oil and olives, peaches, fresh vegetables and baked apples and ginger bread should form part of bill of fare, and there will be no need of castor oil, rhubarb, etc., often an injury to the child.

CHEERFULNESS AND HEALTH.

It is known that intense anger, or great grief or fright, may so poison the milk of a nursing mother that her child is killed by taking that milk into its stomach.

Professor Elmer Gates, recently lecturing before the Smithsonian Institution at Washington, has isolated this poison, and is able to exhibit it in crystals. He has also shown that hateful and unpleasant feelings cause the formation of poisons in the body which are physically injurious to it; that benevolent and happy sensations lead to the creation of beneficial chemical products in the blood and tissues.

All of these can be detected by chemical analysis in the urine and the perspiration.

DIPHTHERIA AND SCARLET FEVER.

A prominent physician claims that there will be no diphtheria, scarlet fever nor worms for children if they eat plentifully of onions every day, especially when there is a scarcity of fresh fruit. He buys the onions by the barrel for his young folks and they are served in every imaginable form.

Diseases of Infants and Children.

SCARLET FEVER.

Definition.—An eruptive contagious disease, brought about by direct exposure to those having the disease, or by contact with clothing, dishes, or other articles used about the sick room.

The clothing may be disinfected by heating to a temperature of 230° Fahrenheit or by dipping in boiling water before washing.

Dogs and cats will also carry the disease and should be kept from the house, and particularly from the sick room.

Symptoms.—Chilly sensations or a decided chill, fever, headache, furred tongue, vomiting, sore throat, rapid pulse, hot, dry skin and more or less stupor. In from 6 to 18 hours a fine red rash appears about the ears, neck and shoulders, which rapidly spreads to the entire surface of the body. After a few days, a scurf or branny scales will begin to form on the skin. These scales are the principal source of contagion.

HOME TREATMENT.

1. Isolate the patient from other members of the family to prevent the spread of the disease.

2. Keep the patient in bed and give a fluid diet of milk gruel, beef tea, etc., with plenty of cold water to drink.

3. Control the fever by sponging the body with tepid water, and relieve the pain in the throat by cold compresses, applied externally.

4. As soon as the skin shows a tendency to become scaly, apply goose grease or clean lard with a little boracic acid powder dusted in it, or better, perhaps, carbolized vaseline, to relieve the itching and prevent the scales from being scattered about and subjecting others to the contagion.

Regular Treatment.—A few drops of aconite every three hours to regulate the pulse, and if the skin be pale and circulation feeble, with tardy eruption, administer one to ten drops of tincture of belladonna, according to the age of the patient. At the end of the third week, if eyes look puffy and feet swell, there is danger of Acute Bright's disease, and a physician should be consulted. If the case does not progress well under the home remedies suggested, a physician should be called at once.

HOME TREATMENT OF DIPHTHERIA.

Definition.—Acute, specific, constitutional disease, with local manifestations in the throat, mouth, nose, larynx, windpipe, and glands of the neck. The disease is infectious, but not very contagious under the proper precautions. It is a disease of childhood, though adults sometimes contract it. Many of the best physicians of the day consider True or Membranous Croup to be due to this diphtheritic membranous disease thus located in the larynx or trachea.

Symptoms.—Symptoms vary according to the severity of the attack. Chills, fever, headache, languor, loss of appetite, stiffness of neck, with tenderness about the angles of the jaw, soreness of the throat, pain in the ear, aching of the limbs, loss of strength, coated tongue, swelling of the neck, and offensive breath; lymphatic glands on side of neck enlarged and tender. The throat is first to be seen red and swollen, then covered with grayish white patches, which spread, and a false membrane is found on the mucous membrane. If the nose is attacked there will be an offensive discharge and the child will breathe through the mouth. If the larynx or throat are involved the voice will become hoarse, and a croupy cough with difficult breathing shows that the air passage to the lungs is being obstructed by the false membrane.

Home Treatment.—Isolate the patient to prevent the spread of the disease. Diet should be of the most nutritious character, as milk, eggs, broths, and oysters. Give at intervals of every two or three hours. If patient refuses to swallow from the pain caused by the effort, a nutrition injection must be resorted to. Inhalations of steam and hot water, and allowing the patient to suck pellets of ice, will give relief. Sponges dipped in hot water and applied to the angles of the jaw are beneficial. Inhalations of lime, made by slaking freshly burnt lime in a vessel and directing the vapor to the child's mouth by means of a newspaper or similar contrivance. Flower of sulphur blown into the back of the mouth and throat by means of a goose quill has been highly recommended. Frequent gargling of the throat and mouth with a solution of lactic acid, strong enough to taste sour, will help to keep the parts clean and correct the foul breath. If there is great prostration, with the nasal passage affected, or hoarseness and difficult breathing, a physician should be called at once.

MEASLES.

Definition.—It is an eruptive, contagious disease, preceded by cough and other catarrhal symptoms for about four or five days. The eruption comes rapidly in small red spots, which are slightly raised.

Symptoms.—A feeling of weakness, loss of appetite, some fever, cold in the head, frequent sneezing, watery eyes, dry cough and a hot skin. The disease takes effect nine or ten days after exposure.

Home Treatment.—Measles is not a dangerous disease in the child, but in an adult it is often very serious. In childhood very little medicine is necessary, but exposure must be carefully avoided and the patient kept in bed in a moderately warm room. The diet should be light and nourishing. Keep the room dark. If the eruption does not come out promptly, apply hot baths.

Common Treatment.—Two teaspoonfuls of spirits of nitre, one teaspoonful paregoric, one wineglassful of camphor water. Mix thoroughly, and give a teaspoonful in half a teacupful of water every two hours. To relieve the cough, if troublesome, flaxseed tea or infusion of slippery-elm bark with a little lemon juice to render more palatable will be of benefit.

CHICKEN POX.

Definition.—This is a contagious, eruptive disease, which resembles to some extent small pox. The pointed vesicles or pimples have a depression in the center in chicken pox, and in small pox they do not.

Symptoms.—Nine to seventeen days elapse after the exposure, before symptoms appear. Slight fever, a sense of sickness, the appearance of scattered pimples, some itching and heat. The pimples rapidly change into little blisters filled with a watery fluid. After five or six days they disappear.

Home Treatment—Milk diet and avoid all kinds of meat. Keep the bowels open and avoid all exposure to cold. Large vesicles on the face should be punctured early and irritation by rubbing should be avoided.

WHOOPING COUGH.

Definition. — This is a contagious disease which is known by a peculiar whooping sound in the cough. Considerable mucus is thrown off after each attack of spasmodic coughing.

Symptoms. — It usually commences with the symptoms of a common cold in the head, some chilliness, feverishness, restlessness, headache, a feeling of tightness across the chest, violent paroxysms of coughing, sometimes almost threatening suffocation, and accompanied with vomiting.

Home Treatment. — Patient should eat plain food and avoid cold drafts and damp air, but keep in the open air as much as possible. A strong tea made of the tops of red clover is highly recommended. A strong tea made of chestnut leaves, sweetened with sugar, is also very good.

1 teaspoonful of powdered alum.
1 teaspoonful of syrup.

Mix in a tumbler of water, and give the child one teaspoonful every two or three hours. A kerosene lamp kept burning in the bed-chamber at night is said to lessen the cough and shorten the course of the disease.

As a rule, the younger the child the more severely will the attack be felt, so that very young children especially should be guarded against infection.

One of the worst features of the disease is the violent straining efforts during the paroxysms of coughing, which dispose to hemorrhage and to rupture.

Those whose experience with the disease has been largest are the readiest to acknowledge that medicines by themselves are of little value. It is all the more important, therefore, that the patient should have good nursing, and all that good nursing implies.

Every day in which the weather permits the child should be taken out-of-doors, and in any event he should have a constant supply of fresh air.

Woolen undergarments should be worn day and night, while daily bathing should be carefully practiced. Counter-irritation of a mild character over the region of the stomach is of great value, and the diet should be of the simplest and most nourishing kind.

Vapors and inhalants rarely do good, but frequently the patient improves after their discontinuance.

MUMPS.

Definition.—This is a contagious disease causing the inflammation of the salivary glands, and is generally a disease of childhood and youth.

Symptoms.—A slight fever, stiffness of the neck and lower jaw, swelling and soreness of the gland. It usually develops in four or five days and then begins to disappear.

Home Treatment.—Apply to the swelling a hot poultice of cornmeal and bread and milk. A hop poultice is also excellent. Take a good dose of physic and rest carefully. A warm general bath, or mustard foot-bath, is very good. Avoid exposure or cold drafts. If a bad cold is taken, serious results may follow.

BED WETTING—ITS CAUSE AND CURE.

1. **Bad Habits.**—Very frequently this affection is the consequence of bad habits; being favored by the free use of fluids during the after part of the day, by exposure to cold in the night, and by lying on the back.

2. **Punishment.**—Never punish a child for bed-wetting; it is cruel and unnatural. Bed-wetting occurs usually toward morning. The child has no control over it and should never be punished. Repeated punishment blights its sense of honor and it soon becomes cowardly and deceitful, and loses all personal spirit.

3. **Cause.**—Bed-wetting may be caused by the presence of worms in the bowels, and sometimes stone in the bladder may occasion the trouble, or weakness of the urinary organs.

4. **Treatment.**—Awake the child at midnight, or very soon after, and have the bladder thoroughly emptied. Do not allow the child to eat or drink anything several hours before bedtime. Do not allow it to sleep on its back. This can be done by tying a towel around the child with a knot over the spinal column, so that when it turns it will be awakened by the pressure. Give the child a cold sponge bath every morning. If these precautions are of no avail, the family physician should be called.

DIARRHEA.

Great care should be exercised by parents in checking the diarrhea of children. Many times serious diseases are brought on by parents being too hasty in checking this disorder of the bowels. It is an infant's first method of removing obstructions and overcoming derangements of the system.

SUMMER COMPLAINT.

1. Summer complaint is an irritation and inflammation of the lining membranes of the intestines. This may often be caused by teething, eating indigestible food, etc.

2. If the discharges are only frequent and yellow and not accompanied with pain, there is no cause for anxiety; but if the discharges are green, soon becoming gray, brown and sometimes frothy, having a mixture of phlegm, and sometimes containing food undigested, a physician had better be summoned.

3. In the first stages give a tablespoonful at bedtime of the following prescription:

> 2 oz. castor oil.
> 2 oz. aromatic syrup of rhubarb.

1. *This is one of the best of domestic remedies*, and should always be kept on hand. Whenever the stomach of children is out of order, a dose of this simple remedy often works magic.

2. Keep the child perfectly quiet and the room well aired.

3. Put a drop of tincture of camphor on a teaspoonful of sugar, mix thoroughly; then add six teaspoonfuls of hot water and give a teaspoonful of the mixture every ten minutes. This is indicated where the discharges are watery, and where there is vomiting and coldness of the feet and hands. Chamomilla is also an excellent remedy.

4. Drink freely of boiled milk, and in bad cases drink no water except that which has been boiled and cooled.

FOR TEETHING.

If a child is suffering with swollen gums, is feverish, restless, and starts in sleep, give nux vomica.

BOOK II.

FIGURE, FORM AND BEAUTY.
CARE OF HANDS, HAIR AND FEET.
RULES ON ETIQUETTE.
HOW TO WRITE INVITATIONS.
HOME AMUSEMENTS.

NATURAL BEAUTY.

PRESERVING THE FIGURE.

These lines are for the lady who is looking for help in the preservation of her figure, which has always been her special pride, until a recent accumulation of surplus "fat" threatens to make it more than becomingly plump.

Remedy.—The remedy for this state of things is within the reach of every one who has time and resolution to spend ten or fifteen minutes every day in certain exercises, which will be given in detail, and which require absolutely nothing else but time and persistence.

Time.—The best time for taking these exercises is in the morning, immediately after leaving one's bed, and before any garments that compress the figure in any way are put on. The air in the room should be pure and sweet, so that the lungs may be benefited, no less than the abdominal muscles, and the blood be purified.

First.—Draw in the abdomen as far as possible; fill the lungs with air, and then raise the arms above the head till the hands meet, without moving or bending the knees; bend the body as far back as possible, and then, allowing the air to escape from the lungs gradually, bend the body as far forward as possible, until the hands approach the floor. Repeat this ten times, following exactly the directions for breathing.

Second.—Place the hands upon the hips, akimbo, draw air into the lungs as before, and bend forward, first to the right as far as possible, allowing the air to escape from the lungs, and then, after filling the lungs again, to the left. Repeat this exercise ten times.

Third.—Place the hands lightly on the breast, draw in the abdomen, fill the lungs, and turn the head and body, without moving the knees or feet, as far, first to the right, and, after filling the lungs again, to the left, as possible. Repeat this ten times.

Fourth.—With the arms at the side, draw in the abdomen, fill the lungs with air, and raise the arms to their height above the head, keeping the lungs fully expanded; then, breathing out, allow the arms to fall slowly to the side again. Repeat this ten times.

These exercises strengthen all the muscles of the abdomen, and cause in them a gradual contraction, which, as it increases, restores symmetry of form, restores the center of gravity to its proper position, and gives the exerciser a command of herself in movement that is very delightful.

A GYMNASIUM DIRECTOR'S ADVICE.

A gymnasium director of long experience disapproves of shoulder-braces.

Instead of artificial shoulder-braces, the director recommends the frequent and persistent use of exercises specially adapted to promote an erect carriage.

It is not enough, he says, to work an hour or so daily in a gymnasium. The proper exercises should be taken many times a day, and therefore should be of a sort that can be practiced anywhere and without special apparatus. Some of the habits and exercises on which he lays stress are as follows:

1. Make it a rule to keep the back of the neck close to the back of the collar.
2. Roll the shoulders backward and downward.
3. Try to squeeze the shoulder-blades together many times a day.
4. Stand erect at short intervals during the day—"head up, chin in, chest out, shoulders back."
5. Walk or stand with the hands clasped behind the head and the elbows wide apart.
6. Walk about, or even run up-stairs, with from ten to forty pounds on the top of the head.
7. Try to look at the top of your high-cut vest or your necktie.
8. Practice the arm movements of breast-stroke swimming while standing or walking.
9. Hold the arms behind the back.
10. Carry a cane or umbrella behind the small of the back or behind the neck.
11. Put the hands on the hips, with elbows back and fingers forward.
12. Walk with the thumbs in the armholes of the vest.
13. When walking, swing the arms and shoulders strongly backward.
14. Stand now and then during the day with all the posterior parts of the body, so far as possible, touching a vertical wall.
15. Look upward as you walk on the sunny side of the street.

The foregoing exercises, it will be seen, are happily varied, and are, many of them, such as can be practiced by anybody in almost any occupation. If he cannot use one, he can another.

Even in a gymnasium a man must be on his guard against forms of exercise that tend to induce a stooping posture.

A Very Simple Cure for Round Shoulders. 249

UNNATURAL POSITION.   NATURAL POSITION.

A VERY SIMPLE CURE FOR ROUND SHOULDERS.

Round shoulders are almost unavoidably accompanied by weak lungs, but may be cured by the simple and easily performed exercise of raising one's self upon the toes, leisurely, in a perpendicular position, several times daily.

Take a perfectly upright position, with the heels together and the toes at an angle of forty-five degrees. Drop the arms lifeless at the sides, animating and raising the chest to its full capacity muscularly, the chin well drawn in. Slowly rise up on the balls of the feet to the greatest possible height, thereby exercising all the muscles of the legs and body; come again into a standing position without swaying the body backward out of the perfect line. Repeat the exercise first on one foot and then on the other.

BEAUTY.

To be beautiful in the real sense means something more than to have facial perfections. The real beauty should start from within and make itself felt with every movement and expression of the body.

Desirable.—Beauty of face and person is desirable, praiseworthy, and attainable by all of us. Nay, it is our imperative duty to be as beautiful, as exquisite, as divinely attractive in soul, body, and mind as we possibly can become. Beauty is a very large word, and covers a broad field not generally understood by the masses of people.

May be Permanent.—It is the desire to excel in all that is good, great, and noble. It is the striving after the highest ideal in life. True beauty is permanent, while the merely physical attractions fade with our years, becoming withered and seamed by the flight of time.

Premature Age.—Have you ever noticed the premature age that comes with fretful, dissatisfied natures; that accompanies a disappointed ambition; that feels they have not been appreciated by the world? And consequently they are cynical, hard, and repellent.

Your Standard.—Let me say to such as these, do not despair, do not feel discouraged, do not let others set a standard for your life, but establish your own ideals of strength, goodness, and beauty, and then work upward to them.

Your Inner Self.—Recognize yourself, your inner self. Make that as near perfection as you can, and the outward will soon grow to correspond with the inner nature, until youth and beauty will become self-renewing and blossom like the bellflower—as you grow physically down life's plane, you will ascend mentally, morally, and spiritually.

Good Advice.—Somebody asked an old lady, whose face is still sweet and rosy at 80, how to be beautiful. Her advice was: "Try a little spiritual exercise. Look at yourself in the mirror four or five times a day. If the corners of your mouth are down and you are an unhappy looking creature, elevate your expression. Think of the pleasantest thing that ever happened to you; the kindest thing that was ever done for you; send out the most generous, sweetest, most helpful thoughts to your friends, then you will be beautiful."

More than Skin Deep.—Beauty is only skin deep, says the old saw, but the source of beauty lies deeper than the superficies of the body. No one ever has or ever can invent unguents, balms, or pigments that shall produce lasting loveliness. Over the footlights, a glowing color, darkened eyebrows, paint here and powder there, may for the time give an illusion of beauty. But the wear and tear of ten years, or even two, must strip off the mask and show the woman as she is.

Physical Beauty.—Physical beauty will come to those who have a beautiful soul, or, as Schiller put it in his "Essays": "Physical beauty is the sign of an interior beauty, which is the basis, the principle, and the unity of the beautiful."

Health and Beauty.—We must be healthy to be beautiful. The tendency to outdoor life is one of the chief agents in cultivating good health and beauty.

An Uplifting Power.—With the broadening of the chest, the expansion of the lungs, a glowing cuticle, a good circulation, an active organism, in short, with a superb physical development governed by a harmonious soul, woman becomes a beautiful, uplifting power in the world that, more than anything else, needs to realize her spiritual energy.

Keeping Fresh.—It is impossible to continue to be beautiful without keeping fresh in mind and body. In this most interesting age, interesting socially, politically, scientifically, ethically, and religiously, there is so much to challenge thought, to keep one abreast of the times, so much to awaken sympathy and demand the fullest exercise of the reasoning faculties, that the days are not half long enough for one who realizes these facts.

Mistress of Circumstances.—There is no need to lose youthful vigor, vim, and good looks, if a woman so orders her life as to be mistress of circumstances, if she studies the laws of hygiene and applies them to the ruling of her household. Let her wisely simplify her habits and apportion her time among her various duties so as to have hours for repose, for recreation, for reading, and for social intercourse.

Seeming Beauty.—Beauty of body and face, which is much to be desired, constitutes a letter of introduction to the people one meets, but does nothing beyond that. A woman who seems to be beautiful may become absolutely ugly by showing herself to be ill-tempered, vain or malicious.

Bad Passion.—Wrinkles upon the face are very often the result of bad passions. The mouth draws down at the corner from malice; the eyes grow small by the lids coming together when one is possessed of a cunning curiosity; the chin doubles itself from gluttony, and the cheeks incline to fold over when one allows one's self to grow cross and to speak with shrill, high notes.

Loud Speaking.—The strain that results from speaking loudly causes the muscles of the throat to over-develop and make it look stringy and unfeminine.

Temper.—So, first of all, she who would be charming must remember that the woman who allows her temper to control her will not retain one single physical charm. It is said that gluttony and anger will deform a face.

Greatest Charm.—The greatest charm and the something which we feel and yet cannot explain, is what is best described as beauty of expression. This delights the eye, but it cannot exist where there are low, sordid feelings, and where encouragement is not given to everything that is high and noble, pure and womanly. After one has cultivated these virtues and made them one's own, then it is necessary to study the physical side of life.

Laws of Life.—Fortunately you are starting out in life with no inherited disease, and with everything in your favor, therefore what remains for you to do is to learn the laws of life, and to live up to them. The treatment you give your body shows, and so you must take special care of the casket holding that jewel, your soul.

TO ACQUIRE A BEAUTIFUL FORM.

Dr. Jacques says, "Take abundant exercise in the open air—free, attractive, joyous exercise, such as young girls, when not restrained by false and artificial proprieties, are wont to take. If you are in the country, or can get there, ramble over the hills and through the woodlands; botanize; geologize; seek rare flowers and plants; hunt bird nests, and chase butterflies. Be a romp, even though you may be no longer a little girl. If you are a wife and a mother, so much the better. Romp with your children. Attend also to your bodily position in standing, sitting, lying and walking, and employ such general or special gymnastics as your case may require. Live, while indoors, in well-ventilated rooms; take sufficient wholesome and nourishing food, at regular hours; keep the mind active and cheerful—in short, obey all the laws of health."

Take a lesson from the English girl, as described in the following extract:

"The English girl spends more than one-half of her waking hours in physical amusements; that is, in amusements which tend to develop and invigorate and ripen the bodily powers. She rides, walks, drives, rows upon the water, runs, plays, swings, jumps the rope, throws the ball, hurls the quoit, draws the bow, keeps up the shuttlecock, and all this without having it forever impressed upon her mind that she is thereby wasting her time. She does this every day, until it becomes a habit, which she will follow up through life. Her frame, as a necessary consequence, is larger, her muscular system better developed, her nervous system in subordination to the physical; her strength more enduring, and the whole tone of her mind healthier. She may not know as much at the age of seventeen as does the American girl; as a general thing she does not, but the growth of her intellect has been stimulated by no hot-house culture, and though maturity comes later, it will last proportionately longer."

Beauty Evanescent.—Beauty is generally spoken of as a fleeting show, an evanescent gleam of celestial radiance, and this is too frequent and true, especially in this country, but all this is contrary to nature's intentions. It is said of the Italian women that instead of presenting a wrinkled and withered appearance, as they grow old, they seem to grow in beauty. In no country in the world are there so many middle-aged beautiful women as in Italy. This is not impossible for our American women. The Italians keep their beauty because they keep their health. In this lies the great secret. American women lose their beauty because they lose their health. If due regard is had to preservation of health, preserved loveliness will not be wanting in our day.

Highest Ambition.—Beauty or strength, casketed in a rounded, complete, and admirable physique, free from excess or deficiency of proportions, stands among the highest ambitions of the woman or man. A perfect form —it is the universal vanity; and "How well you are looking!" is everywhere among the most pleasing of compliments. "We all want to be physically perfect, because we desire that our presence should awaken attention, deference, perhaps admiration, and because, born inevitably to love, we would be capable of awakening love in others. The admiration we bestow on a perfect form, when by chance we meet with one, is a feeling that all know at some time in life. It is a feeling akin to worship —one in which the head has no part or prerogative. We reverence instinctively the largeness of grace, and the perfection of motion, life, and capability of which we perceive that our nature is susceptible."

COSMETICS AND CHEERFULNESS.

Cosmetics are generally good for nothing but the drug business. One merry thought, one kind word, and the smallest contribution to another's happiness, will do more for the complexion than a tableful of cold cream, violet powder, and other skin whiteners. A sweet thought will make the face brighten, and the eyes sparkle, every time it is harbored. It was Alice Cary who sang this old truth so gracefully thirty years ago: Don't mind the cosmetics, little woman; just be as cheerful as you can. Make the best of things. Avoid disagreeable people. Don't read or listen to the horrible. Try to forget the unpleasant things in life. Be cheerful, be gentle, and so be lovely.

Cosmetics.—Young lady, do not deceive yourself. You cannot use cosmetics without the knowledge of your gentlemen friends. They will respect you the more if you forever abandon the use of such subterfuges.

Vegetables Better than Cosmetics.—Ladies all who wish clear complexions, instead of using cosmetics, eat vegetables and fruit, as long as they are in season; and never throw away cucumber water or the juice of any fruit, but rub your face with it whenever you have it.

Eat fruit, girls—good, ripe fruit, however—if you would have and keep a clear and beautiful skin.

Practice smiles, also, not frowns. There is a wondrous charm in a smile. Like charity, it hides a multitude of sins.

PHYSICAL CULTURE.

We may learn much, in spite of our boasted modern civilization, of the old pagan Greeks. They, evidently, were not, like some of the moderns, "ashamed of their bodies;" but rather gloried in them as tenements worthy of the indwelling soul. All the young men of the nation were trained in manly exercises and high honors were bestowed upon those who excelled in them. The most modern of all the moderns, the Americans, adopt a different system. As did the ancient Greeks, we offer prizes or rewards, and bestow honors upon those who excel, but these prizes generally stimulate the already too active mental powers and promote brain-stuffing at the expense of a harmonious development of the whole being.

Standing.—Our "standing" among our fellow-men is quite as important a matter in a physical point of view as in a social or moral sense. An erect carriage is essential, not only to beauty and health, but to grace of movement. Standing may seem to be a little thing, and not worthy of much attention, but when there are so few who stand erect and so many who have wandered so far from nature in this respect, well may we attempt to regain the old paths. The mothers of ancient Greece exhorted their daughters to be virtuous, but they also urged them to hold themselves upright, and put back their shoulders. Not one out of a hundred may pay any attention to the position in standing, but to acquire erectness of body and to promote health attention must be paid to this duty.

Sitting.—A bad position in sitting is quite as common as in standing. Here also there must be an earnest effort made, or one falls in a bad habit and the result is frequently round shoulders and diseases of the lungs.

Walking.—An erect posture in walking requires the use of nearly all the muscles. As a health promoting exercise, walking cannot be undervalued if it is properly engaged in. To make your walks in the highest degree profitable to body and soul, cultivate a love of the beautiful as manifested in nature. Those who would add the beauty of graceful movement to the attractions of face and form must be careful to correct any inelegance of gait to which they may be addicted. American women are too stiff in their walk. Mr. G. W. Courtise says: "An American woman only bends her knees, and hardly that. Her gait gives a movement to her body like the squirming motion of a wounded insect with a naturalist's pin through its midriff. American women hold their arms badly in walking, they generally bring them forward, crossing their hands in front; they have, in consequence, the look of a trussed fowl, and have about as much freedom of motion. If our women were to let their arms fall freely by the side, they would move more gracefully, walk better and look better. The prevailing mode of carrying the arms contracts all proper development of the bust, ruins health, and, what our ladies will be more likely to attend to, destroys beauty of form and grace of movement."

Expanding the Chest.—Many people die for want of breath, when it is their own carelessness alone that prevents them from breathing. Our vitality is in proportion to our respiration, if we only half breathe we only half live. Expanding the chest and increasing our breathing capacity is therefore of the utmost importance. Some noted writer asserts that the development of the chest is an absolute standard of the length of life. It certainly is clear that by expanding it life may often be prolonged and health and beauty promoted.

TAKE LIFE AS IT COMES.

Fretting.—There is one sin which is everywhere and by everybody underestimated and quite too much overlooked in valuations of character. It is the sin of fretting. It is as common as air, as speech; so common that unless it arises above its usual monotone, we do not even observe it. Watch an ordinary coming together of people and we see how many minutes it will be before somebody frets—that is, makes more or less complaining statements of something or other, which most probably every one in the room or the car, or on the street corner, knew before, and which most probably nobody can help. Why say anything about it?

Bringing on Old Age.—It is cold, it is hot; it is wet, it is dry; somebody has broken an appointment, ill-cooked a meal; stupidity or bad faith somewhere has resulted in discomfort. There are plenty of things to fret about. It is simply astonishing how much annoyance and discomfort may be found in the course of every day's living, even at the simplest, if only one keeps a sharp eye on that side of things. Even to the sparks flying upward in the blackest smoke, there is a blue sky above and the less time they waste on the road the sooner they will reach it. Fretting is all time wasted on the road. Not only does fretting worry us and those around us, but remember that nothing brings the wrinkles and makes one old more quickly.

PRACTICAL HINTS ON COMPLEXION.

A well-known writer says, "A woman's gospel is to be lovely in mind and body."

We all know that loveliness of mind is reflected in the

expression of the face and eyes, but as it cannot affect the texture or color of the skin I will give you a few receipts for developing and enhancing the beauty of one, while you alone can cultivate the loveliness of the other.

Bathing.—Fineness of the skin, daintiness of the body and rosiness of the complexion depend almost entirely upon bathing, as a means both of obtaining and retaining them. A cold bath is a good tonic and nerve bracer, but it neither cleanses nor beautifies the skin to any extent. Nor should delicate girls or women think of indulging in it, unless so advised by their physician. The temperature of a beautifying bath should be from 70 to 75 degrees, and it should be of daily occurrence.

Almond Meal Bags.—Ordinary water, that is, water neither particularly hard nor soft, is not considered sufficiently cleansing to the skin, and a French firm has lately introduced dainty bags containing almond meal, oatmeal and orris root to be placed in the water a few moments before the bath is ready. This renders the water very milky and has a wonderfully softening and whitening effect.

Milk, Bran, Starch.—Baths in which milk, bran or starch has been placed are found to refine or whiten the coarsest, reddest skin if persistently used. Softness and firmness of skin may be obtained by the use of a simple unguent made famous by the Greek and Roman women, who centuries ago set us the example of perfect personal cleanliness as the road to beauty. The following can be made with very little trouble, and it is delightfully exhilarating after the bath:

Best white vinegar, one pint; rosemary, rue, camphor and lavender (of each), two drachms. Let the herbs soak in the vinegar for several hours, then strain. Rub thoroughly all over the body and a deliciously comfortable feeling and a dainty perfume will remain with one all day long.

SKIN TROUBLES.

There are many little skin troubles which are both persistent and troublesome, and vex one's very soul by appearing on the face. A greasy skin may arise from various causes, but generally from lack of cleanliness or debility of the skin. Only an astringent has any effect upon it, and a very simple, entirely harmless one may be made from one pint of rosewater, half a pint of white win vinegar and a few drops of essence of rose. This lotion may be applied with a piece of soft linen or a very fine sponge.

Blackheads are very difficult to get rid of, and are caused by the clogging of the pores of the skin, by dust or foreign matter. Alcohol, ninety per cent., applied by means of a piece of chamois skin, will give tone to the skin and remove unsuspected dirt and dust, at the same time stimulating the small glands and removing, by constant use, the blackheads.

Tan and Freckles may be removed by the use of the following lotion. Two drachms of powdered sal ammoniac, four fluid drachms of eau de Cologne, one quart of distilled water. Lemon juice and borax are both very efficacious, and are home remedies.

Lait Virginal.—Many skins will not stand constant washing, but need to be cleaned after a dusty ride or walk by other means than soap and water. Lait Virginal is a delicious preparation and can be made as follows: One pint of rose, orange flower or elder flower water, half an ounce of simple tincture of benzoin and ten drops of tincture of myrrh.

Cream.—After being exposed to harsh or chilling winds it is a good plan, upon retiring, to rub a quantity of fresh cream on the face, removing after five or ten minutes, to be applied again, followed by a generous puffing of rice powder. Remove in the morning by tepid water and Lait Virginal.

Cosmetics.—The use of cosmetics, face powders and rouges cannot be too strongly condemned. They stamp the person using them as silly and vulgar in the eyes of all refined and cultured people, and do not in even the slightest degree enhance or beautify. A good complexion needs no artificial toning or heightening, nature being the cleverest of all artists. A poor skin is kept clogged and its condition impoverished by the application of cosmetics —often, indeed, it is poisoned by the harmful ingredients contained in them.

Arsenic.—Arsenic and white lead are two of the drugs most used in their preparation and two of the rankest poisons which can be introduced into the system.

Free to All.—With good medical advice, plenty of sleep, fresh air, careful diet and scrupulous cleanliness, all women may hope to have complexions fair and sweet to look upon.

How to Obtain and Preserve a Beautiful Complexion. 259

"Why tinge the cheek of youth? the snowy neck,
Why load with jewels? why anoint the hair?
Oh, lady, scorn these arts; but richly deck
Thy soul with virtues: thus for love prepare!
Lo, with what vermil tints the apple blooms.
Say, does the rose the painter's hand require?
Away, then, with cosmetics and perfumes.
The charms of nature most excite desire."

How to Obtain and Preserve a Beautiful Complexion.

1. The great secret in acquiring a bright, beautiful skin, is temperance, exercise and cleanliness.

2. High living and late hours will destroy the most beautiful complexion.

3. Those who desire to be beautiful should never drink strong coffee, nor eat warm bread and butter, fat meat, etc.

4. Moderate diet and frequent bathing will insure a healthy and a beautiful face.

5. If you desire your skin to be perfectly clean and white, bathe it in warm water and bran, adding a few drops of bay rum.

6. To keep the skin and face perfectly soft take the whites of four eggs boiled in rose water, one-half ounce of alum, and one-half ounce of sweet almonds; beat the whole together till it assumes the consistency of paste. Spread this on a cloth and wear it on the face during the night.

7. Another good preparation to produce a soft and beautiful skin is, to take a small piece of the gum of benzoin and boil it in spirits of wine till it becomes a rich tincture. Fifteen drops of this, poured into a glass of water, will produce a mixture which will look like milk, and it also has an agreeable perfume. This will give the face a rich flesh color.

8. A lady who possesses a beautiful face should preserve it by wearing a veil or other covering on going into the open air or sunlight.

9. Do not use strong cosmetics, paints or pastes for adorning the face. They will ruin the best and most beautiful complexion in the world.

10. To powder and paint the cheek of beauty, is a ridiculous and culpable practice. There are many good remedies to produce a good healthy and natural complexion; that is all that is necessary. There is no such beauty as a rosy cheek which nature paints.

A CURE FOR SUNBURN.

This may occur in grade from a slight reddening of the face to an inflammation attended with blistering. Use soothing applications and avoid the sun until well.

HOW TO DEVELOP THE CHEST AND BUST.

The best treatment is gentle rubbing. Great care must be exercised that no chafing or bruising is produced. This gentle friction night and morning, five minutes at a time, will generally produce the desired results. A little linseed oil and rose water may be applied with good effect. Take at the same time, three times a day, small doses of cod-liver oil.

HOW TO REMOVE FRECKLES.

They are always developed on the parts of the body most exposed to the sun, and on some persons disappear in winter. They seldom appear on children before the age of five, and usually disappear in old age.

Remedy: 4 ounces of rose water,
             40 grains of borax,
             ¼ ounce of dilute acetic acid,
             6 grains of corrosive sublimate

Apply with a soft brush or rag every morning and evening, and continue until the freckles disappear.

Caution: Avoid the sun as much as possible during the treatment. Avoid all blistering compounds.

ANOTHER REMEDY FOR FRECKLES.

Sulpho-carbonate of zinc, 1 ounce,
Glycerine, 12 ounces,
Rose water, 12 ounces,
Alcohol, 3 ounces,
Spirit of neroli, ½ drachm.

Mix them. To be applied twice a day, leaving on from half an hour to one hour; then wash off and protect the face with a veil on exposure to strong light.

HOW TO CURE BLACKHEADS.

Blackheads are not worms, as many suppose. They consist of the hardening of the oil in the glands of the skin, and the dust collecting and adhering to the surface gives them a black appearance.

Remedy. Press them out with a hollow key or with the thumb and fingers, and apply a mixture of sulphur and cream every evening. Wash every morning with the best toilet soap, or wash the face with hot water with a soft flannel at bedtime.

HOW TO REMOVE TAN.

Lemon juice, ½ ounce,
New milk, ⅓ pint,
Brandy, ½ ounce.

Mix, and boil and skim off the skum. Apply every night and morning. Or, take a lemon, cut it in two, and rub it over the face. Wash it off and apply magnesia moistened in water and let it dry on the face. When dry, wash it off. Repeat this three or four times successively.

TO REMOVE PIMPLES.

Many pimples are removed by simply washing the face several times a day with warm water.

Sulphur water, 1 oz. White wine vinegar, 2 oz.
Liquor of potassa, ¼ oz. Distilled water, 2 oz.
Acetated liquor of ammonia, ¼ oz.

Apply twice a day.

TO REMOVE BLACK SPECKS OR "FLESH-WORMS."

Wash, and rub thoroughly with a towel and then apply the following twice a day:

White brandy, 4 oz. Cologne, 2 oz.
Liquor of potassa, 1 oz.

TO REMOVE YELLOW SPOTS.

Rubbing the face with common sulphur will often cure the worst forms. If not, apply the following safe remedy:

Strong sulphur water, 1 oz.
Lemon juice, ¼ oz.
Cinnamon water, 1 drachm.

TO REMOVE AND PREVENT WRINKLES.

Put some powder of best myrrh upon an iron plate, sufficiently heated to melt the gum gently, and when it liquefies cover your head with a napkin and hold your face over the myrrh at a proper distance to receive the fumes without inconvenience.

HOW TO PRODUCE BEAUTIFUL EYEBROWS AND LASHES.

The Circassian type of beauty is considered the finest. A preparation to promote the growth of the brows and lashes is made of the following ingredients:

Olive oil, ½ ounce,
Oil of nutmeg, 12 drops,
Oil of rosemary, 12 drops,
Tincture of cantharides, 3 drachms.

PEARL WATER FOR THE COMPLEXION.

1 lb. castile soap,
1 gallon water.

Dissolve, then add alcohol, one quart; oil of rosemary and oil of lavender, each 2 drachms. Mix well.

TOILET HINTS.

Brushing the hair briskly each night.
Warm borax water, for dandruff.
Onion rubbed on the scalp for the hair.
For the hair a tea made of garden box, strained and added to one and one-half ounces of lavender water.
A morning hand-bath in cold, salt water.
Pumice stone, for stained hands.
For the complexion, the milk of fresh, grated cocoa-nut.
For sunburn, the white of one egg and the juice of one lemon heated together.
After peeling onions, rubbing the hands with a stick of celery.
For an oily skin, a little camphor in the wash-water.
To cool the face, bathe it with hot water.

Sunlight is a capital sanitary agent, promotes health and cheerfulness. Therefore light should be admitted in large quantities into sick rooms, except in extraordinary cases. The light, however, should be softened and subdued, not glaring.

In Washing the Face soap should seldom be used, the bran bag sufficing for all purposes of cleanliness. There is nothing better than simple corn meal, not too finely ground; it cleanses the pores of the skin thoroughly and leaves it soft and satiny. Corn meal or bran bags are easily made, and are much less expensive than the bought ones; some bran or corn meal, shaved Castile soap and a little orris root are the necessary ingredients, they should be sewed up in a cheese-cloth bag and rubbed on the face and hands each time they are washed.

Hard Water is one of the most terrible foes to beauty of complexion; but even the hardest water, if boiled twice, or even once, loses much of its hard, coarse nature and is less harmful to the skin. With some the skin is constantly peeling from over-dryness, and this should not be permitted, as wrinkles form when the tissues dry up, and when of this particular type are almost incurable.

Emollients.—There are so many emollients for the skin, all good, and many which act harmlessly on the pores, that innumerable recipes might be given. Glycerine jelly is admirable for that rough type of skin which cracks on the least chill or exposure, but is preferable for the hands and wrists. This is rubbed in after washing, and after a few minutes, lightly bathe off with clear water.

An Excellent Preparation.—The following is an excellent jelly of this type: French gelatine, one-fourth ounce; glycerine, three ounces; dissolve the gelatine in six ounces of distilled water and add powdered borax, one-half drachm; rectified spirits wine, one ounce; attar of rose to perfume, about five drops. This is very easily made, and should be put into small, open-mouthed jars or pots sufficiently shallow for the fingers to reach the bottom.

Druggists' Method.—Druggists prepare glycerine jelly in the following manner; but, although efficacious, it is not as soothing as the first-named and quite as troublesome to prepare, as the oil must be worked in very slowly —in fact, almost drop by drop: Good soft soap, one-half drachm; purified honey, two drachms; pale olive oil, five ounces; perfume as desired.

Cold Cream.—An admirable cold cream, which keeps for some months and may be made firm enough to travel well, consists of: White wax, one ounce; almond oil, one ounce; rosewater, one ounce; glycerine, two drachms.

Almond Meal.—Almond meal, or almond wash powder, as it is sometimes termed, is made in various ways; but the following is an admirable formula: Almond powder (from the blanched almonds ground down fine, after the oil is expressed), eight ounces; the finest almond meal, eight ounces; powdered benzoin, three drachms; orris powder, one ounce; perfume with almond or attar of rose.

How to Take Care of the Teeth.

HOW TO TAKE CARE OF THE TEETH.

1. Teeth should be thoroughly cleansed every morning with a tooth-brush.
2. A wooden or quill tooth-pick should be used after every meal.
3. Professor Miller, an eminent authority on dental science, announces that the decay of teeth is contagious or transferable to others, and that the disease consists of bacilli.
4. When teeth are decayed the dentist should be consulted at once. Powdered charcoal is one of the best and most excellent applications for the teeth. It should be powdered very fine and applied to the teeth with a soft rag.
5. The teeth should never be used for the purpose of cracking nuts, cutting thread, etc.

A GOOD TOOTH POWDER.

Take of Prepared chalk, 7 drachms.
Powdered orris-root, 1 drachm.
Use every other morning.

CLEANING THE TEETH.

When?—It is best to clean the teeth after each meal and just before going to bed. Those who acquire this habit when they are young will not regret it in old age. Mothers should personally see that their children clean their teeth thoroughly and regularly. Children do not realize the importance of such practice and are liable to shirk duty and slight the operation.

How?—There are very few people who know how to clean teeth properly and easily. Just look at them as they swing the brush from side to side at right angles with their perpendicular plane. The proper way to brush and clean the teeth is to brush from the gums downward, for the upper teeth, and from the gums upward, for the inferior or lower teeth. By this method the bristles go between the teeth, touching their approximating surfaces, as well as cleaning the front and sides of the teeth.

It is not less important to brush downward on the palatine-roof surface of the upper teeth, and upward on the lingual-tongue side of the lower teeth, that is to say, brush the inside of the teeth more carefully, if anything, than the outside. Do not brush and clean the teeth for the sole purpose of making them look bright, clean and pretty, but to keep foreign substances from producing caries, or, plainer still, eating holes into the teeth and exposing a highly sensitive tissue, the pulp or nerve. Clean the grinding surfaces of the teeth with the same interested care.

Women in general are supposed to be greatly interested in the preservation of their teeth, and it may be somewhat painful to them for me to inform them that they do not generally possess as strong and dense teeth as do the male sex. That is the rule, the exceptions are rare. Hence the importance of cleanliness on their part is more important.

Mothers.—Then, again, mothers will do well to remember that the bones and teeth of their children are not as firm and compact as are these tissues in adults. There has not been deposited amidst the soft-solids of these textures as much of the carbonate and phosphate of lime as we will find as they grow older. Hence the value of preventing acid formations.

Economy.—If economy is wealth, this is one plain road to that condition. Nay, more, while one saves dental bills he saves, what is infinitely of more value, his teeth. It is not contended that there is no necessity to consult the family dentist. This should be done much more frequently than it is. A small cavity arrested in decay is much better than to have a large decayed spot to fill, or the ultimate loss of the tooth. But the highest art in dentistry is to prevent the formation of cavities, and not to fill them.

Toothpicks.—Do not use pins, needles, metallic toothpicks or any hard substance, or anything as unyielding as a piece of hard wood, like a sliver of beech, oak or walnut, but a thin goose quill, soft basswood picks, or broomcorn. Endeavor to cause the toothpick to rub against the side of each tooth so that anything adhering to the perpendicular walls of the teeth may be removed. Floss or any soft silk thread may also be used to great advantage.

Injurious Substances.—Any acid, like vinegar, will dissolve the lime of the teeth and destroy their solidity. All acid formations should be avoided. One who likes apples can indulge in such fruit, but he should thoroughly cleanse his teeth after eating. Vegetable and animal food remaining between the teeth will, after awhile, become an acid of more or less strength which may prove very injurious to the teeth.

Curious Facts about Teeth.—Damp weather booms the dentist business.

The first false teeth were made on lead plates.

People of the United States have the worst teeth of any nation.

Baltimore is known as the cradle of dentistry and has eight colleges.

Hippocrates, 450 B. C., was the first dentist of whom there is a record.

Gold-filled teeth are found in the jaws of skeletons exhumed at Pompeii.

A child is said to inherit the teeth of its father and the jaws of its mother.

Facial neuralgia is sometimes due to a dead tooth, and may be cured by a dentist.

HOW TO KEEP THE FRONT TEETH PERFECTLY WHITE.

Wipe them off with a clean linen handkerchief, and then wind a corner of the handkerchief around the finger and rub the teeth hard and thoroughly twice a day. The results will be excellent.

AN EXCELLENT TOOTH POWDER.

Suds of castile soap and spirits of camphor, of each an equal quantity, thicken with equal quantities of pulverized chalk and charcoal to a thick paste. Apply with the finger or brush.

HOW TO CURE A BAD BREATH.

Bad breath from catarrh, foul stomach, or bad teeth, may be temporarily relieved by diluting a little bromo chloralum with 8 or 10 drops of water and using it as a gargle, and swallowing a few drops before going out. A pint of bromo chloralum costs fifty cents, but a small vial will last a long time.

How to Take Care of the Hands.

A PERFECT ARM AND HAND.

HOW TO TAKE CARE OF THE HANDS.

To prevent chapping and roughness of the hands, soap should be used very sparingly and the hands should never be washed just before going out of doors. If the hands are inclined to be rough, it is best to use a little mutton tallow after each washing.

Buckskin, kid, dogskin, or other forms of leather, should be worn in cold weather. Silk and woolen gloves and mittens are more likely to produce roughness.

TO WHITEN THE HANDS.

Wash the hands in water containing a few drops of bay rum and ammonia.

Or, take one-half teacupful of cologne water, and another of lemon juice; scrape into it two cakes of Brown Windsor soap. Mix well and let it harden. This will be an excellent soap for whitening the hands.

TO WHITEN THE NAILS.

2½ drams diluted Sulphuric acid,
1¼ drams tincture of myrrh,
4½ ounces rain water. Mix.

First wash the hands with castile soap, and then apply a little of the above wash.

CHAPPED HANDS.

Wash the hands in water as hot as can be borne; then apply mutton tallow, cosmoline or a little carbolic acid and water.

Beautiful Hands.—The first thing one should do, in order to secure beautiful hands, is to see to existing blemishes, and their removal, if that be possible.

Warts.—As for warts, for instance, they are very disfiguring, and should be got rid of at as early an age as possible, so that any scars left may the sooner disappear.

Remedy.—There are many simple remedies for warts, but they are not always effectual. The ordinary milkweed of suburban gardens may be tried. The wart is to be touched with the juice twice or thrice daily.

Second.—If this does not succeed, we go a step further, and try a wash like the following, which not only tends to banish and prevent warts, but is useful for red hands, and helps to do away with clamminess. It is very simple. You take about a dram and a half of sal-ammoniac, and dissolve it in a quart of rain-water. Add a tablespoonful of toilet vinegar. The hands are to be steeped in this—they must have been previously washed and dried—for about a quarter of an hour every morning and evening.

Third.—If obdurate, the warts will want more stringent treatment. There is strong acetic acid to be had at the chemists, in tubes all ready. It should be used with caution—not a drop or half drop being allowed to fall anywhere, for it stains and burns. Touch only the wart gently once a day, and don't let any on the whole skin. But the caustic silver pencil is equally effectual.

Fourth.—If the wart is sufficiently large, it may be removed by winding around it first a silk or silver thread, and after it is dried and shriveled, cauterize with a little nitrate of silver.

The very best treatment, however, is electrolysis, and it is done by a galvanic battery; this should be done by the profession who understand the business.

Moles.—Moles may also be got rid of by acetic acid or even caustic silver; but they are more ticklish things to tackle than warts, so surgical aid should be had. I am much against self-treatment where safety is jeopardized.

Superfluous Hairs are disfiguring. They can be removed by the ordinary depilatories of shops; but these often contain arsenic; they are thus dangerous. Besides, they are dear; and one does not always like to ask for such things. I think the following depilatory as good and safe as any. It is simply a strong solution of sulphuret of barium formed into a paste with powdered starch. It is left on a few minutes and scraped off with the back of a knife. Or here is a French recipe: Crystallized hydrosulphate of soda one part, and three parts of each of powdered starch and powdered quicklime. Make into a paste with water, put on, and let stay on for two minutes; then scrape off with a wooden knife.

Depilatories all require to be handled with caution Touch the skin with oil afterwards, and do all this at night. Hairs may be tweezed out. Then there is electrolysis—a long and somewhat painful process.

Chapped Hands.—Some girls suffer greatly from this complaint, especially during the winter months. They must take the precautions I shall presently give for the preservation of the hands, and they must live in such a way as to increase the general strength and tone of the body, for chapped hands as well as chilblains are often associated with a weakened state of the constitution.

Our Girls.—I may say here at once, that no girl can expect to have pretty hands who lets herself get below par. They will be red and rough, because the heart is not strong enough to receive back the blood as well as it ought. Therefore it gets dammed up in the extremities—and with what results? Why, coldness of hands and feet, clammy feet or hands, red, rough hands, red ears, and—let me whisper it—a red nose. It is surprising how soon, in cases of this sort, improvement may take place from a course of citrate of iron and quinine—three to four grains trice a day in water after meals—the cold or tepid bath after breakfast, an occasional mild liver pill, good solid—not sloppy—food, codliver oil and or unbounded exercise in the open air. Try this treatment and have the grace to think kindly of your "Medicus" for recommending it.

Local Treatment.—But of course for chapped hands some local treatment is also necessary. Well, the camphor ball is as good as anything I know. It soothes, and it allays irritation, too. Then there is almond paste, rubbed well in at night, with gloves worn.

Another little mixture is glycerine mixed with a small quantity of tincture of benzoin and well rubbed in several times a day.

Cosmetics.—Now, I want my readers to disabuse their minds of the notion that cosmetics of any kind whatsoever will permanently whiten or beautify the hands if the health is neglected. I am very earnest in saying this, and I hope you will remember it.

Ordinary Care of Hands.— To begin with, they should be kept very clean. But I do not advise you to be perpetually scouring your hands, nor using too rough a towel. The use of sandsoap or pumice-stone is highly objectionable. Always use the mildest non-alkaline soap; there are many good ones in the market, but do not trust to puffing advertisements, and never buy a cheap soap—cheap and nasty! Always use rain water. Keep your hands gently warm—not hot—while out of doors. Muffs are not always advantageous, as they sweat the hands. If you would avoid roughness and redness, never hold your hands over the fire.

Standing About in Cold Rooms while in evening dress has a most injurious effect both on the complexion and hands. Always, if possible, throw a light, soft shawl around your shoulders. The condition of skin raised by cold, and called "goose-skin," really means temporary paralysis of the cuticle, and is very detrimental if often repeated.

Drinking Hot Tea or hot drinks of any kind when very cold is also bad for hands and face. Such drinks produce a too early reaction, and mischief is done that is difficult to get over.

Nails.— A soft nail-brush should be used in washing the hands. If any instrument be needed for the nails, it should be of ivory, not of steel; if you use a sharp steel instrument you roughen the under surface, and they soon get unsightly, and are more easily soiled.

Trimming.— About once a week is often enough to trim the nails. Do not cut them too much down at the sides, else you may have an ingrowing nail. Trim them oval or filbert, which ever suits the shape of the fingers best. Do not, however, leave them too long, or they may easily be likened to claws by people who don't love you.

Hot Water.— Wash in hot water, and the skin that grows up over the nail may then easily be kept in its proper place by the ivory trimmer.

Lemon Juice and glycerine will clean and soften the hands. When putting glycerine on chapped hands, first wash them thoroughly in soap and water, and when not quite dry rub in the glycerine. This process will be found much better than the old one. Vaseline is also splendid for chapped hands.

Chapped Hands.—At some seasons of the year it is almost impossible to keep the hands from chapping and looking

The Hands.

red when they are in water as frequently as it is necessary to have them. Below is given a most excellent recipe for making laureline, which is simply and easily prepared at home, and very inexpensive:

Laureline.—Two ounces of glycerine, one ounce of alcohol, one-fourth ounce of gum tragacanth, one-fourth to one-half ounce of rosewater or violet perfume, one pint of water; soak the tragacanth in the water two days, then strain and add the other ingredients. Cut the glycerine with the alcohol. If it should be too thick add a little more water and alcohol. Bottle, and it is ready for use.

In very cold weather, if it is too thick to pour easily, heat it by setting over the register or in a bowl of hot water.

Redness.—A good wash for preventing redness of the hands is made of one teaspoonful of muriate of ammonia, one tablespoonful of aromatic vinegar and one quart of tepid soft water. Soak the hands in a little of this for about fifteen minutes every night and morning.

"THE YOUNG DOCTOR."

274　　　　　　　　　　*The Toilet.*

QUEEN ELIZABETH OF ENGLAND,
Known as the Virgin Queen.

HOW LADIES SHOULD DRESS.

1. In the dress of ladies, great latitude is allowed; but the aim of the gentle sex should be simplicity and taste.

2. A lady must always consider what colors will suit her complexion. If she be dark, blue will not look well upon her; or if she be fair, pink will not become her. The most trying color is yellow. Only very pronounced brunettes can wear it. A lady must also take her size into consideration in selecting her dress. Stripes running the length of the dress have the effect of making a short person look taller, and should not be worn by a tall person.

3. The street dress of a lady should be simple and without display. To dress conspicuously or in brilliant colors for the street is a sign of bad breeding. In bad weather, a light India-rubber waterproof with a hood is more convenient and a better protection than an umbrella. To wear much jewelry on the street is vulgar. In large cities it subjects a lady to the danger of robbery or to conspicuous notice.

4. For church the dress should be simple and plain. Very little jewelry should be worn, and the costume should be of quiet colors. It is a mark of bad taste for ladies to attend church elaborately or conspicuously dressed.

5. Modesty in dress and behavior add more charm to woman than the rustle of silk or the glitter of gold.

Hair Dressings OF

QUEEN MARY.
Wife of William III.

QUEEN ANNE.

Different Styles of Wearing the Hair in the 18th Century.

STYLE IN
1776.

STYLE IN
1776.

STYLE IN
1780.

STYLE IN
1790.

Styles of Wearing the Hair in the beginning of the 19th Century.

STYLE IN
1800.

STYLE IN
1800.

STYLE IN
1820.

STYLE IN
1840.

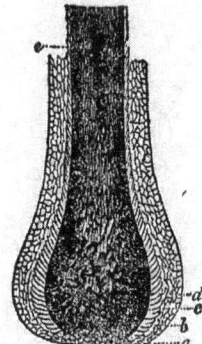

A ROOT OF HAIR.
Representation of a Hair highly magnified.

a, Basement membrane of hair follicle; *b*, layer of cells resting upon it, which become more scaly as they approach *c*, and form the cortex. The medullary substance of the hair consists of cells at the base; at *d* they become elongated and finally fibrous; *e*, coloring matter of hair.

The Structure of the Hair.

1. The whole body, except the palms of the hands and the soles of the feet, is covered with hair. The hair of the head in different individuals embraces a vast variety of color, length and quality.

2. **Root of the Hair.** — The root of the hair is made of two parts, sheath and bulb. The bulb is two or three times the diameter of the hair and is made up of cells.

3. **The Bulb** is the enlargement of the root as shown in the above figure, and the color of the hair is developed in the bulb. In gray hair there is no coloring matter. Thus it is seen that when the bulb becomes diseased, and the root of the hair dies, it must naturally fall out, just as the tree whose root is dead must decay and fall.

4. **Growth of Hair.** — The growth of all hair takes place in the root, which is supplied with blood vessels. A hair is nothing more nor less than a little tube and its growth largely

depends on the condition of health. Many people lose their hair on account of a diseased or debilitated constitution. When the hair commences falling out, it is always well to take a good tonic and keep the constitution in good repair, and it may be possible to preserve the hair for many years.

FALLING OUT OF THE HAIR.

No Absolute Cure.—There are no absolute remedies that will restore hair after it is diseased and has fallen out. A remedy of that kind would be worth millions to the discoverer. There are some hair tonics, however, that are beneficial and have a restorative effect on the hair, if taken in time. When the roots are dead there is no restoration, as there is nothing left to grow. All those patent remedies claiming to restore lost hair are the deceptions of money schemers.

A Common Trouble.—Falling out of the hair is one of the most common troubles. The hair comes out sometimes in spots, but usually there is a general thinning out all over the head, the hair becoming dry and brittle, breaking off and splitting at the ends. This annoying ailment is almost always indicative of one or two things: either a lack of nourishment or else a hot, feverish condition of the scalp.

General Health.—The treatment then must depend on the general condition of your health. If you are in a weak, debilitated state, or if you are suffering from long-continued or severe nervous mental strain, you must overcome these conditions before you can expect any improvement in your hair. Or, on the other hand, if you are in a plethoric state, full blooded, with feverish symptoms, with a sensation of heat in the head, dry, hot skin, etc., you must likewise correct this tendency before you can have healthy growing hair. In either case tone the system by tonics, good food and plenty of rest and sleep; avoid hair restoratives, hair tonics, etc., and take flowers of sulphur in small doses (say a quarter of a teaspoonful twice a day in a little milk).

Use a Soft Brush.—Stimulate the roots of the hair by frequent and long-continued use of a soft brush; clip off the split ends, and keep the scalp clean. There is nothing better for washing the head than tepid water and Castile soap, to which has been added a tablespoonful of alcohol, cologne or bay rum.

HOW TO CARE FOR THE HAIR.

A Housekeeper's Opinion.

Importance.—There is nothing that adds so much to a woman's appearance as an abundance of soft, glossy hair, and more thought and time should be spent in taking care of it than is usually given. Keep it free from dust by wearing a dusting-cap while sweeping, taking up carpets, and similar work. Brushing from five to ten minutes every night and morning will make it glossy and stimulate its growth. I know of two sisters who perform this task for each other regularly, and I have never seen more beautiful hair than theirs. It is more convenient than to brush one's own hair, of course, but those who have no sister within reach, and can not afford a lady's maid, can usually do the work very nicely themselves. The brush should have long, stiff bristles that will remove the dust, and should be kept scrupulously clean. A fine-tooth comb is useful for removing dandruff, which, if allowed to remain, incrusts the scalp, invites disease, and causes the hair to turn gray or fall out. At night it should be braided loosely, tied with soft ribbon, and allowed to hang. Some attention should be given the hairpins, as those that are rough, coarse, or sharply pointed should not be used.

Washing.—The hair will need washing once a month. The following method is very simple, and leaves it in excellent condition. Use plenty of warm, soft water and Ivory soap to get it clean, changing the water as often as necessary. Rinse in clear, soft water, and wipe as dry as possible with a towel. Then spread it over the shoulders and sit near the fire to finish drying. A little vaseline applied after it is dry keeps it from flying about by supplying the oil that has been removed by washing. At no other time is any oil or pomade necessary.

Bleaches.=Preparations containing cantharides cause the hair to grow by stimulating the scalp to healthy action. Many bleaches are injurious, and have been known to seriously affect the brain. Why should any woman wish to change the color of her hair, which usually harmonizes with her features and complexion, simply because fashion declares in favor of blond tresses?

Glossiness.—It is important to give attention to the general healthfulness of the hair and scalp, if we would preserve its early glossiness, instead of trying to restore it when faded and gray. It is said that English women preserve the glossiness of their hair almost to old age by applying once a week, and rubbing in vigorously among the roots of the hair, a cream made as follows: Take a pint of pure glycerine, put it in a quart bottle, and shake it up briskly, with six ounces of lime water. This must be done until it forms a soft, white cream. The hair, after the cream is rubbed into the scalp, is brushed well, and thus the cream is distributed to its very tips.

Dandruff is not, as many people think, a result of negligence or of uncleanliness, for it can certainly be produced by a vigorous use of a harsh brush. Any application, or any treatment that excoriates or irritates the scalp will produce dandruff. A laxative diet, or an aperient medicine, and the use of a soft brush, with one of the dressings given above, will cure any case of dandruff. Sore head—red, inflamed scalp, either in spots or covering the entire head— ringworms, etc., are annoying and painful in the extreme, but a cure is surer and simpler than is generally supposed. A cooling diet, free use of seltzer water and the use of an ointment made according to the recipe given below, will cure the most obstinate cases: Take of lard one tablespoonful and rub in a quarter of a teaspoonful of tar (not coal tar, but pine tar). Rub this salve well into the scalp every night, and by morning the disagreeable odor will be gone.

Remedy.—Where there is a loose scurf and dandruff, apply the following preparation once a week: Yolk of one egg; warm rain water one pint; bay rum one ounce. Beat the ingredients thoroughly together, and use it warm, rubbing the scalp thoroughly. It is always best to avoid all barbers' shampoos, and all other strong liquids manufactured for the purpose of removing dandruff. They are injurious to both hair and scalp. If the hair is dry after washing, apply a little hair oil made of one part castor oil and three parts alcohol.

Hair Oil of all kinds should be carefully avoided; if the hair is very dry and stiff, a little oil made as above may be used, otherwise avoid all oil, grease, or pomades of any kind. If you desire to preserve your natural growth of hair, with a natural healthy gloss, use only water or a weak solution of bay rum.

Dyeing.—If you desire to preserve your hair, carefully avoid all kinds of hair dye; there are some remedies that will darken the hair without injuring it, but any of the regular hair dyes, such as are commonly used, are unsafe and injurious. The color nature has bestowed upon the human hair is more perfect and more beautiful than any imitations which can be produced by any system of dyeing. Gray locks come with age and are an adornment and not a disgrace.

Gray Hairs.—Some persons are given to pulling out solitary gray hairs that make their appearance early. They could not do anything more foolish. The hair is simply broken off at the root, and the decayed nutriment escapes, inoculating the hair in the immediate vicinity. As a consequence, for every gray hair pulled out, five more make their appearance.

There is nothing finer than gray hair on the head of one who is nearing the horizon of life. It is an aureole of glory.

How to Make the Hair Wave.—Soft, natural-looking waves of hair are made by rolling the hair over large, soft papers or kid curlers, rolling from the top of the curl toward the end. The hair should be wet and left on the rolls over night. If that is not done, pinch the curls with a hot iron. If you wish to have the hair set out around the face, turn the teeth of your side combs toward the face, and not away from it. Catch them through the end of your waves, and you can fluff the hair as little or as much as you choose.

HOW TO CLEAN HAIR BRUSHES.

Put a teaspoonful or dessertspoonful of aqua ammonia into a basin half full of water, comb the loose hairs out of the brush, then agitate the water briskly with the brush, and rinse it well with clear water. A few drops of hartshorn put into a little water will clean a hair brush nicely. If very dirty, use a little soap also.

HOW TO TAKE CARE OF THE HAIR.

How to Prepare Your Own Hair Oil, Tonics, Shampoos, and the Different Preparations for the Hair and Beard.

1. Cleanliness is the first requisite to a healthy, vigorous growth of hair. It should be kept clean by brushing, combing and washing the scalp thoroughly with soap and water at least once in two weeks.

2. It is best to trim the ends of the hair once a month to continue a healthy growth.

3. Washing the hair once a day in cold water produces the healthiest, most lasting growth of hair. Avoid the strong shampoo liquids generally used by barbers.

4. There are many cases in which the loss of hair cannot be remedied, but there are cases where an application of good healthy tonics and proper care will restore a new and sufficient growth.

5. If the hair is inclined to come out, avoid all barber's shampoos and sea foams.

6. Avoid hair oils unless the hair is very stiff and dry, and then use it sparingly.

7. Most all hair dyes are very injurious, and unless the growth of hair is vigorous, it should be carefully avoided.

TONICS AND OILS.

We have, as has been seen, discouraged the use of tonics and oils and we would repeat that it is best to avoid their use. Some of them are harmless, but others are injurious. For the benefit of those who would use them we give some of the best and safest recipes.

Hair Tonic or Wash made of the following, bay rum, 4 ounces; rain water, 4 ounces; quinine, 20 grains, is one of the best hair tonics and restoratives for general daily use made. It promotes vigor, growth, and keeps the hair soft and glossy. If the hair is very light, falls out and breaks, the quinine wash should be applied every night before retiring.

Clipping.—When after an illness the hair falls out it should be cut short and kept clipped for at least twelve months. Wash the scalp regularly two or three times a week with the following hair tonic:

Tinct. bloodroot, 2 drachms; tinct. lobelia, 1 drachm; tinct. capsicum, 2 drachms; tinct. cantharides, 2 drachms; glycerine, 2 ounces; alcohol, 7 ounces; bay rum, 7 ounces; sul. quinine, 2 grains.

Dissolve the quinine in the alcohol first, and then add the other ingredients.

Apply at night, rubbing freely into the scalp.

This remedy has been proven to be among the best and can be safely applied under any and all circumstances where the hair shows signs of deadness and is falling out.

Hair Dressing.—In nearly every instance thorough brushing will keep the hair soft, tractable and glossy, but if it is very stubborn and you think you really must have a dressing I advise the use of either of the following as safe—the last one especially is clean and cool, and free from greasiness, being really a fluid neutral soap. It is the very best dressing for children's hair that can be used. Remember that any hair dressing should be used sparingly and well brushed in. Take of castor oil four fluid ounces, alcohol two fluid ounces, add any perfume you like and shake well; or bay rum eight ounces, glycerine two fluid ounces; or pure sweet oil six fluid ounces and limewater two fluid ounces. Shake well every time it is used.

Hair Tonic (Baldness).—Tincture capsicum, 2 drachms; water ammonia (10 per cent.), 1 ounce; pilocarpine hydrochlorate, 5 grains; cologne, 3 ounces. Use on scalp twice a day.

A GOOD HAIR OIL.

Castor oil, 1 quart,
Alcohol, 95 per cent, 3 quarts,
Oil of verbena, 3 drachms.

Mix them thoroughly.

If you desire it colored, use a little Tinct. Alkanet ot.

TO DARKEN THE HAIR.

The following receipt will gradually darken the hair and produce no injurious results.

Rain water, ½ pint,
Alcohol, 1 ounce,
Essence of Rose, 12 drops,
Powdered Blue Vitriol, 1 drachm.

Mix thoroughly.

FINE SHAMPOO LIQUID.

Dissolve ½ ounce carb. of ammonia and 1 ounce of borax in 1 quart of water, then add

2 ounces glycerine,
3 qts. of New England rum,
1 qt. of bay rum.

Moisten the hair with this liquor; shampoo with the hands until a slight lather is formed, then wash off with clean water.

SEA FOAM FOR BARBERS.

4 ounces alcohol, ½ ounce ammonia,
1 ounce castor oil, 1 pint rain water.

Dissolve the castor oil and ammonia in the alcohol, then add the alcohol mixture to the water.

N. B.—Good healthy hair requires no tonics, oil or shampoo liquids; warm water and pure soap only.

DANDRUFF ON BABY'S HEAD.

Grease with chicken oil, or fresh unsalted butter, or sweet cream; then remove by combing.

To Cleanse the Head.—An excellent shampoo is made of salts of tartar, white castile soap, bay rum, and lukewarm water. The salts will remove all dandruff, the soap will soften the hair and cleanse it thoroughly, and the bay rum will prevent taking cold.

**IMAGE EVALUATION
TEST TARGET (MT-3)**

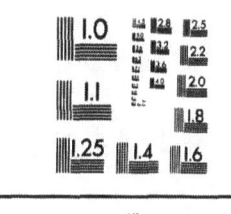

← 6" →

Photographic
Sciences
Corporation

23 WEST MAIN STREET
WEBSTER, N.Y. 14580
(716) 872-4503

PRACTICAL HINTS FOR SHAVING.

How to Sharpen a Razor, Keep the Face Smooth, Color the Beard, Cure Pimples, and Various Preparations for the Face.

1. TO MAKE A GOOD RAZOR STROP, take a piece of an old leather belt, which has been used on some threshing machine or factory machinery, cut it narrow and oil it well. No better strop in use.

2. Take a piece of new kip leather and oil it well with wagon grease. Be sure not to take the grease from the outside of the wheel, as it is filled with too much dust and dirt.

3. No one shaving himself should neglect the use of *Bay Rum*, or a good face wash after shaving. It keeps the skin smooth and soft, and makes shaving an easy task.

4. One of the best and cheapest washes for the face, to use after shaving, is the following:

    2 oz. Glycerine,
    1 oz. Tincture Benzoin,
    1 oz. Rose Water.

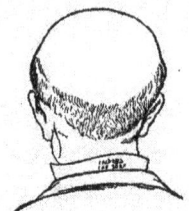

TO PREVENT THE HAIR FROM FALLING OUT.

Wetting the hair thoroughly once or twice a week with a weak solution of salt water will prevent it from falling out.

HAIR TONIC.

TO KEEP THE HAIR FROM FALLING OUT.

Tinct. bloodroot, 2 drachms,
Tinct. lobelia, 1 drachm,
Tinct. capsicum, 2 drachms,
Tinct. cantharides, 2 drachms,
Glycerine, 2 ounces,
Alcohol, 7 ounces,
Bay rum, 7 ounces,
Sul. quinine, 20 grains.

Dissolve the quinine in the alcohol first, and then add the other ingredients.
Apply at night, rubbing freely into the scalp.

A CELEBRATED LIQUID FOR CURLING THE HAIR.

Most receipts for curling the hair are very injurious, but the following is harmless and excellent.

Glycerine, ¼ ounce,
Rectified spirits, 1¼ ounce,
Distilled water, 16 ounces,
Liquor of ammonia, 1 drachm,
Dry salts of tartar, 1 drachm,
Powdered cochineal, ½ drachm,
Essence of rose, ¾ drachm.

Mix and let it stand ten days, then filter and moisten the hair while combing it.

ORIENTAL SHAVING CREAM.

4 ounces oil of almonds.
2 drachms white wax.
2 drachms spermaceti.

Melt, and add rose water, 4 ounces; orange flower water, 1 ounce; used to soften the skin, apply as the last.

LIQUID FOR FORCING THE BEARD.

2 ounces cologne.
1 drachm liquid hartshorn.
2 drachms tincture cantharides.
12 drops oil rosemary.
12 drops lavender.

Apply to the face daily, and await result. Said to be reliable.

A CURE FOR PIMPLES ON THE FACE.

50 drops carbolic acid.
3 ounces glycerine.
1 ounce rose water.

This is one of the best and safest remedies in use. Many of the so-called *Pimple Cures*, do more injury than good.

BARBERS' ITCH OINTMENT.

1 pound olive oil.
1 pound suet.
2 ounces alkanet root.

Melt, and macerate until colored; then strain, and add 3 ounces of alum, nitre and sulphate of zinc, in very fine powder, adding vermillion to color it, and oil of anise seed, lavender and thyme to perfume.

A GOOD RAZOR STROP PASTE.

Wet the strop with a little sweet oil, and apply a little flour of emery evenly over the surface.

CLIFFORD'S SHAMPOO COMPOUND.

¾ pound of borax.
¼ pound of salts tartar.

Mix and dissolve 1 ounce of the mixture in 1 pint of water.

HOW TO TAKE CARE OF THE FEET.

HOW TO CURE CORNS, CHILBLAINS, INGROWING NAILS, COLD FEET, ETC.

Corn Cure.

Soak the feet thoroughly in hot water and remove all the hard skin with a sharp knife and apply kerosene oil. This process repeated twice a week will cure the worst case of corns, providing a loose-fitting shoe is worn.

How to Remove Corns from Between the Toes.

These corns are generally more painful than any others, and are frequently situated so as to be almost inaccessible to the usual remedies. Wetting them several times a day with hartshorn will in most cases cure them.

Do not use those Patent Medicine Cures, they are almost always sure to make you serious trouble.

A Cure for Chilblains.

1. The first thing to relieve distress is gentle rubbing with the hands and the wearing of loose and easy-fitting shoes.

2. If irritation continues, apply a little camphor and water, or a weak solution of carbolic acid and water, or a little kerosene and lard.

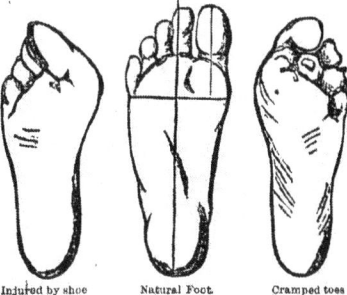

Injured by shoe too short.   Natural Foot.   Cramped toes from tight shoes.

HOW TO CURE BUNIONS.

A bunion is nothing more or less than a large corn, and is generally caused by wearing short, high-heeled, and narrow soled shoes, which throw the weight of the body on the front part of the foot.

Home Remedy.—Take a small, flat and hollow India rubber ring or band and place it over the bunion so as to keep off the pressure of the shoe. A cotton band may be used.

When the pain is severe, it should be poulticed with a bread and milk poultice.

Kerosene treatment recommended for corns is also very efficient. Or touch it with a little Nitrate of silver occasionally.

ANTIDOTES FOR COLD FEET.

Cold feet are generally the result of profuse perspiration. Put small quantities of pulverized alum in the stockings every morning. Bathe the feet every night in warm water and saleratus.

Cold feet are sometimes the result of poor circulation. In that case the general health should be toned up.

AN UNHEALTHY SHOE.

EFFECTS OF TIGHT SHOES.

THE EFFECTS OF WEARING TIGHT SHOES.

The above illustration shows the effects of high-heeled tight shoes. Also the effects of cramping the toes.

No sensible person can really suppose there is anything unpleasant, or even unsightly in the form of a perfect human foot, and yet all attempts to construct shoes upon a sensible model are met with extreme objections. Fashion must be favored with a fashionable shoe, which injures not only the foot, but in many instances results in serious injury of health itself.

The foolish custom of wearing tight and high-heeled shoes is accompanied with more serious results to general health and comfort than almost any other whim of fashion.

Remember that a natural foot in a comfortable shoe will save you much distress, and many hours of discomfort.

HOW TO CURE INGROWING NAILS.

The ingrowing nail is caused by wearing tight shoes or boots, or by an improper mode of cutting the nails.

Remedy.— Scrape the nail in the centre with a sharp knife or piece of glass until it becomes very thin and tender. Keep it scraped in until cured. If it has become very sore the nail should be cut away from the irritated or ulcerated part and dressed twice a day with cosmoline.

SOME POINTERS ABOUT FOOTWEAR.

Dr. Samuel Appleton gives fourteen of them, which every person will derive comfort in heeding:

1. Never wear a shoe that will not allow the great toe to lie in a straight line.
2. Never wear a shoe with a sole narrower than the outline of the foot traced with a pencil close under the rounding edge.
3. Never wear a shoe that pinches the heel.
4. Never wear a shoe or boot so large in the heel that the foot is not kept in place.
5. Never wear a shoe or boot tight anywhere.
6. Never wear a shoe or boot that has depressions in any part of the sole to drop any joint or bearing below the level plane.
7. Never wear a shoe with a sole turning up very much at the toes, as this causes the cords on the upper part of the foot to contract.
8. Never wear a shoe that presses up into the hollow of the foot.
9. Never have the top of the boots tight, as it interferes with the action of the calf muscles, makes one walk badly, and spoils the shape of the ankle.
10. Never come from high heels to low heels at one jump.
11. Never wear one pair of shoes all the time, unless obliged to do so. Two pairs of boots worn a day at a time alternately give more service and are much more healthful.
12. Never wear a leather sole lining to stand upon. White cotton drilling or linen is much better and more healthful.
13. Never wear a short stocking, or one which after being washed is not, at least, one-half inch longer than the foot. Bear in mind that stockings shrink. Be sure that they will allow your toes to spread out at extreme ends, as this keeps the joints in place and makes a strong and attractive foot. As to shape of stockings, the single digital or "one-toe stocking" is the best.
14. Never think that the feet will grow large from wearing proper shoes. Pinching and distorting makes them grow not only large, but unsightly. A proper, natural use of all the muscles makes them compact and attractive.

Rules on Etiquette.

"MY DAUGHTER, REMEMBER, YOUR MANNERS SPEAK LOUDER THAN WORDS."

HINTS AND HELPS ON GOOD BEHAVIOR AT ALL TIMES AND AT ALL PLACES.

1. It takes acquaintance to found a noble esteem, but politeness prepares the way. Indeed, as Montaigne says, courtesy begets esteem at sight. Urbanity is half of affability, and affability is a charm worth possessing.

2. A pleasing demeanor is often the scales by which the pagan weighs the Christian. It is not virtue, but virtue inspires it. There are circumstances in which it takes a great and strong soul to pass under the little yoke of courtesy, but it is a passport to a greater soul standard.

3. Matthew Arnold says: "Conduct is three-fourths of character," and Christian benignity draws the line for con-

duct. A high sense of rectitude, a lowly soul, with a pure and kind heart, are elements of nobility which will work out in the life of a human being at home—everywhere. "Private refinement makes public gentility."

4. If you would conciliate the favor of men, rule your resentment. Remember that if you permit revenge or malice to occupy your soul, you are ruined.

5. Cultivate a happy temper; banish the blues; a cheerful, sanguine spirit begets cheer and hope.

6. Be trustworthy and be trustful.

7. Do not place a light estimate upon the arts of good reading and good expression; they will yield perpetual interest.

8. Study to keep versed in world events as well as in local occurrences, but abhor gossip, and above all scandal.

9. Banish a self-conscious spirit — the source of much awkwardness—with a constant aim to make others happy. Remember that it is incumbent upon gentlemen and ladies alike to be neat in habits.

10. The following is said to be a correct posture for walking: Head erect—not too rigid—chin in, shoulders back. Permit no unnecessary motion about the thighs. Do not lean over to one side in walking, standing or sitting; the practice is not only ungraceful, but it is deforming and therefore unhealthful.

11. Beware of affectation and of Beau Brummel airs.

12. If the hands are allowed to swing in walking, the arc should be limited, and the lady will manage them much more gracefully, if they almost touch the clothing.

13. A lady should not stand with her hands behind her. We could almost say, forget the hands except to keep them clean, including the nails, cordial and helpful. One hand may rest easily in the other. Study repose of attitude here as well as in the rest of the body.

14. Gestures are for emphasis in public speaking; do not point elsewhere, as a rule.

15. Greet your acquaintances as you meet them with a slight bow, and smile as you speak.

16. Look the person to whom you speak in the eye. Never under any circumstances wink at another or communicate by furtive looks.

17. Should you chance to be the rejected suitor of a lady, bear in mind your own self-respect, as well as the inexorable laws of society, and bow politely when you meet her. Reflect that you do not stand before all woman-kind as you do at her bar. Do not resent the bitter-

ness of flirtation. No lady or gentleman will flirt. Remember ever that painful prediscovery is better than later disappointment. Let such experience spur you to higher exertion.

18. Discretion should be exercised in introducing persons. Of two gentlemen who are introduced, if one is superior in rank or age, he is the one to whom the introduction should be made. Of two social equals, if one be a stranger in the place, his name should be mentioned first.

19. In general the simpler the introduction the better.

20. Before introducing a gentleman to a lady, remember that she is entitled to hold you responsible for the acquaintance. The lady is the one to whom the gentleman is presented, which may be done thus: "Miss A., permit me to introduce to you my friend, Mr. B.;" or, "Miss A., allow me to introduce Mr. B." If mutual and near friends of yours, say simply, "Miss A., Mr. B."

21. Receive the introduction with a slight bow and the acknowledgment, "Miss A., I am happy to make your acquaintance;" or, "Mr. B., I am pleased to meet you." There is no reason why such stereotyped expressions should always be used, but something similar is expected. Do not extend the hand usually.

22. A true lady will avoid familiarity in her deportment toward gentlemen. A young lady should not permit her gentlemen friends to address her by her home name, and the reverse is true. Use the title Miss and Mr. respectively.

23. Ladies should be frank and cordial towards their lady friends, but never gushing.

24. Should you meet a friend twice or oftener, at short intervals, it is polite to bow slightly each time after the first.

25. A lady on meeting a gentleman with whom she has slight acquaintance will make a medium bow—neither too decided nor too slight or stiff.

26. For a gentleman to take a young lady's arm is to intimate that she is feeble, and young ladies resent the mode.

27. If a young lady desires to visit any public place where she expects to meet a gentleman acquaintance, she should have a chaperon to accompany her, a person of mature years when possible, and never a giddy girl.

28. A lady should not ask a gentleman to walk with her.

A COMPLETE ETIQUETTE IN A FEW PRACTICAL RULES.

1. If you desire to be respected, keep clean. The finest attire and decorations will add nothing to the appearance or beauty of an untidy person.

2. Clean clothing, clean skin, clean hands, including the nails, and clean, white teeth, are a requisite passport for good society.

3. A bad breath should be carefully remedied, whether it proceeds from the stomach or from decayed teeth.

4. To pick the nose, finger about the ears, or scratch the head or any other part of the person, in company, is decidedly vulgar.

5. When you call at any private residence, do not neglect to clean your shoes thoroughly.

6. A gentleman should always remove his hat in the presence of ladies, except out of doors, and then he should lift or touch his hat in salutation. On meeting a lady a well-bred gentleman will always lift his hat.

7. An invitation to a lecture, concert, or other entertainment, may be either verbal or written, but should always be made at least twenty-four hours before the time.

Rules on Etiquette.

8. On entering a hall or church the gentleman should precede the lady in walking up the aisle, or walk by her side, if the aisle is broad enough.

9. A gentleman should always precede a lady upstairs, and follow her downstairs.

10. Visitors should always observe the customs of the church with reference to standing, sitting, or kneeling during the services.

11. On leaving a hall or church at the close of entertainment or services, the gentleman should precede the lady.

12. A gentleman walking with a lady should carry the parcels, and never allow the lady to be burdened with anything of the kind.

13. A gentleman meeting a lady on the street and wishing to speak to her, should never detain her, but may turn around and walk in the same direction she is going, until the conversation is completed.

14. If a lady is traveling with a gentleman, simply as a friend, she should place the amount of her expenses in his hands, or insist on paying the bills herself.

15. Never offer a lady costly gifts, unless you are engaged to her, for it looks as if you were trying to purchase her goodwill; and when you make a present to a lady use no ceremony whatever.

16. Never carry on a private conversation in company. If secrecy is necessary withdraw from the company.

17. Never sit with your back to another without asking to be excused.

18. It is as unbecoming for a gentleman to sit with legs crossed as it is for a lady.

19. Never thrum with your fingers, rub your hands, yawn or sigh aloud in company.

20. Loud laughter, loud talking, or other boisterous manifestations should be checked in the society of others, especially on the street and in public places.

Rules on Etiquette.

21. When you are asked to sing or play in company, do so without being urged, or refuse in a way that shall be final; and when music is being rendered in company, show politeness to the musician by giving attention. It is very impolite to keep up a conversation. If you do not enjoy the music, keep silent.

22. Contentions, contradictions, etc., in society should be carefully avoided.

23. Pulling out your watch in company, unless asked the time of day, is a mark of the demi-bred. It looks as if you were tired of the company and the time dragged heavily.

24. You should never decline to be introduced to any one or all of the guests present at a party to which you have been invited.

25. A gentleman who escorts a lady to a party, or who has a lady placed under his care, is under particular obligations to attend to her wants and see that she has proper attention. He should introduce her to others, and endeavor to make the evening pleasant. He should escort her to the supper table and provide for her wants.

26. To take small children or dogs with you on a visit of ceremony is altogether vulgar, though in visiting familiar friends children are not objectionable.

CHILDREN SHOULD EARLY BE TAUGHT THE LESSON OF PROPRIETY AND GOOD MANNERS.

Improve Your Speech by Reading.

ETIQUETTE IN YOUR SPEECH.

Don't say Miss or Mister without the person's name.
Don't say pants for trousers.
Don't say gents for gentlemen.
Don't say female for woman.
Don't say elegant to mean everything that pleases you.
Don't say genteel for well-bred.
Don't say ain't for isn't.
Don't say I done it for I did it.
Don't say he is older than me; say older than I.
Don't say she does not see any; say she does not see at all
Don't say not as I know; say not that I know.
Don't say he calculates to get off; say he expects to get off.
Don't say he don't; say he doesn't.
Don't say she is some better; say she is somewhat better
Don't say where are you stopping? say where are you staying?
Don't say you was; say you were.
Don't say I say, says I, but simply say I said.
Don't sign your letters yours etc., but yours truly.
Don't say lay for lie; lay expresses action; lie expresses rest.
Don't say them bonnets; say those bonnets.
Don't say party for person.
Don't say it looks beautifully, but say it looks beautiful.

Don't say feller, winder, to-morrer, for fellow, window, to-morrow.
Don't use slangy words; they are vulgar.
Don't use profane words; they are sinful and foolish.
Don't say it was her, when you mean it was she.
Don't say not at once for at once.
Don't say he gave me a recommend, but say he gave me a recommendation.
Don't say the two first for the first two.
Don't say he learnt me French; say he taught me French.
Don't say lit the fire; say lighted the fire.
Don't say the man which you saw; say the man whom you saw.
Don't say who done it; say who did it.
Don't say if I was rich I would buy a carriage; say if I were rich.
Don't say if I am not mistaken you are in the wrong; say if I mistake not.
Don't say who may you be; say who are you?
Don't say go lay down; say go lie down.
Don't say he is taller than me; say taller than I.
Don't say I shall call upon him; say I shall call on him.
Don't say I bought a new pair of shoes; say I bought a pair of new shoes.
Don't say I had rather not; say I would rather not.
Don't say two spoonsful; say two spoonfuls.

ETIQUETTE OF DRESS AND HABITS.

Don't let one day pass without a thorough cleansing of your person.
Don't sit down to your evening meal before a complete toilet if you have company.
Don't cleanse your nails, your nose, or your ears in public.
Don't use hair dye, hair oil or pomades.
Don't wear evening dress in daytime.
Don't wear jewelry of a gaudy character; genuine jewelry modestly worn is not out of place.
Don't overdress yourself or walk affectedly.
Don't wear slippers or dressing-gown or smoking-jacket out of your own house.
Don't sink your hands in your trousers' pockets.
Don't whistle in public places, nor inside of houses either.
Don't use your fingers or fists to beat a tattoo upon floor, desk or window panes.
Don't examine other people's papers or letters scattered on their desk.

Don't bring a smell of spirits or tobacco into the presence of ladies.
Never use either in the presence of ladies.
Don't drink spirits; millions have tried it to their sorrow.

ETIQUETTE ON THE STREET.

1. Your conduct on the street should always be modest and dignified. Ladies should carefully avoid all loud and boisterous conversation or laughter and all undue liveliness in public.

2. When walking on the street do not permit yourself to be absent-minded, as to fail to recognize a friend; do not go along reading a book or newspaper.

3. In walking with a lady on the street give her the inner side of the walk, unless the outside is the safer part; in which case she is entitled to it.

4. Your arm should not be given to any lady except your wife or a near relative, or a very old lady, during the day, unless her comfort or safety requires it. At night the arm should always be offered; also in ascending the steps of a public building.

5. In crossing the street a lady should gracefully raise her dress a little above her ankle with one hand. To raise the dress with both hands is vulgar, except in places where the mud is very deep.

6. A gentleman meeting a lady acquaintance on the street should not presume to join her in her walk without first asking her permission.

7. If you have anything to say to a lady whom you may happen to meet in the street, however intimate you may be, do not stop her, but turn round and walk in company with her; you can take leave at the end of the street.

8. A lady should not venture out upon the street alone after dark. By so doing she compromises her dignity, and exposes herself to indignity at the hands of the rougher class.

9. Never offer to shake hands with a lady in the street if you have on dark or soiled gloves, as you may soil hers.

10. A lady does not form acquaintances upon the street, or seek to attract the attention of the other sex or of persons of her own sex. Her conduct is always modest and unassuming. Neither does a lady demand services or favors from a gentleman. She accepts them graciously, always

expressing her thanks. A gentleman will not stand on the street corners, or in hotel doorways, or store windows and gaze impertinently at ladies as they pass by. This is the exclusive business of loafers.

11. In walking with a lady who has your arm, should you have to cross the street, do not disengage your arm and go around upon the outside, unless the lady's comfort renders it necessary. In walking with a lady, where it is necessary for you to proceed singly, always go before her.

ETIQUETTE OF CALLS.

In the matter of making calls it is the correct thing:
For the caller who arrived first to leave first.
To return a first call within a week and in person.
To call promptly and in person after a first invitation.
For the mother or chaperon to invite a gentleman to call.
To call within a week after any entertainment to which one has been invited.
You should call upon an acquaintance who has recently returned from a prolonged absence.
It is proper to make the first call upon people in a higher social position, if one is asked to do so.
It is proper to call, after an engagement has been announced, or a marriage has taken place, in the family.
For the older residents in the city or street to call upon the newcomers to their neighborhood is a long recognized custom.
It is proper, after a removal from one part of the city to another, to send out cards with one's new address upon them.
To ascertain what are the prescribed hours for calling in the place where one is living, or making a visit, and to adhere to those hours is a duty that must not be overlooked.
A gentleman should ask for the lady of the house as well as the young ladies, and leave cards for her as well as for the head of the family.

Practical Rules on Table Manners.

1. Help ladies with a due appreciation; do not overload the plate of any person you serve. Never pour gravy on a plate without permission. It spoils the meat for some persons.

2. Never put anything by force upon any one's plate. It is extremely ill-bred, though extremely common, to press one to eat of anything.

3. If at dinner you are requested to help any one to sauce or gravy, do not pour it over the meat or vegetables, but on one side of them. Never load down a person's plate with anything.

4. As soon as you are helped, begin to eat, or at least begin to occupy yourself with what you have before you. Do not wait till your neighbors are served—a custom that was long ago abandoned.

5. Should you, however, find yourself at a table where they have the old-fashioned steel forks, eat with your knife, as the others do, and do not let it be seen that you have any objection to doing so.

6. Bread should be broken. To butter a large piece of bread and then bite it, as children do, is something the knowing never do.

7. In eating game or poultry do not touch the bones with your fingers. To take a bone in the fingers for the purpose of picking it is looked upon as being very inelegant.

8. Never use your own knife or fork to help another. Use rather the knife or fork of the person you help.

9. Never send your knife and fork, or either of them, on your plate when you send for a second supply.

10. Never turn your elbows out when you use your knife and fork. Keep them close to your sides.

11. Whenever you use your fingers to convey anything to your mouth or to remove anything from the mouth, let it be the fingers of the left hand.

12. Tea, coffee, chocolate and the like are drank from the cup and never from the saucer.

13. In masticating your food, keep your mouth shut; otherwise you will make a noise that will be very offensive to those around you.

14. Don't attempt to talk with a full mouth. One thing at a time is as much as any man can do well.

15. Should you find a worm or insect in your food, say nothing about it.

16. If a dish is distasteful to you, decline it, and without comment.

17. Never put bones or pits of fruit on the table-cloth. Put them on the side of your plate.

18. Do not hesitate to take the last piece on a dish, simply because it is the last. To do so is to directly express the fear that you would exhaust the supply.

19. If you would be what you would like to be—abroad, take care that you are what you would like to be—at home.

20. Avoid picking your teeth at the table if possible; but if you must, do it, if you can, where you are not observed.

21. If an accident of any kind soever should occur during dinner, the cause being who or what it may, you should not seem to note it.

22. Should you be so unfortunate as to overturn or to break anything, you would make no apology. You might let your regret appear in your face, but it would not be proper to put it in words.

Giving a Parlor Recitation.

Social Duties.

Man in Society is like a flow'r,
Blown in its native bed. 'Tis there alone
His faculties expanded in full bloom
Shine out, there only reach their proper use.—COWPER.

The primal duties shine aloft like stars;
The charities that soothe, and heal, and bless,
Are scatter'd at the feet of man like flowers.
—WORDSWORTH.

Social Duties.

1. **Membership in Society.**—Many fail to get hold of the idea that they are members of society. They seem to suppose that the social machinery of the world is self-operating. They cast their first ballot with an emotion of pride, perhaps, but are sure to pay their first tax with a groan. They see political organizations in active existence; the parish, and the church, and other important bodies that embrace in some form of society all men, are successfully operated; and yet these young men have no part or lot in the matter. They do not think of giving a day's time to society.

2. **Begin Early.**—One of the first things a young man should do is to see that he is acting his part in society. The earlier this is begun the better. I think that the opponents of secret societies in colleges have failed to estimate the benefit which it must be to every member to be obliged to contribute to the support of his particular organization, and to assume personal care and responsibility as a member. If these societies have a tendency to teach the lessons of which I speak, they are a blessed thing.

3. **Do Your Part.**—Do your part, and be a man among men. Assume your portion of social responsibility, and see that you discharge it well. If you do not do this, then you are mean, and society has the right to despise you just as much as it chooses to do so. You are, to use a word more emphatic than agreeable, a sneak, and have not a claim upon your neighbors for a single polite word.

4. **A Whining Complainer.**—Society, as it is called, is far more apt to pay its dues to the individual than the individual to society. Have you, young man, who are at home whining over the fact that you cannot get into society, done anything to give you a claim to social recognition? Are you able to make any return for social recognition and social privileges? Do you know anything? What kind of coin do you propose to pay in the discharge of the obligation which comes upon you with social recognition? In other words, as a return for what you wish to have society do for you, what can you do for society? This is a very important question—more important to you than to society. The question is, whether you will be a member of society by right, or by courtesy. If you have so mean a spirit as to be content to be a beneficiary of society—to receive favors and to confer none—you have no business in the society to which you aspire. You are an exacting, conceited fellow.

5. **What Are You Good For?**—Are you a good beau, and are you willing to make yourself useful in waiting on the

ladies on all occasions? Have you a good set of teeth, which you are willing to show whenever the wit of the company gets off a good thing? Are you a true, straightforward, manly fellow, with whose healthful and uncorrupted nature it is good for society to come in contact? In short, do you possess anything of any social value? If you do, and are willing to impart it, society will yield itself to your touch. If you have nothing, then society, as such, owes you nothing. Christian philanthropy may put its arm around you, as a lonely young man, about to spoil for want of something, but it is very sad and humiliating for a young man to be brought to that. There are people who devote themselves to nursing young men, and doing them good. If they invite you to tea, go by all means, and try your hand. If, in the course of the evening, you can prove to them that your society is desirable, you have won a point. Don't be patronized.

6. The Morbid Condition.—Young men, you are apt to get into a morbid state of mind, which declines them to social intercourse. They become devoted to business with such exclusiveness, that all social intercourse is irksome. They go out to tea as if they were going to jail, and drag themselves to a party as to an execution. This disposition is thoroughly morbid, and to be overcome by going where you are invited, always, and with a sacrifice of feeling.

7. The Common Blunder.—Don't shrink from contact with anything but bad morals. Men who affect your unhealthy minds with antipathy, will prove themselves very frequently to be your best friends and most delightful companions. Because a man seems uncongenial to you, who are squeamish and foolish, you have no right to shun him. We become charitable by knowing men. We learn to love those whom we have despised by rubbing against them. Do you not remember some instance of meeting a man or woman whom you had never previously known or cared to know—an individual, perhaps, against whom you have entertained the strongest prejudices—but to whom you became bound by a lifelong friendship through the influence of a three days' intercourse? Yet, if you had not thus met, you would have carried through life the idea that it would be impossible for you to give your fellowship to such an individual.

8. The Foolishness of Man.—God has introduced into human character infinite variety, and for you to say that you do not love and will not associate with a man because he is unlike you, is not only foolish but wrong. You are to remember that in the precise manner and degree in which a man differs from you, do you differ from him; and that from his standpoint you are naturally as repulsive to him, as he, from your standpoint, is to you. So, leave all this talk of congeniality to silly girls and transcendental dreamers.

9. **Do Business in Your Way and Be Honest.**—Do your business in your own way, and concede to every man the privilege which you claim for yourself. The more you mix with men, the less you will be disposed to quarrel, and the more charitable and liberal will you become. The fact that you do not understand a man, is quite as likely to be our fault as his. There are a good many chances in favor of the conclusion that, if you fail to like an individual whose acquaintance you make it is through your own ignorance and illiberality. So I say, meet every man honestly; seek to know him; and you will find that in those points in which he differs from you rests his power to instruct you, enlarge you, and do you good. Keep your heart open for everybody, and be sure that you shall have your reward. You shall find a jewel under the most uncouth exterior; and associated with homeliest manners and oddest ways and ugliest faces, you will find rare virtues, fragrant little humanities, and inspiring heroisms.

10. **Without Society, Without Influence.**—Again: you can have no influence unless you are social. An unsocial man is as devoid of influence as an ice-peak is of verdure. It is through social contact and absolute social value alone that you can accomplish any great social good. It is through the invisible lines which you are able to attach to the minds with which you are brought into association alone that you can tow society, with its deeply freighted interests, to the great haven of your hope.

11. **The Revenge of Society.**—The revenge which society takes upon the man who isolates himself, is as terrible as it is inevitable. The pride which sits alone will have the privilege of sitting alone in its sublime disgust till it drops into the grave. The world sweeps by the man, carelessly, remorselessly, contemptuously. He has no hold upon society, because he is no part of it.

12. **The Conclusion of the Whole Matter.**—You cannot move men until you are one of them. They will not follow you until they have heard your voice, shaken your hand, and fully learned your principles and your sympathies. It makes no difference how much you know, or how much you are capable of doing. You may pile accomplishment upon acquisition mountain high; but if you fail to be a social man, you rob yourself and others of many blessings.

Politeness.

1. Beautiful Behavior.—Politeness has been described as the art of showing, by external signs, the internal regard we have for others. But one may be perfectly polite to another without necessarily paying a special regard for him. Good manners are neither more nor less than beautiful behavior. It has been well said that "a beautiful form is better than a beautiful face, and a beautiful behavior is better than a beautiful form; it gives a higher pleasure than statues or pictures—it is the finest of the fine arts."

2. True Politeness.—The truest politeness comes of sincerity. It must be the outcome of the heart, or it will make no lasting impression; for no amount of polish can dispense with truthfulness. The natural character must be allowed to appear, freed of its angularities and asperities. Though politeness, in its best form, should resemble water—"best when clearest, most simple, and without taste"—yet genius in a man will always cover many defects of manner, and much will be excused to the strong and the original. Without genuineness and individuality, human life would lose much of its interest and variety, as well as its manliness and robustness of character.

3. Personality of Others.—True politeness especially exhibits itself in regard for the personality of others. A man will respect the individuality of another if he wishes to be respected himself. He will have due regard for his views and opinions, even though they differ from his own. The well-mannered man pays a compliment to another, and sometimes even secures his respect by patiently listening to him. He is simply tolerant and forbearant, and refrains from judging harshly; and harsh judgments of others will almost invariably provoke harsh judgments of ourselves.

4. The Impolite.—The impolite, impulsive man will, however, sometimes rather lose his friend than his joke. He may surely be pronounced a very foolish person who secures another's hatred at the price of a moment's gratification. It was a saying of Burnel, the engineer—himself one of the kindest-natured of men—that "spite and ill-nature are among the most expensive luxuries in life." Dr. Johnson once said: "Sir, a man has no more right to say a rude thing to another than to knock him down."

5. Feelings of Others.—Want of respect for the feelings of others usually originates in selfishness, and issues in hardness and repulsiveness of manner. It may not proceed from malignity so much, as from want of sympathy, and want of delicacy—a want of that perception of, and attention to, those little and apparently trifling things, by which pleasure is given or pain occasioned to others. Indeed, it may be said that in self-sacrifice in the ordinary intercourse of life, mainly consists the difference between being well and ill bred. Without some degree of self-restraint in society a man may be found almost insufferable. No one has pleasure in holding intercourse with such a person, and he is a constant source of annoyance to those about him.

6. **Disregard of Others.**—Men may show their disregard to others in various impolite ways, as, for instance, by neglect of propriety in dress, by the absence of cleanliness, or by indulging in repulsive habits. The slovenly, dirty person, by rendering himself physically disagreeable, sets the tastes and feelings of others at defiance, and is rude and uncivil, only under another form.

7. **The Best School of Politeness.**—The first and best school of politeness, as of character, is always the home, where woman is the teacher. The manners of society at large are but the reflex of the manners of our collective homes, neither better nor worse. Yet, with all the disadvantages of ungenial homes, men may practice self-culture of manner as of intellect, and learn by good examples to cultivate a graceful and agreeable behavior towards others. Most men are like so many gems in the rough, which need polishing by contact with other and better natures, to bring out their full beauty and lustre. Some have but one side polished, sufficient only to show the delicate graining of the interior; but to bring out the full qualities of the gem, needs the discipline of experience, and contact with the best examples of character in the intercourse of daily life.

8. **Captiousness of Manner.**—While captiousness of manner, and the habit of disputing and contradicting every thing said, is chilling and repulsive, the opposite habit of assenting to, and sympathizing with, every statement made, or emotion expressed, is almost equally disagreeable. It is unmanly, and is felt to be dishonest. "It may seem difficult," says Richard Sharp, "to steer always between bluntness and plain dealing, between merited praises and lavish or indiscriminate flattery; but it is very easy—good humor, kindheartedness, and perfect simplicity, being all that are requisite to do what is right in the right way." At the same time many are impolite, not because they mean to be so, but because they are awkward, and perhaps know no better.

9. **Shy People.**—Again many persons are thought to be stiff, reserved, and proud, when they are only shy. Shyness is characteristic of most people of the Teutonic race. From all that can be learned of Shakespeare, it is to be inferred that he was an exceedingly shy man. The manner in which his plays were sent into the world—for it is not known that he edited or authorized the publication of a single one of them,—and the dates at which they respectively appeared, are mere matters of conjecture.

10. **Self-Forgetfulness.**—True politeness is best evinced by self-forgetfulness, or self-denial in the interest of others. Mr. Garfield, our martyred president, was a gentleman of royal type. His friend, Col. Rockwell, says of him: "In the midst of his suffering he never forgets others. For instance, to-day he said to me, 'Rockwell, there is a poor soldier's widow who came to me before this thing occurred, and I promised her, she should be provided for. I want you to see that the matter is attended to at once.' He is the most docile patient I ever saw."

11. **It's Bright Side.**—We have thus far spoken of shyness as a defect. But there is another way of looking at it; for even shyness has its bright side, and contains an element of good. Shy men and shy races are ungraceful and undemonstrative, because, as regards society at large, they are comparatively unsociable. They do not possess those elegances of manner acquired by free intercourse, which distinguish the social races, because their tendency is to shun society rather than to seek it. They are shy in the presence of strangers, and shy even in their own families. They hide their affections under a robe of reserve, and when they do give way to their feelings, it is only in some very hidden inner chamber. And yet, the feelings are there, and not the less healthy and genuine, though they are not made the subject of exhibition to others.

12. **Worthy of Cultivation.**—While, therefore, grace of manner, politeness of behavior, elegance of demeanor, and all the arts that contribute to make life pleasant and beautiful, are worthy of cultivation, it must not be at the expense of the more solid and enduring qualities of honesty, sincerity, and truthfulness. The fountain of beauty must be in the heart more than in the eye, and if it does not tend to produce beautiful life and noble practice, it will prove of comparatively little avail. Politeness of manner is not worth much, unless it is accompanied by polite actions.

Forms of Invitations to Dinner.

HOW TO WRITE INVITATIONS.

Invitation to dinner conveys a great mark of respect. It is the highest social compliment that can be offered by one person to another.

Dinner parties rank first among all entertainments, and they are a great source of elevation and education.

An invitation to dine should be promptly answered, whether accepted or declined.

FORM OF INVITATION.

Mr. and Mrs. R. C. Hall request the favor of Mr. Jay's company at dinner on Thursday, the 25th, at 2 o'clock.

THE REPLY.

Mr. Jay has the pleasure to accept Mr. and Mrs. Hall's kind invitation to dinner on Thursday, the 25th.

IF DECLINED,
Some Good Reasons should be Given.

Mr. Jay regrets that, owing to previous engagements, he cannot have the pleasure of accepting Mr. and Mrs. Hall's kind invitation for Thursday next.

INVITATIONS.

INVITATION TO SPEND THE EVENING.

Mrs. E. C. Wicks requests the pleasure of Mr. and Mrs. J. L. Nichols' company on Thursday Evening, June 15th, at six o'clock.

Tea at 6:30.

Meriden, Illinois

ACCEPTANCE.

Mr. and Mrs. J. L. Nichols have much pleasure in accepting Mrs. Wicks' kind invitation for Thursday Evening, June 15th.

Young People's Invitation.

Mr. Brown solicits the honor of attending Miss Williams to the lecture on Thursday evening, March 23d.
Tuesday, March 21st.
The bearer will wait for the answer.

Acceptance.

Miss Williams has much pleasure in accepting Mr. Brown's kind invitation to the lecture Thursday evening, March 23d.
Tuesday, March 21st.

Regret.

Miss Williams regrets that she cannot accept Mr. Brown's polite invitation for the lecture Thursday evening, March 23d.
Tuesday, March 21st.

Regret.

Miss Williams regrets that, owing to the dangerous illness of a dear friend, she is unable to accept Mr. Brown's kind invitation to the lecture Thursday evening, March 23d.
Tuesday, March 21st.

INVITATIONS.

To Meet Visiting Friends.

Mr. and Mrs. John C. Sawyer request the pleasure of Mr. W. N. Tarnutzer's company, on Friday evening, November 19th, from eight to eleven o'clock, to meet Wm. Emerich.

Broad and Walnut Sts., Philadelphia.

EXCURSION.

Mr. Weber would be pleased to have your company on Thursday, Sept. 14th, to visit the park.

Carriages will be in waiting at the Continental Hotel at 4 o'clock P. M.

Continental Hotel.   R. S. V. P.

Mr. Taylor solicits the honor of attending Miss Lyman to the Opera on Thursday evening next.

Tuesday, Nov. 7.

The bearer will wait for the answer.

---

* R. S. V. P. French, "Answer if you please."

If the parties are very intimate friends, the formal and ceremonious style may be dropped and that of a familiar letter adopted, as in the following:

Saturday Morning, May 10.

Dear Carrie,

We are going to Irving's Cliff this afternoon for wild flowers. Will you oblige us by making one of our little party? If so, we will call for you at two o'clock. Do go.

Yours affectionately,
Belle.

Please answer by bearer.

My dear Sir,

If you can come next Sunday, we shall be equally glad to see you, but do not trust to any of Martin's appointments in futures. Leg of lamb as before, at half-past four, and the heart of Lamb for ever.

Yours truly,
C. Lamb.

30th March, 1897.

A MODEL INVITATION.

1. This model is printed in common script type in order to illustrate the best style of engraved billets.
2. These invitations should always be printed in script type and never written except by a skillful penman.
3. Wedding invitations are issued ten days or more before the ceremony.
4. If an answer is expected "The favor of an answer is requested," or the letters R. S. V. P. should be written or printed on the bottom.

Mr. & Mrs. Wm. Radley
request your presence
at the marriage of their daughter

Elizabeth
to
Dr. W. H. Simpson,
on Friday Morning, January sixth,
at ten o'clock.

St. Bartholomew's Church.

Reception
from half-past ten till one,
at 814 Irving Place.

Model 2.—*Ceremony.*

Mrs. Mary H. Collins

requests the pleasure of your company at the marriage ceremony of her daughter

Alice C. Cass

to

Thomas W. Clark,

on Tuesday afternoon, May sixteenth, 1897, at four o'clock.

Waverly Terrace.   Baltimore.

Enclosing a reception card as follows:—

Reception

On Monday, May twenty-second,

day and evening.

Or, "Mr. and Mrs. Henry J Clark at home at a certain time and place.

Model 3.—*Ceremony and Reception.*

CEREMONY,

First Congregational Church, Earlville Ills., on Tuesday, May sixteenth, at ten o'clock.

❀ AT HOME, ❀

Tuesdays and Fridays in June, at the residence of Dr. Charles C. Porter, Seymour Avenue.

LEROY MATHER.   ANNA J. WILLIAMS.

318   *How to Amuse Little Children.*

Teach your children to play with a design or purpose.
Have them always make or construct something.

urpose.
hing.

HOW TO AMUSE
LITTLE CHILDREN.

A busy child is always happy, and whoever possesses the faculty to keep a child busy has a great advantage in a household.

We will enumerate some very simple methods for amusing small children: A block of wood, a saucerful of tacks, and a small tack hammer will give a child more amusement than almost anything that can be devised. It may make a little noise in the house, but it will amuse the child for a long time every day. A pair of blunt pointed scissors, with plenty of newspaper pictures, or other pictures, to cut out, will give amusement of which children rarely ever tire. A cheap box of paints for coloring the pictures is an excellent diversion and a good practice.

Little ones find great pleasure in stringing buttons, and they can soon learn to make ornamental work by sewing them on cloth in simple designs.

Little girls are always delighted with a doll, but many parents make mistakes by not teaching them to dress and undress the dolls, and make jackets, dresses, etc., for them. For little children a heap of clean sand will afford an unending source of amusement. Children will dig it over and over again, mold it in all sorts of shapes and forms, and seemingly never tire of it. The older children will extract pleasure from it also.

Empty spools, both large and small, can be utilized to form many a little toy carriage, engine, and the like. A nice set of blocks, home made or purchased, affords one of the best amusements for children. In order to give the best results there should be from twenty-five to fifty blocks; different forms are preferable.

The simplest toys will generally afford as much amusement as expensive ones, and in the homes where money can purchase every conceivable luxury there is probably no more happiness among the children than in the humblest homes of the poor, if the parents will but utilize what facilities they have in preparing playthings for their children.

RING GAMES AND FROLICS FOR CHILDREN'S PARTIES.

The mother or hostess who has kept herself in touch with the play life of her child, and has assisted it rightly, need not fear to undertake the direction of such plays and games as are suited to make a child's birthday party a happy and long-remembered holiday.

The simple games are always best—the games you and your children have played over and over again. Old games, like "Blind Man's Buff," "Puss-in-the-Corner," "London Bridge," and their like, never seem to lose their interest. Any game which, like "Thumbs Up," has been played by children since the days of Nero must, indeed, be worth playing today. Then, again, kindergarten literature is full of new and delightful suggestions for play and songs, so that mothers have no end of resources for entertaining their own children and their child friends.

Game of Flowers.—Children never tire of ring games. They like the simple ones best—those that do not tax the memory to any great extent. They prefer something with a catching swing in the rhythm, carrying the same words through many verses, with just enough verbal change to indicate the progress of the game.

The game of flowers is simple and sweet. It is played similar to "London Bridge." Two children stand opposite to each other and raise their joined hands. Those forming the ring pass under, while all keep saying or singing, suiting the action to the words they sing:

"We're looking about for a daffodil,
 A daffodil, a daffodil.
We're looking about for a daffodil,
 We've found one here."

At the word "here" the raised arms come down and inclose the head of the child who happens at that moment to be passing underneath their hands. Then all sing:

"We find one here; we find one here;
 We're looking about for a daffodil,
 And find one here."

"Daffodil" now takes the place of one of the children who caught him or her, then calls out "Buttercup." The children all understand that buttercup, instead of daffodil, is the word, so they make the lines:

"We're looking about for a buttercup,
 A buttercup, a buttercup," etc.

The leader may hold a bouquet and give to each child the flower chosen.

The next child, "Buttercup," being duly "found," takes the place of "Daffodil," and the child who has held that place goes into the ring. The newcomer calls out the name of some flower, like bright blue-bell, daisy flower or mignonette, and substituting the word, they sing as before. Each child tries to be ready with the name of some favorite flower, and the game may close when each child flower has been "found."

Fox.—A game in which the children can run is always a favorite. "Fox" is another ring play, so easy that the smaller children can play it without help. One of the children "fox" stays outside the ring and slyly slaps the shoulder of one of the children. "Fox" runs to the left, the child to the right. They meet, pass each other going at full speed around the ring. The one who gets back to the "den" (the place in the ring where the child was standing) may hold that place, and the other must be the fox and try a race with some other child.

"Jingle Bells" is another frolic which pleases little ones. Let mamma or the hostess harness up the children for a "team." They have a string of small bells around their necks, and a cambric or tarletan rope is used for the "tackle"—the children taking hold of it by twos, except the last in line, who acts as "driver." The pianist plays the well-known college glee, "Jingle bells, jingle bells, jingle all the way," and the children trot away at a merry pace. The leaders hurry on, making devious turns to right and left, supposably through snowdrifts and over high hills and down in deep valleys. The children sing the chorus, and the trip proves so delightful that they are never ready to stop until a very long journey has been made.

The above games may all be successfully played by a large party of children.

Whatever new plays the children may learn they dearly love the old, old games:

"Buffy" and "Puss" and the "Needle's eye,"
"Tag" and "Thimble" and "Halt! I spy,"
"Ring-round-a-rosy," and "Making a cheese,"
"Bean-porridge-hot" and "Slave, on your knees!"
"Man on your castle," "Stage-coach" and "Gool,"
Noon-hour games at the old village school.

Fun with Peanuts.—A peanut hunt is lots of fun for an

evening party. The hostess hides peanuts in all sorts of queer places about the room, sometimes putting two or three nuts in the same place. Then she provides each of her guests with a little basket tied with gay ribbons, and then the "hunt" begins. Sometimes a march is played, and the hunters must keep step to the music, stopping when it stops, and starting again when it starts. After a certain time the finds are compared. The one who has the largest number wins the first prize, while the "booby" prize is fittingly awarded to the one having the fewest.

Some other trials that are great sport are often introduced. One is to see who can carry the most peanuts in one hand from one table to another. A boy ought to win this. Forty-two is a good number.

Children's March.—By all means let the guests be punctual, so that all the children may be ready to join in the opening march. Let a good pianist lead off with familiar airs, and, if the hostess will remember to provide a rope made out of strips of cambric or tarletan lightly twisted, the children may all grasp it with the right hand; then walking, say two feet apart, and keeping the rope mildly taut, they have but to follow their leader or the one just in front, and a march with many turnings will not confuse the little ones in the least. A very simple and pretty march for young children is formed as follows: Let the children march in a circle six times around the room; then diagonally across the room by four ways, the path along each side of the room joining the four diagonals; then in serpentine paths from north to south six times across, again from east to west the same. March by narrowing circles to the center of the room; then, passing to the left, retrace directly the same path until all are led to form again a full circle about the outer edge of the room. By turning to right and left the children may march to form scallops reaching around the entire room. The march closes with a general hand-clapping accompaniment to a lively tune, the rope being dropped upon the floor.

The hostess who entertains a large number of little people needs the help of a half dozen grown-up girls to start the march and games and assist the smaller children to join in them. They are also needed during the refreshment hour.

As a rule invited children should not proffer birthday

gifts, unless their families happen to be relatives or particularly intimate friends; the privilege of gift-making belongs to home friends.

A QUOTATION HUNT.

This game is best described by one who was present and enjoyed its pleasures.

Upon entering, by invitation, a friend's parlor one evening last June, I was puzzled by the sight of the numerous little slips of paper that seemed to be everywhere—pinned to curtain, chair, mantel lambrequin and cushions, over table and piano cover, on p'cture-frames and on bric-a-brac the little slips found lodgment. Presently the guests arrived, and our hostess informed us that on each slip was written one-quarter of a familiar quotation. We might pick up any slip we wished and proceed to find the rest of the quotation of which it formed a part. We were allowed to ask for parts of quotations, the one asked being obliged to hand over the slip asked for if he or she happened to have it. At a given signal we started and a lively time ensued, the object being to see who could match the greatest number of quotations. I first picked up a slip on which I read, "to see oursels," I found "Oh! wad sae power" in the hands of one of the company. "The giftie gie us" had taken refuge in the corner of a white picture-frame, and "as ithers see us" was nestled comfortably in a fold of a portiere.

The prizes were appropriate, but inexpensive, the most elaborate one being a dainty booklet for the most successful searcher, while the member of the company who had been least successful received a pair of steel-rimmed spectacles, to which was attached a note expressing the hope that they would aid in future searches.

DISTINGUISHED GUESTS.

Not long since I accepted an invitation to spend the evening at a neighbor's. At eight o'clock we found ourselves in the pleasant parlor of our hostess. In the course of an hour other guests came until we numbered fifteen.

The two young ladies, our hostesses, stated that a number of distinguished guests had been invited, but being unable to come had sent their cards to represent them. The younger sister then passed a tray of cards, on which were the names of friends who could not be with us. Each one present had the privilege of drawing a card, but was not allowed to look at the name on it. The elder sister stood, paper of pins in hand, ready to fasten the card on the back of the lady who had drawn it. Thus each of us carried about, not on our faces, but on our backs, the characters we were to personate, nor could we find out, except by discreet questioning, whom we were representing.

The remark that some of us were dead, some living, some real and some fictitious, set our brains in a whirl. One lady, queenly in her bearing, who was labeled "Queen Victoria," in due time discovered her identity. The Duke of York, Gladstone, Lord Tennyson and his "Maud" were present. One lady, to her own satisfaction, turned out to be Susan B. Anthony. Even the Infanta and her Duke were with us, and also Mr. and Mrs. Potter Palmer and Miss America. Peggotty and Barkis had great difficulty in finding out who they were, and though both were "willin'" could not guess their identity. Adam himself was there and his dear Eve, whom he found after many trials.

It can be easily imagined what funny blunders were made until we learned what names we bore, and that there was no possible chance for stiffness among the guests can be readily surmised.

Refreshments were served in another room, where the English ladies and gentlemen sat at one small table, the Infanta and Duke of Veragua at another, Adam and Eve at a third. Sweet peas were scattered loosely over each table. Ice cream and cake were served and later coffee. Nothing could have been simpler nor more expressive of genuine hospitality than this charming and unique entertainment of distinguished people.

CROSS QUESTIONS AND CROOKED ANSWERS.

The company sit around, and each one whispers a question to his neighbor at the right, and then each one whispers an answer; so that each answers the question propounded by some other player, and of the purport of which he is, of course, ignorant. Then every player has to recite the question he received from one player and the answer he got from the other, and the ridiculous incongruity of these random cross questions and crooked answers will frequently excite a good deal of sport. One, for instance, may say, "I was asked 'Are you going tomorrow,'" and the answer is, "It is in the cupboard." Another may declare, "What had you for dinner?" and the answer is, "Sleeve and cuff buttons." A third, "I was asked, 'Did you see the carriage pass?'" and the answer is, "He came yesterday!"

TO PLACE WATER IN A DRINKING GLASS UPSIDE DOWN.

Procure a plate, a tumbler, and a small piece of tissue or silver paper. Set the plate on a table, and pour water into it up to the first rim. Now very slightly crumple up the paper, and place it in the glass; then set it on fire. When it is burned out, or rather just as the last flame disappears, turn the glass quickly upside down into the water. Astonishing! the water rushes with great violence into the glass! Now you are satisfied that water can be placed in a drinking glass upside down. Hold the glass firm, and the plate also. You can now reverse the position of the plate and glass, and thus convince the most skeptical of the truth of your pneumatic experiment Instead of burning paper a little brandy or spirits of wine can be ignited in the glass; the result of its combustion being invisible, the experiment is cleaner.

GUESSING.

Guessing is a game that whiles away many an hour pleasantly, as the children gather around the kitchen fire while the evening work is being done. One of the party thinks of an object and gives the first letter of its name. For instance, one thinks of a ship and says, "I have thought of something and it begins with S." The rest then question him and he must answer as best he can unless the question comes too close and he declares it would be "telling." They may ask: What color is it? Is it something made, or does it grow? Has it legs? Does it move about, or is it stationary? Is it vegetable, animal or mineral? Have we one? Of course some will be easily guessed and others will tax the ingenuity of the best guessers. In a compound word the first letter of each word should be given.

Mothers with the little ones trooping around them can make the evening exceedingly pleasant and something to look back upon with pleasure in after years.

BOOK III.

THERE IS NO PLACE LIKE HOME.
(FEATHER YOUR NEST WELL.)

THE HOUSEKEEPER.
HOME ADORNMENTS.
THE BEDROOM.
THE DINING-ROOM.
THE KITCHEN AND KITCHEN UTENSILS.
FAMILY RECEIPTS.

THE HOUSEKEEPER.

A woman who is at the head of a household has vast power and responsibility placed in her hands. It rests with her to make the home a place where there shall be gained rest and strength for the battle of life; a place inexpressibly dear to each member of the family, where all shall feel that there is perfect freedom, yet where there is also perfect order. Some are born housekeepers, while others must work hard to train themselves for their many duties. But it matters not whether one be a trained or a natural housekeeper; if the work be done well and lovingly, the spirit of the head of the house pervades every part. One cannot always define it, but one certainly feels it. Love, sympathy and charity must be there, else the best appointed household will fail to be a home for its members. The housekeeper must be patient, unselfish and industrious.

Reward.—Her reward will be the consciousness that her duty has been well done, and the possession of the love and respect of her family and friends. To my mind there is no position in the world of higher importance, or in which a woman can do more good.

Exacting.—The occupation of a housekeeper is most exacting. In nothing else does there seem to be the necessity for such varied knowledge. Even under the most favorable circumstances the position is at times exceedingly trying. What must it be, then, when undertaken without the least preparation? The perplexity, disappointment and mortification through which the inexperienced housekeeper passes are both disheartening and demoralizing.

Method.—One of the secrets of the ample leisure many housekeepers have is the system of methods adopted. A day for everything and everything on its day. Monday—Wash day will leave time to clean the bath room, stairs and laundry. Tuesday—After ironing is finished the linen closet can be cleaned and the clothes folded and replaced. Wednesday—For cleaning silverware and putting the china closet in order, repapering pantry shelves and with the midweek change of table linen, the dining room might receive special attention. Thursday—Sweeping bed-rooms, and while this is being done it is a good plan to air all the bedding thoroughly; this adds greatly to the freshness of the nicely swept and well dusted sleeping apartments. Friday—Sweep the parlors, reception and sitting rooms, have the rugs well cleaned and windows and mirrors polished. Saturday—Bed linen and table linen changed, towels and soiled clothing gathered, baking done and special preparation made for the day of rest. This will afford the satisfaction of having conducted a well ordered system and will leave some time each day for reading, sewing, visiting and resting.

A MODEL HOUSEWIFE.

In the first place she is the most thoroughly cheerful and happy-looking woman you will meet in a day's travel; and although she is thirty-five years old she does not look thirty. This is because she never allows the petty cares of housekeeping to worry and plow lines across her face. She does one thing at a time, never making the error of undertaking a dozen duties at once.

Good Judgment.—The model housewife keeps a scrupulously neat home, but in no room is comfort sacrificed for the sake of appearance. She has neither too much furniture nor bric-a-brac. She dresses her children neatly but plainly.

Agreeable and Systematic.—This very sensible woman is a loving wife and agreeable companion to her husband. She knows how to save time and thus finds opportunity to read, and is able to discuss topics of interest with her husband in the evening by the fireside. She is a gentle mother to her little ones, and when she says "no" she keeps her word. She is never impatient with the baby when he is sleepy and clings to her skirts. Instead of spanking him, she takes the tired little form to her arms and rocks it to sleep.

Taste and Sympathy.—Her husband is not very wealthy and she does not strain the last nerve to dress as well as her more wealthy neighbors, but her taste is so correct that these same neighbors envy her stylish appearance. She is also a neighbor and does not gossip. If there is sickness she is willing to aid the suffering, and she does not forget the old and poor in the neighborhood.

HOW TO MANAGE TO BE HAPPY.

During the early years of married life many are often very unhappy, and the cares of housekeeping seem a burden greater than they can bear.

Simplification is the first step toward happiness. In furnishing a house try not to have anything too good to use. If you can afford to keep but one servant, dispense with elaborate draperies, brass and bric-a-brac, the care of which means too much work for one pair of hands. Do not crowd your rooms with useless little tables and delicately-covered furniture, but rely upon sunshine, easy chairs, an open fire and a few good pictures to make home charming.

Individuality.—One mistake is common to young homemakers. Through imitation they make all manner of domestic misfits. When calling on a friend they mentally compare her household plenishings with their own, and wonder how they can create, from limited resources, the things of beauty by which they are surrounded.

They do not like to invite to their plain house the friend who has married a merchant prince, because they fear she would miss the luxuries of her costly environment. They have no Persian rugs, no Satsuma teacups, no Oriental hangings to show her, and the fact both distresses and mortifies them.

They try, therefore, with a limited income, to follow in her footsteps. They exchange the cozy house, on the unfashionable street, for what the agent called a "desirably-located flat."

They give up the happiness and comfort of their families for door-openers and electric bells. The fretfulness of the children, who suffered from the substitution of modern conveniences for fresh air and sunshine, the complaints of the maid who could hardly turn around in the tiny kitchen, and the effort to live beyond means, make them irritable and unhappy. At last they agree with the clever woman who declared that there was such a thing as sacrificing good living to bad frescoes.

There is a homely saying to this effect: "Cut your coat according to your cloth." An experienced housekeeper says:

That is what I now try to do. I copy no one, but keep house with reference to *my* income, and the needs of *my* husband, *my* children. The wonderful methods which others pursue, and the achievements of my neighbors no longer make me envious, or arouse emulation. In acting well my part, I find satisfaction and success. It used to try me greatly to have the shades of my mother-in-law, and the aunts evoked, who in their day were notable housewives. I failed utterly until I gave up trying to adapt the ways and means of the past to the necessities of the present. You cannot successfully conduct a modern by applying to it the methods of the past generation. This I ascertained distinctly and fully.

Training Children.—I train my children to helpfulness, and teach the boys, as well as the girls, to sweep, dust, mend and care for their clothing. There is nothing unmanly in a boy learning to do those things which will make him comfortable and independent when away from home.

It is surprising how greatly my labors are lightened by their assistance, and how much more unselfish and considerate the children are growing under the discipline.

Slave of Circumstances.—It used to trouble me very much if anything interfered with the routine of the household. I worshiped days and seasons, and was determined that no meal in my house should be a movable feast. As a consequence, I became the unhappy slave of my own laws.

Method a Servant.—Now, method is my servant, not my master. I try to curb an abnormal appetite for dirt, and overcome the domestic sin of excessive cleanliness. My home may not be so immaculate in each minute and unseen part, but it is a pleasanter place to live in.

Books and Music.—In all my economy of time and money, I leave a margin for the higher life. I buy and read the best books, and hear good music. Every day I make a point of going to my room, lying down and resting mind and body. This brief withdrawal from the thick of the family life keeps me fresh for the evening, when my husband and children naturally expect to find me, in some degree, companionable. I make it my point to save something for myself for those who make my home as well as for the things which make it.

Persistent Cheerfulness.—The crowning grace of the home, in my opinion, is persistent cheerfulness, and I try to see the funny side of every annoyance. My children are often ill, but I discourage anxious inquiries after the health of the members of the family, believing that it is possible to talk yourself and others into any number of diseases.

The breakfast table is not a bulletin board for the curing of horrible dreams and depressing symptoms, but the place where a bright key-note for the day is struck. The supper table is not made a battle-field, but a pleasing panorama of what has occurred during the day in the outer world.

Forgetting the Disagreeable.—I make a habit of forgetting disagreeable things as quickly as possible. One great factor in this result is never talking about them. I keep the genie in the bottle, for the grievances that are aired grow with every airing. In dealing with Bridget's faults it does not yield me any moral support to dwell on the atrocious acts of her predecessor.

Leaving the past to bury its dead I live simply in the present, trying to take no anxious thoughts for the morrow, thereby exhausting in advance my nervous force. So,

> "I build a fence of loving trust
> About today;
> I fill it full of happy work,
> And therein stay."

These Three.—Simplification, individuality and persistent cheerfulness make it possible for a woman to keep gray hairs and wrinkles at bay, and she can manage to be happy, though a busy housewife.

GOOD RULES FOR THE MISTRESS.

1. When engaging a servant be careful to explain her work to her, and let her understand that the work must be done in your way and not in the way of any former mistress she may have had, and this explanation must be made so that it shall not reflect upon the routine of any other household.

2. Try to arrange the housework so that each servant may have an opportunity to attend church on Sunday.

3. When your servants do well encourage them to do better by a few words of praise.

4. Do not allow them to have visitors until after certain hours in the evening.

5. Give your orders for the day to the cook as early in the morning as possible.

6. Insist upon being informed when anything is broken or lost.

7. See that the chambermaid is wearing a clean apron while making the beds, and that she knocks at the bedroom doors before entering.

8. Order the maid who opens the door, not to leave visitors standing in the hall, nor to give parcels to strangers without previous instruction.

9. When you reprove, do so firmly and decidedly.

10. Only allow your rules to be broken once; let dismissal, with customary notice, follow the second offense.

11. Retain your temper under all circumstances.
12. Insist upon the punctuality of the family as well as upon the punctuality of the cook.
13. Be kind to your servants when they are ill, and thoughtful of them always; in nine cases out of ten the considerate mistress will be rewarded by faithful service.
14. Pay your servants' wages regularly. Do not allow them to go out without first obtaining your permission.

GOOD RULES FOR THE SERVANT.

1. Be punctual. Keep your brooms, brushes, dusters, pots, kettles and pans clean and sweet. Obey your mistress in every particular; go to her when you are in doubt. If your fellow servants shirk their duties, and their doing so affects your work, take the first opportunity you have of explaining this to your mistress, being careful not to exaggerate.
2. Do not do rough work while wearing a white apron. Have large gingham aprons for such purposes, and keep your white one hanging where it can be easily gotten at.
3. Never give away anything that belongs to your mistress without first obtaining her permission.
4. If you wish to invite a friend to eat with you, first obtain permission.
5. During the day, when opportunity offers, devote a little time to the care of your bedroom; see that it is kept well aired.
6. Do not take hold of the pots and pans with your apron; it is a dirty and dangerous habit.
7. If you break anything tell your mistress at once.
8. Let your working dresses be made of material that will wash.
9. Retire early; rise early.
10. Be truthful.
11. If you have a lover, confide in your mistress and obtain her permission to have him spend his evenings with you; do not meet him on the street, or try to "smuggle" him into the kitchen.
12. Be careful of all that is intrusted to you while in service; when the day comes for you to leave it for a home of your own, you will find any lessons of economy and neatness that you may have learned very valuable, and any good habit that you may have formed very helpful.

THE SERVANT QUESTION.

The vexed question of "domestic service" is a serious one, and like its companion problem, the "labor question," its solution can hardly be satisfactorily accomplished in this country, where our servants and our "lower classes" are made up of aliens, many of whom are untrained and unfitted for the positions which they undertake to fill.

American-Born Women instinctively object to domestic service as a means of livelihood. They are usually fairly well educated, as our excellent public school system gives opportunities to all. The American girl would do anything rather than domestic service; she considers it menial and beneath her, and so, when she starts out for herself in the world, she undertakes type-writing, or telegraphy, or clerking in an office, or she becomes an amanuensis or a factory hand, or does everything else rather than the work for which she is thoroughly well equipped both by experience and inheritance. It is a very rare thing to find an American girl in service; and when she is discovered, what a joy she is to the finder, for we are sure we have in our house honesty, energy, and often great capability.

Foreigners.—It would seem that no honest work faithfully performed could be beneath any one, and the domestic servant in America has many privileges which a clerk or a factory girl cannot enjoy. However, this is not a popular opinion, and so our domestics are mostly foreigners, who come to this country only to make money, who look upon us merely as a means to that end, and the sooner that end is accomplished the better for both of us.

Practical Knowledge.—If in the elaborate scheme of a daughter's education a little time were given to a practical knowledge of household affairs, it would be found of inestimable service all through her life. Possibly the fault of which we complain does not lie so much with the servant as it does with the mistress. How can we expect our maids to know more than we know ourselves? They are very much like children, and they soon discover our ignorance, and impose upon us. Try to teach a child anything, and see how utterly impossible it is unless you yourself know thoroughly the subject you are trying to impart.

Lack of System.—Another great trouble with the average young housekeeper is lack of system. Her education is doubtless at fault in this, and she has never learnt business principles. But one's house must be run with method if one wishes to run it satisfactorily. Inexperienced women make demands which are often quite impossible to be complied with, not realizing what work their domestics are doing at the moment, which must be neglected if their request is regarded.

Who is Responsible?—There are nearly three million women working for their living in this country, and of this three million a full third are in domestic service. And, oh, sorrow and shame to the housekeeper! the ranks of the fallen, whom the charitable women go down into the slums to reform, receive, according to statistics, more than half their recruits from domestic servants. Why leave your home to go and rescue these after they have sinned? Why not make sure first that all those who serve you are guarded by the strong aegis of your protection from this sorrowful fate; are being led upward by your example; are receiving your full sympathy and care? Surely it is more important to prevent the fall than to rescue the penitent after it. Does it not behoove you to examine yourself, your life, your influence, with the most searching care, to divine what it is that makes the service of ladies peculiarly demoralizing to those who serve them?—such a terrible thought!

The Mistress.—It is evident that the solution of the problem is largely in the hands of the mistress of the house. The servant is capable of feelings, sensibilities, ambitions and hopes as well as the mistress. Let the attitude of the mistress of the home change and the whole question will necessarily change.

A Friendly Interest can always safely be shown to those who serve us. While familiarity of intercourse is demoralizing, it is as truly work as well worth doing as any done in the slums to show sympathy in trouble, help and kindness in sickness, and interest in their interests about their own family and friends. There at once springs up a different spirit in those who serve us when they learn that we are really interested in their welfare.

The Servant's Room.—It pays to make the servant's room as cozy and home-like as possible. A very little money and pains make all the difference between a dull, uninviting den and a dainty, pleasant chamber—curtains and carpets past their wear in the lower rooms, or if newly furnishing, why, cheap drugget and a bit of cheap muslin, make them homelike. A few cheap pictures, perhaps a shelf for a bright, innocent novel or two and last month's magazines. We know from our experience how much we value our own special corner, which is ours alone.

"Like Mistress; Like Maid" is an old, but true, saying pains to teach the easiest and most skillful means of ac- the age, but frequently may be found nearer home. Taking pains to teach the easiest and most skillful means of accomplishing necessary work. Helping each to make his work an art rather than a drudgery. Not afraid of quiet blame, but not sparing either of due thanks and praise for service well done. It is not well to say, Why should I thank her? she is paid to do this. No money can purchase or pay for that cheerful, proud, affectionate help, that loyal devotion to the household interests, which some wise housewives receive by means of friendly gratitude and recognition. Such a mistress and such servants are banded together to produce and preserve that nearest likeness on earth to the dreams of heaven—a home.

HOME ADORNMENTS.

There are in the United States 11,483,318 dwellings in which 12,690,152 families live. Imagine, if you please, the variety of scenes from the stately mansion of the rich to the hovel of those in abject poverty. We Americans too often think that wealth is all that is needed to produce a home. This is a great mistake. There are many model homes found where great self denial is necessary to "make ends meet" and there are many families of wealth in which the true spirit of the home is not found.

A True Home.—A furnished house is not always a home. Carpets and furniture may be of the latest styles and costly and yet the home may be anything but "home-like."

Individuality.—It is only when a house has been occupied long enough to have an individuality imparted to it by its occupants when a vast number of little articles suggested by the daily wants of the family have been made that the rooms have the aspect of home. Many of the articles cannot be bought nor are they expensive, but the wide-awake housekeeper will ever be on the alert and will supply these little conveniences that make the home attractive to its occupants.

Home Decorations.—The so-called esthetic craze and decorative fads are no longer looked upon as objectionable features, but are recognized necessities of the home life. The unadorned home is now the exception; and while at one time the American housewife was criticised because of over-decoration, it is noticeable that even the average home is showing how rapidly the masses are being educated to appreciate the truly artistic in home adornment. Nor does a slender purse debar one from possessing many decorative trifles. We cannot all possess Sevres and Royal Worcester, and costly paintings may be beyond us; still, there is no excuse for filling our rooms with inartistic crockery and "chromatic chromos" until they look like a "teastore arranged by an earthquake." The main thing is to buy with taste and discretion, and to ornament and arrange according to our best artistic lights.

Well-Chosen Bric-a-Brac.—Nothing can equal a few well-chosen bits of bric-a-brac in giving character to a room. Needle-work must have its place, but it is not alone sufficient for adornment; besides, we do not all possess either time or skill for this sort of decoration.

There is much satisfaction in possessing a few bits of real china, or a slender vase of undoubted Venetian glass; but if our purses are shallow, we can satisfy our artistic longings in some very pretty imitations. Doubtless we should draw John Ruskin's thunders on our devoted heads by expressing any delight in make-believes, but often enough there is little difference, save in the price.

Newly Married People.—As a rule, newly-married people have a good many trifles in ornamental china, in the way of wedding presents, either artistic or the reverse, as the donor's taste may incline. So the only thing the possessors have to decide upon is the question of arrangement. In a well-filled modern house there is usually a cabinet or over-mantel above the fireplace, especially in a well-appointed dining-room, and this is the best position for showing off china. If an over-mantel cabinet is beyond one's reach, the next best thing is a drapery falling from a curtain pole at the back of the mantel; a continuation of this forms the mantel scarf. This is especially desirable when the wall is light-colored. A dark felt or plush curtain of harmonious shade forms such an admirable background. Of course, this is intended chiefly for throwing into relief the china on the mantel, though it has a decorative effect on the whole room.

Wall Decorations.—We can obtain very good effects with china plates or placques as wall decoration in any nook or corner where they may be comparatively isolated. They lose something of their effect when mingled with a lot of pictures. A very striking over-mantel decoration may be made where the chimney piece projects from the wall by putting a curtain rod up against the ceiling and dropping a curtain from this to the mantel. On this curtain drapery arrange china plates that are handsomely decorated, fastened, of course, by invisible placque hangers. The curtain may be felt, plush or any of the artistic draperies in vogue; it need not necessarily be expensive, for the best effects, appropriateness and artistic blending with the wall coloring is of first importance.

Another form of the same idea is to have a beveled mirror the width of the mantel, and about two feet high, put at the back to reflect the mantel ornaments, with the curtain descending from the ceiling to the mirror. The mantel drapery should match the curtain.

Furniture.—With the walls, ceilings, floors and windows of our house beautiful properly treated, it would indeed seem an easy task to supply just the right kind and amount of furniture—if only the purse were well filled. Not so. No amount of money can produce a beautiful, satisfactory and elevating home unless a clear and cultivated mind directs its expenditures.

Arrangement.—The style and air most conducive to the beauty and comfort of a room is in no small degree dependent upon the arrangement of its furniture. Any number of suggestions, but few explicit directions, for producing the desired results can be given; for while certain rules must be adhered to, success is far less dependent upon technical knowledge than upon the artistic sense and cleverness of the woman who produces them.

Simplicity.—That "simplicity is three-fourths of beauty" is never more apparent than in furniture. Indeed, simplicity of design is the essence of good furniture. More than this, while furniture good in design, material and workmanship is seldom low-priced, it is always beautiful and durable, and it is unquestionably wiser, even for those who must economize closely, to have rooms scantily supplied with furniture that is really good than filled with the "regulation" number of half-made, showy pieces. Expensiveness is not an essential factor in achieving artistic results. With taste, judgment, a well-defined plan, patience and time you are sure to attain success.

Folly of Fashion.—Fashion is responsible for any amount of bad furniture. For the wealthy it is Marie Antoinette and other period furniture, or Turkish, Japanese and other ornate eastern styles, none of which are adapted to our habits and surroundings.

Size and Uses of Room.—The size and uses of a room must determine the kind and amount of furniture to be put into it. Furniture should be beautiful in itself, and beautiful as considered in connection with everything else in the room. A piece of furniture good in design, material and workmanship is always beautiful when appropriately used. Let use be the first consideration. Make no purchases hastily. Have a definite idea of what is both suitable and good; of the needs of the room and the sum you can afford to expend. Prefer hard wood and good workmanship every time to cheap decorations. If you must economize closely, let fashion be neither the first, second nor third consideration.

The Mistress.—The individuality of the mistress should be plainly manifest in her parlor. Give little attention to parlors in general, and none to the opinion of Mrs. Grundy. After arranging the larger pieces of furniture in the most favorable positions, place the chairs at whatever angle best conforms to the remaining space and tends to heighten the general effect. If in doubt as to how this should be done, study the arrangement of the chairs the next time they are vacated by some of your "dear congenial friends," and see if you cannot catch the air of ease and sociability they carry.

Avoid Regularity.—Avoid apparent regularity. Don't think because you place a sofa across one corner of a room that you must treat any or all the other corners similarly. While a scheme of arrangement is essential, care must be taken to conceal it. Large pieces of furniture are not appropriate for small rooms; nor is any piece seen at its best unless there is room for its individuality to assert itself. In a library that is only used as a reading and writing room, and in a dining-room, the table is properly placed in the center of the floor, but not in any other apartment. A dining-room side-table should be placed in a corner conveniently near the pantry door. Table for card-receiver in main hall should stand conveniently near the front door or the entrance to the parlor. If the hall is used merely as an entrance, stand the chair or chairs against the wall. If used as a waiting or reception room, treat in a less formal manner.

Sitting-Room.—In the sitting or living room the comfort and convenience of the family must decide the arrangement of furniture.

Bedroom.—In the ordinary bedroom, windows are the only means of ventilation, and the location of these should go far to determine the most desirable place for the bedstead. Placing the head of a bedstead against the wall causes little discomfort to the occupants, but there should be a free circulation of air on all the other sides. Put the wash stand in the most inconspicuous corner, and conceal with a large screen, if the room is large enough to do so without making a nuisance of the latter.

Kitchen Furniture.—Kitchen, pantry and laundry furniture should be arranged in the way that best conduces to the convenience and comfort of those who labor in them.

To save time and strength is to be wise as well as economical.

Fancy Articles.—A great many think that economy cannot be used in making fancy articles. Many pretty things, both useful and ornamental, may be made at very little expense. Art in every form, and particularly in house decoration, is seemingly carrying everything before it. Dried grasses, leaves, and berries are much used in decorating fancy baskets.

Pot-pourri of Roses.—Gather the rose petals in the early morning, and place them in a cool, shady place for an hour to dry. Toss them lightly, and then put them in layers, with salt sprinkled freely between, in a large covered glass dish. You may add fresh petals to this every morning. When you have a sufficient quantity, let the whole stand ten days, shaking thoroughly every morning. Now, in the bottom of a glass fruit jar place two ounces of whole allspice, crushed, and two ounces of stick cinnamon, broken coarsely. Fill the jar with the rose petals and salt. This must now stand six weeks, or even longer, when it may be prepared for the permanent jar. During these six weeks the jar should be perfectly air tight.

Mix together one ounce each of ground cloves, allspice, cinnamon and mace; one ounce of orris root, shredded and bruised; two ounces of lavender flowers. These are the proportions to be used to one quart of the rose petals. Place this mixture in alternate layers with the contents of the glass fruit jar, in the more ornamental jar that is to be used permanently. If you choose you may add a few drops of the oil of your favorite flower, rose, geranium or violet, and pour over the whole one-quarter of a pint of good cologne. This pot-pourri will last for years. From time to time you may add a little lavender water or any nice perfume. The fragrant odor from a rose jar filled with leaves and fragrant spices is very penetrating, and is particularly pleasant in large drawing rooms and halls. The odor is not only refreshing but delightful as well. A rose jar filled with a good stock should never be allowed to remain constantly open; if the covers are removed for an hour at a time twice a day, your rooms will become permeated with a sweet, reviving odor, that will be a delight to all who enter your home.

Now, one word. When you select your rose jar, the best are those with double covers without perforations in either cover. You will find them with a single cover; with a double cover, the inner one perforated, and with a double cover, the outer one perforated; and the best of all is the one which I have mentioned. In conclusion, let me say, if you own a rose bush, by all means have a rose jar. It is not only a delightful thing to prepare, but once prepared, you will find it

"A thing of beauty, and a joy forever."

A Rustic Flower Stand.—A neat stand can be made by taking a crotched stick having three branches as shown in the accompanying figure. The branches should come from the main trunk at about the same point, and be equally distant from one another at their lower ends. Such a stick can easily be found in the forest, and with a little labor an ornamental and serviceable flower stand can be had without any outlay of money.

Sewing Box.—This is a simple and very useful and convenient addition to the utensils of the busy housewife. It can be made at home by any one with very little skill at carpenter work. Make a box out of common pine lumber 24 inches in length by 16 inches wide and 16 inches high. Make the arms as shown in the picture 27 inches high. The cover is put on hinges and straps prevent its falling backward; castors are placed under the corners. Tack a sheet of wadding over the boards inside and out, and then cover with denim or cretonne, using brass-headed nails and white tape as illustrated on the following page. The inside is fitted with strips of tape and pockets of every size and shape to form a safe retreat for scissors, thread, needles, tapes, elastic, buttons, hooks and eyes, etc.

When the cover is down, it forms a pretty chair and no one would suspect that it contains undarned stockings and all the family mending awaiting a leisure hour to be attended to.

Home Adornments.

The accompanying illustration, we hope, will prompt some to make this convenient and useful adornment of the home.

Sweet Potato Vine.—If the beauty of the foliage of this vine were more widely known, it would be more frequently used as an ornamental plant. It can be used in water or in earth in a pot. Select a sound potato of good size. Let it rest upon the edge of the vessel with its lower end just touching the water. Considerable heat is required to start it. Then give it a sunny place and plenty of water. If it is to be trained to run up over the window, remove all except two or three of the strongest sprouts. It is a beauty if grown in a vase set upon a bracket. In this case a number of small and tender shoots are preferable to a few large ones. All the care needed is to supply it with water which the leaves take up and evaporate rapidly.

Decorating with Natural Objects.—Nature has provided abundant material of the greatest variety from which skillful hands and artistic taste can devise and plan thousands of articles that make home attractive. And these need not be confined to the homes of the wealthy, but the humblest home in the land with proper care and forethought can be made more homelike by taking free that which is offered in nature's storehouse. The shells of the ocean; the leaves, twigs and bark of trees; the grasses and flowers of fields and meadows; the mosses of the rocks, and the insects of the woods are all at our service. A home-made bird nest bracket, a shell bracket, a bracket made of ferns, grasses, leaves, mosses and set off with butterflies or other insects may add beauty and bring cheerfulness where most needed.

Ferns.—Ferns whose exquisite beauty of form and grace of outline cannot be destroyed are abundant in our shaded woodlands and in sheltered nooks. They should be pressed very carefully when nearly full grown. These, when painted with pale green paint, mixed with linseed oil, may be tastefully arranged in brackets of straw and splints, or simply glued on a pasteboard frame with moss, grasses or leaves. Do not use turpentine to thin the paint. It will give the ferns an unnatural color. Ferns can, in this way, be used for decorating picture frames, mantels and beautifying unsightly corners. They can be arranged by a network of string held in place by small wire nails.

Autumn Leaves.—Leaves should be collected before the rains bleach them. After being carefully pressed and dried, they can be prepared by being dipped into a mixture of white wax and a little gamboge. Keep the wax at proper temperature, so that it does not set in lumps on the leaves, or, on the other hand, curl or crimp them.

Grasses should be collected as soon as they become wiry and stiff. The prettiest grasses are found in marshes and along the sea shore. They can be bleached by being dipped into strong boiling soda water and then laid on racks in a tight box where a little sulphur is burned under them. They are then dried in a hot sun. It is often necessary to repeat the process. Some flowers are bleached by using strong castile soap suds instead of soda. Be sure that your grasses are thoroughly bleached before coloring them. The best method of coloring them is by using the aniline dyes. Some colors take in a few minutes, while others require much boiling before the colors are set. These grasses made up into bouquets, or used in a variety of ways, provide adornments for rooms. At little or no cost your home can be made more homelike by their use. Try it!

HYGIENE OF THE BEDROOM.

Dr. W. C. Lyman says: This doesn't consist chiefly in airing the room and bedding, after their use during the night. That is a very good, important thing in its way. But it is not the matter a neglect of which brings on the characteristic bedroom smell. The bedroom odor, noticeable in three out of every five bedrooms in the land, is mostly derived from the urine that is allowed to stand in uncovered, or but partly close receptacles, 12 out of each 24 hours, in these rooms. Urine contains several volatile and also highly poisonous and malodorous elements. Those not only pass readily into the air of bedrooms, but are absorbed by mattresses, carpets, hangings, plaster, and upholstered furniture. Airing a room thus charged and saturated is better than not airing it. But it is not beginning at the more available end of the problem. This is not a matter to be minced about, or politely overlooked, when bedroom hygiene is being discussed. To speak of the (slightly!) increased exhalations of the body during sleep, as if they were what had mainly to be dealt with, is to divert attention from a matter that is all too little appreciated, and is really primary. The extent to which this source of mischief in bedrooms is overlooked by people otherwise highly particular in their housekeeping is indicated by the number of delicately shaped, finely decorated and coverless pieces of pottery sold to well-to-do people for use in their bedrooms. A wide inquiry into the subject has convinced the writer that the bedroom odor to be found in most houses is there because the idea of urine as a source of smell has never occurred, or been suggested to housekeepers generally.

The means of obviating the nuisance are too obvious to need mention, and the only further comment called for is that prevention here is emphatically better than cure. Once this matter is seen to, a carpeted, upholstered bedroom, with ever so many woolen hangings, if reasonably aired, can be kept as sweet, both in summer and winter, as the general sitting-room, with its two to three times as many occupants. Try it and see.

Beds and Bedding.—The beds and bedding should sometimes have special care. The blankets that have been put away all summer must be hung on the clothes-line some bright day. Give them a good shaking or beating and let them air for several hours. If comforters are used they must have the same treatment. When it is possible, however, discard comforters and use only blankets, which are more healthful and cleanly. Have the mattresses, pillows and bolsters thoroughly beaten and aired. Dust the springs of the beds, and when the form of the springs is such that you can do so, make a covering of strong calico. It should be sewed at both ends and one side. Slip the springs in at the open side, which should then be sewed up. This prevents the accumulation of dust on the springs, saving an immense amount of trouble. Get the wide, light prints that upholsterers use for the covering of fine stuffed furniture. It is a little more expensive than common calico, but it pays in the end. This covering also protects the mattress from rust. Make covers of strong unbleached cotton for mattresses, and have these covers washed twice a year. They must be made open on the side, and, when the mattress is slipped in, the sides must be basted together.

While the bedding is airing, take down the bed and dust it thoroughly. Lay the head, foot and side pieces on the floor, grooved sides up, and pour naphtha into all the grooves and creases. It will not hurt the floor or carpet if it should run over upon them. Have the windows open, of course, whenever you use naphtha. Let your bed stand this way for several hours; then set it up and bring in the mattresses and other bedding. There is not the slightest danger in using naptha if the windows in the room and adjoining hall or rooms be opened, that the gases shall escape, and if there be no light or fire in the rooms. If you have some blankets to be washed, select a bright, windy day, and if this be their first washing, rip off the bindings, if colored cotton or worsted, and bind the blankets anew with the lossely-woven white braid that comes for flannels.

Airing the Sleeping Room.—In cold weather there is possibly a tendency to be a little neglectful in the matter of fresh air for the sleeping rooms, especially if they are so situated as to get but little artificial heat.

But in winter, even more than in summer, the poisonous exhalations of the body during sleep must be gotten rid of, or the air breathed at night becomes very impure. Why is it that the tone of the system is generally lowered, and that many people need a tonic or a "blood purifier" in the spring? Simply because the manner of living has not been in accordance with the strict laws of health, and largely because the sleeping rooms have not been sufficiently aired.

Hygiene of the Bedroom.

How to Do It.—In the first place, then, the bed should be opened, the blankets and sheets taken off one by one, and well shaken, and arranged carefully in such a way that the air can blow upon them. Shake the pillows well, and if possible leave them in a sunny, breezy spot; take off the blanket or quilt that covers the mattress, and lastly, the mattress itself should be thrown up so that the air may get around it. Then open the windows, and let the room be purified.

Go Far Enough.—A woman of my acquaintance used to arrange her bedding in the way mentioned above, and would then open the window in the farthest corner of the room, three or four inches. When the room was cold, she called it well aired. She congratulated herself vastly on her excellent method. It was all right as far as it went, but it did not go far enough. The windows ought to be opened enough to make a good draught through. Then, after a while, the poisonous air—containing possibly many disease germs—will give place to the sweet, fresh, vitalizing air that sustains life in vigor.

Dr. Abernethy.—There is a story told of the eminent Dr. Abernethy, who was as blunt as he was learned. He was called to prescribe for an old lady in failing health, who prided herself upon being, and who looked, the very pink of neatness. Her dress was spotless, and her cap immaculate, and her friends spoke of her as that "sweet old lady." After much questioning, which was almost impertinent, and a careful diagnosis of the case, the doctor said, gruffly: "Madam, you are ill because of filth." Of course she was horrified, but he went on: "Your bed is not properly aired, and in consequence you are being slowly poisoned to death."

Before Breakfast.—The smart housewives who make their beds before breakfast, so as to have their work "out of the way early," are not unknown to most of us.

Closet Door.—When the windows are open, open also the closet door, for, besides dispelling the odors that will gather in a closed closet, light and air are very discouraging to the naughty little silver moths, for they truly "love darkness rather than light."

Punctilious.—In caring for the furnishing of the sleeping room, one can not be too punctilious. The washstand, and all the dishes belonging to it, should be kept perfectly sweet and clean. Let no stale water remain in the room, or soiled towels, or clothing. Indeed, nothing which can taint the room in any degree should be allowed where, more perhaps than in any other room in the house, there ought to be an abundance of sweet, wholesome, and refreshing air.

Home Made Mattresses.—The advantages of the home-made mattresses over the store mattresses is that one has the satisfaction of knowing what is in them, which cannot be said of the purchased ones. Then, too, by making one's own mattresses one has more money to buy the springs and bedding. I have had many of my friends copy my mattresses, which I make of the best of fancy blue stripe ticking. Cut the proper length and width, with side and end pieces as wide as you wish. When sewed up with an opening in the top piece, fill with as much excelsior as you can press in, sew up the opening, and tie just as the store ones are. Use an upholsterer's needle. I knot with three or four strands of colored warp, which makes them look prettier. The "filling" can be procured for a song generally. Tie a row of knots around the sides and ends, and when your work is complete you will vote them the prettiest mattresses you ever saw. To make my beds more comfortable I make top mattresses of 6-cent tennis flannel, putting twelve rolls of cotton in each one and knotting like comfortables. They are far superior to feather beds, as the latter never get renovated often enough. When I want to wash them I take them out in the shade on a big table and scrub them on both sides with a new scrub brush made of broom splints, and they are easily and quickly cleansed. Now hang them on a wire line and pour on cold water, rinsing in this way until the water runs off clear. I wash comforts the same way, excepting the cheese-cloth ones; these I wash with my "pounder" washer, which gets them nice and white, and they are as light as a feather. No need of taking them apart, it is tedious and unnecessary. Sanitary laws require the inside to be clean, too.

Spare Bed.—Don't let your guests sleep in the spare bed without first giving it a good airing. A good way to test the sheets for dampness is to lay a hand mirror between them. If it comes out blurred, give them some other bed.

Guest Chamber.—Something interesting to read is a desirable provision for the guest chamber. A bright novel, the latest magazine, or a book of short stories will always be appreciated by the guest who does not always wish to stay with the family to entertain or be entertained. A scrap book will furnish something of interest; also a portfolio of engravings.

THE DINING ROOM.

Too much stress can hardly be laid upon the desirability of having the dining room bright and cheery. The dainty touches that make the difference between the home and the hotel table should not be lacking.

Best Results.—There is much to be said in this direction, both for the behavior at table, and the refinement of setting and bringing out the best results from what we have on hand. To the millionaire, of course, all this is plain sailing; the fashionable caterer is called in, the date fixed, number of guests decided upon, the best results gained, and the newest fads presented on the evening in question. Many times there is no consultation at all; the whole affair is handed over to the chef in charge, and he and the florist bring all their best and most original ideas into play, making the house and table resplendent with beauties and delight.

Less Fortunate.—But to the less fortunate of mankind and women, who have to study the lights and shades, the materials and forces on hand, to those I address myself. To give an entertainment, large or small, there are a few points to be observed.

We Eat to Live.—'Tis a long and well-established fact that we eat to live, and to do this well, food should be well and properly cooked, as our mental and physical condition greatly depends on the purity of what we take as nourishment.

Live to Eat.—I must confess, however, judging from some people in this world, from their habits and behavior at table, that they "live to eat." Now, there is no doubt that eating is one of the necessities of life; so to enjoy our meals, good manners and an amount of good sense should rule the head as well as the stomach.

Requisites.—Still, to really enjoy the food we eat, several things are requisite. We must have the desire for food—appetite—and to possess this, we must have health, and health is only to be attained by leading temperate lives, eating and drinking judiciously—avoiding excesses of all kinds.

Well Cooked Food.—To this we may add that the food should be well cooked. By this I do not mean well done, for some dishes, especially beef and game, are better when

The Dining Room.

"rare done," but properly cooked, and carefully prepared previous to the cooking.

Good Quality.—Nor can we hope for a good dinner, or other meals, unless the materials comprising it are of themselves of a good quality—no strong butter, stale eggs, meat that is under a cloud. Nor will coarse brown sugar make a delicate cake or jelly. Such a condition of things must of necessity produce an inferior meal.

White China.—Pure white china, dainty and pretty, is taking the place of the ornate china that has been so long in vogue.

Simplicity.—The simpler the appointments of a dining room are, the better it is. It is comfort rather than show that is to be considered.

The Appointments of the table should be of the best you can command—the linen of snowy whiteness, the silver bright and shining, sparkling glass clear and clean, with well-polished and sharpened cutlery. These give an air of refinement and elegance to the simplest repast, and are a crown of luxury to the feast.

"Hot."—Then this rule should be followed out in the various dishes, served with neatness and care, and not the least in consideration, all should be placed on the table "hot."

Punctuality should be the motto, and the table should not be kept waiting for any belated guest. Flowers are always a beautiful adjunct to the table, from the simplest rose, standing all alone in its beauty, to the bevy of lovely flowers just gathered, dripping with dew, from the garden. To this we add a prevailing spirit of friendliness and harmony, with refinement of manners.

Enjoyment Complete.—If these requirements be fulfilled, the pleasure, I am sure, will be more than realized, and your enjoyment be complete.

Napkins and Doilies.—For ordinary dinners the doilies should be three-fourths of a yard in size, and marked, if marked at all, with letters an inch and a half long.

Luncheon and breakfast napkins are five-eighths of a yard square.

Tea napkins should not be longer than half a yard square.

The little fringed designs are prettiest for this purpose. Never introduce any colors except in flowers.

Never employ heavily-scented blossoms for table decoration, as the strong perfume is very nauseating to some people.

PRACTICAL METHODS AND RECIPES FOR THE CARE OF KITCHEN UTENSILS.

1. Attention to details is very necessary.
2. Sand or bath brick is excellent in cleaning wooden articles, floors, tables and the like.
3. If you use limestone water, an oyster shell in the tea kettle will receive the lime deposit.
4. Boil in the coffee pot, occasionally, soap, water and washing soda. It should always be bright to insure good coffee.
5. Pans made of sheet-iron are better to bake bread and cake in than those made of tin.
6. If skillets are very greasy, a little sal soda in the water will neutralize the grease, and so make them much easier to wash.
7. Bottles and cruets are cleaned nicely with sand and soap suds.
8. Iron pots, stoneware jars and crocks should have cold water and a little soda placed in them on the stove and allowed to boil, before using them.
9. Never allow the handles of knives to be placed into hot water.

10. A discolored brass kettle can be cleaned nicely by scouring it with a little vinegar and salt and washing it well afterward with hot water and soap.

11. Scrape the dough from your rolling pin and wipe with a dry towel, rather than wash it.

12. Steel or silver may tarnish in woolen cloths. A chamois skin or tissue paper is very much better.

13. Don't put your tinware or iron vessels away damp, always dry them first. And scald out your woodenware often.

14. Don't use a brass kettle for cooking until it is thoroughly cleaned with salt and vinegar.

15. Don't allow coffee or tea to stand in tin.

16. Don't allow knives with wooden, horn or bone handles to lie in hot water, wash the blades in as hot water as you please, but keep it off the handles as much as possible.

17. Don't heat new iron vessels too quickly. Heat them gradually and they are not so liable to crack.

18. **Milk in Tumblers.**—When milk is used in tumblers wash them first in cold water, afterward rinse in hot water.

19. **Cleaning Fruit Jars.**—A handful of carpet tacks will clean fruit jars or bottles readily. Half fill the jars with hot soapsuds, put in the tacks, cover, give vigorous shaking and rinse well.

20. **To Clean Knives,** take a potato, cut in halves and dip in brick dust and rub the knives, the potato affording just enough moisture.

21. **Silverware.**—Put a lump of camphor in the case with the silverware when packing it away for the summer months. If this be done the silver will be less liable to become discolored.

22. **Ammonia for Silver.**—One teaspoonful of ammonia to a teacup of water applied with a rag will clean silver or gold jewelry perfectly.

23. **For Cleaning Tinware** there is nothing better than dry flour applied with a newspaper. First wash the tin in hot soapsuds, wipe thoroughly dry, and then scour with flour and well crumbled newspaper.

24. **Bread and Cake Bowls,** or any dishes in which flour and eggs have been used, are more easily cleaned if placed in cold water after using.

25. **Glass Dishes.**—Dissolve a tablespoonful of turpentine in two quarts of hot water and use for washing glass dishes and globes.

It gives them a beautiful luster.

26. **Cut Glass.**—To wash cut glass and have it clear and shining you should have a soft brush, and dry it lastly, after using a linen towel, with tissue paper.

27. **Covers** should not be left on cooking utensils when they are put away, as in this way the fresh air is kept out, and that which is kept in grows stale and ill-smelling.

28. **Pitchers, Bowls, Pans** and other utensils used for milk should have cold water stand in them for an hour or so, then be washed in plenty of clean, soapy water, be scalded with boiling water, wiped dry, and placed in the open air and sun, if possible. Then you may be sure they are clean and sweet, and fit to receive milk.

29. **Fish and Onions.**—Pans in which fish or onions have been boiled should be rinsed at once, then filled with cold water, into which a teaspoonful of cooking soda or Pearline has been placed, set on the range, and allowed to stand until time for washing; then wash them thoroughly in warm, clean, soapy water, rinse and wipe, and dry in the open air.

30. **To Cleanse Your Sink** dissolve a pound of copperas in a gallon of boiling water and use freely. The copperas can be bought for a few cents, but it should be labeled "poison" and kept out of the reach of children. It is a great disinfectant and purifier.

31. **Ivory Knife-Handles,** and other ivory handles that have become yellow, may be bleached by placing them under a tall glass in the sun. If the ivory is carved, and the crevices have become dirty and discolored, wash them with warm water and powdered pumice-stone. If very little soiled, moisten a flannel with water, dip it in finely powdered salt, rub the article lightly with it, and it will both cleanse and whiten the ivory.

32. **Economic Points.**—Housekeeping carried on on a cash basis always pays. If you cannot pay cash for an article, do not buy it. Have tin canisters for your spices, tea, coffee, etc. Oatmeal, rice, cracked wheat and the like are kept better in close covered glass jars, as they are liable to get wormy, if loosely covered. Meal and flour keep best in wooden receptacles. Do not allow groceries to stand around in paper bags or packages. It is not economical to buy sugar and coffee in quantities less than a dollar's worth. Do not buy potatoes and apples by the peck, but by the bushel, unless they are very high in price, or you have no room for them. Do not buy oat meal in large quantities.

HOUSEHOLD MEASURES AND WEIGHTS.

Below we give the weights and measures in ordinary use among housekeepers:

2 teaspoonfuls equal 1 tablespoonful.
2 tablespoonsfuls equal 1 ounce.
16 tablespoonfuls equal 1 cupful.
2 cupfuls equal 1 pint.
1 pint equals 1 pound.
16 ounces equal 1 pound.
4 gills equal 1 pint.
2 pints equals 1 quart.
4 quarts equal 1 gallon.
An ordinary tumblerful equals 1 cupful.
1 quart flour equals 1 pound.
8 or 10 ordinary sized eggs equal 1 pound.
1 tablespoonful salt equals 1 ounce.
4 tablespoonfuls equal 1 wine glass.
4 wine glasses equal 1 coffee cupful

Recipes often call for weights and measures, in fractions, of a pound or a cup. If the cook is not accurate in her measurements more or less of failure results. The following have been carefully verified and can be relied upon, Girls who are learning to cook will find them helpful, if kept close at hand for reference.

A teaspoonful, tablespoonful or teacupful is one filled, then slightly shaken until rounded on the top. A heaped teaspoonful, etc., is all that will lie on, and a level one a heaped one leveled with a knife.

Nine heaped tablespoonfuls of granulated sugar make a teacupful, and two teacupfuls weigh a pound.

Two and three-quarters teacupfuls of powdered, two and one-half of good brown sugar weigh a pound.

Four heaped tablespoonfuls of butter make a teacupful, and two teacupfuls weigh a pound.

Four teacupfuls of sifted flour fill a quart measure, and a quart of flour weighs a pound.

Two teacupfuls of raisins weigh a pound, and two and two-thirds teaspoonfuls of currants weigh a pound.

A teacupful of rice weighs half a pound, and a quart of oatmeal weighs one pound.

One teacupful makes half a pint, sixteen tablespoonfuls of liquid make a teacupful. Three teaspoonfuls make a tablespoonful, and ten and two-thirds tablespoonfuls make a teacupful. Four tablespoonfuls of liquid are equal to a wineglassful. A tablespoonful holds half a fluid ounce. Two rounded tablespoonfuls of flour weigh an ounce.

Amateur cooks are perplexed by the direction so often given, "salt and spice to taste." The proportion of salt to a quart of soup or gravy is one teaspoonful. A teaspoonful of flavoring extract, or a teaspoonful of spice is sufficient for one cake.

A tablespoonful of broken cinnamon, a tablespoonful each of peppercorns, celery seed, whole cloves and mustard seed, will spice strongly a quart of vinegar for sour pickles.

A tablespoonful of commercial mixed spices will spice a quart of vinegar.

One level teaspoonful of soda will sweeten a pint of buttermilk or sour milk.

Three teaspoonfuls of baking powder are used for a quart of flour.

A quick oven, to sear roast meats, should turn a white paper brown in three minutes, for bread and pastry in five minutes.

To test for cake, white paper should turn yellow in five minutes, if the oven is the right temperature.

HOW TO EAT ORANGES.

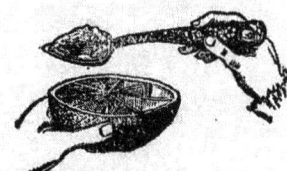

Cut the oranges across the sections as shown in the above illustration. Then take a small spoon, and it will fit into each section, and the meat is easily and daintily removed.

There are special orange spoons, which are very nice for those who can afford them. An ordinary teaspoon will answer the purpose very nicely.

HOUSEHOLD HINTS.

Throw flour on kerosene flames.
Try molasses for grass stains.
Ripe tomatoes will remove ink stains.
Remember, slamming the door of the oven makes cake fall.
A few drops of lemon juice make cake frosting very white.
A hot shovel held over varnished furniture will take out white spots.
Try sprinkling powdered cloves about the places infested by red ants.
A little flour dredged over the top of a cake will prevent the icing from running.
There should be just as much conscience put into dusting a room as in managing an estate.

The ivy-decked house is picturesque, but the dampness and insects that linger in the greenery are not.

Early-rising means a whole day's work done before noon, a consideration that hot weather makes desirable.

Hard-finished walls may be cleaned by using one-half cupful of ammonia in a pail of water.

When polishing mirrors, windows or picture glass with whitening, the best way to use it is to have it in muslin bags. Dampen the glass lightly, then rub with the bag and polish off with a crumpled newspaper.

Window panes.—Warm water into which a small quantity of turpentine has been poured will clean glass globes, window panes and mirrors in the most satisfactory way. A few drops of alcohol in warm water is also good for burnishing glass.

To Prevent Frosted Windows.—Apply a very thin coating of glycerine to both sides of the glass and no moisture will settle thereon.

To Remove Wrinkles from Woolens.—Stretch the garments and hang them over night in a heated room.

To Polish Iron.—A solution of vinegar and salt is the best thing to clean polished iron as well as copper. Heat the salt and vinegar in the frying pan or other dish. Rub off the stains, then wash it off and scour it with sand soap.

SALT.

Salt puts out a fire in the chimney.
Salt in the oven under baking-tins will prevent their scorching on the bottom.
Salt and vinegar will remove stains from discolored teacups.
Salt and soda are excellent for bee stings and spider bites.
Salt thrown on soot which has fallen on the carpet will prevent stains.
Salt put on ink freshly spilled on a carpet will help to remove the spot.
Salt in whitewash makes it stick.
Salt thrown on a coal fire which is low will revive it.
Salt used in sweeping carpets keeps out moths.
Salt sprinkled upon the kitchen range will stop the smoke and smell of substance burning.

SODA AND CHARCOAL.

A box of washing soda in the kitchen and another in the bath room closet are great aids in cleanly housekeeping. Greasy pots and pans, or those to which something has burned or fastened itself so firmly that scraping is a disagreeable necessity, are easily cleansed if a small lump of the soda is put in the pan and covered with cold water. Set the utensil over the fire until after dinner and you will find that all the grease or crust is loosened. Granite ware and tin last much longer when cleansed in this way, which is preferable to the pot-cleaner that is a network of iron or steel rings. The soda is also excellent to cleanse and whiten unvarnished and unpainted floors, tables, and other surfaces, and quite indispensable in flushing the waste pipe in the bathroom and kitchen sinks once or twice a week. In this case the soda should be dissolved in boiling water and used at once.

Charcoal is another simple and inexpensive purifying agent that is most useful in keeping a house free from smells of various kinds. A few good-sized pieces in a refrigerator occasionally purify and preserve it. If you have that abomination, an enclosed dark place under the sink for pots, etc., put some charcoal there, as well as in the cupboard where you keep cooked food.

HOW TO HAVE LAMPS BURN BRIGHTLY.

In these days when lamps are used so much, the care of them is quite an important matter. If the lamps be good and have proper attention, one cannot wish for a more satisfactory light; but if badly cared for they will be a source of much discomfort. The great secret of having lamps in good working order is to keep them clean and to use good oil. Have a regular place and time for trimming the lamps. Put a folded newspaper on the table, so that any stray bits of burned wick and drops of oil may fall upon it. Wash and wipe the chimneys and shades. Now take off all loose parts of the burner, washing them in hot soap-suds and wiping with a clean soft cloth. Trim the wicks and turn them quite low. With a soft, wet cloth, well soaped, wipe the burner thoroughly, working the cloth as much as possible inside the burner, to get off every particle of the charred wick. Now fill the lamps within about one inch of the top, and wipe with a damp towel and then a dry one. Adjust all the parts and return them to their proper places. Whenever a new wick is required in a lamp, wash and scald the burner before putting in the wick. With a student lamp, the receptacle for waste oil, which is screwed on the bottom of the burner, should be taken off at least once a week and washed. Sometimes a wick will get very dirty before it is half consumed. It is not economy to try to burn it; replace it with a fresh one. The trouble and expense are slight, and the increase in clearness and brilliancy will repay the extra care. When a lamp is lighted, it should not at once be turned up to the full height; wait until the chimney is heated. Beautiful shades are often cracked or broken by having the hot chimneys rest against them. Now, when lighting a lamp, be careful that the chimney is set perfectly straight, and does not touch the shade at any point. The shade should be placed on the lamp as soon as it is lighted, that it may heat gradually.

Lamp Burners.—At least once a month lamp burners should be boiled in strong, soapy water; lamp wicks should as often be washed in soap suds; lamp chimneys should not be washed, but moistened with steam, wiped with soft linen, and polished with paper. A cloth and kerosene give a good bright surface.

Keep Your Oil Lamp Full.—Scarcely a day passes but

that we hear of fearful accidents and disastrous fires occasioned by the explosion of kerosene lamps. A fruitful source of danger from this course lies in the neglect to keep the lamp full. If a lamp is neglected and allowed to burn low, inflammable gas gathers over the surface, which a slight jar inflames, and an explosion follows. Lamps in daily use should be filled every morning.

HOW TO TRIM LAMPS.

In trimming the wicks, leave a thin coat of the brown edge. It takes a steady hand to trim a wick, so that it will burn with an even and steady flame. The wick should always be turned down. If it is above the burner, the kerosene will flow down the sides of the lamp more or less.

TO TOUGHEN LAMP CHIMNEYS AND GLASSWARE.

Immerse the article in a pot filled with cold water, to which some common salt has been added. Boil the water well, then cool slowly. Glass treated in this way will resist any sudden changes of temperature.

TO MAKE AN OLD LAMP BURNER AS GOOD AS NEW.

Dissolve an ounce of sal-soda in a quart of rain water. In this boil the burner for ten minutes, then wipe with a cotton cloth. Soak the wick in strong vinegar, dry thoroughly, and it will not smoke.

HOW TO CLEAN A STOVE.

A little soap is as useful in cleaning a stove or range as in cleaning other kitchen ware. A flannel rubbed with soap and then dipped into stove polish will lighten labor when the stove is to be made bright. Of course, the finishing touch must be a dry brush or cloth, applied with energy. Stoves so blackened are said to retain their polish much longer.

HOW TO KEEP STOVES FROM RUSTING,

By applying kerosene with a rag when you are about to put your stoves away for the summer you will prevent them from rusting.

THE YOUNG PHOTOGRAPHER.

Family Receipts. 361

ALL KINDS OF FAMILY RECEIPTS AND REMEDIES.

A SURE CURE FOR CAR SICKNESS.

Take a sheet of writing-paper large enough to cover both the chest and stomach, and put it on under the clothing, next to the person. If one sheet is not large enough paste the edges of two or three together, for the chest and stomach must be well covered. Wear the paper thus as long as you are traveling, and change it every day if your journey is a long one. Those who have tried it say that it is a perfect defense.

A HEALTHY SPRUCE BEER.

½ pint essence of spruce,
4 ounces bruised pimento,
4 ounces ginger,
3 gallons water.

Boil five or ten minutes, then strain, and add eleven gallons of warm water, a pint of yeast, and six pints of molasses. Allow the mixture to ferment for twenty-four hours.

How to Remove Stains, Etc.

NEW AND SCIENTIFIC METHODS
For Taking Out all kinds of Grease Spots, Fruit or Ink Stains, Paints, Oils, Etc.

The left column shows the kind of stain and the top column the kind of cloth.

Kind of Stain	From Colored Cotton	From Colored Woolen.	From Linen.	From Silks.
Grease Spots.	Soap and Water or Benzine.	Soap and Water or Benzine.	Soap Suds or Benzine.	Chloroform, Benzine or Chalk.
Fruit Stains or Red Ink	Warm Soap Suds or Ammonia and Water	Warm Soap Suds or Ammonia and Water.	Warm Chlorine Water.	Warm Water mixed with Ammonia or warm Soap Suds.
Oil Paint or Varnish.	Turpentine or Benzine.	Turpentine.	Turpentine.	Ether or Soap or Benzine.
Ink Stains.	A solution of Citric Acid. Wash repeatedly.	Dilute Hydrochloric Acid.	A warm solution of Oxalic Acid.	No remedy.
Iron Stains.	A solution of Citric Acid. Wash repeatedly.	Dilute Hydrochloric Acid.	A warm solution of Oxalic Acid.	No remedy.
Wagon Grease or Coal Tar.	Rub with lard then Soap it and apply Turpentine.	Rub with lard then Soap it and then wash alternately with Water and Turpentine.	Soap or Turpentine or Benzine.	First lard it, then soap it, then wash alternately with Water and Benzoin instead of Benzine.
Nut Shell Stains.	Wash alternately with water and diluted Chlorine water.			

Removing Stains.

Grease Spots.—Cold rain water and soap will remove machine grease from washable fabrics.

Stains from Acids can be removed by spirits of hartshorn, diluted. Repeat, if necessary.

Iron Rust.—Dip the rusty spots in a solution of tartaric or citric acid; or wet the spots and rub on hard, white soap; expose it to the heat; or apply lemon juice and salt, and expose it to the sun.

To Take Out Scorch.—Lay the article scorched where the bright sunshine will fall upon it. It is said it will remove the spot, and leave it white as snow.

Mildewed Linen.—This may be restored by soaping the spots; while wet, covering them with fine chalk scraped to powder, and well rubbed in.

To Remove Mildew.—Remove mildew by dipping in sour buttermilk and laying in the sun.

Coffee Stains.—Pour on them a small stream of boiling water before putting the article in the wash.

Grass Stains.—Wash the stained places in clean, cold, soft water, without soap, before the garment is otherwise wet.

Tea Stains.—Clear, boiling water will remove tea stains and many fruit stains. Pour the water through the stain, and thus prevent its spreading over the fabric.

Medicine Stains.—These may be removed from silver spoons by rubbing them with a rag dipped in sulphuric acid, and washing it off with soap suds.

Fruit Stains.—Freezing will take out all old fruit stains, and scalding with boiling water will remove those that have never been through the wash.

Ink Stains.—Ink stains may sometimes be taken out by smearing with hot tallow, left on when the stained articles go to the wash.

Ink in Cotton, Silk and Woolen Goods.—Saturate the spots with spirits of turpentine, and let it remain several hours; then rub it between the hands. It will crumple away without injuring either the color or the texture of the article.

To Remove Paint Stains on Windows.—It frequently happens that painters splash the plate or other glass windows when they are painting the sills. When this is the case, melt some soda in very hot water and wash them with it, using a soft flannel. It will entirely remove the paint.

To Remove Grease from Coat Collars.—Wash with a sponge moistened with hartshorn and water.

To Clean Wall-Paper.—Tie a soft cloth over a broom, and sweep down the walls carefully.

Stains on the Hands.—A few drops of oil vitriol (sulphuric acid) in water, will take the stains of fruit, dark dyes, stove blacking, etc. from the hands without injuring them. Care must, however, be taken not to drop it upon the clothes. It will remove the color from woolen, and eat holes in cotton fabrics. To remove ink or fruit stains from the fingers, take cream of tartar, half an ounce; powdered salt of sorrel, half an ounce; mix. This is what is sold for salts of lemon.

Removing Grease From Silk.—Apply a little magnesia to the wrong side, and the spots will disappear.

To Clean Furs.—Shake and whip them well; then brush; boil some flax seed; dip a rag in the water and wipe them slightly. This makes them look nearly as good as new.

To Preserve Furs.—First, hang them out in the sun for a day or two; then give them a good beating and shaking up, to be sure no moth is in them already. Then wrap up a lump of camphor in a rag, and place in each; then wrap up each in a sound newspaper and paste together, so there is no hole or crevice through which a moth can gain entrance.

To Clean Velvet.—Wet a cloth and put it over a hot flat-iron, and a dry one over that; then draw the velvet across it, brushing it at the same time with a soft brush, and it will look as nice as new.

Wrinkled Silk.—Wrinkled silk may be rendered nearly as beautiful as when new, by sponging the surface with a weak solution of gum-arabic or white glue; then iron on the wrong side.

To Make Cloth Water-Proof.—In a pail of soft water put half a pound of sugar of lead, half a pound of alum; stir this at intervals until it becomes cool; then pour it into another pail and put the garment therein, and let it be in for twenty-four hours, and then hang it up to dry without wringing it.

To Color Kid Gloves.—Put a handful of logwood into a bowl, cover with alcohol, and let it soak until it looks strong —one day, perhaps. Put one glove on the hand, dip a small woolen cloth or sponge into the liquid, wet the glove all over, rub it dry and hard until it shines, and it will be a nice purple. Repeat the process, and it will be black.

Washing Kid Gloves.—First, see that your hands are clean, then put on your gloves and wash them as though you were washing your hands, in a basin of spirits of turpentine. This method is used in Paris. The gloves should be hung in the air, or some dry place, to carry away the smell of turpentine.

Grease spots in cloth may be taken out by applying a solution of salt in alcohol.

Paint on Clothing.—Soak in kerosene a while previous to washing; also paint brushes. If on the hands, dampen with it and it will wash off easily.

Inkstains on a white surface should be wet with milk and rubbed with salt, allowing it to remain on for some time. Two or three applications may be found necessary.

Alcohol for Grass Stains.—It is claimed that alcohol will immediately remove grass stains from any white material.

Grease Spots on Velvet.—Grease spots on velvet or cloth can be removed by dropping a little turpentine over the place, and rubbing it dry with a piece of clean flannel. Continue this until the grease has vanished. If the nap of the velvet has become flattened, raise it by damping the wrong side, stretching it out, and ironing it on the wrong side. This is best done by standing the iron on end and passing the velvet over it.

Removing Paint from Woolen Goods.—Turpentine will remove paint from woolen goods and silk fabrics. Saturate the spot with spirits of turpentine and allow it to remain for hours. Rub the cloth between the fingers and the paint will crumble off without injuring the goods.

Grease Spots on Wall Paper.—A great many housewives are very often annoyed at finding grease spots on the pretty wall paper adorning their rooms. A good way to remove these spots is put powdered French chalk, wetted with cold water, over the places, and let it remain for twelve hours or more. When you brush off the chalk, if the grease spots have not disappeared, put on more chalk, place a piece of coarse brown paper or blotting paper on this, and press for a few minutes with a warm iron.

Or apply a little powdered pipe clay only dampened enough to make it stick, and brush the dried powder off later. The ugly grease spots will be gone.

Wall paper that has become bruised or torn off in small patches, and cannot be matched, may be repaired with ordinary children's paints. Mix the colors till you get as nearly as possible the desired shade, and lightly touch up the broken places, and at the distance of a foot or two the disfigurement will be quite unnoticed.

Scratches of Matches.—If matches have been scratched on bare walls by careless hands, cut a lemon in two, rub the marks off with the cut end, wash the acid off with clear water, and when dry rub with a little whiting till the faintest mark is removed.

BORAX.

Borax is very useful as a medicine. But to the housekeeper it is unspeakably more valuable.

Meats and fruits are now sent long distances when packed in it, and even fish are sent in its solution a thousand miles. The happy possessor of a garden can lay away her early summer fruits—her currants and gooseberries and cherries, her blueberries, her damsons—in layers of dry borax, and have them fresh and sweet in the middle of winter, carefully brushing and washing them before bringing them to the table, and her borax is good for another season. The laundress finds it softening hard water, whitening her clothes without destroying them, and removing the dreaded fruit stains, giving transparency to her muslins, and renovating her laces; the kitchen maid finds it cleansing both her porcelain saucepans and her coffee-urn, and its occasional use sweetening the tea-kettle and every pot she uses; the table girl finds it giving a new luster to her glass, lays her silver in a hot solution of it, and then does not have to cleanse it laboriously half so often; and the housemaid finds it renewing the brightness and color of her oil-cloth, and taking, as if by magic, all the finger marks and soiling from wood-work.

TO REMOVE TEA STAINS.

Mix thoroughly soft soap and salt, say a tablespoonful of salt to a teacupful of soap, rub on the spots and spread the cloth on the grass where the sun will shine on it. Let it lie for two or three days, then wash. If the spots are wet occasionally while lying on the grass, it will hasten the bleaching.

The Broom Should Hang.—Some of the daintiest housekeepers neglect to enforce the rule that a brush or broom should never be stood brush-part down on the floor, where the straws or hair gather dust or dampness. Every one of these articles should hang from its own hook, and, as this is apt to bring the soiled part against the wall, it is well to stretch a breadth of muslin or calico along the wall from the floor up, so that even the washboard is protected from stain. The muslin, of course, is washed whenever necessary. As all brooms and brushes are not provided with "hangers," a Yankee

Household Receipts.

woman has invented a contrivance which can be fitted to any handle. It is a wire loop with a string attached, and when the string once grips the handle the loop is ready for use. The invention costs but a few cents, and is of real value in hanging troublesome whisk brooms, brushes, umbrellas, and the various impediments which were born to be hung.

If your room be stuffy because it has been lived in too much, or because *homo domesticus* has indulged too freely in the soothing nicotine, you may easily render it sweet and habitable once more by placing one half ounce of spirits of lavender and a lump of salts of ammonia in a wide-mouthed fancy jar or bottle, and leaving it uncovered. This makes a pleasant deodorizer and disinfectant, filling the room with a delicate perfume which will be soothing to the nerves and senses, especially during the warm weather.

To Purify Water.—Sprinkle a tablespoonful of powdered alum in a barrel of water, stirring the while. All impurities will be precipitated to the bottom, leaving it clear and fresh. A smaller amount of alum may be used for a less quantity of water.

Kitchen Utensils, which every housekeeper, if able, should have, are: Bread box; biscuit cutter; cake turner; cake cutter, two sizes; double kettle for cooking grains; funnels; grater; jelly cake tins; clock; can opener; corkscrew; chopping knife; egg beater; flour scoop; tin dipper; pitcher; bowls; soup strainer; gravy strainer; colander; lemon squeezer; meat board; beefsteak pounder; wooden spoons; iron spoons.

Hot Water.—A very important duty of housekeeping is the providing of plenty of hot water on the stove. Has your patience ever been taxed when in a great hurry for a cupful of boiling water you turned to the kettle to find it dry? The remedy is found in keeping kettles and reservoirs filled. The old lady's advice may be ridiculed, but, nevertheless, if followed, it would do away with much of worry and taxing of nerves. As she was about to die, and almost speechless, she beckoned her daughter to bend over her to receive her final message and murmured with her last breath: "Always—keep—the kettle —full—of—hot—water."

HOW TO CLEAN BRASS.

First rub over with a little lemon-juice, and then dry thoroughly; then place the article in paraffin, and let it soak for three or four hours. Take it out, and while wet rub thoroughly with emery powder. The ordinary knife powder will do. Use a piece of old flannel, or new, if you have no scraps of anything else. When clean rub the article well with a clean duster, so as to remove all the powder, and then finish off with a leather. Of course the rubbing in of the powder takes time, but the result is perfection.

Rust may be removed from steel by rubbing the article with kerosene oil and leaving it for twenty-four hours. Then rub thoroughly with a mixture of kerosene and fine emery powder.

HOW TO SHINE SILVER, BRASS, COPPER, TIN, ETC.

Dissolve a quantity of alum in water so as to make a pretty strong brine, and skim it carefully, then add some soap to it, dip a linen rag in it and rub over the silver.

A WASH FOR CLEANING SILVER

½ ounce fine salt.
½ ounce powdered alum.
½ ounce cream of tartar.

Mix together, put into a large white-wa ; pitcher, and

How to Clean Various Metals.

pour on two quarts of water and stir them frequently till entirely dissolved. Then transfer the mixture to clean bottles and cork them closely. Before using it, shake the bottles well. Pour some of the liquid into a bowl and wash the silver all over with it, using an old, soft fine linen cloth. Let it stand about ten minutes, and then rub it dry with a buckskin. It will make the silver look like new.

TO WASH GREASY TIN AND IRON.

Pour a few drops of ammonia into every greasy roasting-pan, after half filling the pan with hot water. A bottle of ammonia should always be kept on hand near the sink for such uses; never allow the pans to stand and dry, for it doubles the labor of washing; but pour in water and use the ammonia, and the work is half done.

TO CLEAN BRASS.

Finely-rubbed bichromate of potassa, mixed with twice its bulk of sulphuric acid, and an equal quantity of water, will clean the dirtiest brass very quickly.

TO POLISH NICKEL PLATE.

Scour with pulverized borax; use hot water and very little soap; rinse in hot water, and rub dry with a clean cloth. By this quick process a bright polish may be had.

TO CLEANSE BRASSES, TINS, COPPERS, ETC.

Mix rotten-stone, soft soap and old turpentine to the consistency of stiff putty. The article should be first washed in hot water to remove grease, then rub the metal with the mixture, mixed with a little water; then rub off briskly with a dry, clean rag or leather, and a beautiful and durable polish will be obtained. The stone should be very fine, or the articles will become worn or scratched. Very fine emery will answer the same purpose.

TO REMOVE RUST FROM KNIVES, FORKS, RAZORS, ETC.

Cover with sweet oil, well rubbed on, and let it remain for forty-eight hours; then rub with unslaked lime, powdered very fine until the rust disappears.

370 *How to Make All Kinds of Furniture Washes.*

HOW TO MAKE ALL KINDS OF FURNITURE WASHES AND REMOVE STAINS, BRUISES, MOTHS, Etc.

W. W. WICKLE'S FURNITURE POLISH.

1½ qts. raw linseed oil, 1 qt. turpentine,
½ qt. boiled linseed oil, 3 ozs. bees wax.

FURNITURE POLISH.

Equal quantities of common wax, white wax and white soap, in the proportion of one ounce of each, to a pint of water. Cut the above ingredients fine, and dissolve over a fire until well mingled. Bottle and label.

A good temporary wash is kerosene oil.

TO REMOVE STAINS, SPOTS AND MILDEW FROM FURNITURE.

Take ½ pint of 98 per cent. alcohol,
¼ ounce of pulverized resin,
¼ ounce gum shellac.

Add ½ pint of linseed oil, shake well, and apply with a brush or sponge. Sweet oil will remove finger marks from varnished furniture, and kerosene from oiled furniture.

TO TAKE BRUISES OUT OF FURNITURE.

Wet the part with warm water, double a piece of brown paper five or six times, soak it and lay it on the place; apply on that a hot flat-iron till the moisture is evaporated. If the bruises be not gone, repeat the process. After two or three applications, the dent or bruise will be raised level with the surface.

Household Receipts. 371

A POLISH FOR NEW FURNITURE.

1 pint of alcohol.
1 ounce shellac.
1¼ ounces copal.
1 ounce dragon's blood.

Mix and dissolve. Apply with sponge or soft brush.

A POLISH FOR WOOD OR LEATHER.

1 pint alcohol.
3¼ sticks sealing wax.

Dissolve by heating it, and apply warm with sponge.

N. B.—The sealing wax should be the color of the leather, black, red or blue.

TO REMOVE MOTHS FROM FURNITURE.

Moths may be exterminated or driven from upholstered work, by sprinkling this with benzine. The benzine is put into a small watering pot, such as is used for sprinkling house plants; it does not spot the most delicate silk, and the unpleasant odor passes off in an hour or two into the air.

Care must be used not to carry on this work near a fire or flame, as the vapor of benzine is very inflammable. It is said that a little spirits of turpentine added to the water with which the floor is washed will prevent the ravages of moths.

TO CLEAN MIRRORS, WINDOW GLASS, ETC.

Take a soft sponge, wash it well in clean water and squeeze it as dry as possible; dip it into some spirits of wine and rub over the glass; then have some powdered blue tied up in a rag, dust it over your glass, and rub it lightly and quickly with a soft cloth; afterwards finish with a silk handkerchief.

TO REMOVE STAINS IN TABLES.

Wash the surface with vinegar; the stains will then be removed by rubbing them with a rag dipped in spirits of salts. To repolish, proceed as you would with new work. If the work be not stained, wash the surface with clean spirits of turpentine and repolish it with furniture oil.

TO TAKE SMOKE STAINS FROM WALLS.

An easy and sure way to remove smoke stains from common plain ceilings is to mix wood ashes with the whitewash just before applying. A pint of ashes to a small pail of whitewash is sufficient, but a little more or less will do no harm.

FURNITURE POLISH.

A simple furniture polish for common use is made by mixing two tablespoonfuls of sweet or linseed oil with a tablespoonful of turpentine. Rub on with a piece of flannel and polish with a dry piece.

HOW TO MAKE OIL FINISHED FURNITURE LOOK NEW.

Many good housekeepers are often at a great loss in knowing how to keep varnished furniture, and the kind generally known as "oil finished," looking fresh and new, without going to the expense of having it re-varnished or gone over by a finisher. Here is a never-failing polish; After thoroughly dusting the article and cleaning off whatever specks may be on it, she should mix and apply the following: Take one teaspoonful of pure cider vinegar and add to it one gill of pure raw linseed oil. Shake thoroughly until mixed. Apply with a soft woolen rag, rubbing gently. It is only necessary to dampen the rag with the mixture and not to thoroughly wet it. It soon dries and leaves the article with a bright, new face. This preparation has the advantage of not gumming, but giving a fresh look to every article of furniture it is applied to.

HOW TO STAIN A FLOOR.

Take one-third turpentine and two-thirds boiled linseed oil, with a little japan dryer added. Buy a can of burned sienna, and blend it thoroughly with this mixture. This gives a rich reddish brown. Mix the paint quite thin, so that it will run readily. Lay it on with a good-sized brush, stroking the brush the way of the grain of the wood. Put on several coats, allowing each one to become perfectly dry. Lastly, give the floor a good coat of varnish, and when thoroughly dry it will be found as satisfactory as a stained floor can be and easily kept clean.

THE CARE OF HARDWOOD FLOORS.

Parquetry Floors.—The parquetry inlaid floors are much more easily cared for, as well as more durable, when polished with wax than any other preparation.

In laying a new floor the best paste filler should be thoroughly applied by one who understands his business and then floor wax applied with a flannel cloth without the use of varnish, shellac or hard oil. It requires a heavy-weight floor brush to give a polish, but persistence and perseverance will give better results and less liability to scratching than any other method. This method has been in use in the old country many years.

Plain Oak.—A plain oak floor can be treated in the same manner.

To clean a floor never use soap and water, the dirt can be removed with turpentine or the use of some of the patent "restorers" furnished by the manufacturers of hardwood floors. Apply the turpentine or restorer with a woolen cloth and plenty of elbow grease, then use the wax. A thin coating of wax should be rubbed over the entire surface of the floor with a woolen cloth and then polished with the brush. The brush should be moved in straight lines first one way and then the other.

To Give the Finishing Touch.—Place a clean flannel cloth under the brush and rub the floor with this.

In an ordinary room that has very hard use once a month is often enough to polish a floor. In bedrooms or where the floor is almost entirely covered with rugs once in every three months is sufficient.

HOW TO BREAK A STRING.

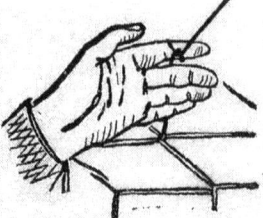

It is easy to break a string, if you know how. Woman need not hunt for a knife or a pair of scissors after tying a bundle, nor saw the string over the edge of the counter. The grocer's loop does the business. Hook the first finger of the left hand over the string, giving the finger a twist, or rather, bring the palm upward. Then roll the finger over backward until it is tight against the bundle, drawing tight the cord, which is held in the right hand all the time. Press the thumb against the loop; then jerk the cord suddenly with the right hand, and the string cuts itself.

HOW TO MAKE A PERMANENT OUT-DOOR WHITEWASH.

Take good lime and slake it in sour milk, and when slaked dilute with water until it is of the consistency of ordinary whitewash, then apply with a brush.

Another Method.—Slake the lime with sufficient water to make a thick mush. While still hot stir into it a pound or more of tallow to a peck of lime. Then thin the lime with water and apply with a brush. It is best to have a little fire to keep the lime warm while using it.

HOW TO PURIFY SINKS AND DRAINS.

To one pound of common copperas add one gallon of boiling water, and use when dissolved. The copperas is deadly poison, and should always be carefully labeled, if kept on hand. This is one of the best possible cleansers of pipes and drains.

HOW TO CLEAN GILT FRAMES.

When the gilt frames of pictures or looking-glasses, or the gilt mouldings of rooms have specks of dirt upon them, from flies or other causes, they can be cleaned with the white of an egg, gently rubbed on with a camel-hair pencil.

HOW TO MAKE A PERFECT HOLE IN A PIECE OF GLASS.

First cover the glass with a little stiff clay or putty where you desire to drill the hole. Then make a hole into the clay, or putty, the size of the desired hole to be made through the glass. Then pour into this hole a little melted lead, and unless the glass is very thick, it will make a perfect and regular hole.

HOW TO POLISH WOOD.

Take the plain surface of any timber or board and soak it in linseed-oil for a week, and then rub it briskly for a few minutes with a new cloth every day for ten days, and it will produce a beautiful glossy surface.

HOW TO REMOVE OLD VARNISH.

    5 parts of 36 per cent. silicate of potash,
    1 part of sal ammoniac,
    1 part of 40 per cent. soda lye.
Mix, and apply.

TO REMOVE GLASS STOPPERS.

When the stopper on a glass decanter is too tight, a cloth wet with hot water and applied to the neck will cause the glass to expand, and the stopper may be removed. In a phial, the warmth of the finger may be sufficient. Tapping the stopper with a penknife often has the desired effect, or, slowly revolve the neck of the bottle in the flame of a burning match. Remove the stopper before the heat reaches it. Thick glass may require a second match. Never fails, nor does harm. Best thing I ever learned of.

WHITEWASH THAT WILL NOT RUB OFF.

Mix up a pailful of lime and water ready to put on the wall; then take one-fourth pint of flour, mix with water, then pour on it a sufficient quantity of boiling water to thicken it, and pour it while hot into the whitewash; stir all well together and use.

TO REMOVE FLY SPOTS.

Dip a camel-hair brush into spirits of wine, and apply it to remove fly spots.

HOW TO PREPARE KALSOMINE.

Soak one pound of glue twelve hours; then dissolve it in boiling water, and add eighteen or twenty pounds of paris white. Then dilute with water until the mixture is of the consistency of milk. To this mixture add any coloring that may be desired.

A BEAUTIFUL REDWOOD FINISH.

One quart spirits of turpentine.
One tablespoonful raw linseed oil.
One tablespoonful of brown japan,
One-fourth pound burnt sienna,
One pound of corn starch.

Mix thoroughly, and apply with a brush.

HOW TO CLEAN CARPETS, MATTING, ETC.

1. Sprinkle salt over it; then sweep it well and it will make an old carpet look almost like new.

2. Take warm water and pour in a little ammonia and wipe carpet with a large sponge or soft rag. This will also take out grease spots should there be any.

3. A weak solution of alum or soda will brighten up the colors wonderfully. Use warm water.

4. Fresh green grass dampened a little and spread upon the carpet and then swept up will brighten and beautify a carpet. It is much better than tea leaves, for it will leave no stains.

5. Never use soap or hot water on oil cloth.

6. Always beat a carpet on the wrong side first.

KEROSENE STAINS IN CARPETS.

Kerosene stains in carpets may be removed by sprinkling buckwheat flour over the spot. If one sprinkling is not enough, repeat.

SPONGING CARPETS.

Carpets need seldom know the wear and tear of a broom, if sponged once a week, and will look brighter and really be cleaner than if swept by a broom. Take a pail of water and put in a little soap to soften it, or two teaspoonfuls of liquid ammonia. Begin in one corner, using the sponge so that it will not drip, and wipe over a space about two feet square, then pick from the sponge all the hair, lint, and other substance that adheres to it. Go over the remaining space in the same manner. A carpet-sweeper is indispensable to every well-regulated household, particularly when one has been sewing to such an extent as to litter the floor.

STRAW MATTING.

Straw matting should not be washed any oftener than is absolutely necessary, and then it should be wiped dry with a clean cloth.

Straw matting can be cleaned beautifully by using warm water and salt and then rubbing dry with a cloth to avoid turning yellow.

A SUGGESTION FOR SWEEPING DAY.

When sweeping a room there is nothing better to aid in collecting the dust than newspaper. Take a sheet of newspaper at a time, wet it in hot water and press between the hands until it ceases to drip, then tear it into pieces and throw them over the carpet. Then sweep, and most of the dust will gather on the wet paper. On matting if large pieces of wet paper are pushed ahead of the broom they will take the light fluff that is likely to fly back and lodge.

A CARPET CLEANING MIXTURE.

The following is an excellent mixture for cleaning carpets:

Dissolve four ounces of white castile soap (or any pure make) in four quarts of boiling water. When cool add five ounces of aqua ammonia, two and one-half ounces alcohol, same amount of glycerine, and two ounces ether. Cork tightly. To clean a carpet use about a teacupful to a pail of water. To clean a soiled coat, or black garment, use two tablespoonfuls to a pint of strong black coffee. To remove grease spots, use without diluting.

Practical Rules and Receipts for Builders, Carpenters, Wood-Workers and House-Keepers.

1. Moisture-proof glue is made by dissolving sixteen ounces of glue in three pints of skim milk. To make the glue still stronger add a little powdered lime.

2. Shellac and borax, boiled in water, will make a good stain for floors or other wood-work.

3. Porch floors should be made of narrow boards, and the joints laid in white lead.

4. A common brick will absorb about a pint of water, and a house built of brick, without a dead wall, is liable to be very damp.

5. A closet, finished with red cedar shelves and drawers, is sure proof against moths and other insects.

6. Oak floors will stand dampness better than maple.

7. It is much better to oil floors than to paint them. A monthly rubbing will keep them as good as new.

8. Do not construct solid doors of two kinds of hardwood. Changes in the weather will cause one to warp more than the other, and consequently great difficulty will be experienced.

TO FILL CRACKS IN PLASTER.

Use vinegar instead of water to mix your plaster of Paris. The resultant mass will be like putty, and will not "set" for twenty or thirty minutes, whereas, if you use water, the plaster will become hard almost immediately, before you have time to use it. Push it into the cracks and smooth it off nicely with a tableknife.

Household Receipts. 379

TO PREVENT RUST ON IRON OR STEEL.

Take 1 pint of fat oil varnish, mixed with five pints of highly rectified spirits of turpentine, and rub with a sponge. This varnish may be applied to bright stoves, and even to mathematical instruments, without hurting their delicate polish, and they will never contract any spots of rust.

HOW TO POLISH NICKEL PLATE.

Apply rouge with a little fresh lard on a piece of buckskin. Rub the nickel, using as little of the rouge and oil as possible, and then wipe off with a clean rag slightly oiled.

HOW TO POLISH ZINC.

4 ounces powdered rotten stone,
2 ounces pumice stone,
4 ounces oxalic acid.

Add 2 quarts of rainwater. Mix thoroughly, and let it stand two days before using. Apply the polish to the zinc with a dry woolen cloth or chamois skin.

HOW TO REMOVE RUST FROM IRON.

Take the iron and immerse it in a bath of nearly saturated solution of chloride of tin and leave it there from twelve to twenty-four hours, according to the thickness of the rust.

HOW TO CLEAN RUSTY STEEL.

Apply and cleanse with the following preparation:
8 parts of prepared buck's-horn.
10 parts of tin putty,
25 parts of spirits of wine.

Mix into a paste and apply, and then rub off with a soft blotting paper.

IMAGE EVALUATION
TEST TARGET (MT-3)

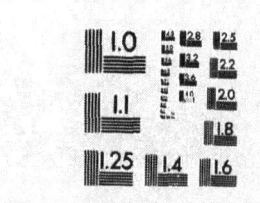

6"

Photographic
Sciences
Corporation

23 WEST MAIN STREET
WEBSTER, N.Y. 14580
(716) 872-4503

How to Make Vinegar.

HOW TO MAKE ALL KINDS OF VINEGAR.

Cider Vinegar.

Vinegar making is easy enough if you have good cider and patience. Keep the barrel in a warm place, filled up to the bung, refilling as needed. When done working draw off into an old vinegar barrel, filling it not over two-thirds full. Keep the bung hole covered with a piece of screen to exclude vinegar flies. If kept in a warm place it may make good strong vinegar in less than six months' time. In an ordinary cellar it will take longer.

Common Vinegar.

8 gallons rain water,
3 quarts molasses,
2 yeast cakes.

Shake well. Put in a warm place, and in ten days add a sheet of wrapping paper covered with molasses and torn into strips; it makes the mother.

Vinegar for Pickles.

4 quarts of vinegar; 2 cups of sugar; 3 nutmegs, grated; 2 large onions, sliced; ½ cup of grated horse-radish; 1 ounce of mustard seed; 1 ounce of celery seed; 1 ounce of salt; ¼ ounce of mace, ½ ounce of black pepper; 1 ounce of allspice.

Vinegar for Sweet Pickle.

6 pounds of fruit; 2 pounds of sugar; 1 quart of vinegar; 2 ounces of cassia buds or cloves.

Vinegar for Spiced Tomatoes.

1 quart of vinegar; 2 ounces of sugar; 1 ounce of cloves; 1 ounce of cinnamon; 1 ounce of allspice; 1 ounce of ground black pepper.

Vinegar for Green Tomato Pickle.

3 chopped red peppers; a handful of grated horseradish; ½ gallon of vinegar; ½ pound of sugar.

Vinegar for Sweet Pickled Peaches and Apples.

4 pounds of sugar; 1 quart of vinegar; 2 ounces of unground cinnamon.

TO MAKE VINEGAR WITHOUT FRUIT.

Inexpensive methods for making vinegar without the use of any fruit.

1. Molasses, one quart; yeast, one pint; warm rainwater, three gallons; put all into a jar or keg, and tie a piece of gauze over the bung, to keep out the flies and let in the air. In hot weather set it in the sun, in cold weather by the stove or in the chimney-corner. In three weeks you will have good vinegar.

2. The cheapest mode of making good vinegar is to mix five quarts of warm rainwater with two quarts of New Orleans molasses and four quarts of yeast. In a few weeks you will have the best vinegar you ever tasted.

3. To make vinegar from acetic acid and molasses, take of acetic acid two pounds, of molasses one-half gallon, and put them into a twenty-gallon cask. Fill it up with rainwater; shake it up and let stand from one to three weeks, and you will have good vinegar. If this does not make it as sharp as you like, add a little molasses. Acetic acid is concentrated vinegar. Take one pint of this acid, and add seven times as much soft water, and you have just as good a pure white vinegar as can be made from cider, and that instantaneously.

HOW TO RAISE CANARIES AND KEEP THEM HEALTHY AND IN GOOD SONG

1. In summer keep them out of doors in some cool and shady place.
2. In fall, winter or spring, hang the cage so that no draught of air can strike the bird.
3. Give nothing to healthy birds but rape, hemp, canary seed, water, cuttle-fish bone, and gravel paper or sand on the floor of the cage.
4. A bath three times a week.
5. The room should not be ove   ed.
6. When moulting keep warm   avoid all draughts of air.
7. Give plenty of German summer rape seed. A little hard boiled egg mixed with cracker, grated fine, once or twice a week, is excellent.
8. Feed at a certain hour in the morning.

DISEASES AND CURES.

9. **Husk or Asthma.**—The curatives are aperients, such as endive, water cresses, bread and milk and red pepper.
10. **Pip.**—Mix the pepper, butter and garlic and swab out the throat.
11. **Sweating.**—Wash the hen in salt water, and dry rapidly.
12. **Costiveness.**—Plenty of green food and fruit.
13. **Lice.**—Keep a saucer of fresh water in the cage, and the bird will free itself.

Fresh Flowers. 383

14. **Overgrown Claws or Beak.**—Pare carefully with a sharp knife.

15. **Moulting.**—Give plenty of good food and keep warm. Saffron and a rusty nail put into their drinking water is excellent.

16. **Loss of Voice.** Feed with paste of bread, lettuce and rape seed with yolk of egg. Whisky and sugar is a good remedy.

17. To keep insects out of bird cages, tie up a little powdered sulphur in a bag and hang it in the top of the cage.

TO KEEP FLOWERS FRESH.

To keep flowers fresh exclude them from the air. To do this, wet them thoroughly, put in a damp box, and cover with wet, raw cotton or newspaper, then place in a cool spot. To preserve bouquets, put a little saltpetre in the water you use in your vases, and the flowers will live for a fortnight.

Flower Hints.—Always pull the leaves off the stalks of flowers before putting them in water—those which would be in the water, not those above it. And with flowers from any hard-stalked sort of shrub the bark should be peeled off as well as the leaves. The flowers live ever so much longer if these precautions are taken. A scrap of charcoal in the water is also a great preservative.

When Flowers Wilt.—Cut the stems and plunge them into hot water. It is marvelous what a reviving effect this will have.

THE DELINEATOR.

HOW TO ENLARGE PORTRAITS AND PICTURES FOR PAINTING AND DRAWING.

Also How to Enlarge Embroidery, Braiding Patterns, Mats, Engraving Capital Letters, Scrolls, Music, Etc.

1. The Delineator, as shown in the above engraving, is fastened to a table or board with a little screw or awl. The little steel point at "A" rests on the picture or work to be copied. The pencil in the hand copies as fast as the steel point traces the small picture. The Delineator is set to enlarge four times by the little finger screws "B" and "C." If you wish your picture the same size as the copy, put the screws at number one. If you wish your picture twelve times as large as the copy, put the screws in number twelve in each of the four bars.

2. Keep the pencil sharpened under the hand. It is not necessary to watch the pencil in the movements of the hand, but to watch the steel point at "A."

3. Now any one can easily make a delineator, by going to the hardware store and securing a few little screws, as shown in the cut, and then making or securing four little pieces of wood, as shown in the illustration, of about two feet in length. If pictures are to be very much enlarged, the sticks may be made larger, so that the delineator may enlarge twenty-five or one hundred times.

How to take Measures for Patterns. 385

HOW TO TAKE MEASURES FOR PATTERNS.

Dresses, Coats, Vests, Pants and Shirts.

To Measure for a Lady's Basque or any Garment requiring a Bust Measure to be taken:—Put the measure around the body, over the dress, close under the arms, drawing it closely—not too tight.

To Measure for a Lady's Skirt or Overskirt:—Put the measure around the waist, over the dress.

To Measure for a Lady's Sleeve:—Put the measure around the muscular part of the upper arm, about an inch below the lower part of the arm's-eye, drawing the tape closely—not too tight.

Take the measure for Misses' and Little Girls' Patterns the same as for Ladies'. In ordering, give the ages also.

To Measure for a Boy's Coat or Vest:—Put the measure around the body, under the jacket, close under the arms, drawing it closely—not too tight.

To Measure for a Boy's Overcoat:—Measure about the breast over the garment the coat is to be worn over.

To Measure for Trousers:—Put the measure around the body, over the trousers at the waist, drawing it closely—not too tight.

To Measure for a Shirt:—For the size of the neck, measure the exact size where the collar encircles it, and allow one inch—thus, if the exact size be fourteen inches, use a Pattern marked fifteen inches. In other words, give the size of the collar the shirt is to be worn with. For the breast, put the measure around the body, under the jacket or coat, close under the arms, drawing it closely—not too tight.

25

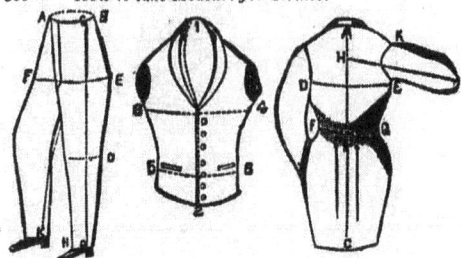

HOW TO TAKE THE MEASURE FOR A SUIT OF CLOTHES.

Take these Measures over the Vest: Inches.

From 1 at center of back of neck, round the inside edge of the collar, to height required from top button ....
From top button to 2 for length in front................
From 3 to 4 round breast...............................
From 5 to 6 round waist................................

MEASURE FOR PANTS.

From A to B round waist...............................
From C to D, top to bottom............................
From center to fork, close up, down to K, for length of leg inside, the leg straight down....................
F to G round the seat..................................
L round the knee......................................
From H to I round bottom.............................

Take these Measures outside the Coat:
From A to B..
Continuing on to C for full length......................
From H to I for elbow joint............................
Continuing on to K for length of sleeve................

Take these Measures under the Coat:
From D to E round the breast..........................
From F to G round the waist...........................

FOR AN OVERCOAT.

Take the last two measures over the undercoat; the others same as above.

HOW TO CLEAN NECKTIES, RIBBONS, ETC.

Get a quart fruit-jar with rubber and cover; half fill it with naphtha and put the ties in, the white ones by themselves and first of all. Having screwed the cover down tightly, shake the jar about for some minutes, when the dirt will almost be entirely removed. If necessary, repeat the process. Smooth them out carefully, and pat any streaked or discolored places with a bit of cloth—an old handkerchief will do nicely. Then hang them in the air to dry and allow the odor to evaporate. It is best to leave them out some days. A bit of mosquito-netting or cheese-cloth will be required to cover them from dust or flies. The darker ties may be put in the same naphtha. It is well to have two jars: one for first washing, another for the second dipping if necessary. The naphtha should be kept in a close-stoppered bottle, and such work should always be done by daylight in a room without a fire and with open windows, if possible, as the vapor from naphtha is highly inflammable.

HOW TO CLEAN SILK.

To Remove Grease Spots.—Scrape French chalk fine; moisten to a stiff paste with soap-suds; make into small flat cakes, and dry in the sun or oven. When a spot is to be cleaned, scrape one of the cakes to a powder, cover the spot with it, laying the silk on a linen or cotton cloth. Lay several folds of tissue paper upon the chalk, and press with a hot iron for several minutes, taking care it does not touch the silk.

To Wash Silk.—Mix together two cups cold water, one tablespoonful honey, one tablespoonful soft soap, one wine-glass alcohol. Lay the silk on a board, sponge both sides with it, rubbing it in well. Shake up and down in a tub of cold water. Shake dry but do not wring it. Iron on the wrong side while it is very damp.

How to Dye Cloth in Permanent Colors.

HOW TO DYE ALL KINDS OF CLOTH IN PERMANENT COLORS.

For Cotton Goods, Woolen, Silk, Etc.

YELLOW.

To color yellow, take one ounce of bichromate of potash and two ounces of sugar of lead. Dissolve them separately in as much hot water as will cover the goods. Dip into potash water first.

The above will color two pounds of cotton goods.

BLUE.

Dissolve one ounce Prussian blue and two ounces oxalic acid in enough cold water to cover the goods. Will color two pounds of cotton goods.

GREEN.

Dissolve one ounce of Prussian blue in cold water. Let goods remain in over night, then proceed as for yellow.

BLACK.

Soak the cloth in acetate of iron mordant, and then boil in a decoction of madder and logwood.

FOR WOOLEN GOODS, SILKS, LINENS, ETC.

Use Diamond Dyes. The colors will remain permanent in woolens, silks and linens, but for cotton cloth they are not satisfactory.

HOW TO MIX PAINTS OF VARIOUS COLORS.

A correspondent asks us a question on this subject, and we have no doubt there are numerous painter's manuals, or books of instruction, in existence; but many of these are not very reliable. We give the following table of compound colors, showing the simple colors which produce them, which may be of some service to our inquirer.

Buff—White, yellow ochre and red.
Chestnut—Red, black and yellow.
Chocolate—Raw umber, red and black.
Claret—Red, umber and black.
Copper—Red, yellow and black.
Dove—White, vermilion, blue and yellow.
Drab—White, yellow ochre, red and black.
Fawn—White, yellow and red.
Flesh—White, yellow ochre and vermilion.
Freestone—Red, black, yellow ochre and white.
French Grey—White, prussian blue and lake.
Grey—White lead and black.
Gold—White, stone ochre and red.
Green Bronze—Chrome green, black and yellow.
Green Pea—White and chrome green.
Lemon—White and chrome yellow.
Limestone—White, yellow ochre, black and red.
Olive—Yellow, blue, black and white.
Orange—Yellow and red.
Peach—White and vermilion.
Pearl—White, black and blue.
Pink—White, vermilion and lake.
Purple—Violet, with more red and white.
Rose—White and madder lake.
Sandstone—White, yellow ochre, black and red.
Snuff—Yellow and vandyke brown.
Violet—Red, blue and white.

In the preceding table of the combination of colors required to produce a desired tint, the first-named color is always the principal ingredient, and the others follow in the order of their importance. Thus in mixing a limestone tint, white is the principal ingredient, and the red the color of which the least is needed. The exact proportions of each color must be determined by experiment with a smaller quantity. It is best to have the principal ingredient thick, and add to it the other paints thinner.

HOW TO TAN HIDES WITH HAIR ON.

A cheap and simple process is to apply to the flesh side, when fresh and wet, a mixture of two parts of saltpetre and one part alum. These should be finely pulverized and sprinkled over every part of the skin; double in flesh to flesh, roll up and let it lie a day or two; then with a dull knife remove the flesh and fat, if any has been left. When about half dry, commence rubbing and continue working until dry. The skin will be found very nice, white and pliable, and the hair firmly set.

HOW TO MAKE ALL KINDS OF GLUE, PASTE, MUCILAGE, ETC.

TO CEMENT BROKEN CHINA, ETC.

Beat the whites of eggs well to a froth, let them settle; add soft grated or sliced cheese and quicklime; beat them well together, and apply a little to the broken edges. This cement will endure both fire and water. Another good receipt, and which is nearly colorless, is the following: Dissolve ½ ounce of gum acacia in a wineglass of boiling water, add plaster of Paris sufficient to form a thick paste, and apply it with a brush to the parts required to be cemented together.

CHEAP WATERPROOF GLUE.

Melt common glue with the smallest possible quantity of water; add, by degrees, linseed oil, rendered drying by boiling with litharge. While the oil is being added, the ingredients must be well stirred, to incorporate them thoroughly.

PAPER AND LEATHER PASTE.

Cover 4 parts, by weight, of glue with 15 parts of cold water and allow it to soak for several hours; then warm moderately until the solution is perfectly clear, and dilute with 60 parts of boiling water, thoroughly stirred in. Next prepare a solution of 30 parts of starch in 200 parts of cold water, so as to form a thin homogeneous liquid, free from lumps, and pour the boiling glue solution into it with thorough stirring, and at the same time keep the mass boiling.

CHEAP AND BEAUTIFUL INK.

INDELIBLE INK FOR MARKING CLOTHING.

5 scruples nitrate of silver,
2 drachms gum arabic,
1 scruple sap green,
1 ounce distilled water

Mix together. Before using on the article to be marked, apply a little of the following:

½ ounce carbonate of soda,
4 ounces distilled water.

Let this last, which is the mordant, get dry; then with a quill pen write what you require.

HOW TO MAKE INVISIBLE INK FOR POSTAL CARDS.

2 ounces of water,
¼ ounce of cobalt, dissolved in a little muriatic acid,
½ drachm of mucilage of gum acacia.

Write on paper with this liquid and it remains invisible until heated. On cooling it becomes invisible again.

INK FOR MARKING PACKAGES.

Take lamp black and mix thoroughly with sufficient turpentine to make it thin enough to flow from the brush. Powdered ultra marine blue makes a fine blue marking ink.

Inks.

HOW TO MAKE YOUR OWN INKS AT A TRIFLING COST.

Black Ink.

Take one package of Diamond Slate Dye and dissolve in a pint of boiling water. It will make a pint of excellent jet black ink at the small cost of ten cents.

Red, Green, Purple, Blue or Yellow Ink.

Take ten grains of the desired color of aniline and mix with one ounce of soft water, in which about fifteen grains of gum arabic have been dissolved. A bottle of ink of any of the above colors can be made at a cost of five cents.

White Ink.

Mix pure Flake White with water containing enough gum arabic to prevent the immediate settling of the substance.

Five cents' worth of Flake White will make a bottle of ink.

Gold or Silver Ink.

Take ten cents' worth of gold or silver bronze and mix with water containing gum arabic to the thickness of ordinary mucilage, and apply to pen with a small brush or stick.

Many of the *high-priced inks* that are advertised and sold as *mineral inks* are nothing more or less than the above preparations.

Indelible Ink.

Nitrate of silver, 50 grains; tartaric acid, 40 grains; carmine, No. 40, 5 grains; liquor ammonia, ½ ounce; mucilage of gum arabic, ½ ounce. Dissolve the nitrate of silver in the ammonia, and add the tartaric acid; then rub the carmine with the solution, then add the mucilage.

HOW TO MAKE ALL KINDS OF BLACKING, OIL, AND DRESSING FOR BOOTS AND SHOES.

TO MAKE SHOES OR BOOTS WATERPROOF.

Melt together, equal quantities of beeswax and mutton suet. While liquid rub it over the leather, including the soles.

TO SOFTEN BOOTS AND SHOES.

Kerosene will soften boots and shoes which have been hardened by water, and render them as pliable as new.

LIQUID BLACKING.

2 pounds ivory black,
1 pound sweet oil,
2 pounds molasses.

Rub together till well mixed; then add oil of vitriol, ¾ pound, coarse sugar ½ pound; dilute with beer bottoms. This cannot be excelled.

WATERPROOF COMPOUND, FOR LEATHER BOOTS, SHOES, ETC.

8 ounces suet,
8 ounces linseed oil,
6 ounces yellow beeswax,
1½ ounces neatsfoot oil,
1 ounce lamp black,
½ ounce litharge.

Melt together, and stir till cold.

BLACKING FOR LADIES' SHOES.

3 ounces of Gum Shellac,
1½ ounces of Aqua Ammonia,
10 ounces of water.

Boil until the shellac has dissolved. Then add a little black Aniline for coloring, and add water enough to make about twenty ounces.

PREPARED GLUE FOR CONSTANT USE.

To any quantity of glue use common whiskey instead of water. Put the bits of glue, well broken up, into a bottle; fill up with the spirit, and set it in a closet, or where it is warm, for a week; then it will be ready to use without the application of heat.

Glue thus prepared will keep for years, and will be fit for use at all times, unless the weather is very cold, then place the bottle in boiling water for a few moments. To obviate the difficulty of the stopper becoming tight from the glue, it is a good plan to make the glue in a tin box, and the cover will fit on tightly without sticking. It must be closed tight or the spirit will evaporate.

MUCILAGE FOR LABELS.

2 ounces dextrine,   1 ounce alcohol,
1 drachm glycerine,   6 ounces water.

PASTE FOR PAPERING BOXES.

Boil water and stir in batter of wheat or rye flour. Let it boil one minute, take off and strain through a colander. Add, while boiling, a little glue or powdered alum. Do plenty of stirring while the paste is cooking, and make of consistency that will spread nicely.

PASTE FOR SCRAP BOOKS.

Take half a teaspoonful of starch, same of flour, pour on a little boiling water, let it stand a minute, add more water, stir and cook it until it is thick enough to starch a shirt bosom. It spreads smooth, sticks well and will not mold or discolor paper. Starch alone will make a very good paste. Adding ten drops of oil of clover to ½ pint of this preparation will make it more permanent.

COMMON MUCILAGE FOR HOME AND BUSINESS USE.

Take one ounce of gum arabic and reduce it to the consistency of common mucilage by pouring warm water on it, and let it stand a few hours. This makes a very good mucilage, and it costs but a trifle.

HOME-MADE MUCILAGE.

Boil a good-sized onion for a short time and squeeze the juice out. It is adhesive and answers the purpose as well as the bought article.

Gum Arabic and gum tragacanth in equal parts, dissolved in hot water, make the best and most convenient mucilage to keep in the house.

HOW TO IMPROVE LEATHER.

To Soften Leather.—Castor oil is the best thing with which to soften leather.

To Remove Grease Stains from leather apply benzine and afterward the beaten white of an egg.

Best Dressing.—Vaseline is said to be one of the best dressings for russet shoes, and spirits of turpentine the correct thing for cleaning and brightening patent leather.

You Can Tell a Woman by Her Shoes.—Slovenly shoes a slatternly person; neat and clean shoes, a natty and nice little woman. So it is well to look after this small detail. If your kid "uppers" lack the freshness of the new article, the following will be found a cheap and good renovator: Yolk of one egg, one ounce of castor oil, one drachm of turpentine, two drachms of gum arabic, three ounces of writing ink.

Something About White Shoes.—A light evening toilet is not complete without white shoes or slippers; and a white shoe that is soiled is execrable. There are many popular fallacies in this world; one is that raw eggs are not good to eat, and another that white shoes are perishable. Perishable, indeed! My white shoes have lasted me longer than any shoes I have ever had, and with nothing more than a little "elbow grease" to preserve them. Any druggist will sell you ten cents worth of pipe clay. And who does not possess an old tooth brush? With these two articles there is no excuse for the dustiness of your white shoes. Use the pipe clay dry, taking care always to rub the way of the grain, so as not to roughen the suede. Do not be afraid to brush hard, or to get too much of the clay on the shoe. You cannot get too much on, and unless you are an athlete, with an arm of iron, I do not believe you can brush too hard. Pipe clay, used in the same way, will also clean trimmings of white cloth if they are excessively soiled. Use the clay wet; it will make them look badly at first, but if brushed carefully with a clean brush and fresh water, it will dry off in a most satisfactory manner. I have kept a little white broadcloth waistcoat, collar and cuffs clean in this way for two years. White undressed kid gloves may also be cleaned in this way. It is with pipe clay that the men in the British army keep their white gloves and the white in their uniforms so immaculately clean.

STATUARY AND MARBLE.

To Clean Statuary.—Use a very *weak* solution of oxalic acid applied with a soft tooth brush. This will cleanse the finest pieces of statuary.

1. **To Clean Marble** mix two parts of powdered whiting with one of powdered bluing and half a pound of soft soap and allow it to come to a boil; while still hot apply with a soft cloth to the discolored marble and allow it to remain there until quite dry; then wash off with hot water and soap in which a little salts of lemon has been dissolved. Dry well with a piece of soft flannel and your marble will be clean and white.

2. **To Clean Marble.**—Take two parts of common soda, one part of pumice stone, and one part of finely powdered chalk; sift it through a fine sieve, and mix it with water; then rub it well all over the marble, and the stains will be removed; then wash the marble over with soap and water, and it will be as clean as it was at first.

Marble May Be Cleaned by mixing up a quantity of the strongest soap-lees with quicklime, to the consistence of milk, and laying on the marble for 24 hours; clean it afterwards with soap and water.

Caution.—While these are excellent for cleaning ordinary marble, they would ruin fine statuary. For cleaning fine statuary see above.

To Take Ink Stains Out of Mahogany.—Put a few drops of spirits of nitre in a teaspoonful of water, touch the spot with a feather dipped in the mixture, and on the ink disappearing, rub it over immediately with a rag wetted in cold water, or there will be a white mark, which will not be easily effaced.

To Take Ink Stains Out of a Colored Table-Cover.—Dissolve a teaspoonful of oxalic acid in a teacup of hot water; rub the stained part well with the solution.

To Take Ink Out of Boards.—Strong muriatic acid, or spirits of salts, applied with a piece of cloth; afterwards well washed with water.

398

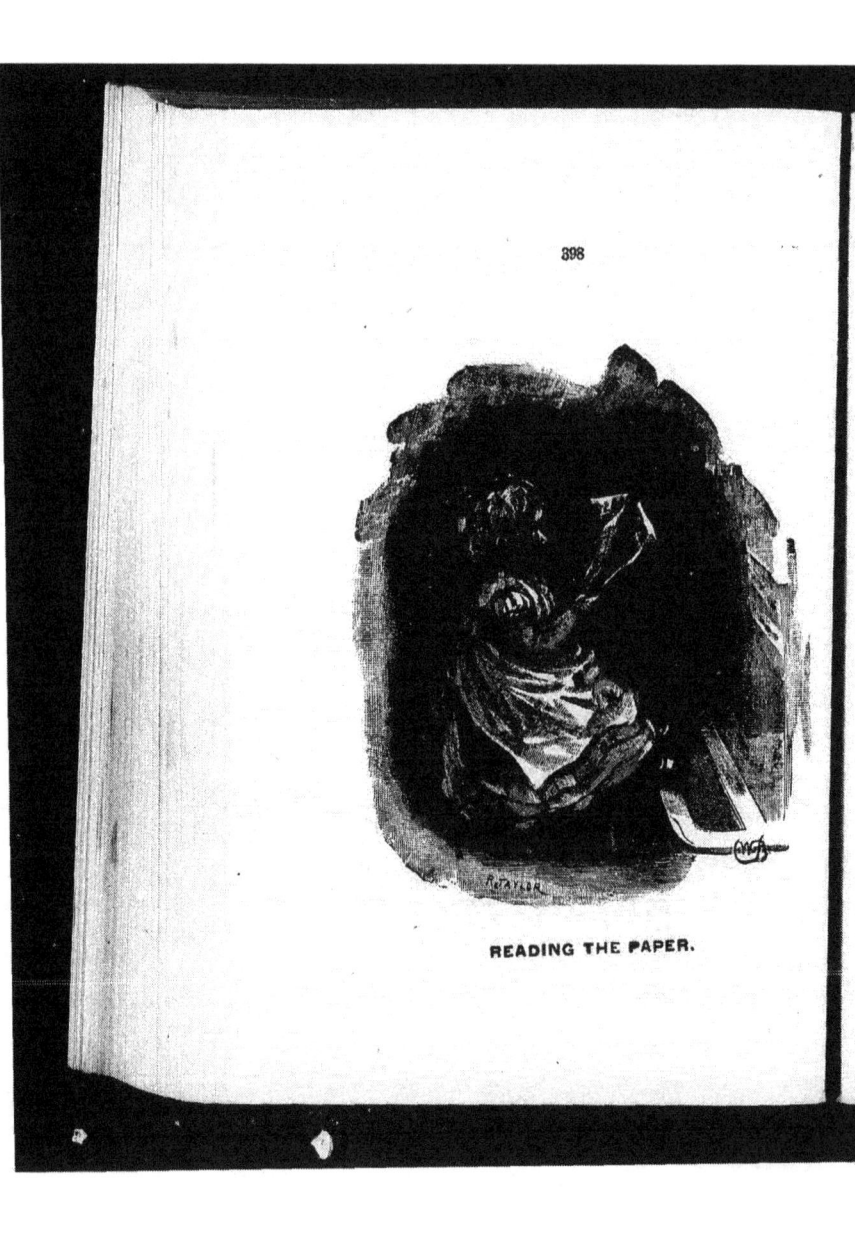

READING THE PAPER.

BOOK IV.

WOMAN'S FRIEND.

A COMPLETE COOK BOOK.

THE ART OF COOKING.

"The number of inhabitants who may be supported in any country upon its internal produce depends about as much upon the state of the art of cookery as upon that of agriculture; but if cookery be of so much importance, it certainly deserves to be studied with the greatest of care. Cookery and agriculture are arts of civilized nations. Savages understand neither of them."—Count Rumford's Works, Vol. 1.

The importance of the art of cookery is very great; indeed, from the richest to the poorest the selection and preparation of food often becomes the chief object in life. The rich man's table is luxuriously spread; no amount of money is spared in procuring the rarest delicacies of the season. Art and nature alike contribute to his necessities. The less wealthy have, indeed, fewer resources; yet these may be greatly increased by the knowledge of what may be called trifling details and refinement in the art of cookery, which depends much more on the manner of doing a thing than on the cost attending it. To cook well, therefore, is immensely more important to the middle and working classes than to the rich, for they who live by the "sweat of their brow," whether mentally or physically, must have the requisite strength to support their labor. Even to the poor, whose very life depends upon the produce of the hard-earned dollar, cookery is of the greatest importance. Every wife, mother or sister should be a good plain cook. If she has servants she can direct them, and if not, so much the more must she depend upon herself. To such we venture to give a few general hints. An old saying (to be found in one of the earliest cookery books): "First catch your hare, etc.," has more significance than is generally supposed. To catch your hare well you must spend your income judiciously. This is the chief thing. In our artificial state of society, every income, to keep up appearances, has at least half as much more to do than it can afford. In the selection of provisions, the best is generally the cheapest. Half a pound of good meat is more nutritious than three times the amount of inferior. As to vegetables, buy them fresh. Above all, where an income is small and there are many to feed, be careful that all e nourishment is retained in the food that is purchased. This is to be effected by careful cooking. Cleanliness is an imperative condition. Let all cooking utensils be clean and in order. Uncleanliness produces disorder, and disorder confusion. Time and money are thus wasted, dinners spoiled, and all goes wrong.

very great; in-
e selection and
ef object in life.
; no amount of
lelicacies of the
to his necessi-
r resources; yet
wledge of what
nt in the art of
the manner of
To cook well,
the middle and
who live by the
 or physically,
ort their labor.
upon the prod-
of the greatest
er should be a
an direct them,
pend upon her-
neral hints. An
arliest cookery
as more signif-
atch your hare
ly. This is the
ciety, every in-
it half as much
ection of provi-
Half a pound of
nes the amount
sh. Above all,
any to feed, be
in the food that
areful cooking.
et all cooking
liness produces
ind money are
rong.

HINTS FOR THE COOK.

Tumblers that have been used for milk should never be put into hot water until they have been first rinsed in cold water. The heat drives the milk in, and gives a cloudy appearance to the glass, which cannot be removed.

Meats never allowed to boil will be more tender than those that cook hard. Tough meats become tender by proper cooking, while the reverse of this is equally true. Hard boiling in salt water will toughen the best piece of meat ever sold.

An excellent substitute for potatoes at a dinner is rice, cooked in milk and well salted, put into a dish and browned in the oven. Make a hot lemon sauce and pour it over the rice when it is taken from the oven and just before the dish is sent to the table.

Old potatoes are made mealy by being soaked for an hour in cold water after being peeled. When boiling they should be cooked in salted water; when the potatoes are soft, turn off the water, leave the potatoes in covered kettle to dry off all steam. They will be nearly as nice as new ones.

Butter that has become stale may be made sweet for pastry by boiling it in plenty of water and a little soda, a teaspoonful being enough for four or five pounds. Let it get cold, take the cake off and boil again in clear water. When it is cold, scrape the bottom dry and pack away for use.

HINTS ON SEASONING.

Sliced onion fried in butter or in butter and flour, and rubbed through a sieve and put into soups just before serving, gives a fine flavor and good color.

A dash of black pepper greatly improves vanilla ice cream.

Make snow cake with arrowroot flour; the flavor is delicious.

Bean soup is much improved by adding a little mace just before serving.

When making corn bisque, use cayenne with a little sugar for seasoning.

Add a cup of good cider vinegar to the water in which you boil fish, especially salt water fish.

Boston baked beans can be greatly improved by adding a cup of sweet cream the last hour of baking.

Place on top of fish when baking thin slices of salt pork; it will baste the fish and the seasoning is fine.

Put sugar into the water used for basting meats of all kinds; it gives a good flavor to veal more especially.

To give a fine flavor to corn beef hash use good soup stock for moistening, with a pinch of salt, sugar and cayenne.

Three tablespoons of freshly-made Japan tea, with a bit of nutmeg, gives an indescribable flavor to an apple pie.

Put a few sticks of cinnamon bark and a little lemon juice with crab apple when making jelly; the flavor is good, or use pineapple instead of the lemon.

To give an appetizing flavor to a broiled beefsteak, cut an onion in half, and rub it over the hot platter with the melted butter.

When flavoring has been forgotten in a pudding or cake, the fault may be remedied by rubbing the desired extract over the outside of the cake as soon as it is taken out of the oven.

GOLDEN RULES FOR THE KITCHEN.

Without *cleanliness and punctuality* good cooking is impossible.

Leave nothing *dirty; clean and clear as you go.*

A time for everything and everything in time.

A good cook wastes nothing

An hour lost in the morning has to be run after all day.

Haste without hurry saves worry, fuss and flurry.

Stew boiled is stew spoiled.

Strong fire for roasting.

Clear fire for broiling.

Wash vegetables in three waters.

Boil fish quickly, meat slowly.

ADVICE TO COOKS.

Importance of Cooking.—No matter how large the establishment, no person holds a more important part than the cook, for with her rests not only the comfort, but the health of those she serves, and we would warn all cooks not to make light of their responsibilities, but to study diligently the tastes and wishes of all those for whom they have to prepare food.

Cleanliness.—A dirty kitchen is a disgrace, both to mistress and maid, and cleanliness is a most essential ingredient in the art of cooking. It takes no longer to have a clean and orderly kitchen than an untidy and dirty one, for the time that is spent in keeping it in good order is saved when cooking operations are going on and everything is clean and in its place.

Dress.—When at your work, dress suitably; wear short, plain gowns, well-fitting boots, and large aprons with bibs, of which every cook and kitchen maid should have a good supply, and you will be comfortable as you never can be with long dresses, small aprons, and slipshod shoes, the latter being most trying in a warm kitchen.

Kitchen Supplies.—Do not let your stock of pepper, salt, spices, seasonings, etc., dwindle so low that there is danger, in the midst of preparing dinner, that you find yourself minus some very important ingredient, thereby causing much confusion and annoyance.

MEATS.

There seems to be a general impression that a continued meat diet is absolutely essential and with some it seems to be unwise to omit it for a single meal.

There is no civilized country in the world in which so much meat is eaten or in which so much is wasted by bad cooking, by profusion, or by absolute unthrift.

We all eat too much meat, too much for our health, probably, and certainly too much for the well-being of our pocketbooks. Great, brawny Scotchmen live month after month on oatmeal and buttermilk, and a healthier, harder working class of men it would be difficult to find. The general health of the American would be greatly improved if the diet were to consist more of vegetables, grains and fruit and not so much of meat.

Cooking Meat.—We are profuse in our provision of meat and then we are apt to cook it in the most wasteful way. With many the sum total of a knowledge of cooking is to get a joint or a steak and roast or broil—say, rather, to bake or fry it, at a range or cooking

Meats.

stove. Meat is often spoiled in the cooking. A very little piece of meat, nicely broiled, with gravy in it, well seasoned with pepper and salt, a very little butter on it, and served up quite hot, will make a better and more nourishing meal than four times the amount badly cooked in the frying pan.

The Frying Pan has almost, times without number, spoiled a good piece of meat. The frying pan is indispensable for some things, but very bad for chops and steaks.

A Golden Recipe.—In the cooking of meat by any process whatever, remember, above all, to cook the juices *in it* not *out* of it.

Roasting.—In roasting meat, the gravy may be retained in it by pricking the joint all over with a fork and rubbing in pepper and salt. Mutton and beef may be overdone; veal and pork must be well cooked. Young meat generally requires more cooking than old; thus, lamb and veal must be more done than mutton and beef. In frosty weather meat will require a little more time for cooking. All joints for roasting will improve by hanging a day or so before cooking.

Broiling.—Broiling is the most nutritious method of cooking mutton and pork chops, or beef and rump steaks, kidneys (which should never be cut open before cooking), etc. Have the gridiron clean, and put over a clear fire; put the meat on it; "keep it turned often." This last is a common direction in books, but the reason why is never stated; it is to keep the gravy in the meat. By permitting the one side of a steak to be well done before turning, you will see the red gravy settled on the top of the steak, and so the meat is hard and spoiled. This is cooking the gravy out of, instead of keeping it in, the meat to nourish the consumer. Never stick the fork into the meaty part; you will lose gravy if you do so. Be sure to turn often, and generally the chop of steak is done if it feels firm to the fork; if not done it will be soft and flabby. It is economical to broil well.

Boiling Meat.—If you put a piece of lean meat into cold water and heat it slowly, you find that much of the nutriment has been drawn out by the water and the meat has of course just in that proportion been made poor. The longer and slower the warming process, the more the nutritious substance is extracted.

Soup Making.—This is the process when it is desired to have good soup. After some hours of cooking the meat becomes tasteless. A dog fed on that alone could not live many days.

Another Method of Boiling Meat.—Put a piece of meat into boiling water and continue the boiling. The surface of the meat suddenly whitens and the nutritious substance is thereby not permitted to escape from the meat. The outside of the meat is seared and the juices are kept in. The temperature must now be lowered or the meat will be "overcooked." If meats are allowed to boil too fast they toughen, all their juices are extracted, and only the flesh fiber, without sweetness, is left; if they boil too long they are reduced to a jelly and their nourishing properties are transferred to the water in which they are boiled. Nothing is more difficult than to boil meat exactly as it should be; close attention and good judgment are indispensable.

Frying in Fat.—If we put a thin piece of meat, as a cutlet coated with eggs and bread crumbs, into boiling fat, the albumen in the surface or rather in that of the egg surrounding it is thickened or coagulated and the juices will be retained in the meat. For frying always use an abundance of fat in the pan. This is no waste, as the same fat can be used over and over again by pouring it through a strainer into a crock kept for the purpose.

To Bake Meat.—Make some beef fat hot in an iron pan or broad kettle. Put the meat into it, and with a fork stuck into the fat, turn it rapidly till it is on all sides a fine brown, then put it into a hot oven, elevating it above the pan on a meat rack, or a few iron rods. Now comes the process called basting; in five minutes or less you will find that the top of the meat has dried, and you must now dip, with a spoon, the hot fat from the pan over the top. Do this every few minutes, adding no water to the pan; you will find your meat well cooked in from 12 to 15 minutes to the pound. It is done when it has lost in the middle the blue color, and becomes a fine red. Only salt and pepper should be used to season such roasts, and must be added when the meat is half done; earlier it toughens the fibers.

Meat and Soup.—To make soup crack the bones and cut up the meat into small pieces and put on the stove in *cold* water, cook slowly several hours, cool, remove the fat and rewarm, adding flavors to taste before serving Do not remove the scum which rises while boiling, as this is the most nourishing part. The soup meat may afterward be chopped, moistened with some of the soup, flavored with spices, lemon, etc., and pressed while warm and will make nice cold meat for tea.

HOW TO MAKE MEAT TENDER.
(A NEW METHOD.)

It is well known that meat must be kept some time after killing to make it tender. In winter, a large piece of beef or mutton will keep for six weeks if hung in a dry, cool place. Indeed, this is the time allowed in England for the Christmas "shoulder of mutton," and every few days it is rubbed over with salt and vinegar. In summer, unless the butcher will keep the meat for you, you must resort to other means.

STUFFED BEEF'S HEART.

If fire is no object, you may boil a beef's heart, it will take all day. Put into cold water and bring slowly to the simmering point and keep it there. Next day it may be stuffed with well-seasoned bread crumbs and baked three quarters of an hour.

HOW TO SERVE ROAST BEEF A SECOND TIME.

Heat the gravy, put the roast in it. After trimming it into shape again, cover closely and put into a hot oven for ten minutes, or less, according to size of piece.

Or, cut in slices and lay in hot gravy, only long enough to heat them through.

HAM CAKES.

Take one cup finely chopped boiled ham, two cups of breadcrumbs, two eggs, pepper and salt, and enough milk to make quite moist.

To use. First: Fry on a griddle in small spoonfuls, and turn as pancakes.

Second: Use mashed potatoes instead of breadcrumbs, and fry as above.

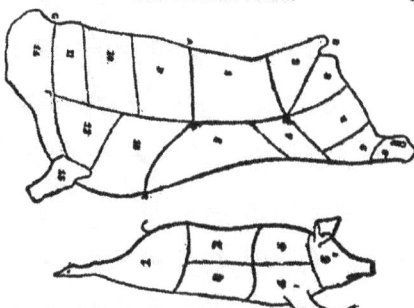

Showing the Sections into which Pork should be cut.

HOW TO PICKLE BEEF.

A. S. Barnard's Celebrated Recipe.

To 3 gallons of water add 8 pounds of salt, 2 ounces of saltpetre and one pine of molasses—same proportion for larger quantities.

Method.—Pack the meat without salt. Prepare the brine as above, scald it, skim it, let it cool and cover the meat.

HOW TO PICKLE HAMS.

Take to 100 pounds of ham, 4 quarts of fine salt, ½ pound of saltpetre and 1 quart of molasses and mix thoroughly.

Method.—Rub the hams with the mixture and pack them closely. Put the remaining mixture upon them and let them lie 10 days, then turn them and let them lie 20 days—take them up and smoke them with corn cobs.

HOW TO PACK PORK.

Pack the pork closely together and put in plenty of rock salt, then pour on cold water to cover the meat.

HOW TO PICKLE TONGUES.

For each tongue take: 6 ounces of salt; 2 ounces of bay salt; 1 ounce of saltpetre; 3 ounces coarse sugar.

Cloves and allspice to taste, keep the tongue in the above pickle two weeks or 20 days.

SAUSAGE.

Two pounds lean pork, two pounds lean veal, two pounds beef suet, peel of half a lemon, one grated nutmeg, one teaspoonful black pepper, one teaspoonful cayenne pepper, five teaspoonfuls salt, three teaspoonfuls sweet marjoram and thyme, mixed, two teaspoonfuls of sage, juice of a lemon. Grind the meats and thoroughly mix in the other ingredients. Stuff in cases.

BOLOGNA SAUSAGE—COOKED.

Mix well together and let boil twelve hours: 5 pounds beef finely chopped, 1¼ pounds pork finely chopped, 2 teaspoonfuls of powdered cloves, 1 teaspoonful of powdered mace, 1¼ ounces of ground black pepper, salt to taste. Stuff this mixture into muslin bags eight or twelve inches long and three inches in diameter. Lay them in a ham pickle four or five days, and then smoke them six or seven days. Hang up in a dark place.

ROASTED TURKEY.

Stuff a nicely cleansed turkey with dressing, made of two pints of bread crumbs, one cup of butter, and moistened with water; to this add one egg, and salt and pepper to taste, and also a pint or more of oysters, if convenient. Mix this well before using. Rub butter over the outside of the turkey, place in the dripping pan with a little water, and baste frequently while cooking.

SMOTHERED CHICKEN.

Prepare the chicken as you would for boiling it whole, and place, with a little water, into a dripping pan, after seasoning it with butter, pepper and salt. Put thin slices of tomato over it, dredge with flour, cover it very closely to keep in the steam, and place in the oven to cook until tender. When done, remove the cover, to let brown nicely. Make a nice gravy from the drippings, to serve with them.

FRICASSEED CHICKEN.

Clean, wash, and cut up a pair of young chickens. Lay in clear water for half an hour. If they are old, you cannot brown them well. Put them in a saucepan, with enough cold water to cover them well, and set over the fire to heat slowly. Meanwhile, cut half a pound of salt pork in strips, and fry crisp. Take them out, chop fine, and put in the pot with the chickens. Fry in the fat left in the frying-pan one large onion, or two or three small ones, cut into slices. Let them brown well, and add them also to the chicken, with a quarter teaspoonful of allspice and cloves. Stew all together slowly for an hour or more, until the meat is very tender; you can test this with a fork. Take out the pieces of fowl and put in a hot dish, covering closely until the gravy is ready. Add to this a great spoonful of walnut or other dark catsup and nearly three tablespoonfuls of browned flour, a little chopped parsley, and a glass of brown Sherry. Boil up once; strain through a cullender, to remove the bits of pork and onion; return to the pot, with the chicken; let it come to a final boil, and serve, pouring the gravy over the pieces of fowl.

DEVILED TURKEY.

Take the first and second joint of a roast turkey and cut deep gashes in them, and into these put a little mixed mustard, a little salt and cayenne pepper. Lay on a broiler until heated through, then place on a very hot dish, and spread with butter.

PREPARED FOR ROASTING.

HOW TO COOK ALL KINDS OF POULTRY.

1. Poultry should never be eaten in less than twelve hours after it has been killed; but it should be picked and drawn as soon as possible.

2. After picking and drawing chickens it is well to wash them in three waters, adding a little soda in the last water.

3. When buying turkeys notice carefully the legs; if they are rough and reddish the bird is old; if smooth and black it is young.

4. If the fowl is old or tough, a little soda in which it is boiled will make it tender.

5. A pan of water placed in an oven with a roasting fowl will keep it from scorching.

6. Wild game first fried in butter before boiling will greatly improve the flavor.

7. Chickens, unless of the very tenderest spring brood, and Ducks and Turkeys are far better when dressed, stuffed and steamed until tender, then brown nicely in the oven. This makes an easy Sunday dinner, as all the labor may be done on Saturday with only a half hour's cooking Sunday.

8. Young fowls should never be fried but always broiled. Split down the back, butter and broil over clear coals. They may be finished in the oven after four or five minutes broiling. The flavor is finer and they digest much easier when fried. Use the bones for soup.

HOW TO CARVE TURKEYS, DUCKS, CHICKENS, ETC.

"Conversation is but carving;
Give no more to every guest
Than he's able to digest.
Give him always of the prime,
And but little at a time.
Carve to all but just enough,
Let them neither starve nor stuff.
And that you may have your due,
Let some neighbor carve for you."

1. It is a very easy matter to divide and separate the parts of a baked fowl, but it is another matter to do it easily and elegantly.

2. Every man and woman, boy and girl, should be familiar with the art of carving.

3. A good skillful carver places the fork in the fowl and does not remove it until the whole is divided.

4. First cut off the leg and wing on one side and then shave off the breast in nice thin slices. Then turn the bird and cut the other side in the same manner.

5. Never rise from your seat while carving.

6. To hit the joints while carving and separating the wings and legs, the bird should be thoroughly studied before cooked, and the lesson learned as to the location of the joints, after which no trouble will ever be experienced in separating any of the joints or parts in the fowl.

7. In a turkey the thigh should be separated into three portions, one with the bone, and two without, and a piece of this, with a slice from the breast, will be sufficient for one person, unless it is known that they do not prefer any of the parts thus separated.

8. The wing may be divided in a similar way, unless preference is otherwise expressed.

9. Always lay the pieces with skin side up and add a spoonful of stuffing.

414 *Stewed Chicken and Dumplings.*

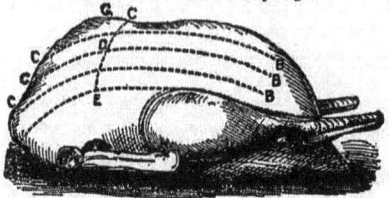

SHOWING THE SECTIONS IN WHICH THE BREAST IS TO BE CUT.

10. If there are old persons at the table, the choice part just below the thigh, which is easily removed, should be given them.

11. The best way to learn to carve is to watch a good, skillful carver, and then practice at every opportunity offered.

STEWED CHICKEN AND DUMPLINGS.

Cut a chicken into pieces suitable for serving, wash it, and put it into a deep stew pan, add three pints of water. Put on to boil, in another sauce pan, three slices of carrot, three of turnip, and one large onion, cook slowly for half an hour, then take up the vegetables in a strainer and place it in a stew pan with the chicken and dip some of the water into it. Mash the vegetables with the back of a spoon and rub as much as possible through the strainer. Now skim two spoonfuls of chicken fat and put it into the pan in which the vegetables were cooked. When boiling hot add three tablespoonfuls of flour, stir it in with the chicken, and simmer until tender. Season well with pepper and salt and butter. The stew must not boil hard, but only simmer about two hours. Ten minutes before serving, put it on the front of the stove and put the dumplings in and cook ten minutes.

HOW TO PREPARE AND COOK ALL KINDS OF FISH.

HOLLANDAISE SAUCE.

Put two tablespoonfuls of butter into a frying pan; when melted, add two tablespoonfuls of flour, stir until smooth, then pour in two cupfuls of cold water and stir steadily until it thickens, add a little salt and pepper, take from the fire and add the beaten yelks of two eggs and the juice of half a lemon, stirring steadily.

FRIED WHITEFISH.

Split a large whitefish and place in a dish with salt and pepper, squeeze over it the juice of two lemons and let it stand for an hour. Drain them, flour them all over, dip in egg and fry to a light brown. Serve with the above sauce.

BOILED FISH.

Unless you have a fish kettle the fish must be pinned in a stout piece of white cloth, and not boiled hard, but simmered. Serve with egg sauce.

HOW TO USE CANNED SALMON.

SALMON ON TOAST.

Flake the fish, season with pepper and salt, and heat it with a little milk or cream. Have some hot milk in a flat pan. Toast several slices of bread, which dip quickly into the hot milk, place on a hot dish, spread with butter and pour over it the heated fish.

SALMON CROQUETTES.

One can of salmon; one egg, well beaten; one-half cup of fine bread crumbs; salt, cayenne pepper; nutmeg; juice of half a lemon. Drain off the liquid and mince the fish. Melt and work in the butter; season, and if necessary moisten with a little of the liquid; add the crumbs. Form the parts into rolls, which flour thickly, and stand them in a cold place for an hour. Fry in hot fat and serve on a hot platter, garnished with fresh parsley or lettuce.

SALMON SALAD.

One cup of cold salmon minced and mixed with an equal quantity of chopped celery or cabbage. Line a dish with lettuce leaves, turn into it the mixed salmon and celery or cabbage, and over all pour dressing made of two tablespoonfuls of oil, three tablespoonfuls of vinegar, salt and pepper. A mayonnaise dressing may be used, but with salmon the plain dressing is to be preferred.

FISH BALLS.

The favorite dish is prepared by adding to cooked codfish, finely shredded, a like quantity of mashed potatoes. Make into balls, season and fry on a griddle or in boiling fat.

Any other fish can be used in the same way.

CODFISH SOUP.

Cook one tablespoonful of flour in one tablespoonful of butter. Add one and one-half quarts of milk, or milk and water, and when it boils stir in one teacup of cold boiled codfish that has been freed from skin and bones and then chopped fine. Add salt and pepper to taste.

OYSTERS.

OYSTER SOUP.

THE EDIBLE OYSTER.

Put the liquid of one quart of oysters and two pints of water in a kettle; let it boil and skim it, then add two quarts of milk and one dozen rolled crackers, with two tablespoonfuls of butter; put in a little salt and pepper. When near boiling point put in the oysters. When it begins to boil take up at once.

OYSTERS ON TOAST.

Put in a stew pan one quart of oysters with their liquid; when they come to a boil put in one pint of milk, one tablespoonful of butter mixed with two tablespoonfuls of flour and a little salt and pepper. Let it boil up and then pour over slices of nicely browned and buttered toast. Serve hot.

ROASTED OYSTERS.

Oysters are roasted in the following manner: Select large oysters and have them scrubbed thoroughly; then place them in the oven in a large tin with the round side of the shells down, so that when they open the liquor will not be lost. As soon as they do open remove the upper shell, sprinkle them with salt, pepper and chopped parsley, add a little butter and serve hot as possible on a bed of watercress. Oysters served in this way make an excellent first course at dinner if accompanied by thin slices of brown bread and butter.

OYSTER PATTIES.

Line patty pans with paste, put a cover of paste over and pinch the edges; bake in a quick oven, take as many large oysters as you have patties, stew them in their own liquid, then cut in pieces and add one tablespoonful of flour, the same of butter, the grated rind of one lemon, a little salt, pepper and minced mace, and three tablespoonfuls of cream; mix together well and into each of the patties put a tablespoonful of the mixture. Serve hot.

LOBSTER CUTLETS.

MADE FROM CANNED LOBSTERS.

Mince the meat of the lobsters fine, season with salt and spice, melt a piece of butter in a sauce pan, mix with it one tablespoonful of flour, add the lobster and a little finely chopped parsley, add a little stock also, and let it come to a boil; remove from the fire and stir into it the yolks of two eggs, spread this mixture in a shallow pan; when cold cut into cutlets, shape, dip carefully in beaten eggs, then in cracker crumbs and fry to a rich brown color in hot lard.

BAKED SALMON.

One can of salmon, two eggs, one tablespoonful melted butter, one cup bread crumbs, pepper, salt and minced cucumber pickle. Drain the liquid from the fish and set aside for the sauce. Pick the fish to pieces, then work in the melted butter, seasoning, eggs, and crumbs. Put in a buttered bowl, cover tightly and set in a pan of boiling water. Cook in a hot oven one hour, then stand the bowl in cold water for a moment to loosen the pudding, and turn out on a hot dish.

For the sauce make a cup of drawn butter, to which add the liquid from the can, a beaten egg, pepper, salt, a chopped pickle and some minced parsley, cabbage or lettuce. Boil up and pour over the fish or serve in a gravy tureen.

CORN OMELET.

HOW TO MAKE ALL KINDS OF OMELETS.

CORN OMELET.

For this take young tender sweet corn; shave off the kernels, scrape out the rest with a dull knife, being careful not to get in any of the cob. For 4 large ears, add 3 well-beaten eggs, 2 tablespoonfuls cream, or the same amount of milk with a tablespoonful butter, a pinch of salt and a little pepper. Place a tablespoonful butter in a spider, and when hot pour in the omelet. As soon as it sets, turn or fold it over and take up on a hot platter. Omelet is best if eaten hot.

VEGETABLE OMELET.

Cold cooked asparagus, French beans, carrots, cabbage, cauliflower sprigs, spinach, sorrel, tomatoes, mushrooms, etc., are all suitable to introduce into an omelet. Chop very finely the vegetable or vegetables in question—for a mixture is often preferred to only one kind—then mix thoroughly with the eggs; be careful to add appropriate seasonings, and proceed as already directed, serving with sauce, or not, just according to taste and convenience. Always continue the beating for some time after the last addition has been made to insure the ingredients being thoroughly blended, as this is the most important point.

FISH OMELET.

The remains of almost any kind of fresh fish may, with great advantage, be used for this purpose, and only a very small quantity is required—about two large teaspoonfuls for four eggs. After carefully removing the bones and every particle of skin, mince the fish very finely or tear it into tiny shreds with two forks, and add to it the other ingredients, then fry, and serve in the usual manner; or, if preferred, dish up without a paper under, and pour a few tablespoonfuls of some rich, boiling-hot fish sauce round—but not over—the omelet just at the last minute.

OMELETS WITH MEAT.

It is almost impossible to get wrong in the making of

OMELET.

these, as the remains of all sorts of meat, poultry, and game may be used, providing they are carefully prepared, very finely minced, and pleasantly seasoned previously to being added to the eggs. Cook in the usual way, serve as fancy dictates.

CHEESE OMELETS.

These form a particular appetizing little dish, and are deservedly very popular. To four eggs allow two dessert-spoonfuls of grated cheese, a teaspoonful of finely minced parsley, and a seasoning of salt and pepper; then, when sufficiently beaten, fry, and serve in the ordinary way.

SWEET OMELETS.

These are prepared, cooked, and served in precisely the same manner as described above, only substituting sweet ingredients for the savory. A tablespoonful of fine white sugar, a pinch of salt, and a few drops of some favorite flavoring essence added to the eggs will make a most delicious plain omelet; but, if prepared, about two tablespoonfuls of some delicate preserve may be used, or any kind of fresh fruit which has been partially cooked and sweetened, the omelet, of course, taking its name accordingly.

NEW EGG DISHES.

EGG ON TOAST.

Put one quart of boiling water and one tablespoonful of salt in a frying-pan. Break the eggs, one by one, into a saucer and slide carefully into the salted water. Cook until the white is firm. Lift out carefully and place on toasted slices of bread. Serve immediately.

SALAD EGGS.

Boil the eggs hard, turning them several times to prevent the yolks from settling on one side. When cool peel off the shells, cut across neatly with a sharp knife, remove the yolks and mash them smooth, mix with them some good salad dressing, taking care not to make the mixture too thin.

Return this mixture into the white part, and place the two halves together neatly, so as to look as if it had never been cut. Lay each egg in a fresh lettuce leaf. Excellent for picnics and luncheons.

CREAMED EGGS.

Boil six eggs twenty minutes. Make one pint of cream sauce. Have six slices of toast on a hot dish. Put a layer of sauce on each one, and then part of the white of the eggs, cut in thin strips; and rub part of the yolks through a sieve onto the toast. Repeat this, and finish with a third layer of sauce. Place in the oven for about three minutes. Garnish with parsley, and serve.

STUFFED EGGS.

Cut six hard-boiled eggs in two. Take out the yolks and mash them fine. Add two teaspoonfuls of butter, one of cream, two or three drops of onion juice, and salt and pepper to taste. Mix all thoroughly. Fill the eggs from the mixture, and put them together. There will be a little filling left, to which add a well-beaten egg. Cover the other eggs with this last preparation, and roll in cracked crumbs. Fry in boiling lard till a light brown.

New Dishes of Rice.

NEW DISHES OF RICE.

RICE.

Rice is the most digestible of all vegetable foods, and on that account is valuable alike for the table, nursery and sick-room. It is very rich in starch, but not as nutritive as wheat and some other cereals. It may be prepared in a variety of ways.

TO MAKE A RICE BORDER.

Wash one cupful of rice in cold water, and drain it; put in a saucepan and pour over one quart of boiling stock, let boil rapidly for 15 minutes; then stand on the back of the stove for 15 minutes longer; drain, season with salt and pepper and press into a well-buttered mold. Put in the oven and bake 15 minutes. Take up, turn out on a dish, fill the center with stewed chicken.

RICE CROQUETTES.

Wash a cupful of rice, put in a saucepan with a quart of milk and boil until thick; add the yolks of four eggs and cook ten minutes longer. Take from the fire, add a tablespoonful of chopped parsley, a little salt and pepper; mix well, turn out on a plate and set aside until very cold. Form in croquettes, dip first in beaten egg, then in grated bread crumbs and fry in boiling lard.

RICE SOUFFLE.

Put half a pint of cream on to boil. Beat two ounces of butter, five ounces of sugar, three ounces of ground rice and the yolks of six eggs together until light, stir into boiling cream, and stir until thick. Take from the fire, add a teaspoonful of vanila and half a teaspoonful of salt. Beat the whites of six eggs, stir them carefully into the mixture and turn in a glass bowl.

SNOWBALLS.

Wash a cupful of rice and put in a saucepan with a cupful of milk; boil until tender, add a pinch of salt and put in small cups to cool. When cold, turn out in a dish and pour over boiled custard. Serve with whipped cream or sauce.

RICE MERINGUE.

Boil a cupful of rice in a quart of water until tender, drain in a colander; add a pint of milk, a tablespoonful of butter and the yolks of six eggs beaten with two cupfuls of sugar, with the juice and rind of a lemon; pour in a baking-dish and bake in a quick oven. Beat the whites of the eggs with a teacupful of powdered sugar and heap over the top; set in the oven to brown.

POTATOES.

We in our country need not feel as bitter against the potato as do the scientists of Europe, for we are not obliged to use it to excess, and considering its cheapness and availability, it is for us a good vegetable, and on these accounts, though it makes a poor enough showing as to food value, we must rank it next to the bean in importance. The quality of the potato is of great importance, and none but the best should be used. It should be of a mealy variety and perfectly ripe.

How Potatoes May be Spoiled.—In a bulletin issued by Professor Snyder, of the Minnesota State Agricultural College, he makes a point of interest to the housewife. He shows that where potatoes are peeled and started boiling in cold water there is a loss of 80 per cent. of the total albumen, and where they are not peeled and are started in hot water this loss is reduced to two per cent. A bushel of potatoes, weighing 60 pounds, contain about two pounds of total nitrogenous compounds. When improperly cooked one-half of a pound is lost, containing six-tenths of a pound of the most valuable proteids. It requires all of the protein from nearly two pounds of round beefsteak to replace the loss of protein from improperly boiling a bushel of potatoes.

Scalloped Potatoes.—Peel and slice thin, then lay in a stew pan a layer of potatoes, sprinkle with pepper, salt, a little flour and a piece of butter the size of a walnut, then another layer of potatoes, then the seasoning, and so on until the pan is full. Fill the pan half full with sweet milk, put into the oven and bake twenty or thirty minutes.

POTATO SOUP.

Ingredients.—Six large potatoes peeled, 1 large onion, 1 heaping teaspoon salt, ¼ teaspoon pepper. For a richer soup add ¼ pound salt pork cut in bits (in this case put in less salt), or add 1 cup of milk or a beaten egg. Chopped celery leaves give a good flavor.

Boil potatoes, onions and salt in a little water, and when very soft mash; then add, a little at a time, and stirring to keep it smooth, a quart of hot water and 1 tablespoon beef fat, in which 1 tablespoon flour has been cooked; or use the fat for frying bread dice, which add at the last minute.

Most cooks fry the sliced onion before putting it in the soup, but the difference in taste is so slight as not to be worth the few minutes' extra time, if time is an object.

NEW WAYS FOR COOKING POTATOES.

POTATO CAKES WITH PREPARED FLOUR.

Mix together one pint each of milk, mashed potato and prepared flour, four eggs beaten light, an even teaspoonful of salt, and bake the cakes like biscuit.

POTATO PUFFS.

Melt two heaping tablespoons of butter in half a cupful of cream, stir it into a pint of hot, mashed potato, with an even teaspoonful each of salt and white pepper, two eggs, beaten to a foam and enough prepared flour to make a dough, which can be rolled out and cut in thin biscuits; bake them in a rather moderate oven, so they cannot burn, and serve them hot with butter.

RAW POTATO FRITTERS.

Peel and grate under water a pint of raw potatoes, drain off the water through a towel and wring the potato pulp in it; mix the liquid with three heaping tablespoons of flour and three eggs beaten light, salt and pepper to taste, and fry the batter at once in enough smoking-hot fat to float the fritters; serve them hot, dusted with powdered sugar.

POTATO CUSTARD PIE.

To a pint of mashed potato and two eggs beaten light, add half a cupful of warm milk containing half a cupful of sugar and a heaping teaspoonful of butter; flavor the custard with grated nutmeg and bake it in a bottom crust, to be eaten either hot or cold, like other custard pie.

DELICIOUS DISHES OF SWEET POTATOES.

Scalloped Sweet Potatoes.

Take large sweet potatoes, boil, peel and slice. Put a layer in the bottom of a deep pan, put over a layer of butter and sugar, then more potatoes, butter and sugar until the pan is full. Set in the oven to brown. Sift sugar and grated nutmeg over the top.

Sweet Potatoes a la Province.

Slice raw sweet potatoes thin and lay in a dish with bits of butter; sprinkle with salt and pepper, pour over milk to cover. Wet bread crumbs in cream, add a beaten egg, pour over the top. Set in the oven and bake until done.

Sweet Potato Custard.

Take a quart of sweet milk, beat the yolks of four eggs with a teacupful of sugar, put in a saucepan and set on the stove, let come to a boil; mash a teacupful of boiled sweet potatoes and mix it; take off the fire and stir until cool; flavor with nutmeg. When ready to serve, put in glasses and pile meringue over the tops.

Sweet Potato Pie.

Boil large sweet potatoes, peel and slice; place evenly on the bottom of a deep pie-pan lined with crust, cover with butter and sugar, then add another layer of sweet potatoes butter and sugar until full. Bake in a slow oven.

Sweet Potato Custard Pie.

Take one pint of mashed sweet potatoes and a teacupful of sweet milk. Beat the yolks of four eggs, and cream a teacupful of sugar and butter together; mix with the potatoes. Flavor with nutmeg. Beat the whites to a stiff froth and stir in. Pour in pie-pans lined with crust and bake quickly.

Sweet Potato Pudding.

Take two pounds of boiled sweet potatoes, mash and mix them with half a pound of butter, six eggs, a teacupful of milk and one grated lemon. Put in a pudding-dish, bake, and serve with wine sauce.

VEGETABLE SOUPS.

If any meat bones are on hand or trimmings of meat not otherwise needed, simmer them from one to two hours in water and use the broth thus obtained instead of water in making any of the following soups:

Vegetable Soups.

Most important are those made from the dried bean, pea and lentil, the three pod-covered vegetables.

Bean Soup.—Ingredients: One pound beans, 1 onion, 2 tablespoonfuls beef fat, salt and pepper. Additions, to be made according to taste; ¼ pound pork, or ham bone, a pinch of red pepper, or, an hour before serving, different vegetables, as carrots and turnips, chopped and fried.

Soak the beans over night in 2 quarts water. In the morning pour off, put on fresh and cook with the onion and fat till very soft, then mash or press through a cullender to remove the skins, and add enough water to make two quarts of somewhat thick soup. Season.

This soup may also be made from cold baked beans. Boil one-half hour, or till they fall to pieces, then strain and season.

Green Vegetable Soup.—The water in which vegetables have been cooked should never be thrown away, with the exception of that used for cooking beets, and potatoes boiled without peeling; even cabbage water can be made the basis of a good soup.

General Method.—Boil the vegetables until very tender, mash or press through a cullender, thin sufficiently and season.

Flour and Bread Soups.—Ingredients: 1 tablespoon beef fat, 1 heaping tablespoon flour, 2 sliced onions, 2 pints water, 1 pint milk, 1 cupful mashed potato, salt and pepper.

Fry the onions in the fat until light brown; remove, pressing out the fat. In same fat now cook the flour till it is yellow, and add, a little at a time, the water. Put back the onions and let it stand awhile, then add milk and potato. Salt well.

Green Pea Soup.—This is a delicious soup, and very nutritious. Large peas, a little too hard to be used as a vegetable, may be utilized in its manufacture.

Ingredients: 1 pint shelled peas, 3 pints water, 1 small onion, 1 tablespoon butter or fat, 1 tablespoon flour. Salt and pepper.

Put peas and onions in boiling water and cook one-half hour to an hour, till very soft. Press through cullender and season.

Peas and Tomato Soup.—Add to the above when done 1 pint stewed tomatoes and a little more seasoning. This is an excellent soup, having the nutrition of the pea and the flavor of the tomato.

Tomato Soup.—Valuable for its fine flavor, and may be made nutritious also by adding broth, milk or eggs.

A FEW NOVEL VEGETABLE DISHES.

GENERAL DIRECTIONS.

Great care should be used in picking out all the defective or rotten portions of vegetables before cooking. It is better to soak vegetables an hour or two before cooking. The water should always boil before putting in the vegetables.

Hold onions under water while peeling, as it will prevent the odor from affecting the eyes.

BAKED BEETS.

Beets are nearly always boiled, but if baked right, they are excellent. Wash them well, and place in a dripping pan to roast, as you would meat, with a little water, replenishing it as it cooks away. Bake slowly in a moderate oven for three hours, and when soft, peel them and season to taste, with quite a little butter, pepper and salt.

STEWED CELERY.

Use only the tender stalks, which should be cut into small pieces and stewed in beef broth. When cooked tender, dress with: ½ pint of cream, 1 teaspoonful of butter, 1 teaspoonful of flour, pepper and salt to taste.

SCALLOPED VEGETABLE OYSTERS.

Cut the scraped roots into small pieces and boil until tender. Place in a deep dish a layer of rolled crackers or bread crumbs and layers of oysters, consecutively, seasoning each layer with pepper, salt, butter and parsley or celery leaves. When the dish is full, pour over it two pints of sweet milk, and bake an hour and a half or two hours in a medium oven.

SMOTHERED CABBAGE.

Cut a small head of cabbage fine and put into a pan where meat has been fried; put on a very little sweet milk, season with pepper and salt, and butter about the size of an egg. Cover it tightly and let it stand on the back of the stove fifteen or twenty minutes.

NEW WAYS FOR COOKING CORN.

BAKED CORN.
1 quart corn, cut from cob.
2-3 cup of cream.
1 tablespoonful of butter.
Season with pepper and salt to taste. Bake one hour. Stir it several times while baking.

FRIED CORN.
Put into a skillet containing hot butter, corn that has been cut from the cob. Season with pepper and salt, and stir it often, to prevent it burning. It should be kept covered.

CORN OYSTERS.
Grate the corn into a dish, and season with salt and pepper. Drop a spoonful into a well buttered skillet, in form of oysters, and as soon as they are brown, turn them over to brown, the same on the other side. Serve hot.

HULLED CORN.
To every pint of corn, add a half tablespoonful of baking soda, and enough water to cover it. Let it soak over night and in the morning boil in this solution, until the hulls will rub off, which will require about two hours.

CORN CUSTARD.
After cutting the corn from the cob, mix it medium thick with milk, pepper and salt to taste. Then add three well beaten eggs, and bake twenty-five or thirty minutes.

CORN CAKES.
Mix well: 1 pint of grated corn; 1 teaspoonful of melted butter; 3 tablespoonfuls of sweet milk; 2 eggs, well beaten; 3 tablespoonfuls of rolled crackers. Fry in hot butter.

CORN FRITTERS.
Core and press out the pulp of one dozen ears of sugar corn, add to this one cupful of sifted flour, one cupful of milk, half a teaspoonful of salt, one teaspoonful of sugar, a pinch of black pepper and the beaten yolks of two eggs. Beat well, stir in carefully the two whites beaten to a stiff froth, and one teaspoonful of baking powder. Fry them like any other fritter, in smoking hot fat, and drain them on brown paper.

HOW TO MAKE SAUER KRAUT.

Take off the outer leaves of the cabbage and the core, and cut it very fine on a slaw cutter; put it down in a keg or large jar, and sprinkle a little salt between each layer, and pound each with a masher or mallet. When the receptacle is full place some large cabbage leaves on top, and a thick cloth, first wrung out of cold water; then cover it and put on a very heavy weight. It should stand for six weeks before using, and it should have every bit of scum removed by washing the cloth and weight. Before it is used, the water should be drained off and fresh put on.

ROASTED ONIONS.

Onions are very good roasted in ashes, without removing the skin. When they are done, take off the skin and flavor with pepper, salt and butter.

TOMATO SUCCOTASH.

To every half pint of tomatoes, a pint of corn, cut from the cob; let them cook twenty or twenty-five minutes, then add a very little bread crumbs, pepper, salt and butter about the size of an egg.

TOMATO TOAST.

Toast some nice pieces of bread, and pour over them the tomatoes prepared as follows:

Cook together, four medium sized tomatoes and one medium sized onion, pared and sliced fine, for three-quarters of an hour; when done pour off the water and season to suit the taste; then add one cup of sweet cream, or milk, and a tablespoonful of butter.

FRIED TOMATOES.

Cut the tomatoes in slices, without skinning, sprinkle pepper, salt and flour over them, and fry in butter until brown. After they are taken up, pour cream into the butter and juice, and while boiling hot pour over the tomatoes.

STUFFED TOMATOES.

Take large tomatoes of even size, scoop out the top of the tomato as much as you can without spoiling the shape, and fill with stuffing made as follows:

Fry a small chopped onion in a little water; when nearly done, add some bread crumbs moistened with a little milk and season with pepper and salt; put a little butter on each and bake twenty minutes, or until a nice brown.

TOMATO FRITTERS.

Scald and peel the tomatoes, put them in a chopping bowl and chop them fine, season with pepper, salt, and stir flour, with one-half teaspoonful of soda, to make a thin batter. Fry in butter or lard over a quick fire, and serve as soon as possible after taking from the fire.

HOW TO MAKE ALL KINDS OF CATSUPS, PICKLES, SALADS, AND SALAD DRESSINGS.

TOMATO CATSUP.

Boil together for one hour, then strain through a sieve; 4 quarts of tomatoes, ½ dozen red peppers, 3 tablespoonfuls of mustard, ½ cup of salt, ½ cup of unground pepper, 1 teaspoonful of allspice. Bottle and seal when cold.

TOMATO CATSUP.

Skin the tomatoes, and cook them well. Press them through a sieve, and to each five pints add three pints of good cider vinegar. Boil slowly for about two hours, or until it begins to thicken; then add one tablespoonful of ground cloves, one of allspice, one of cinnamon, and one of pepper, and three grated nutmegs. Boil until very thick (six or eight hours), and add two tablespoonfuls of fine salt. When thoroughly cold, bottle, cork and seal.

CURRANT CATSUP.

Boil together for twenty minutes: 1 gallon of currant juice, 3 cupfuls of vinegar, 7 cupfuls of sugar, 3 teaspoonfuls of cinnamon, 2 teaspoonfuls of cloves, 2 teaspoonfuls of pepper, 2 teaspoonfuls of grated nutmeg. Cork and seal.

CHOPPED PICKLE.

One peck of green tomatoes, two quarts of onions and two of peppers. Chop all fine, separately, and mix, to which add three cups of salt. Let them remain over night and in the morning drain well. Add half a pound of mustard seed, two tablespoonfuls of ground allspice, two of ground cloves, one cupful of grated horse-radish and three quarts of boiling vinegar.

PICKLED CUCUMBERS.

Soak ten dozen cucumbers in brine five or six hours, then scald in the following mixture: 3 quarts of cider vinegar, 1 cup of sugar, 2 tablespoonfuls of unground cloves, 2 tablespoonfuls of unground cinnamon, 2 tablespoonfuls of unground black pepper, 2 tablespoonfuls of chopped horse-radish, 4 red peppers. When the vinegar is scalding hot, take out the cucumbers, put them in jars and pour the vinegar over them. Keep closely covered or seal.

SOUR CREAM SALAD DRESSING.

One cupful of sour cream, one teaspoonful of salt, a speck of cayenne, one tablespoonful of lemon juice, three of vinegar, one tablespoonful of sugar. Mix thoroughly. This is nice for vegetables.

ASPARAGUS SALAD.

Boil two bunches of asparagus with one quart of water, and one tablespoonful of salt for twenty minutes. Take up and drain in a cullender. When cold, cut off the tender points and arrange them on the dish. Pour on the cream salad dressing

SALMON SALAD.

Pour over a pound of canned salmon, a dressing made as follows: ½ cup cider vinegar, 1 tablespoonful melted butter, 1 teaspoonful mustard, 1 tablespoonful sugar, 3 eggs, ½ teaspoonful salt. Cook all together until it creams up nicely, when cool add a half cup milk or cream. Garnish with tender lettuce leaves.

LETTUCE SALAD.

Four heads tender lettuce, chopped fine, the yolks of three hard-boiled eggs, rubbed fine. Season with salt, pepper and mustard. Heat together and add one cup of vinegar, one tablespoonful butter. Mix well and garnish with the whites of the eggs cut in rings.

CELERY SALAD.

1 boiled egg, 1 raw egg, 1 tablespoonful salad oil, 1 teaspoonful white sugar, 1 saltspoonful salt, 1 saltspoonful pepper, 4 tablespoonfuls vinegar, 1 tablespoonful made mustard. Rub the yolk to a paste, adding by degrees the other ingredients. Beat the raw egg to a froth and stir in lastly the vinegar. Cut the celery into bits about half an inch long. Eat at once.

POTATO SALAD.

2 cups of mashed potatoes, rubbed through a cullender, ¼ of a cup of chopped cabbage—white and firm, 2 tablespoonfuls of cucumber pickle, also chopped, yolks of two hard boiled eggs, powdered fine. Mix well.

DRESSING.

1 raw egg, well beaten, 1 saltspoonful of celery seed, 1 teaspoonful white sugar, 1 tablespoonful of melted butter, 1 teaspoonful of flour, ½ cupful of vinegar, salt, mustard and pepper to taste. Boil the vinegar and pour it upon the beaten egg, sugar, butter and seasoning. Wet the flour with cold vinegar and beat into this. Cook the mixture, stirring until it thickens, then pour, scalding hot, upon the salad. Toss with a silver fork and let it get very cold before eating.

FRENCH SALAD DRESSING.

3 tablespoonfuls of oil, 1 of vinegar, 1 saltspoonful of salt, ½ a saltspoonful of pepper. Put the salt and pepper into a cup, to which add 1 tablespoonful of oil. Mix thoroughly and then add the remainder of the oil and the vinegar. This is dressing enough for a salad for six persons.

POTATO SALAD.

Ten potatoes, cut fine; the French dressing, with 4 or 5 drops of onion juice in it, and 1 tablespoonful chopped parsley.

COOKED VEGETABLES IN SALAD.

Nearly every kind of cooked vegetables can be served in salads. They can be served separately or mixed. They must be cold and well drained before the dressing is added.

A NEW SALAD DRESSING.

1 pint of vinegar, sugar to taste, butter size of an egg, 2 teaspoonfuls salt, 1 teaspoonful mixed mustard, pepper, celery, salt. Heat together. Beat three eggs light with one cup sour cream, pour into the hot vinegar the eggs and cream and let it all slowly thicken. This should be cooked in a double boiler; makes a quart and will keep any length of time if kept covered.

COLD SLAW.

To a small cup of vinegar add a well-beaten egg, a teaspoonful of mustard, one of sugar, a small lump of butter, season with pepper and salt. Let these ingredients come to a boil, and pour over nicely chopped cabbage, while hot.

WARM SLAW.

Boil together and pour over fine cut cabbage the yolks of two eggs, one cup of vinegar, two tablespoonfuls of sour cream, two teaspoonfuls of butter, and three table-spoonfuls of sugar.

PEACHES, PEARS AND SWEET APPLE PICKLES.

For six pounds of fruit use three of sugar, a pint of vinegar and about five dozen cloves. Bring the vinegar and sugar to a boil. Put the fruit into this, having first stuck two cloves into each peach, pear or apple. Cook until tender.

SWEET TOMATO PICKLE.

One peck of green tomatoes and six large onions sliced. Sprinkle with one cupful of salt, and let them stand over night. In the morning drain. Add to the tomatoes two quarts of water and one quart of vinegar. Boil fifteen minutes, then drain again and throw this vinegar and water away. Add to the pickle two pounds of sugar, two quarts of vinegar, two tablespoonfuls of cloves, two of allspice, two of ginger, two of mustard, two of cinnamon, and one teaspoonful of cayenne, and boil fifteen minutes.

COFFEE.

Next to the quality of the coffee, it is of importance that it should be freshly ground and browned. If you buy it browned reheat it before grinding. The easiest and most economical way of making is to grind it very fine and put it into a bag made of woven stuff. Heat this in your coffee pot as hot as you can without burning. Pour on boiling water and keep it hot and close covered for 15 or 20 minutes. Boiling coffee increases its strength but does not improve its flavor.

A GOOD CUP OF TEA.

How Easily it May be Made with a Little Care.

Have good tea to begin with; then be sure that you have freshly drawn, pure and filtered water of which to make the beverage. The water must not have been standing for hours exposed to the weather nor simmering on the range. It must be fresh, and then, if you have a brisk fire or the hot flame of an alcohol lamp, bring it quickly to the boil. A flat bottomed kettle is to be preferred, as it has a broad surface to expose to the heat, and the boiling is soon accomplished. Water is boiling when it bubbles and the steam comes in white puffs from the spout of the kettle. It does not boil when it begins to simmer and to sing. That is only the sign that it is near to boiling. You must make your tea when the water has just boiled. A kettle which has been standing on the back of a stove all day, filled up now and then by a dipper or two more of water, will not make good tea. You must boil the water on purpose.

An earthen pot is better for tea than a metal one. Pour a little boiling water in the pot to heat it, and after a minute or two pour it out. Now put a teaspoonful of tea for every cup of hot water—an even, not a heaping, spoonful—and add an extra one for the pot. Pour on as much water as will fill the number of cups you wish to make. Let it stand two minutes; then, with a long handled spoon, stir the leaves once through the water and instantly cover the pot again. Three minutes more, and your tea is done. Never let tea steep or boil or stand a long time. It is a quick, neat, nice process from beginning to end.

BREAD.

Prize Bread Recipe.—At a bread contest held in an eastern city not long ago, a milling company offered prizes ranging from five to one hundred dollars for the best loaves of bread. The recipe used by the winner of the prize of one hundred dollars was: Three pints of water, one half pint of milk, one tablespoonful of lard, one tablespoonful of sugar, two tablespoonfuls of salt, one yeast cake, and the necessary quantity of flour to make three loaves. The ingredients, which were first thoroughly mixed, and then kneaded ten minutes, were raised over night in a covered bread-pan. In the morning the dough was kneaded ten minutes and made into three loaves. Three other loaves entered for the contest were awarded seventy-five-dollar prizes. One of these loaves seems to have been prepared in a somewhat unusual way. The ingredients for the dough were two-thirds milk to one-third water, compressed yeast and a little salt and sugar, and were mixed with enough flour to make a stiff dough. This dough was mixed, kneaded, and set to rise at night. When light it was chopped thoroughly with a chopping-knife, made into loaves, and set to rise the second time; when this was light it was baked forty minutes.

BREAD.

Sift four quarts of flour into your bread-pan, leaving cavity in the center. Stir in equal parts of two quarts warm milk and water and, lastly, stir in three pints of potato yeast, beating thoroughly for about five minutes; when light add a teaspoonful of salt, piece of butter size of an egg or one tablespoonful of lard, one tablespoonful of sugar; knead well (for about twenty minutes) and let rise; when light knead again, let rise and knead again. The fourth or last time let rise and put in tins, allowing to stand until light; rub over the top of loaves a light coating of drawn butter, bake in oven moderately heated for one hour.

GRAHAM BREAD.

Four teacups graham flour, one-half teacup brown sugar, one-half teacup molasses, one teaspoon salt, one teaspoon soda dissolved, one pint sour milk or buttermilk; bake in a slow oven two hours.

CORN BREAD.

Two cups of sour milk, two cups graham flour, two cups corn meal, half cup molasses, one teaspoon rounding full of soda, steamed three hours; brown in oven.

COFFEE CAKE.

When mixing bread save one cup of yeast, add two eggs, one small cup sugar, one-half cup butter or melted lard, one pint of warm sweet milk, one teaspoonful salt. Stir in flour to make a stiff batter, set to rise until light; then beat well and put in bread or cake pans; let rise again; when light put small bits of butter and a sprinkling of sugar and cinnamon on top. Bake in a moderate oven half an hour.

GRAHAM GEMS.

One bowl of sour milk, one teaspoonful baking soda, one egg, graham flour to make quite stiff; pour one tablespoonful of hot lard on the mixture and beat well; have the pans hot. Bake in a quick oven.

DELICATE CORN MEAL GEMS.

3 eggs, ½ cup sugar, butter the size of an egg, 1 cup white flour and 1 of cornmeal, 1½ teaspoons baking powder. Bake in gem irons.

FRITTERS.

2 tablespoonfuls of sugar, 3 eggs, 2 cups of sour milk, 1 teaspoonful of soda, ½ teaspoonful of salt. Flour enough to make a thick batter. Beat well, fry in hot lard until a light brown. Roll in powdered sugar when done

CRULLERS.

2 cups of sugar, 1 cup of butter, 2 eggs, 2 cups sour milk, 1 teaspoonful soda dissolved in hot water. Flour to roll out tolerably stiff.

APPLE FRITTERS.

1 cup of flour mixed with 1 teaspoonful baking powder, add 1 cup of milk with yolk of 2 eggs stirred in; add 1 cup or 1½ cups of chopped apples; last of all add the whites of two eggs beaten very light; drop with spoon into very hot lard. Any fruit can be used.

MUFFINS.

1 pint milk, 1 egg, a tablespoonful lard, ½ cup yeast, flour for a stiff batter, 1 teaspoonful salt. Set to rise over night. Bake in muffin-rings.

STEAMED CORN BREAD.

2 cups Indian meal, 1 cup flour, 2 tablespoonfuls white sugar, 2½ cups buttermilk, 1 teaspoonful soda, 1 teaspoonful salt, 1 heaping teaspoonful melted lard. Beat well and put into a buttered mould. Place in a steamer over a pot of boiling water. Steam 1½ hours, and set in oven about 10 minutes. Eat while warm.

JOHNNY CAKE.

3½ cups buttermilk or sour milk, ½ cup molasses, 1 egg, 1 teaspoonful salt, 1 teaspoonful soda, 1½ cups cornmeal, then add flour enough to make thicker than cake dough.

WAFFLES.

2 cups milk, 2 eggs, 3 cups flour, 1 teaspoonful cream-tartar, ½ teaspoonful soda, 1 saltspoonful salt, 1 tablespoonful melted butter. Sift the cream tartar with the salt into the flour, add soda dissolved in a little hot water, milk and eggs. Add the flour the last thing. If the batter is too stiff, put in more milk.

RICE WAFFLES.

1 cup boiled rice, 1 pint milk, 2 eggs, lard the size of a walnut, ½ teaspoonful soda, 1 teaspoonful cream tartar, 1 teaspoonful salt, flour for a thin batter.

GRAHAM GEMS.

Thicken with graham flour, 2 cups of sour milk, 1 large teaspoonful of soda, 2 tablespoonfuls of molasses. Bake in gem pans.

RICE GRIDDLE CAKES.

Mix together: ½ cup of flour, 1 cup of boiled rice, 1 teaspoonful of soda, 2 teaspoonfuls of cream-tartar, 1 egg. Sweet milk enough to make a batter of the right consistency.

BREAKFAST CAKES.

Beat well together: 1 egg, ½ pint of sweet milk, 1 cup of flour, 1 pinch of salt. Heat gem irons very hot, well greased, and bake them in a hot oven.

HOW TO MAKE ALL KINDS OF CAKES, COOKIES, DOUGHNUTS, ETC.

A FEW PRACTICAL RULES.

Powdered sugar is better than granulated for baking cake. It dissolves more quickly.

Always remember that baking powder and sweet milk go together, and sour milk and soda.

Do not use butter to grease baking pans. The salt in the butter makes the cake stick to the pan. Always use fresh lard.

If eggs are kept in a cool place they always beat better when broken.

Continually opening the oven door makes a cake fall. The oven door should never be opened for at least ten minutes after placing the cake into it.

If molasses is used in cakes they should never be baked in a hot oven as they will burn very quickly.

WALNUT CAKE.

H. B. J. writes: Take 2 teacupfuls of white sugar, ¾ teacupful butter, 1 teacupful milk, 3 teacupfuls flour, whites of 8 eggs, 2 teaspoonfuls baking powder, Filling: Make a boiled frosting and stir in 1 lb. chopped English walnuts.

SPONGE CAKE.

One cupful of sugar, two cupfuls of sifted flour, half a cupful of cold water and three eggs, with a teaspoonful of baking-powder; flavor with lemon; bake in a moderate oven.

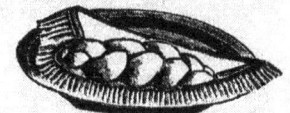

COFFEE CAKE.

Work in a quart of bread dough, a tablespoonful of butter, half a cupful of sugar, with one cupful of dried currants; add flour to make dough, make in cake, shake, rub with melted butter, put in a pan and let rise. Rusks. —In one pint of milk dissolve one yeast cake, add three eggs, one cupful of sugar and beat together; sift in flour to make dough, add two ounces of butter; let rise, work well, make in rusks, put in a pan to lighten, bake in a quick oven; sprinkle with sugar.

LEMON CAKE.

Beat to a cream: 1 cup of sugar, ½ cup of butter. Then stir in: 4 well beaten eggs, 1 grated lemon, 2 cups of flour. Bake in greased pans, in a quick oven.

How to Make All Kinds of Cake.

ECONOMY CAKE.

1 cup of sugar, 1 cup of buttermilk, 1 egg, butter the size of an egg, 2 cups of flour, 1 teaspoonful of soda.

BOSTON CAKES.

Beat to a cream: 1 teacup of butter, 3 cups of sugar. Then add: 1 cup of cream or milk, 6 well beaten eggs, 4 teacups of sifted flour, a little salt, ½ pound of currants, 1 teaspoonful of soda dissolved in one tablespoonful of milk. Bake in a moderate oven.

MARBLE CAKE—LIGHT.

1 cup white sugar, ½ cup of butter, ½ cup of milk, whites of three eggs, 2 cups prepared flour.

DARK.

½ cup brown sugar, ¼ cup butter, ½ cup molasses, ¼ cup milk, ½ nutmeg, 1 teaspoonful cinnamon, ½ teaspoonful allspice, ½ teaspoonful soda, 2 cups flour, yolks of 3 eggs. Fill the pan with alternate spoonfuls of light and dark batter.

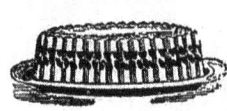

JELLY OF TWO COLOURS.

BREAD CAKE.

Into 2 teacupfuls of light bread dough, work with the hands 1½ teacupfuls sugar, 1 of butter, half a teacupful of milk, 2 well-beaten eggs, 1 teaspoonful baking powder, nutmeg to taste and a teacupful seeded raisins. A little more flour may be needed. Place in pan it is to be baked in and let rise again, and when light, bake in a moderate oven 40 or 50 minutes.

PLAIN CAKE.

CORNFLOUR CAKE.

CAKE-MOULD.

SILVER CAKE.

One cupful of sugar, half a cupful of butter, the whites of three eggs, half a cupful of cornstarch, dissolved in nearly half a cupful of milk; one and a fourth cupfuls of flour, half a teaspoonful of cream of tartar, one-fourth of a teaspoonful of soda, and vanilla or almond flavor. Beat the butter to a cream and gradually beat in the sugar. Add the flavor. Mix the flour, cream of tartar and soda together, and sift. Beat the whites to a stiff froth. Add the corn starch and milk to the beaten sugar and butter, then add the whites of the eggs and the flour. Mix quickly and thoroughly. Have the batter in sheets, and about two inches deep. Bake in a moderate oven for about half an hour. A chocolate frosting is nice with this cake.

GOLD CAKE.

One cupful of sugar, ½ cupful of butter, the yolks of three eggs and 1 whole egg, ½ cupful of milk, ¼ of a teaspoonful each of soda and cream tartar, 1¼ cupfuls of flour. Mix the butter and sugar together, and add the eggs, milk, flavor and flour, in the order named. Bake the same as the silver cake. A white frosting is good with this cake.

ANGEL CAKE.

The whites of 11 eggs, 1½ cupfuls of granulated sugar, 1 cupful of pastry flour, measured after being sifted 4 times; 1 teaspoonful of cream tartar, 1 of vanilla extract. Sift the flour and cream of tartar together. Beat the whites to a stiff froth. Beat the sugar into the eggs, and add the seasoning and flour, stirring quickly and lightly. Beat until ready to put the mixture in the oven. Use a pan that has little legs at the top corners, so that when the pan is turned upside down on the table, after the baking, a current of air will pass under and over it. Bake for 40 minutes in a moderate oven. Do not grease the pan.

WATERMELON CAKE.

White Part.—One teacupful each of butter and milk, two teacupfuls sugar, three and one half teacupfuls flour, 3 teaspoonfuls baking powder, 1 teaspoonful extract of lemon and the whites of 8 eggs. Red Part.—One cupful red sugar, ½ cupful butter, 1-3 cupful milk, 2 cupfuls flour, 2 teaspoonfuls baking powder and a teacupful raisins; bake in a pan with a tube in the center. Place the red part around the center of the pan and the white around the outside of this. Frost when done.

FRUIT CAKE.

HOLIDAY CAKE.

A SMALL FRUIT CAKE.

½ cup of sugar, ½ cup of butter, 4 tablespoonfuls of molasses, ¼ of a teaspoonful of soda dissolved in it, 4 eggs, ½ cupful of citron cut fine, ½ pound of seeded raisins, ¼ pound of well washed currants and blanched almonds, 1 grated nutmeg, 1 tablespoonful each of cloves and cinnamon, 2 cups of sifted flour. Flavor with lemon essence, and at the very last add the whites of the eggs, well beaten. Bake one hour in a moderate oven.

COFFEE CAKE.

Mix quite stiff, and bake in a moderate oven for one hour; 1 cup of brown sugar, 1 cup of molasses, 1 cup of butter, 1 egg, 1 cup of strong coffee, 2 cups of raisins, ½ ounce of powdered cloves, ½ ounce of powdered cinnamon, ½ ounce of soda, 1 grated nutmeg, 4 or 5 cupfuls of flour.

SUNSHINE CAKE.

This is made almost exactly like angel cake. Have the whites of 11 eggs and the yolks of six, 1½ cupfuls of granulated sugar, measured after sifting; 1 cupful of flour, measured after sifting; 1 teaspoonful of cream of tartar and 1 of orange extract. Beat the whites to a stiff froth, and gradually beat in the sugar. Beat the yolks in a similar manner, and add to them the whites and sugar and flavor. Finally, stir in the flour. Mix quickly and well. Bake for fifty minutes in a slow oven, using a pan like that for angel cake.

CITRON CAKE.

Beat separately the whites and yolks of 4 eggs, 3 cups of sugar, 1 cup of butter, ½ cup of sweet milk, 3 cups of flour, 2½ teaspoonfuls of baking powder, 1½ cups of chopped citron, rolled in flour. This is best baked in pans about twice as long as wide. The pan should be large enough so as to have the batter about 2½ inches thick.

NUT CAKE.

2 cups of sugar, 1 cup of butter, 1 cup of milk, 3 eggs, 3 cups of flour, 2 teaspoonfuls of baking powder, 2 cups of any kind of nut kernels.

CHOCOLATE CAKE.

2 cups of sugar, ¾ cup of butter, 1 cup of milk, 2 cups of flour, 1 cup of corn starch, yolks of 5 eggs. Beat the butter and sugar to a cream, then put in the eggs, stirring them well together; add the milk and corn starch, then the flour, first mixing it with the baking powder. Bake in jelly tins. For the icing: ¼ cake of Baker's chocolate, ½ cup of sweet milk, 1 teaspoonful of corn starch, 1 teaspoonful of vanilla. Grate the chocolate into the milk and dissolve it, heat the milk to the boiling point; stir the corn starch in a little cold milk, and add to the chocolate and milk.

SNOW CAKE.

Cream ¾ teacupful of butter with 2 teacupfuls sugar; add 1 teacupful each of sweet milk and corn starch, 2 teacupfuls flour, 1½ teaspoonfuls baking powder, and flavoring to taste; lastly add the well beaten whites of 7 eggs. Stir these in lightly and bake in a dish, preferably one with a pipe. Bake 40 to 45 minutes.

PUFF CAKE.

Beat to a cream ½ teacupful butter and 1 teacupful sugar; add in the order named, the yolks of two eggs well beaten, ½ teacupful milk, 1½ teacupfuls sifted flour, the whites of two eggs beaten stiff, and 1 heaping teaspoonful baking powder, sifted in the last thing. Flavor with vanilla, and bake in a loaf.

WHITE SPONGE CAKE OR "ANGEL FOOD."

One-and-a-half cupfuls pulverized sugar, one cup flour, twelve whites of eggs, one teaspoonful cream of tartar, one teaspoonful flavoring.

DIRECTIONS FOR PREPARING.

Sift the sugar and flour three times separately, then mix and stir in the well-beaten whites of twelve eggs. Stir the cream of tartar in with the sugar and flour before putting in the eggs. Add the flavoring and bake in a medium oven.

ORANGE CAKE.

Mix smoothly one teacupful granulated sugar with half a teacupful butter, add the well-beaten yolk of three eggs, ¾ cup of milk, a tablespoonful lemon juice, and 2½ cups flour, with which is sifted 2 teaspoonfuls baking powder. Lastly add the whites beaten stiff. Bake in four layers. For a filling, to be put in when the cakes are cold, chop fine 3 or 4 peeled oranges, sweeten and spread them over 3 of the layers, cover these and the top layer with a soft boiled frosting made with the whites of the eggs, sweetened to taste and flavored with a little grated lemon peel. Pile these together adding frosting to sides as well as on top.

RELIABLE SPONGE CAKE.

Beat three eggs 3 minutes, add 1½ teacupfuls sugar and  beat 5 minutes; then stir in a teacupful flour with which is sifted one teaspoonful cream of tartar. Beat three minutes before adding ½ teacupful of cold water in which is dissolved ½ teaspoonful soda; lastly stir in 1 teacupful flour and mix thoroughly. Bake in a moderate oven.

SPONGE CAKE.

COCOANUT CAKE.

Cream two cupfuls of sugar and half a cupful of butter together, sift in three cupfuls of flour with two teaspoonfuls of baking-powder, pour in a cupful of milk, flavor with lemon, and lastly, add the well-beaten whites of eight eggs. Bake in jelly-pans, and spread grated cocoanut and powdered sugar, mixed between.

WHITE MOUNTAIN CAKE.

Cream one pound of sugar and a half a pound of butter together; sift in one pound of flour with two teaspoonfuls of baking-powder, add half a cupful of milk and the stiffly-beaten whites of ten eggs. Flavor with bitter almond extract. Pour in cake-mold and bake 40 minutes.

LAYER CAKES.

CREAM CAKE.

2 cups powdered sugar, 2-3 cupful butter, 4 eggs, ½ cupful milk, ½ teaspoonful soda, 1 teaspoonful cream tartar, 3 cups flour. Bake in layers as for jelly cake, and when cold spread the following mixture between the layers: ½ pint of milk, 2 small teaspoonfuls corn starch, 1 egg, 1 teaspoonful vanilla, ½ cup sugar. Let the milk come to a boiling point, and stir in the corn starch wet with a little cold milk. Beat the egg and sugar together, take out a portion of the boiling mixture and gradually beat it into the eggs and sugar; return to the rest of the custard, and boil, stirring constantly until quite thick. When cool season with vanilla and spread between the layers.

COCOANUT CAKE.

2 cups powdered sugar, ½ cup butter, 3 eggs, 1 cup milk, 3 cups flour, 2 tablespoonfuls cream tartar, 1 teaspoonful soda. Bake in jelly tins.

Filling.—1 grated cocoanut. To one-half of this add whites of three eggs, beaten to a froth, and one cup of powdered sugar. Spread between the layers. Mix the other half of the grated cocoanut with four tablespoonfuls powdered sugar, and strew thickly on top of cake.

JELLY CAKE.

Beat to a cream: 2 cups of sugar, ½ cup of butter, then add three-quarters of a cup of milk, 1 large tablespoonful of baking powder, mixed in two and a half cups of flour. The frothed whites of eight eggs. Bake in jelly pans, and when cool, spread jelly between the layers.

Strawberry Cake.

Mix into a dough: 5 cups of flour, 1 teaspoonful of salt, 4 well beaten eggs, enough milk to make it roll nicely. Roll them, and place a crust in the bottom of a shallow pan, then a thick layer of strawberries sugared to taste. Cover with a thin layer of crust, then another layer of strawberries and sugar. Cover the whole with another layer of crust, and bake in a quick oven, twenty minutes.

Custard Cake.

2 eggs, 1 cup of sugar, ¼ cup of water, 1 cup of flour, 1 heaping tablespoonful of baking powder. Bake in layers.

Custard.—½ cup of sugar, ¾ cup of milk, 1 tablespoonful of corn starch, butter the size of a hickory nut. Flavor with lemon. Boil until as thick as jelly. Spread between the layers when they are cool.

Hickory Nut Cake.

2 cups of sugar, ½ cup of butter, 4 eggs, 4½ cups of flour, 2 teaspoonfuls of baking powder. Bake quickly in jelly pans.

For the Filling.—Beat together 1 cup of sugar, 2 eggs, ¼ cup of corn starch, 1 cup of fine chopped hickorynut kernels, 1 pint of milk. Boil until a custard, and when cool spread between the layers of the cake.

Jam Cake.

1½ cups of sugar (brown), 2-3 cup of butter, ½ cup of jam (strawberry preferred), ½ cup of sour cream, 3 eggs, 2 cups of flour, 1 teaspoon of soda, 1 teaspoon of cinnamon, ½ teaspoon of cloves, ½ nutmeg. Bake in layers. Put together with icing.

HOW TO MAKE ALL KINDS OF FROSTING.

Boiled Frosting.

White of 1 egg beaten to a stiff froth, 1 cupful of granulated sugar, moistened with 4 tablespoonfuls of hot water; boil sugar briskly for five minutes, or until it "jingles" on the bottom of the cup when dropped in cold water; then pour the boiling syrup on the egg in a small stream, beating hard at the same time.

Gelatine Frosting.

Dissolve a teaspoonful of gelatine in ¾ of a cup of boiling water; strain, thicken with a cup of sugar, and flavor with lemon.

Every Day Frosting.

Beat the whites of 3 eggs stiff; add 2½ cups of powdered sugar gradually, beating briskly all the time. Flavor with vanilla.

Frosting.

Beat the whites of 2 eggs to a stiff froth, add gradually ½ pound of pulverized sugar, beat very thoroughly, flavor with lemon juice. To color a delicate pink, use the juice of strawberries, currants or cranberries or a very little cochineal.

FROSTING.

Whites of 4 eggs, 1 pound of powdered sugar, lemon, vanilla or other flavoring. Break the whites into a broad, cool dish. Throw a small handful of sugar upon them, and begin whipping it in with slow steady strokes of the beater. In a short time throw in more sugar, and keep adding it until it is all used up. Beat perseveringly until icing is of a smooth, fine and firm texture. If not stiff enough put in more sugar. Lemon juice whitens the icing.

PLAIN FROSTING.

Beat the white of one egg to a stiff froth, then stir in ten heaping teaspoonfuls pulverized sugar, well heaped, but not all you can take up on the spoon, and one of cornstarch; be sure that it is thoroughly beaten before taking the cake from the oven. Invert a milkpan, place the cake on the pan and apply frosting; it will be as smooth as glass, and adhere firmly to the cake.

CHOCOLATE FROSTING.

¾ cup of grated chocolate, 3 cups of powdered sugar, the whites of four eggs. Beat the whites but very little, they must not become white, and stir in the chocolate, then pour in the sugar gradually, beating to mix it well.

YELLOW FROSTING.

The yolk of one egg to nine heaping teaspoonfuls of pulverized sugar; flavor with vanilla. Use the same day it is made.

FROSTING WITHOUT EGGS.

Place one cup of sugar in a basin, add three tablespoonfuls of milk, put it on the stove and let it boil five minutes; take off, and stir until perfectly white, adding any flavor. You can make a chocolate frosting of it by adding a square of Baker's chocolate, well shaved or melted, just as you take it from the stove.

HOW TO MAKE ALL KINDS OF COOKIES.

ECONOMICAL COOKIES.

1 cup of sugar, ½ cup of butter, 1 cup of water, 2 teaspoonfuls of baking powder, flavor with lemon. Flour enough to roll out thin, cut with a biscuit cutter.

NICE COOKIES.

2 eggs, 1 cup of sugar, ½ cup of butter, 2 tablespoonfuls of sweet milk, 2 teaspoonfuls of baking powder, flour enough to stiffen. Mix soft and flavor with vanilla.

COOKIES.

2 cups of sugar, 1 cup of butter, 2 eggs, ½ cup of milk, 1 teaspoonful of cream tartar, ½ teaspoonful of soda, flour to roll stiff.

MOLASSES COOKIES.

1 cup of butter, 2 cups of molasses, 1 teaspoonful cloves, 1 tablespoonful ginger. Sufficient flour to make a soft dough. Mould with the hands into small cakes, and bake in a steady rather than quick oven, as they are apt to burn.

SOFT GINGER COOKIES.

1 pint of molasses, 1 cup of lard, 1 cup of water, 1½ teaspoonfuls of cream tartar, ½ teaspoonful soda, 1 tablespoonful of ginger. Flour enough to roll as stiff as possible.

How to Make All Kinds of Cookies.

GINGER SNAPS.

Melt a quarter of a pound of butter, the same of lard, and mix them with: ¼ pound of brown sugar, 1 pint of molasses, 2 tablespoonfuls of ginger, 1 quart of flour. Dissolve two teaspoonfuls of saleratus in a wine-glass of milk, and strain it into the cake. Add sufficient flour to enable you to roll it out very thin, cut into cookies, and bake in a slow oven.

GINGER SNAPS.

1 cup of molasses, 1 cup of sugar, 1 cup of butter and lard mixed, 1 egg, ½ cup of boiling water, 1 teaspoonful of soda dissolved in water, 2 teaspoonfuls of ginger. Flour enough to mould rather soft.

GINGER SNAPS.

2 cups of molasses, 1 cup of butter, melted into it, ½ cup of water, 2 teaspoonfuls of soda, 3 teaspoonfuls of ginger, flour enough to roll soft. Bake with a hot fire. Watch carefully as they burn very easily.

GINGERBREAD.

SOFT GINGER BREAD.

2 well beaten eggs, 1 cupful of molasses, ½ teacupful of lard, ½ teacupful of butter, 1 tablespoonful of ginger, 1 teaspoonful of cream tartar, 1 teaspoonful of soda, dissolved in ½ teacupful of milk, a pinch of salt, 3 cups of flour. Bake slowly for half an hour. Watch that it may not burn.

PLAIN GINGERBREAD.

2 cups of molasses, ½ cup lard, ½ cup butter, 2 tablespoonfuls soda, dissolved in hot water, 2 tablespoonfuls ginger, 1 cup sour milk, thicken with flour to a stiff dough. Warm the molasses, lard, butter, and ginger and beat them well for about ten minutes before adding the milk, soda, and flour. Roll into shape and bake in a quick but not too hot oven. Brush over with white of egg while hot.

RISEN DOUGHNUTS.

1 pound butter, 1¾ pounds sugar, 1 quart sweet milk, 4 eggs, 1 large cup yeast, 1 tablespoonful mace or nutmeg, 2 teaspoonfuls cinnamon, flour to make stiff as bread dough, 1 teaspoonful salt. Beat the sugar and butter to a cream, add the milk, yeast, and a quart of flour. Set to rise over night. In the morning add the eggs, well beaten, spice, and the rest of the flour. Let rise until light; roll into thick sheets, cut into shape and fry in hot lard.

DOUGHNUTS.

1 cup sour cream, 1 cup sugar, 1 egg, a small teaspoonful of soda, ½ teaspoonful of salt, flavor to taste. Mix soft, roll three-quarters of an inch thick, cut out with a round cookie cutter with a hole in the center. Fry in hot lard.

FRIED CAKES.

One coffee cup of not too thick sour cream or one of sour milk, and one teaspoonful butter, two eggs, a little nutmeg and salt, one teacup sugar, one small teaspoon of soda dissolved; mix soft.

DOUGHNUTS.

Three eggs, one cup sugar, one tumblerful sweet milk, one teaspoonful soda, two teaspoonfuls cream tartar, two large iron spoonfuls melted lard; stir sugar and eggs to a cream, then add other ingredients, and last just flour enough to roll nicely; cut in rings and fry in hot lard.

PIES AND TARTS.
PASTRY.

The water used in making pastry should always be cold and in summer ice water is best. The cook must be dexterous as well as skilled, for so much depends upon the handling, that although pastry be made ever so well, unless it gets into the oven quickly, it will lose its elasticity and become heavy. Fruit and filling should always be cold when put into the crust.

PIE CRUST.

Three teacupfuls of flour, half the quantity of butter, and half a teacup of lard; work the lard and butter into the flour and pour in a teacupful of cold water; knead into a firm dough with the least possible handling; roll out a thin sheet and place all over it pieces of butter set closely together; fold up and roll out again as before, repeating the process until the butter has been thoroughly assimilated with the dough, using a slight sprinkling of flour when needed.

APPLE CUSTARD PIE.

Make a very smooth apple sauce; to each cupful add two eggs beaten light, and half a cup of fresh milk. Line a pie-plate with paste and fill with the custard. Bake without upper crust.

DATE PIE.

Soak one pound of dates over night and stew until they can be strained; mix with a quart of milk, three eggs, and add a little salt and nutmeg. Bake with an undercrust only. This will make three pies.

LEMON PIE.

Two tablespoonfuls of flour, two-thirds of a cupful of water, one teacupful of sugar, yolks of three eggs, the grated rind and the juice of one lemon. Bake in a hot oven. Mix the whites of the eggs, well beaten, with three teaspoonfuls of sugar. Spread over the top of the pie when done, and return it to the oven until nicely browned.

COCOANUT PIE.

To a pint of scalded milk add half a teacupful of sugar, the yolks of two eggs and a dessertspoonful of corn starch dissolved in milk; beat all together; cook in the boiling milk and add a teacupful of grated cocoanut which has been soaked in milk over night; bake with the lower crust only. Beat the whites of the eggs to a froth, mix with two teaspoonfuls of sugar and spread over the pie when baked, return to the oven until nicely browned.

CREAM PIE.

A scant half cup of corn starch, thoroughly mixed with one cup of sweet cream and half a cup of sugar. Flavor with lemon. Bake with one crust.

PUMPKIN PIE.

Stew the pumpkin until soft. Strain through a sieve and for every pint take two eggs, one and one-half cups of sugar, one and one-half pints of milk, one-half teaspoonful of ginger, and two teaspoonfuls of cinnamon. Beat well and bake without upper crust.

MINCE PIE.

One pound each of raisins, currants and sugar; stone and chop the raisins; one pound of suet chopped very fine, two-thirds of an ounce each of candied lemon and orange peel, two large apples, chopped fine, one-third of an ounce cinnamon, two-thirds of a nutmeg, the juice of one lemon and two-thirds of a gill of cider. Bake with two crusts.

TARTS.

COMPOTE OF APPLES.

Roll the paste very thin, line small patty pans, and bake. When done and cold, fill with any kind of preserves, jelly or marmalade.

CHOCOLATE TARTLETS.

Four eggs, one-half cake of chocolate, grated; one tablespoonful corn starch, dissolved in milk; three tablespoonfuls of milk; four tablespoonfuls of sugar; a heaping teaspoonful of butter, a pinch of salt, flavor to suit. Rub the chocolate smooth in the milk, heat over the fire and add the cornstarch wet with more milk. Stir until thickened, then pour out. When cold beat in the yolks of the eggs, sugar and flavoring. Bake in small patty pans lined with paste. Cover with the whites beaten to a froth to which a little sugar has been added.

HOW TO MAKE ALL KINDS OF PUDDINGS.

CHOCOLATE PUDDING.

For one quart of sweet milk take a teacupful bread crumbs, two-thirds cupful of grated chocolate, the yolks of 4 eggs and one teacupful sugar. Heat milk and crumbs to moderate warmth and stir into them the sugar, chocolate and yolks, well beaten together with a tablespoonful of corn starch previously moistened with a little milk or water. Stir until scalding hot, then pour into a dish and cover the top with the egg whites beaten stiff and sweetened. Bake brown. Serve cold.

"BROWN BETTY."

A very simple but palatable dessert is made thus: Cut stale bread in very small squares or slices, and place a teacupful in the bottom of an earthen pudding dish. Over this put a thick layer of sliced sour apples; sprinkle them thickly with sugar and cinnamon and a few bits of butter; then more crumbs, apples, etc., until the dish is full. Finish with the crumbs, and then pour over half a pint boiling water, cover closely and bake in a moderate oven. When the apples begin to soften, remove the cover and bake to a delicate brown. To be eaten cold with cream or milk, preferably the former.

SUET PUDDING.

One cup of sugar, one cup of suet, chopped fine, one cup of raisins or English currants, chopped fine, one-half cup of sweet milk, two eggs, one teaspoonful of soda. Stir with flour like cake. Steam three hours.

THE QUEEN OF PUDDINGS.

1½ cup white sugar, 2 cups fine dry bread-crumbs, 5 eggs, 1 tablespoonful of butter, vanilla or lemon seasoning, 1 quart fresh milk and one-half cup jelly. Rub the butter into a cup of sugar; beat the yolks very light, and stir these together to a cream. Add the bread-crumbs soaked in milk and the seasoning. Bake in a large buttered pudding dish, filling it about two-thirds full, until the custard is "set." Draw to the mouth of the oven, spread over the jelly or other nice fruit conserve. Cover this with a meringue made of the whipped whites and a half cup of sugar. Shut the oven and bake until the meringue begins to color. Eat cold with cream. You may, in the fruit season, substitute the fresh fruit for preserves.

SNOW PUDDING.

Dissolve in one pint of hot water one-half ounce of gelatine. After it has cooled add the beaten whites of three eggs, one teacupful of sugar, and the juice of two lemons. Pour the whole into a mould. When set put into a dish, pour over it a quart of custard, flavored with vanilla, and set on the ice until served.

BREAD PUDDING.

2 cups of grated bread crumbs, 3 eggs, sugar to taste, season with nutmeg or cinnamon, milk to make very thin. Bake about thirty minutes. The white of one of the eggs may be saved and beaten to a stiff froth to which add a tablespoonful of powdered sugar. This may be spread on the top of the pudding when it is done. Place it back into the oven a moment to brown.

Home Pudding.

2 eggs, 1 cup of sugar, ½ cup of milk, 1½ cups of flour, 2 teaspoonfuls of baking powder, 1 tablespoonful of melted butter. Bake twenty or thirty minutes. Serve with cream and sugar or with lemon sauce.

Raisin Pudding.

Pour 2 cups of boiling milk over 1 teacupful of bread crumbs, add 3 tablespoonfuls of butter. Let stand until perfectly cool; then add: 1 cupful of seeded raisins, 1 cup of sugar, 1 cup of cream, the yolks of ½ dozen eggs, lastly the well whipped whites. To be served with sauce.

Chocolate Pudding.

Sweeten 1 quart of sweet milk with 1 cup of white sugar and let come to a boil; when it boils pour into it 4 tablespoonfuls of corn starch dissolved in one well beaten egg and a little milk; add 1 cup of boiling milk and 2 cups of grated chocolate. When it is done pour into a mold. Serve with cream and sugar when cold.

Corn-starch Pudding.

4 tablespoonfuls of corn-starch, 1 quart of milk, 4 eggs (whites and yolks separate), ¾ cup of sugar, nutmeg and cinnamon, 1 tablespoonful of butter. Let the milk come to a boil, stir in the corn-starch dissolved in a little cold milk. Let boil three minutes, stirring all the time. Remove from the fire and add the butter. Set away until cold; beat the eggs very light—the sugar and seasoning with them; stir into the corn-starch, beating thoroughly to a smooth custard. Turn into a buttered dish and bake half an hour. Eat cold, with powdered sugar sifted over it.

Graham Pudding.

1 cup of raisins seeded and chopped, 1 cup of molasses, 1 teaspoonful of soda dissolved in 1 scant cup of sweet milk, ½ teaspoonful salt, 2 cupfuls of graham flour. Steam three hours. Serve with cream or hot sauce.

Peach Pudding.

Stir peaches into a batter made of ½ cup of sugar, 3 tablespoonfuls of melted butter, 1 cup of milk, 1 egg well beaten, 1 pint of flour, 3 teaspoonfuls of baking powder. Bake in loaf. Serve with cream.

Green Corn Pudding.

With a sharp knife cut lengthwise through the kernels of six large ears of corn; then slice off the slit kernels and with back of knife scrape the rest from the ear. Mix thoroughly with this pulp 2 well beaten eggs, 2 tablespoonfuls each of sugar and butter, ½ teaspoonful salt, 6 rolled crackers and 1 teacupful milk. Bake three hours in a greased pudding dish. Eat with a hot sauce.

Pie-plant Pudding.

Peel the stalks and cut them into small pieces; allow same weight of sugar as of pie-plant. Cover the bottom of an earthen pudding dish with the cut plant and sugar, then spread on a layer of bread crumbs and bits of butter; next more pie-plant, and so on alternately until the dish is full, finishing with bread crumbs. Cover and bake in a moderate oven until the pie-plant is cooked; then remove and brown the top. When ready for the table, a boiled custard may be poured over it, though the dish is good without.

Taylor Pudding.

1 cup of milk, 1 cup of molasses, 1 cup of suet, chopped fine, 2 cups of raisins stoned and chopped, 3 cups of sifted flour, with 3 teaspoonfuls of baking powder, 1 teaspoonful of salt, and 1 teaspoonful each of allspice, cinnamon and nutmeg. Boil in a mold four hours, and eat with a liquid sauce.

Boston Pudding.

1 cup of chopped suet, 1 cup of sweet milk, 2 cups of raisins, 1 cup of molasses, 3 cups of sifted flour, 1 teaspoonful of soda, 2 teaspoonfuls of salt. For extra occasions add 1 cup of currants and ½ cup of sliced citron. Season with cloves and cinnamon to taste. Boil three hours. Eat with hard sauce.

Bread Pudding.

1 quart of milk, 2 cups of fine bread crumbs (dry and stale), 4 eggs, 2 tablespoonfuls melted butter, nutmeg to taste, ½ teaspoonful soda dissolved in hot water. Beat the yolks very light and mix with the bread crumbs which have previously been well soaked in the milk. Stir these together; then add the butter, seasoning, soda and the whites in the order named. Bake to a fine brown, and eat hot with sweetened cream or with pudding sauce.

Apple Tapioca Pudding.

Soak one cup of tapioca in three pints of water (cold) over night. In the morning let boil twenty or thirty minutes, or until it looks clear. Add 1½ quarts of pared and quartered apples, 1 cupful of sugar, 1 teaspoonful of salt. Flavor with lemon. Bake 1¼ hours in a buttered dish. Serve when cold, with sugar and cream.

Rice Pudding.

1 coffee-cup rice, 2 quarts milk, 8 tablespoonfuls sugar, 1 teaspoonful salt, butter the size of an egg (melted), nutmeg or cinnamon to taste. Soak the rice in one pint of the milk two hours, then add the rest of the milk, the sugar, salt, butter and spice. Bake two hours. Eat cold.

A Splendid Pudding.

Bake a common sponge cake in a flat buttered pudding dish, or take stale cake on hand, cut in six or eight pieces. Split and spread with butter and return them to the dish. Make a custard with four eggs to a quart of milk, flavor and sweeten to taste. Pour over the cake and bake about thirty minutes. The cake will swell up and fill the custard.

Apple Pudding.

Remove the core of as many apples as you wish and cut them just in half, place them in a pudding dish, the round side down. Fill the hollow places with a little butter, sugar and cinnamon. Pour a milk and egg custard over all, and bake for twenty-five or thirty minutes. Serve with cream and sugar.

SAUCE.

Two tablespoonfuls of flour, seven tablespoonfuls of sugar, two tablespoonfuls of butter, a little nutmeg. Stir all together and pour on boiling water and let it boil on the stove. When ready to serve, add to the sauce one large teaspoonful of your favorite jelly.

OLD ENGLISH PLUM PUDDING.

Take one-half cup of lard and one-half cup of butter, two cups of English currants. Mix all these (currants and shortening), dry through some flour, add water to make a dough as stiff as pie crust; take one-third of this mixed dough and roll out in a large, round sheet. On it put a cup and a half of sugar and two-thirds of a cup of butter and a cup of currants. Draw the crust around this like a dumpling; roll out the rest of the dough and wrap it around the dumpling; tie this up securely in a cloth, to boil three hours. To be eaten with sauce or simply with moistened sugar.

CHRISTMAS PLUM PUDDING.

One coffeecup of raisins, stoned and cut up, one cup of molasses, one cup of sweet milk, one cup of chopped suet (or if you have it, a half cup of butter), three cups of flour, one teaspoonful of saleratus, one teaspoonful each of salt, cinnamon, cloves and nutmeg. Steam three hours. To be eaten with a rich sauce.

DELMONICO PUDDING.

Heat a quart of milk to boiling and stir into it 3 tablespoonfuls corn starch previously moistened; let it boil a few minutes, then add the yolks of 5 eggs beaten with 6 tablespoonfuls sugar and half a teaspoonful extract of vanilla. Place the whole in a pudding dish and bake. Beat the whites stiff, add 2 or 3 tablespoonfuls sugar and a few drops extract of lemon; spread this over the pudding as soon as done, or lay it on in spoonfuls; return to oven and bake to a nice yellow.

tablespoonfuls of
ittle nutmeg. Stir
and let it boil on
the sauce one large

JDDING.

cup of butter, two
ese (currants and
d water to make a
hird of this mixed
heet. On it put a
of a cup of butter
around this like a
ough and wrap it
rely in a cloth, to
ice or simply with

DDING.

cut up, one cup of
p of chopped suet
hree cups of flour,
onful each of salt,
three hours. To

NG.

tir into it 3 table-
ned; let it boil a
ggs beaten with 6
oonful extract of
sh and bake. Beat
s sugar and a few
er the pudding as
eturn to oven and

How to Make All Kinds of Puddings.

STEAMED INDIAN PUDDING.

One pint each of sour milk and of Indian meal, 1 teacupful rye flour (or in absence of rye flour use white flour), 1-3 teacupful molasses, one teaspoonful salt and a large one of soda. Dissolve the soda in a little warm water and stir it in after the other ingredients are well mixed. Lastly add half a teacupful raisins. Steam in a mold 3 or 4 hours. For a sauce take a teacupful molasses, half as much water, 1 tablespoonful butter, a pinch of salt, 3 tablespoonfuls vinegar. Boil together 15 or 20 minutes.

A GLACE CHERRY PUDDING.

One-half cup of butter, one cup of sugar, one-half cup of milk, one and one-half cups of flour, one teaspoonful of baking powder, one teaspoonful of vanilla flavoring. Bake in the round lids of baking powder tins. While these are baking, boil two tablespoonfuls of sugar, three-fourths of a cup of milk, one large tablespoonful of corn starch and the beaten white of one egg. Flavor with one-half teaspoonful of vanilla extract. When the puddings are baked, and while this mixture is still hot, spread one large teaspoonful smoothly over the top of each pudding.

Have white glacé cherries cut into halves. Place about six of these pieces around the top of each pudding. For the sauce, boil three-fourths of a cup of sugar, one and one-half cups of milk, two tablespoonfuls of butter, one tablespoonful of corn starch, the yolks of three eggs, and one teaspoonful of vanilla extract. Pour the sauce around each little pudding. Serve hot. These quantities are sufficient for twelve persons.

BREAD AND BUTTER PUDDING.

Cut bread in rather thin slices, remove crusts, lay the buttered slices in a pudding dish and sprinkle currants liberally over the bread layers. When the dish is nearly full, pour a boiled custard over it; bake 15 to 20 minutes. Serve with sauce.

BLACKBERRY SPONGE.

Cover half a box of gelatine with a cupful of cold water and soak for half an hour, pour over a pint of boiling water, add half a cupful of sugar and stir until dissolved; strain in a pint of blackberry juice, mix, and pour in a tin pan. Set on ice until thick, then beat to a froth, add the beaten whites of four eggs and mix smooth. Pour in a mold and set on ice to harden. Serve with vanilla sauce.

CHERRY AND TAPIOCA PUDDING.

Soak one teacupful tapioca over night in its bulk of cold water; in the morning put it on the fire adding 2 teacupfuls of hot water and bring to a boil; add 1½ pounds stoned cherries, and sugar enough to sweeten. When the cherries are cooked through take up in a mold and set in a cool place to stiffen. Serve with sugar and whipped cream.

QUICK PUDDING.

Set a quart of milk to cook on the stove, and when it boils stir in flour smoothly until it becomes quite thick. Salt and sugar to taste. An egg may be added if desired. Serve hot with a sauce made as follows: Beat a tablespoonful of sugar and a piece of butter about the size of a walnut to a cream. Then pour on a pint of milk and let boil ten minutes.

COCOANUT PUDDING.

1 pint of milk, yolks of two eggs (well beaten), two tablespoonfuls cocoanut, ½ teacup of rolled cracker crumbs. Sweeten and flavor to taste. Bake thirty minutes. Make a frosting of the whites of the eggs, beaten to a froth, and a cup of sugar. Spread over the top.

TAPIOCA PUDDING.

Soak one-half cupful of tapioca in luke-warm water over night. In the morning put into it 1 quart of sweet milk, 4 eggs, whites and yolks well beaten and added separately, ½ cup of sugar, ½ teaspoonful of salt. Boil until it creams, stirring constantly with a wooden spoon. Jelly laid on in spoonfuls may be added, or it may be eaten with cream and sugar.

HOW TO MAKE ALL KINDS OF PUDDING SAUCES.

LEMON SAUCE.

Beat together, until light: The yolks of two eggs, 1 cup of sugar, ½ cup of butter, 1 tablespoonful of corn starch, the juice of one lemon. Stir this into one cup and a half of boiling water, until sufficiently thick for the table.

VANILLA SAUCE.

Beat the whites of two eggs to a stiff froth, and then beat in ½ cup of powdered sugar, the yolk of one egg, 1 teaspoonful of vanilla.

APRICOT SAUCE.

1 cupful of canned apricots, 1 cupful of sugar, 1 cupful of milk, 1 tablespoonful of corn starch, ½ cupful of water. Put the milk on to boil. Mix the corn starch with a little cold milk, and stir into the boiling milk. Cook ten minutes. Boil the sugar and water together for twenty minutes. Rub the apricots into a sieve, and stir it into the syrup. Beat well, and then beat it into the boiled milk and corn starch. Place the sauce pan in cold water and stir eight minutes, and set away to cool.

CREAM SAUCE.

1 cupful of powdered sugar, 1 egg, 2 cupfuls of whipped cream. Beat the white of the egg to a stiff froth. Add the yolk and sugar and beat well. Flavor with vanilla, or lemon, and add the cream last of all.

COLD CREAM SAUCE.

1 cup of sugar, 1 cup of butter well beaten, 1 cup of good cream. Stir all well together, and place it where it will keep cool.

PUDDING SAUCE.

One spoonful of flour wet with a cup of milk, one half cup of sugar, one half spoonful of butter. Boil slowly and flavor with extracts to taste.

PUDDING SAUCE.

1 pint water made into a smooth starch with a heaping tablespoon flour. Cook ten minutes, strain if necessary, sweeten to taste and pour it on 1 tablespoon butter and juice of a lemon or other flavoring. If lemon is not used add 1 tablespoon vinegar.

This can be made richer by using more butter and sugar; stir them in a cream with a flavoring, then add the starch.

APFEL KUCHEN. NUDELN.

HOW TO MAKE FROZEN OR OTHER DESSERTS.

FOR FREEZING ICE CREAM.

Have ice pounded in small pieces (pound in a bag), pack around the tin can a layer of ice about five inches deep, then a thin layer of salt, and so on until the tub is full, packing down well. For a gallon can use three pints of rock salt and about ten quarts of ice. If packed solid no more ice or salt is needed. Do not drain off the water while freezing. If more salt is used the cream freezes sooner, but will not be so rich and smooth.

BOILED ICE CREAM.

Take two quarts of sweet milk and one pint of sweet cream and let come to a boil. Take four tablespoonfuls corn starch and dissolve in a little milk, five eggs, well beaten, one and one-half cups of sugar, beat thoroughly. Pour into the boiling milk and cream, stirring well and let come to a boil once more. Set away to cool, when thoroughly cold, freeze.

Any flavoring to suit the taste may be added, before cooling.

STRAWBERRY ICE CREAM.

Mash two pints of strawberries, and one pint sugar together, and let them stand one and one-half or two hours. Then rub through a strainer into one quart of cream and freeze.

ICE CREAM.

Take one quart of milk, and one quart of cream, sweeten and flavor to taste. Let stand in the freezer fifteen minutes before commencing to freeze.

LEMON WATER ICE.

Take two lemons and rasp them on sugar, the juice of six lemons, the juice of one orange, one pint of clarified sugar and half a pint of water. Mix all together, strain through a fine sieve and freeze. When nearly frozen add the white of three eggs.

CURRANT ICE.

Take two pounds of ripe, red currants and half a pound of raspberries, rub through a fine sieve into an earthen dish, add about one pint of thick sugar syrup. Put into a freezer and freeze in the ordinary way.

ALMOND CREAM.

Blanch and pound fine, with a little water, one and a half pounds of almonds; beat the whites of two eggs to a froth, beat into this five ounces of powdered sugar, and to both add one quart of milk. Boil gently over a slow fire until reduced one-quarter, then add the almond paste and boil five minutes longer. Flavor to taste, and when cold sprinkle thickly with granulated sugar and brown, garnish with whole almonds.

SNOW PYRAMIDS.

Beat the whites of half a dozen eggs to a stiff froth; add a teacupful of currant jelly, and whip all together; fill saucers half full of cream, dropping into the center of each a tablespoonful of the egg and jelly in the shape of a pyramid.

TUTTI FRUTTI ICE CREAM.

Two quarts of cream, one quart of new milk, three cups sugar, flavor with vanilla, one-half cup of nut meat (any kind), one-half cup chopped raisins and citron, one-half cup candied cherries; when cream is partly frozen add fruit and nuts well mixed. Very nice.

LEMON ICE.

Juice of eight lemons, two quarts of water, sugar to make a very sweet lemonade; partly freeze this mixture, then add the whites of five eggs beaten stiff, finish freezing and pack with ice until time to serve. Any fruit juice may be used in the same manner, but with most other fruits the juice of two or three lemons makes a great addition to the flavor.

PINEAPPLE SHERBET.

Take one large pineapple, add three quarts water, one ounce of dissolved gelatine, four lemons and the whites of six eggs; make very sweet and freeze. Oranges can be used instead of lemons if preferred.

FROZEN PUDDING.

Make a plain egg and milk custard, three pints, add a cupful of partially chopped, blanched almonds and pour into the freezer. When just beginning to freeze add two cups of whipped cream. Stir often while freezing so that the fruit will be well distributed.

CAUTION FOR CANNED FRUITS.

Never allow the contents of a tin can of fruit, or canned goods of any kind, to remain in the cans after they are opened.

HOW TO CAN ALL KINDS OF FRUIT.

1. Always pick the fruit when it is perfectly dry, for when it is rain-soaked it spoils very easily and will not keep as well.
2. Look it over very carefully, removing all insects and hulls, and if sandy, place it in a cullender and turn cold water over it, and the sand will pass through the holes in the bottom.

How to Can All Kinds of Fruit.

3. Add sugar at the rate of two teacupfuls to a quart of fruit, but more or less may be added according to taste and kind of fruit.

4. Place the fruit in porcelain or granite-ware kettles, and heat till cooked through.

5. Wring a towel, or piece of cotton cloth, out of cold water, and wrap it tightly around the can, then set the can into a tin containing one-half inch of water.

6. Now place a long-handled spoon into the can and then with a small tin cup fill as rapidly as possible. When nearly full give it a good stir with the spoon to bring all the air bubbles to the top; fill full, turn down the cover as tight as you can and set aside to cool.

7. When cool, tighten the cover again and set away in a cool, dry, dark place. Look at the cans occasionally, and if they show signs of working, re-cook them.

8. If your cans are perfect and the cover as tight as you can turn it down upon the rubber, you will have no trouble; the fruit will keep perfectly well.

How to Make Jellies. 469

9. If the fruit settles somewhat in the cans do not be alarmed, as most fruit shrinks some, strawberries most of all. If there is considerable juice left after the cans are all filled, it can be made into jelly, or it may be put with an equal amount of pieplant, cooked and canned. This makes a very palatable sauce for winter.

HOW TO MAKE ALL KINDS OF JELLIES, JAMS, MARMALADES, APPLE BUTTER, ETC.

Grape Jelly.

Boil the grapes in a porcelain kettle and to every four quarts of grapes use half a pint of water. Boil until soft and then strain through a sieve or cloth. Boil the juice twenty minutes, and add a pound of sugar to every pound of juice. Then let it boil ten minutes and pour into jelly glasses.

Currant Jelly.

Put the currants into a vessel and put this vessel into another containing boiling water. Boil until thoroughly scalded, then squeeze them through a cloth. Put a pint of sugar into every pint of juice and boil on the fire, stirring it frequently. Five minutes boiling is sufficient.

Blackberry Jelly.

Mash the berries thoroughly, squeeze and strain the juice from them, put it on to boil a half hour with sugar, pint for pint. Pour into jelly glasses and place a piece of paper dipped in brandy over the top, before fastening the lid.

Strawberry Jelly.

To every two pounds of sugar add three quarts of strawberries. Mash and let stand for two hours. Then press the juice from the berries. Then dissolve one box of gelatine in half a pint of cold water. Then mix, and add the juice of a lemon. Strain, and pour into glass dishes to harden.

Raspberry Jelly.

Raspberry jelly is made the same as strawberry.

Lemon Jelly.

Cut 6 bananas lengthwise. Slice 6 oranges. Dissolve a little more than ½ box of gelatine in ½ pint of cold water; then add ½ pint of boiling water, the juice of 3 lemons, and sweeten to taste.

Clear Apple Jelly.

Pare and core 6 dozen of sour apples, put into a pan with water to cover them, boil gently until soft, let cool, and strain through a bag; to each pint of juice add one pound of sugar and the peel of two lemons, boil to the stiffness of calf's foot jelly, skim, and add the juice of one lemon.

Fruit Jelly.

Pare and slice very thin 8 oranges and 6 bananas, and arrange in layers in a charlotte-russe mold. Make a jelly of half a box of gelatine soaked in half a pint of cold water for two hours, then add half a pint of boiling water and the juice of 3 lemons; sweeten to taste; when it has partly cooled, pour this jelly over the fruit and set away in a cool place to harden.

Orange Jelly.

The juice of 8 oranges, juice of 2 lemons, 1 pound of white sugar, ¾ of a box of gelatine, soaked in 1 pint of water for half an hour, then add ¾ of a pint of boiling water, stir thoroughly, and strain through a flannel bag into molds.

Cider Jelly.

Let 3 pints of cider come to a boil, and pour it over a box full of gelatine, that has been soaked in cold water for two hours, and add two cupfuls of sugar. Strain, pour into molds and put aside to harden.

Tomato Jam.

Stew 1½ gallons of apples, and 1 gallon of tomatoes separately. Then put them together in a kettle, and add 6 pounds of sugar, 1 ounce of ground cloves, and 1 ounce of ground cinnamon.

Cherry Marmalade.

Strain the cherries and add to every 3 pounds of cherries ¼ of a pint of currant juice. Now add ¾ of a pound of sugar to every pound of fruit. Put on the fire and stir thoroughly. When it has boiled to thick jelly pour it into jars.

Apple Butter.

Stew your apples as you would for sauce, and to every 2 gallons of cooked apples add 3 cups of cider vinegar and 4 pounds of sugar. Boil this down about one-third, or until there is about 1½ gallons. Flavor, when nearly done, with essence of, or ground cinnamon.

Currant and Raspberry Jam.

Ingredients.—To every pound of red currants allow ¼ pound of raspberries, weighed after the stalks are removed, and 1 pound of loaf sugar.

Mode.—Place the fruit in the above proportion in the preserving pan, with 1 pound of sugar to every pound of fruit, stir and boil for three-quarters of an hour after the mixture boils fast; remove the scum as it rises. Put the jam in pots.

Grape Jam.

Ingredients.—Unripe grapes, sugar.

Mode.—The grapes must not be quite ripe, and they should be most carefully picked and gently washed, all unsound ones being taken out. Allow half a pound of sugar to one pound of grapes. Put the fruit into a preserving-pan, without water, layer for layer with sugar. Boil rather quickly, stirring always. Pour, when cool, into pots as usual.

HOW TO MAKE ALL KINDS OF PRESERVES.

PRESERVED CHERRIES.

Stone the cherries, preserving every drop of juice. Weigh the fruit, allowing pound for pound of sugar. Put a layer of fruit for one of sugar until all is used up; pour over the juice and boil gently until the syrup begins to thicken.

The short-stem red cherries, or the Morellas are best for preserves. Sweet cherries will not do.

PRESERVED STRAWBERRIES.

Pound for pound. Put them in a preserving kettle over a slow fire until the sugar melts. Boil twenty-five minutes fast. Take out the fruit in a perforated skimmer and fill a number of small cans three-quarters full. Boil and skim the syrup five minutes longer, fill up the jars, and seal while hot. Keep in a cool, dry place.

PEAR PRESERVES.

Weigh the pears after they are pared, and to every pound add three-quarters of a pound of loaf sugar, water enough to prevent them from burning, and the peel of a small lemon cut very thin. Let them stew gently for six or seven hours.

PEACH PRESERVES.

Pare, stone and quarter ripe free-stone peaches. To six pounds of peaches allow three pounds of brown sugar. Put the sugar over the peaches and let them stand over night; next morning place them in a preserving-kettle and boil for two hours, keeping it well skimmed.

CRAB APPLE PRESERVES.

If Siberian crabs, wipe them only; if French, they must be pared. Put the apples in and let them simmer until they are done, into a boiling syrup, made from two pints of lump sugar and one pint of cider. Reduce the syrup, and skim until it is thick enough, and pour it over the fruit which has been placed in earthen or glass jars.

RHUBARB PRESERVES.

Slice six oranges into a stew pan, with the rind cut very small, a quart of rhubarb, cut fine, and two pounds of sugar. Boil the whole down as any other preserves.

PRESERVED APPLES.

Firm, well-flavored pippins or bell-flower apples make an excellent preserve, prepared in the same manner as quinces. A few quinces cut up among them or the juice of two lemons to every three pounds of fruit improves them.

QUINCE PRESERVES.

Into two quarts of boiling water put a quantity of golden pippin apples, not cut very thin, and not pared, but wiped clean. Keep them closely covered, boil quickly till the water becomes a thick jelly, then scald. To every cupful of apple jelly put a half pound of sugar; boil it and skim it clear. Put those quinces that are to be done whole, into the syrup, and let it boil very fast; those that are to be in half by themselves; skim it, and when the fruit is clear, put some of the syrup into a glass to try whether it jellies, before taking from the fire. The quantity of quinces is to be a pound to a pound of sugar, and a pound of jelly already boiled with the sugar.

RIPE TOMATO PRESERVES.

7 lbs. round yellow or egg tomatoes—peeled.
7 lbs. sugar and juice of three lemons.

Let them stand together over night. Drain off the syrup and boil it, skimming well. Put in the tomatoes and boil gently twenty minutes. Take out the fruit with a perforated skimmer, and spread upon dishes. Boil the syrup down until it thickens, adding, just before you take it up, the juice of three lemons. Put the fruit into jars and fill up with hot syrup. When cold, seal or tie up.

GREEN TOMATO PRESERVES.

8 lbs. small green tomatoes. Pierce each with a fork.
7 lbs. sugar.
4 lemons—the juice only.
1 oz. ginger and mace mixed.

Heat all together slowly, and boil until the fruit is clear. Take it from the kettle in a perforated skimmer, and spread upon dishes to cool. Boil the syrup thick. Put the fruit into jars and cover with hot syrup.

IMAGE EVALUATION
TEST TARGET (MT-3)

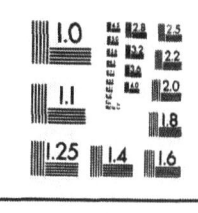

← 6" →

Photographic
Sciences
Corporation

23 WEST MAIN STREET
WEBSTER, N.Y. 14580
(716) 872-4503

HOW TO MAKE ALL KINDS OF DRINKS FOR THE SICK.

FROM TOKOLOGY.

LEMONADE.

Juice of half a lemon, one teaspoon sugar, one glass of water, either hot or cold, as the case requires. Hot lemonade is an excellent remedy for colds and biliousness.

ORANGE WHEY.

Juice of one orange, one pint sweet milk. Heat slowly until curds form. Strain and cool.

EGG LEMONADE.

Juice of one lemon, one glass of water, white of one egg, one tablespoon sugar. Beat together.

JELLY WATER.

Sour jellies, or the canned juice of any fruit, make pleasant drinks when reduced with water and sweetened.

OATMEAL TEA.

Two tablespoons raw oat-meal, one quart water. Let stand two hours in a cold place, then drain off as wanted.

TOAST WATER.

Toast a thin slice of bread very brown. Let it stand in a bowl of cold water an hour before using.

TAPIOCA MILK.

Soak three tablespoons tapioca one hour in cold water. Add three cups boiling milk, sugar and flavoring to taste, and simmer slowly thirty minutes. Eaten warm. Sago can also be used in the same way.

FLAXSEED LEMONADE.

Pour one pint boiling water over two tablespoons whole flaxseed, when cool strain and add the juice of two lemons, and two tablespoons honey. Used for coughs, colds and suppressed urine.

BEEF TEA.

Cut one pound lean beef in pieces, cover tightly in a bottle, placed in a pot of cold water. Heat slowly to a boil, which should be continued steadily four hours. When salted it is ready for use. It is a mild stimulant, but not very nourishing, and a patient confined to it *long* will slowly starve.

RICE GRUEL.

Steep two tablespoons rice slowly in one quart water, one hour. Strain, and add salt and a little cream.

CORN TEA.

Common corn parched brown. Grind it, and pour on boiling water. Can be used with or without cream. Used in nausea, vomiting and diarrhea.

BRAN GRUEL.

Bran of white wheat, one pint. Boil half an hour in three pints water. Strain, and salt it. May be thinned and flavored with lemon juice.

CORN MEAL OR "WATER GRUEL."

Wet one tablespoon sifted corn meal in cold water. Prepare one quart boiling water in a gruel pan. Stir one spoonful of this cold batter into the boiling water, let it boil up, then add another, stirring thoroughly, and so on until the gruel is thick enough. Let it boil hard twenty minutes or longer. Salt and add a little cream.

Gruel can be made of graham the same way.

MILK PORRIDGE.

Into one quart boiling *milk* stir one and one-half tablespoons flour, wet in cold water. Salt to taste. Can be made of "whole-wheat flour," arrow root, corn-starch, etc.

BUTTERMILK.

For some forms of dyspepsia, in fevers, and in cases of diabetes buttermilk is an excellent food. May be sealed like fruit in glass jars and kept some time.

OATMEAL GRUEL.

Two tablespoons oatmeal in one quart boiling water. Sift in slowly and boil one hour, then strain and season.

HOT MILK.

Reduce the milk by adding one-tenth water. Heated in a double boiler to 110° F., or as hot as one can sip it slowly, it is a most valuable drink for any invalid. Especially would it be well for nursing mothers to try, instead of the beer or porter so often ignorantly recommended to them. By its means mothers have been enabled to gain flesh during the nursing period, which usually is such a draught upon the strength and flesh.

CHICKEN BROTH.

Boil the dark meat of half a chicken in one quart of water with little rice or barley. Take off the fat and use as soon as the rice is well cooked. Add bits of brown toast.

MACARONI SOUP.

Break into small pieces a handful of macaroni. Boil one hour. Strain two cups stewed tomatoes, and add to it, with one cup of cream just before serving.

FARINA SOUP.

One half cup of farina, half cup of cream or one beaten egg, added to any soup stock, and boiled gently half an hour.

TOMATO SOUP.

One quart water, one pint tomatoes heated to boiling. Thicken with Graham flour—three tablespoons mixed with cold water. Add one quart of milk and stir until it boils. Season.

How to Cook All Kinds of Relishes for the Sick.

LEMON JELLY.

Stir into one pint of boiling water two tablespoons cornstarch, wet in cold water. Add part of a cup of sugar and juice of two lemons, with a little grated rind. Set in molds to cool.

ANOTHER RECIPE FOR LEMON JELLY.

Dissolve one ounce of gelatine in one quart water. Let it come to a boil in a saucepan. Add juice of three lemons, a little grated rind, and one cup of sugar, pour into molds, and set on the ice to cool.

HOW TO COOK ALL KINDS OF RELISHES FOR THE SICK.

FROM TOKOLOGY.

CRACKED OR ROLLED WHEAT.

Cracked wheat should be stirred into boiling water and cooked in a double kettle 3 hours. Salt and serve either hot or cold in molds with fruit sauce, or cream and sugar. Rolled wheat may be cooked the same way, only it does not require to cook so long.

Do not soak in cold water, but stir into boiling water, as all the grains should be. Wheat is excellent for constipation or biliousness.

INDIAN MEAL MUSH.

Cornmeal stirred into boiling water slowly and cooked thoroughly one hour—not less.

OATMEAL MUSH.

Prepared the same as wheat with the same distinction between the cracked oats and the rolled. It should not be stirred while cooking.

GRAHAM MUSH.

Prepared the same as above. Let it boil ten minutes, then beat thoroughly before taking up. Serve with fruit juice, or cream and sugar.

FARINA MUSH.

Half a cup farina, one quart boiling water. Cook fifteen minutes in double kettle without stirring; add half a cup of cream just before removing from fire.
Serve with stewed fruit or fruit juice.

WHEATLET MUSH.

Use water or equal parts milk and water. Salt to taste. Have it boiling hot, then sprinkle in wheatlet enough to make a thin pudding. Boil hard for five minutes, then set it back ten minutes to cook slowly.

WHEATLET PUDDING.

Break up cooked wheatlet, add milk enough to make a thin pudding. Two eggs, currants, raisins to suit. Brown in a moderate oven.

WHEATLET PUDDING.

In a deep pudding dish put layers of cold cooked wheatlet (cracked wheat may be used), and tart apples sliced thin. Sugar to taste. Raisins if desired. Fill the dish thus having wheatlet at the top. Bake until well done and browned.
Rice and apples may be prepared the same way.

RICE AND RAISINS.

Boil together, one cup rice, half cup raisins, one cup sweet milk, in three cups boiling water. Serve warm or cold with cream or fruit sauce.

RICE SNOW BALLS.

Boil two cups rice two hours in two quarts water and one pint of milk. Mould in small cups. Serve with boiled custard or fruit sauce.

RICE OMELET.

Two cups boiled rice, one cup sweet milk, two eggs. Beat with the egg beater, and put into a hot buttered skillet. Cook slowly ten minutes, stirring frequently.

HOMINY.

One cup hominy, three and a half cups boiling water. Salt. Cook four hours in a double kettle.

RICE AND BERRY PUDDING.

Work together two cups cold rice and two cups sweet milk. Then stir in the beaten yolks of two eggs with one-third cup of sugar, also the well whipped whites. Stir in two cups blueberries, currants, strawberries, seeded cherries, or chopped apples. Bake one hour in a pudding dish, set in a pan of boiling water. Serve warm or cold with or without cream.

BOILED RICE.

Two cups of rice to three pints boiling water. Salt to taste. Cook in double kettle four hours. The Japanese method of cooking rice is to cover a dish tightly and cook in a steamer with only a very little water in the rice. Each kernel turns out separate, and bursts open like a mealy potato.

GRAHAM MUFFINS.

Stir together one pint new milk and one pint graham or "entire wheat" flour. Add one beaten egg and bake in hot muffin rings. Salt must not be used with any bread that is made light with egg.

BEST GRAHAM BISCUIT.

Make a thick Graham mush as above. Take it out on the moulding board, and knead into it more Graham flour, roll about an inch thick and cut into biscuits, and bake in a hot oven.

LIGHT GRAHAM BISCUIT.

Make the dough of Graham yeast, beat a trifle stiffer, roll and cut into biscuits. When light bake thirty minutes.

BOSTON BROWN BREAD.

Three cups Graham flour, one cup cornmeal, one cup molasses, two cups sweet milk, one cup sour milk, one teaspoon soda. Steam three hours, then bake until brown.

OATMEAL SNAPS.

Mix one cup sweet cream and three tablespoonfuls sugar; add fine oatmeal until stiff; knead slightly. Roll to the thickness of an eighth of an inch. Cut in shapes and bake crisp in a moderate oven.

GRAHAM FRUIT CRACKERS.

Make a stiff dough of equal parts graham and white flour, two-thirds cup sweet cream, three-fourths teaspoonful of baking powder (or one-fourth teaspoon soda to one-half of cream of tartar). Roll out thin; cover thickly with dried currants. Roll on another sheet of dough and pass the rolling pin over it. Cut in shapes. Prick deeply. Bake in a moderate oven.

GRAHAM WAFERS.

Mix graham flour with pure cold water. No salt. Roll very thin, cut in squares and bake quickly. These will keep months in a dry place and are excellent for dyspeptics. May be heated over before eating.

GRAHAM GRIDDLE CAKES.

Sour milk or buttermilk with just enough soda to make it bubble a little. One egg well beaten, and graham flour stirred in to make a batter. Excellent with maple syrup for constipation.

MILK TOAST.

Toast graham bread or gems split in two. Boil one pint of milk and half a cup cream. Thicken with one teaspoon corn-starch. Salt to taste. Pour over the toast and serve hot.

OYSTER TOAST.

Pour stewed oysters over graham gems or bread toasted. Excellent for breakfast.

Codfish cooked in milk is also excellent on toast. Also stewed tomatoes.

EGGS ON TOAST.

Soften brown bread toast with hot water. Serve on a platter with poached or scrambled eggs. Add salt, butter and a little cream. Set in the oven to warm just before serving.

ASPARAGUS ON TOAST.

Stew tender asparagus thirty minutes. Add half a cup of cream, salt and butter to taste. Turn over graham toast.

BOILED EGGS.

Eggs furnish the most perfect food as well as milk. They should never be boiled hard. Place in boiling water and set back ten minutes, and they will be cooked to perfection and easily digested.

EGGS POACHED IN MILK.

One cup milk, half a cup of water, when boiling break in six eggs. Cook slowly and serve on toast, well seasoned.

EGG OMELET.

Beat whites of six eggs. Beat yolks with three tablespoonfuls of milk and one of flour, stir in the whites lightly. Cook in a hot buttered skillet. When the edge is cooked turn over carefully. In two minutes more double together on a hot platter. Jelly may be spread between if desired. Use no salt.

GRAHAM GEM PUDDING.

Break up six cold gems into small pieces, and pour over them a pint of hot water and half a cup of sugar. Stir in six large tart apples, cut in thin slices. Bake brown.

APPLE TAPIOCA PUDDING.

Soak a cup of tapioca in a quart of warm water three hours. Stir in lightly six tart apples sliced thin, add half a cup of sugar, and bake in a pudding dish.
Serve with whipped cream, warm or cold.

ORANGE PUDDING.

Pare and slice five large oranges, removing seeds. Lay in a deep dish and sprinkle with sugar, let them stand two hours. Make a custard of one pint milk, yolks of three eggs and two tablespoons corn-starch; when cool pour over oranges. Beat the whites with two tablespoons powdered sugar, and place on top.
Brown quickly in the oven.

BROILED OYSTERS.

Put large oysters on a toaster. Hold over hot coals until heated through. Serve on toast moistened with cream. Very grateful in convalescence.

PIE FOR DYSPEPTICS.

Four tablespoons of oatmeal, one pint of water, let stand till the meal is swelled. Then add two large apples, pared and sliced, a little salt, one cup of sugar, one tablespoonful of flour, nutmeg if desired. Bake in a buttered dish, when well mixed together. Makes a most delicious pie, which can be eaten with safety by the sick or well.

APPLE SNOW.

Bake tart apples till soft and brown. Remove skins and cores. When cool beat them smooth and fine. Add half a cup of granulated sugar and the white of one egg.

Beat till the mixture will hold on your spoon. Serve with whipped cream or soft custard.

BAKED PIE PLANT.

Cut pie plant into a pudding dish. Sprinkle over it a cup of sugar, and cover with bread crumbs. Bake in a quick oven. Pie plant may be steamed with sugar and make a nice sauce.

FRUIT ICE.

Apples, pears, pineapples or any fruit grated fine, sweetened to taste and frozen, are delicious. Useful in fever or inflammation.

SCALLOPED TOMATOES.

Bake in a pudding dish alternate layers of tomatoes (fresh or canned) and bread crumbs. Seasoned well. Have the top layer of tomatoes.

The following are taken by permission from "Prize Essay of American Health Association," by Mrs. Mary Hinman Abel, published by the American Public Health Association:

BILLS OF FARE.

For family of six; average, 78 cents per day, or 13 cents per person.

1.   SATURDAY, MAY.

BREAKFAST.
Flour Pancakes with Sugar Syrup.
Coffee.

DINNER.
Bread Soup.
Beef Neck Stew.
Noodles.

SUPPER.
Browned Flour Soup with Fried Bread, Toast, and Cheese.

2.   SATURDAY, SEPTEMBER.

BREAKFAST.
Oatmeal Mush with Milk and Sugar.
Bread.
Coffee.

DINNER.
Pea Soup.
Mutton Stew.
Boiled Potatoes.
Bread.

SUPPER.
Bread Pancakes.
Fried Bacon.
Tea.

BILLS OF FARE.

For family of six; average, $1.38 per day, or 23 cents per person.

1.   SATURDAY, MAY.

BREAKFAST.
Oranges.
Egg Omelet on Toast.
Boiled Rice with Milk and Sugar.
Coffee.

DINNER.
Beef Soup with Egg Sponge.
Macaroni with Cheese.
Dandelion Greens.
Bread.

SUPPER.
Sour Cream Soup.
Meat Croquettes (of soup meat).
Graham Bread and Butter.
Tea Cake.

2.   TUESDAY, MAY.
   BREAKFAST.   DINNER.
Buttered Toast.   Sorrel Soup.
     Coffee.   Fried Catfish.
  Canned Fruit.   Noodles.
                                 Bread.
                          Swell Rice Pudding.

            SUPPER.
          Fried Mush.
        Stewed Rhubarb.
     Fresh Rusks and Butter.
             Tea.

3.   SATURDAY, SEPTEMBER.
   BREAKFAST.   DINNER.
Hominy Mush with   Plum Soup.
   Sugar Syrup.   Broiled Beefsteak.
    Stewed Pears.   Boiled Green Corn.
 Toasted Crackers.   Turnips and Potatoes.
      Coffee.   Bread.
                                Apple Pie.

            SUPPER.
          Irish Stew.
  Biscuit and Butter.   Yeast Doughnuts.
             Tea.

4.   SUNDAY, SEPTEMBER.
   BREAKFAST.   DINNER.
Sour Milk Pancakes with   Green Corn Soup.
   Sugar Syrup.   Fricasseed Chicken.
 Sausage. Bread.   Potatoes and Carrots
   Cucumbers.   with Fried Onions.
     Coffee.   Bread.

            SUPPER.
       Fried Farina Pudding.
   Water Toast.   Radishes.
             Tea.

5.   SATURDAY, JANUARY.
   BREAKFAST.   DINNER.
 Buckwheat Cakes   Roast Fresh Pork.
 and Sugar Syrup.   Apple Sauce.
 Bread and Butter.   Mashed Potatoes.
      Coffee.   Indian Pudding. Bread.

            SUPPER.
    Herring and Potato Salad.
 Lentils with Prunes.   Bread and Butter.
             Tea.

6. SUNDAY, JANUARY.

BREAKFAST.
Buckwheat Cakes.
Sausage.
Coffee.
Apple Sauce.

DINNER.
Pea Soup.
Roast Beef.
Baked Potatoes.
Canned Tomatoes.
Barley Gruel.

SUPPER.
Potato Soup with Egg and Bread Balls.
Brown Bread and Butter.
Canned Fruit.   Tea.

COLD DINNERS.

If a man is to eat a cold dinner for months or even for weeks, it is quite worth while to make that dinner as good as it can be, and to pack it nicely for carrying. Every one knows how it can take the edge off even a keen appetite to find his sandwich smeared with apple pie, or his cake soaked with vinegar from the pickles. That a box or basket of given dimensions shou'd hold as much as possible, and keep the different kinds of food separate, it must be divided into compartments.

COLD DINNERS FOR SUMMER.

1. Bread and Butter.
Salad of Potatoes and
Cold Baked Fish.
Cold Boiled Beef.
Molasses Cookies.
Apple Soup.

2. Bread and Butter.
Cold Veal.
Hard Boiled Eggs.
Pickled Beets.
Cherry Pie.

COLD DINNERS FOR WINTER.

3. Bread.
Cold Baked Beans.
Doughnuts.
Apple Pie.
Cold Coffee.

4. Biscuit and Butter
with Honey.
Cold Corn Beef and
Rye Bread.
Dried Apple Tarts.
Cheese.

HOW TO MAKE YOUR OWN CANDIES.

1. It is very easy for people to prepare and make their own candies. They will know of what they are made, and how they are made. In reference to extracts, flavors, acids, etc., they can be procured of your own druggist whom you personally know, and consequently no deleterious drugs will enter into the composition of the candies.

2. It is very necessary that a few things should receive special attention in making candy.

3. Sugar boiled down to a sufficient thickness for candy will remain perfectly clear if not stirred. If it is in any way disturbed by dropping in nuts or other articles, it is liable to go back to sugar.

4. Vinegar or other acids can be added to the sugar, and this will keep it perfectly clear, no matter how much it is stirred or disturbed. Never disturb candy that is intended to be perfectly pure and clear.

5. Boil the sugar in a thick pan, or in a granite or porcelain kettle.

WHY HOME-MADE CANDY IS BEST.

The chief constituents of candy, as will have been observed, are butter and sugar. The rest are merely incidents. This being so, no home should ever be without its candy. And what is there that children love better than to see their mother engaged in making candy? How

they hover around her and watch her every movement! How their little mouths water in blissful anticipation! I do not know whether the idea that home-made bread is better than baker's bread can be applied to candy. There is this to be said about it, however, that one knows just exactly what the candy is when made at home, which is more than can be said of sweets retailed by many of the small-fry confectioners. It is better and safer to make you own candy than to buy cheap mixtures. It is the same with confectionery as with clothes. There are different grades, and the good grades represent a certain amount of money laid out in their manufacture.

Home-made candy is cheaper, in that the cost of labor is saved. But after all, little or no candy is made in the home for the purpose of economy, or of avoiding poor kinds of confectionery. When made at all, it is made for pleasure and amusement. On cold winter evenings a festive "taffy-pull" infuses warmth and gladness into the little ones. Even the older people derive much merriment and amusement from it. In this connection I might mention that butter is better to use for covering the hands than flour. The latter makes no end of bother for the housemaid after the fun is all over.

HOME-MADE HOREHOUND CANDY.

At the season of coughs and colds, how many women know that a good horehound candy, soothing to tired or inflamed throats, can easily be made at home? Boil two ounces of dried horehound, which can be procured at a druggist's, in a pint and a half of water until its flavor is extracted; that will be in about half an hour. Strain through muslin until perfectly clear. Add to this extract or tea three pounds and a half of brown sugar, and boil over a quick fire until the syrup will harden when a little of it is dropped in cold water. Pour into a buttered tin, and when the candy is partially cooled mark into squares. This is a very good rule to add to the list of candies that the children may make for a frolic.

A DELICIOUS CHOCOLATE CANDY.

A very delicious chocolate candy can be made that shows bewitchingly through the cut glass of a French bonbon dish, and is far superior in taste to many makes of chocolate, and much less expensive. Take one cup of grated chocolate, three cups of granulated sugar, a piece of butter the size of a walnut, a cup of hot water, a pinch of salt, and a teaspoonful of vanilla. Boil down to the consistency of candy. Stir constantly, and allow it to boil for ten minutes only. Try it in a cup of cold water, and so soon as it is of the consistency of thickened molasses pour into buttered tins. Take a silver knife and stir back and forth until it sugars. When this takes place, mark off into little squares and put away to cool.

CHOCOLATE VANILLA CREAMS.

Take two cups of pulverized sugar and a half cup of cream. Boil for five minutes, and divide off into balls while hot. Take as much grated chocolate as is necessary and steam over a tea kettle. When soft, cover the balls and set them away to harden. If you wish to have a vanilla flavor, add the extract before putting on stove.

COCOANUT CREAM CANDY.

Take one and one-half pounds of granulated sugar, and the milk from a cocoanut. Mix together, and heat slowly until sugar is melted; then boil for five minutes. When boiled, add one cocoanut, finely grated, and boil for ten minutes longer, stirring constantly to keep it from burning. When done, pour on buttered plates and cut into squares. This will take about two days to harden.

SOME TOOTHSOME GINGER CANDY.

Take one cup of water to one and one-half cups of sugar, and boil until, on applying your finger to the syrup, taking a little on the tip and quickly dipping it into water, it will roll up into a small ball. Flavor with essence of ginger or powdered ginger. Rub some of the sugar against the sides of the pan with a wooden spoon until it turns white, then pour into buttered tins and put away in a cool place. Lemon, peppermint, or almond candy is made in the same way.

NEW ORLEANS MOLASSES CANDY.

Take one cup of New Orleans molasses, one cup of sugar, a piece of butter the size of an egg (sweet, not salt), and a tablespoonful of vinegar. Boil these together, but do not stir until the mass hardens when dropped into cold water. When done, stir in a teaspoonful of soda, and beat well. Pour into buttered pans, and when cool cut into sticks. If flavoring is desired, it should be added just before pouring out to cool.

HONEY CANDY.

Take one pint of white sugar, with water enough to dissolve it, and four tablespoonfuls of honey. Boil until it becomes brittle on being dropped into cold water. Pour off into buttered pans to cool.

CREAM CANDY.

Take one pound of white sugar, one tablespoonful of vinegar, one teaspoonful of lemon extract, and one teaspoonful of cream of tartar. Add a little water to moisten the sugar, then boil until brittle. The extract should be added just before turning the mass quickly out on buttered plates. When cool, cut in squares.

FOR A GOOD TAFFY PULL.

Some excellent taffy may be made by taking one quart of molasses, and half a pound of butter, and boiling the two until the mass thickens. This will take about half an hour. Then stir with a spoon until, on taking out a little taffy, it becomes hard on immersion in cold water. Take half a teacup of vinegar, pour into the mass, and stir for half a minute. Then pour the taffy into buttered tins, or dishes, and set aside to cool.

TO MAKE BUTTER SCOTCH.

Take three pounds of sugar, a quarter pound of butter, half a teaspoonful of cream of tartar, and add sufficient water only to dissolve the sugar. Boil without stirring until it will easily break when dropped into cold water. Then pour into a well-buttered dripping-pan, and, when almost cold, cut into small squares. If desired, a dash of lemon may be added into the mixture before putting on to boil. Eight drops will be sufficient.

HICKORY NUT CANDY.

Take one cup of hickorynut meats, two cups of sugar, half a cup of water. Boil the sugar and water together without stirring, until thick enough to spin to a thread. Flavor, if desired; then set in cold water. Stir quickly until white, then throw in the nuts. Pour into flat tins, and cut into squares.

MAPLE SUGAR CANDY.

Boil maple sugar until it becomes sufficiently thick. Then add a teacupful of vinegar for every two quarts of syrup; smaller amounts proportionately. When the candy has reached a sufficient consistency, pour out. Any kind of nuts may be dropped into it, or different flavors may be used, to make almost any kind of candy preparation

FIG CANDY.

1 pound of sugar,
1 pint of water.

Set over a slow fire. When done add a few drops vinegar and a lump of butter, and pour into pans in which split figs are laid.

RAISIN CANDY.

Can be made in the same manner, substituting stoned raisins for the figs. Common molasses candy is very nice with all kinds of nuts added.

SCOTCH BUTTER CANDY.

1 pound of sugar,
1 pint of water.

Dissolve and boil. When done add one tablespoonful of butter, and enough lemon juice and oil of lemon to flavor.

MOLASSES CANDY.

Two and a half cups of molasses, one tablespoonful of sugar; stir occasionally while boiling; before taking from the fire add butter half the size of an egg, and one-third teaspoonful of soda. Pour into buttered tins, and when cool pull it until well whitened.

MOLASSES CANDY.

Two and a half cups of sugar, one cup of molasses, one and a half cups of water; after it begins to boil add one-fourth teaspoonful cream tartar; cook in the usual way, but do not stir; before taking from the fire add butter, half the size of an egg. Do not butter your hands while pulling.

CARAMELS.

One cup of molasses, two of sugar; boil ten minutes. Add one large tablespoonful of flour, butter the size of an egg. half-pound chocolate; boil twenty minutes.

BOOK V.

THE OLD STYLE OF WASHING.

IN THE LAUNDRY.
HOUSE INSECTS.
YARD AND GARDEN.
PRACTICAL RULES FOR KEEPING
POULTRY.

HOW TO MAKE HARD SOAP FROM SOFT.

7 pounds of good soft soap,
4 pounds of sal-soda.
2 ounces borax,
1 ounce hartshorn,
½ pound resin.

Dissolve in twenty-two quarts of water and boil about twenty minutes.

HOW TO MAKE THE BEST SOAP FOR WASHING FINE LINEN.

To make the best washing soap, and one that is suitable for either laundry or toilet purposes, will not soil the finest fabric, or injure the most delicate complexion, use the following:

Take 10 pounds white bar soap,
2 gallons of soft water,
5 pounds sal-soda (common washing soda).

Dissolve four ounces of borax and one ounce of salts of tartar in a little water; cut the soap into slices, and boil until dissolved; then add the soda and salts of tartar, and mix thoroughly; pour into a box or mold, or cut into bars. This makes twenty-five pounds of soap which has no equal.

Directions: Put the clothes to soak in warm water; soap each in proportion to the amount of dirt it contains—only the dirtiest will need rubbing. Rinse thoroughly, and your clothes will look better and wear longer than washed in any other way. Try it once, and you will never use any other soap.

HOW TO POLISH OR ENAMEL SHIRT BOSOMS.

To Polish or Enamel Shirt Fronts.

1 ounce of white wax,
2 ounces of spermaceti.

Melt together. Heat gently and turn into a very shallow pan: when cold cut or break into pieces. When making boiled starch the usual way, enough for a dozen bosoms, add to it a piece of the polish the size of a hazel nut.

THE WASHING OF FLANNELS.

There are few things more annoying to even phenomenally patient mortals than the discovery that their flannels are growing beautifully less with each successive visit to the laundry. This tendency to shrinkage on the part of flannels has been a boon to the funny men on the comic papers, but to others a source of woe.

Certain rules should always be observed in the washing of flannels, if you would have them keep their original color, size, and softness:

In the first place, shake the dust thoroughly from each article before washing—and you will be amazed, by the way, at the capabilities of one small garment in the way of holding extraneous matter. Then make a strong soap solution by boiling half a cake of any pure, reliable soap in water enough to dissolve it. Add this, with one tablespoonful of borax or four tablespoonfuls of liquid ammonia, to half a tub of water just hot enough to bear the hand in it comfortably. Put the white and gray flannels in and cover, as the retained steam aids in softening and removing grease. After a half hour's soaking wash out, drawing the fabric back and forth through the hands, but on no account putting soap on the garment or rubbing it on the board. If very much soiled, wash in two suds, being extremely careful that the temperature of the water remains the same. If any spots are particularly difficult about coming out, they can be laid on the board and rubbed with a soft brush. Then rinse through two waters, still of the same temperature, being careful that all the suds are out. In washing baby flannels add a very little bluing to the last rinsing-water. Shake, stretch out, pass carefully through the wringer without twisting, and hang lengthwise to dry in warm, sunshiny air, or else in the laundry. Never hang them in cold or frosty air, as that would surely shrink them. When nearly dry, they can be pressed gently with a moderately warm iron; but do not shove the iron over them, nor use a very hot iron, as you do not wish to generate steam.

All kinds of woolens can be washed in the same way, only in worsted goods do not wring, but let them hang and drain. While still a little damp bring in and press smoothly with an iron as hot as you can use without scorching the goods.

To wash flannels that have become yellow, boil four tablespoonfuls of flour in four quarts of water, stirring thoroughly. Pour half the liquid while still warm over the flannels, letting them stand half an hour covered. Rub the flannel with the hands, but use no soap. Rinse the flannel in several clear waters of the same temperature. Then heat the remainder of the liquid, pour over the flannel again, and proceed as before, rinsing thoroughly; then hang out to drain and dry.

HOW TABLE LINEN SHOULD BE LAUNDERED.

The careful housekeeper never entirely intrusts her table linen to her help at home nor to her laundress abroad; she always prefers to superintend its washing and ironing, and has it done under her personal direction, for the reason that no matter how handsome it may look when new, it immediately loses its beauty if poorly laundered.

All stains should be removed by first filtering cold water slowly through tea and coffee stains

Wine stains may be removed by covering the stain while fresh with salt and then filtering the water through it.

Linen should be very slightly starched, or, better still, ironed while quite damp until perfectly dry, this will give sufficient stiffness, and is the method employed by the best French and Swiss laundresses.

In folding, fold the napkins square, and the tablecloth first lengthwise.

If possible do not have small folds, one line each way from the center is enough.

Have perfectly dry and aired before putting away.

Embroidered doilies, centerpieces, and carving cloths have become fashionable pieces of fancy-work, and many of them are so handsome that they should receive the care necessary to preserve their beauty.

If the cloth has been stained with fruit or coffee, the stained portion should be placed over a basin, and boiling water poured over it, allowing the water to run into the basin. Or, if a little salt and a few drops of lemon juice are put on it while still fresh, and the linen placed in the sunshine for an hour or two, all traces of the stain will usually disappear.

Table-linen should not be used long enough to become badly soiled, as the hard rubbing necessary to get it clean is destructive to its beauty. Make a lather of soft water and ivory soap, and wash it between the hands—never on the wash-board. Rinse through two waters, with a little bluing in the second. If any starch is thought necessary, make it very thin. Hang linen where the wind will not whip it out, and iron while it is quite damp. The embroidered parts should be ironed on the wrong side to make the pattern show to the best advantage. Be sure it is thoroughly dry before putting in the linen closet, or it will mildew.

Silk Handkerchiefs and ribbons that are washed in salt and water and ironed wet give better results than the ordinary method.

Another good way of washing silk handkerchiefs so as to preserve the fine colors in them is as follows: Pour a small quantity of boiling water on a bag of bran, leave the water until cool, then remove the bag, and wash the handkerchiefs in the lather. Wring out quickly, fold in a cloth to dry, and iron as soon as possible.

How to Wash Silk Socks.—Dissolve a moderate amount of castile soap in luke-warm water. Squeeze and press the water through the articles. Rub the deepest stains very lightly. Rinse thoroughly in clear cold water. Extract the water by rolling and twisting in a coarse heavy towel. Stretch into good shape, and dry without any exposure to the sun whatsoever. To add luster, take a soft, dry piece of flannel and rub in one direction when the article is nearly dry. Never use a hot iron unless the article is folded inside a thick cloth.

Lace-woven Stockings in white and delicate tints should be washed with benzine or naphtha instead of the ordinary washing water. Turn them wrong side out, shaking out all the dust, then lay them flat in a dish, and cover with naphtha. Stir violently for a minute or two, then turn and wash the other side in clean naphtha. Hang out in the air until all the odor of the cleansing fluid has disappeared.

Turpentine.—A little turpentine mixed with starch will give gloss to collars and cuffs.

A spoonful of it to a pail of warm water cleans paint excellently, and a little in the boiler on washing-day whitens the clothes.

Grease Spots.—Cold rain water and soap will remove machine grease from washable fabrics.

Starch.—Boiling starch is much improved by the addition of sperm or salt, or both, or a little gum arabic dissolved.

Cotton Fabrics.—The colors of cotton fabrics will become "set" if salt and water is employed—three gills of salt to four quarts of water. The calico is dropped into the water while hot, and there remains until it is cold.

Flannels.—To shrink baby flannels or white flannels of any sort, indeed, they should be put into an earthen basin and have boiling water poured over them; let them lie until the water is quite cold; in drying them don't wring, but shake, stretch and fold smoothly to keep the fabric even and then hang out. Bring them in while still damp, roll smoothly and in about half an hour iron with nearly a cold iron.

To Whiten Clothes.—To improve the color of white cloths and clothing that have been washed, a spoonful of borax dissolved in a little hot water should be added to the last water in which they are rinsed. It will whiten the clothes very much.

Shrinking of Flannels.—Many housekeepers, otherwise experienced and careful, have very vague ideas as to what is going on in the laundry, or as to the necessity of varying processes for the cleansing of different fabrics.

If you should examine the fiber of wool through a microscope, you would discover a series of tiny irregular sheaths with serrated edges, all running in the same direction. With the application of heat these miscroscopic sheaths expand and reach over one another; but with an exposure to a lower change of temperature they hurriedly contract, catching and knotting and pulling each other, producing the effect known as "fulling." Twisting, wringing, or rubbing flannels vigorously also tends to entangle the little scales, and to give to the article an unpleasant diversified surface.

INEXPENSIVE AND DELIGHTFUL.

"My! what a flowery whiff. That handkerchief must have been literally steeped in violets!" exclaimed one girl to another who had just shaken from its folds a fragrant square of linen.

"Not steeped in violets, my dear," was the answer, "but boiled in orris water. The effect is the same, so where's the odds? On washdays, I supply the laundress with a good-sized piece of orris root, and she throws it into the water where my handkerchiefs are boiling. When they come up off of the ironing board they are as redolent of orris as can be. Then I slip them between the folds of a sachet filled with violet powder, and they never lose their fragrance. Violet and orris scent together, I've discovered, can make a real violet's odor faint with envy."

HOW TO DESTROY ALL KINDS OF HOUSE INSECTS.

1. Insects do not grow by imperceptible increase in size as a bird or a cat. All insects pass through several changes from the egg to the perfect state. The horrid caterpillar that crawls in our path today will soon be seen flitting among the flowers in the form of a beautiful butterfly.

2. To destroy house pests successfully, the history of the insect, from the egg to the perfect state, must be well known. The successful housekeeper must always be a close observer and a careful student in order to keep her house free from noxious insects.

HOW TO AVOID FLEAS.

1. There are no human fleas in North America. The dog and the cat flea are the only species that annoy us.

2. The eggs of the flea are very small, white and oblong, and are laid on the dog or cat, and, being sticky, adhere to the hair until they are ready to hatch, when they fall to the ground. They hatch in about a week, and in less than two weeks attain their growth. They then pass through a pupal stage, and in

498 *How to Destroy All Kinds of House Insects.*

two weeks more the perfect flea appears. They flourish best in sandy soil.

3. Remedy. Put olive oil on the dog or cat or both, as the case may be, and rub it into the hair thoroughly and after a few hours wash out with warm water and soap.

4. Dalmation Insect Powder rubbed into the hair and sprinkled around the dog's kennel or the cat's sleeping place is also a good remedy.

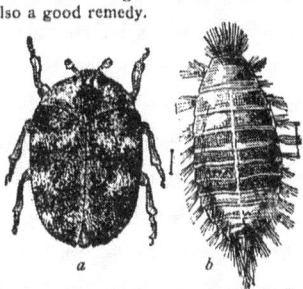

HOW TO EXTERMINATE THE CARPET BUG.

The Carpet Bug (Anthienus Scrophulanæ) or Buffalo Bug, as it is sometimes called, was first noticed in the city of Buffalo, New York.

The grub which does the damage is about one-fourth of an inch in length. It is covered with hair as shown in the above illustration a, b. It spins no cocoon like the caterpillar, but when full grown the skin splits on the back and shows the insect. A few weeks later the skin bursts again, and the perfect little bug, as shown in a, appears. It is marked with red, black and white spots and is less than one-eighth of an inch in length.

Remedy. When once in a carpet it is a very difficult insect to destroy. In some houses carpets cannot be used, as they are eaten as fast as they can be put down. Tallowed paper placed around the edges of the carpet is a very good preventive.

ouse Insects.

ars. They flourish

og or cat or both,
he hair thoroughly
rm water and soap.
I into the hair and
the cat's sleeping

CARPET BUG.
ulanæ) or Buffalo
rst noticed in the

about one-fourth
h hair as shown in
o cocoon like the
splits on the back
ter the skin bursts
)wn in a, appears.
: spots and is less

is a very difficult
:ts cannot be used,
ut down. Tallow-
e carpet is a very

How to Destroy All Kinds of House Insects. 499

When a carpet is cut as if with scissors following the seams in the floor, the simplest and safest remedy is to pour benzine in very small quantities along the seams; also running a hot flat iron over along the seams of the carpet is very destructive to both the insect and the eggs. Sprinkling the paper with benzine before the carpet is tacked down is an excellent precaution. Pour half a pint of turpentine into your hot-water pail, and scrub the boards with your long-handled brush, and add another half-pint when you mop it all up. Then no buffalo moths will attack the carpets you have prepared floors for.

HOW TO DESTROY CLOTHES MOTHS.

One of the greatest enemies of the housewife is the clothes moth. It is very small and makes its way through the smallest crevices. The female moth finds its way in early summer among the clothes and furs, suitable for food for its young, and there deposits about fifty or more eggs. In about a week the eggs hatch and the young worms begin to eat upon the cloth upon which the eggs were laid. It spins a sort of case which it lengthens and enlarges. Not content with eating and making a house for itself upon the cloth upon which it lives, it cuts its way in various directions through the cloth and drags its case after it. As the weather gets warmer the little worm closes its case at the ends and in three weeks the perfect moth will make its appearance.

Remedy. Beat the garments well early in the spring and occasionally during the summer. It is better to keep the articles in a large paper bag. Occasional airing is good.

For clothes packed in boxes or trunks, put a little oil of cedar on a piece of paper and roll up and wrap with other paper to avoid soiling the garments, and put several of these rolls into each box or trunk. Carbolic acid, turpentine or benzine is equally good, used in the same manner.

Black pepper, a piece of camphor gum, or a handful of snuff wrapped up with the clothes is excellent.

Caution. Camphor should never be used in keeping seal skin, as it takes the color out of the fur.

A close closet lined with tar paper is the best for furs. It is also excellent for clothes.

THE COMMON MOTH.

In May the clothes-moth begins to fly about our rooms. It is a small, light, buff-colored "miller," dainty and beautiful on close inspection. Its highest mission seems to be to teach us to set our affections only upon incorruptible treasures which "moth and rust cannot destroy." But it is necessary to keep a sharp lookout for the safety of our furs and flannels, and we must wage war upon it. In the first place, we must carefully put away everything we can, upon which it will lay its eggs. If we pack away our furs and flannels early in May, before the moth has begun to lay its eggs, and leave them in boxes and bags so tight that the flying moth cannot squeeze in, no further precaution is necessary. Clean paper bags are recommended for this purpose—those used for flour and meal bags. They should be without holes or opening anywhere. These bags, when filled and closed firmly, may be put away on closet shelves or in loose boxes, without danger to their contents, so far as moths are concerned, without need of camphor or other strong odors to drive the moths away. Furs are usually sold in boxes in which they may be kept. Beat them well when you finally put them away for the season. If you delay putting them away until June, examine the furs well, and shake and beat them thoroughly, in order that any moth eggs that may possibly have been laid in them may be thoroughly removed or killed. Furs sealed up early in May need no camphor or tobacco or other preventive. Muff and tippet boxes should be tied up securely in bags, or made safe by mending holes and pasting a strip of paper around the juncture of the cover with the box below, so as to close all openings. Woolen garments must not hang in closets through the summer, in parts of the country where moths abound. They should be packed away in tight trunks or boxes, or sealed up in bags. Woolen blankets must be well shaken and carefully put away, unless they are in daily use. Early in June the larvae of the moth begin their ravages, and then, unless you dwell in places where moths are not found, look sharp, or you will find some precious thing, that you have forgotten—some good coat unused for a few weeks, or the woolen cover of a neglected piano—already riddled by the voracious moths. It is their nature to eat until they have grown strong enough to retire from the eating business, and go into the chrysalis condition.

is.

about our rooms.
dainty and beauti-
ssion seems to be
pon incorruptible
destroy." But it
the safety of our
war upon it. In
ay everything we
we pack away our
e moth has begun
and bags so tight
, no further pre-
are recommended
and meal bags.
; anywhere. These
nay be put away
ut danger to their
, without need of
: the moths away.
they may be kept.
hem away for the
ly until June, ex-
them thoroughly,
ossibly have been
d or killed. Furs
or or tobacco or
es should be tied
ending holes and
:ture of the cover
penings. Woolen
ugh the summer.
ind. They should
s, or sealed up in
iken and carefully
. Early in June
ces, and then, un-
e not found, look
thing, that you
for a few weeks,
)—already riddled
iture to eat until
e from the eating
lition.

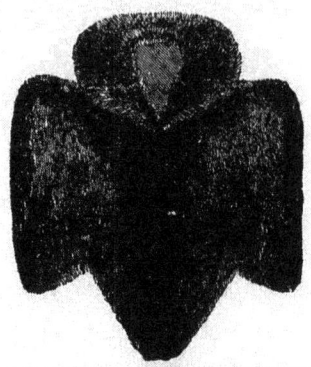

HOW TO KEEP FURS FROM MOTH.

Moths will avoid light and sunshine. Before packing away furs, sun them several hours in the open air, then tie them tightly in a linen, cotton or paper bag, which is whole. A little snuff placed in the bottom is a good thing.

If moth are already at work, fumigate with sulphur placed on live coals. Close the room in which the furs are placed, and be careful not to inhale the fumes. Fumigating rooms after scarlet fever or other contagious diseases is said to destroy all the disease germs.

Moth Preventive.—In this age of fearful moth-preventive smells, it is worth while to know that moths will never go where there are lavender bags. Even where they have begun their ravages in furs or feathers, a lavish sprinkling of the articles with good lavender water will prevent further damage. No one can ask for a purer or pleasanter odor about garments. A liberal distribution of lavender sachets in closets, drawers and trunks will give you the satisfaction of making sweeter your belongings with the weapon which drives away their depredators. Put a lavender sachet in your piano if you fear moths will ravage the felt.

Another Infallible Remedy is compounded of the fol

lowing sweet-smelling things: Lavender, thyme, rose, cedar shavings, powdered sassafras, cassia, and lignea in about equal quantities, with a few drops of attar of roses thrown upon the whole.

Tansy Leaves, spread freely among woolens and furs, are a protection against moths.

Turpentine is an excellent preventive against moths, although naphtha is preferable, the odor leaving much sooner; it will drive ants and cockroaches away, if sprinkled about the shelves and cupboards.

Whole Cloves are now used to exterminate moths, and some say they are much better than tobacco, camphor, or cedar shavings.

The Best Preventive of moths is care. Cedar chests, camphor, and pepper avail nothing if a garment is laid away with the egg of the moth in it. If it is, in season, shut up in paper or cloth so that no millers can possibly reach it, there will be no need of pungent odors. Benzine is the best remedy if the moths have stolen a march and are ravaging carpets or furniture. Pour it freely upon any carpet or upholstered furniture and it will not stain.

The Buffalo Moths, the most destructive of all household foes, try equal quantities of borax, camphor, and saltpetre, mixed. Wash the floor with a strong solution of it, and scatter it under the edge of the carpet and in your closets and drawers. The beetle that lays the eggs comes early in February and then the fight must begin. Naphtha is considered an efficient remedy, but it must be repeatedly used in order to destroy each successive generation.

HOW TO GET RID AND KEEP RID OF BEDBUGS.

1. The eggs of the bedbug are white in color and oval in shape. The young resemble the parents, and it takes about eleven weeks to get its full growth. Like reptiles, they can live many years without food. Mr. Goeze, of Germany, has kept them six years in a bottle without a particle of nourishment of any kind.

2. Keeping the bedding and bedstead perfectly clean is the best preventive.

3. **Remedy.**—Pour hot water into the crevices and then apply benzine to the different parts of the bedstead.

4. Unpurified petroleum mixed with a little water is also a sure remedy. Corrosive sublimate is a very good, but a very poisonous cure.

HOW TO EXTERMINATE SPIDERS.

Take a small common kerosene lamp and light it, and late in the afternoon or early in the evening look over the corners and places where spiders are commonly found, and when one is seen hold the lamp chimney directly beneath it, and it will fall at once into the chimney and be instantly destroyed. It is not difficult in this way to destroy all the spiders in the house in a few evenings. It avoids killing them by sweeping them down, and staining the walls or carpet. Early in the evening is the best time.

HOW TO PRESERVE BOOKS FROM BOOK MOTHS.

The little Bristle Tail or Silver Fish has a little, long, slender body covered with a delicate silver scale; it has no wings and passes through no changes. It feeds on the paste of the binding of books, devours leaves, eats off the labels in Museums and is generally destructive to both books and papers.

Books are also eaten by the larva of a little bug that produces a ticking sound like a watch—it is called the "Death Watch," as it is usually heard in the night ticking like a watch.

Remedy. A little rag saturated with benzine or carbolic acid placed along the back of the shelves will clear the library of all insects. Insect Powder sprinkled over the books will destroy the little "Silver Fish" insect instantly.

MIXTURE FOR DESTROYING FLIES.

1 pint infusion of quassia,
4 ounces brown sugar,
2 ounces ground pepper.

To be well mixed together, and put in small shallow dishes when required.

504 *How to Destroy All Kinds of House Insects.*

HOW TO KEEP OUT MOSQUITOES.

If a bottle of the oil of pennyroyal is left uncorked in a room at night, not a mosquito, or any other blood-sucker, will be found there in the morning.

A DOMESTIC REMEDY FOR DESTROYING FLIES.

½ tablespoonful black pepper, in powder,
1 teaspoonful brown sugar,
1 tablespoonful cream.

Mix them well together, and place them in the room on a plate, where the flies are troublesome, and they will soon disappear.

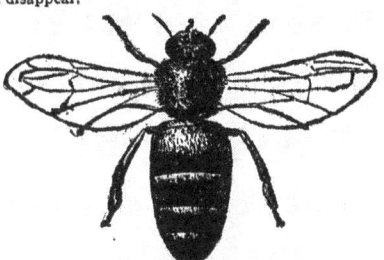

TO BANISH THE FLIES.

The following is vouched for: Take one ounce of camphor gum, one ounce of corrosive sublimate, one pint of oil of turpentine; grind the sublimate thoroughly, put into a strong bottle and add the camphor gum. Pour on the turpentine and shake occasionally. It should be fit for use in 36 hours. Heat a piece of iron and drop a few drops on it in the stable and all flies will leave. Flies may be driven out of the house by dropping a few drops on a hot stovelid. Practiced every other day will, it is said, soon drive out all flies.

A CURE FOR BEE AND WASP STINGS, SPIDER BITES, ETC.

Apply ammonia or common soda and water. If there is much inflammation and redness, apply a solution of borax and warm water. Apply with a rag saturated with the solution.

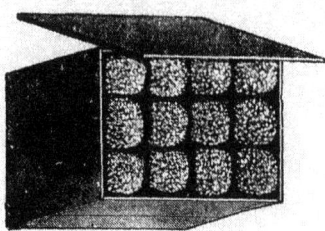

A BOX OF SPONGES.

A NEW WAY OF TRAPPING ANTS.

1. Ants are very difficult pests to expel from the house. There have been many recipes and experiments tried, but without any satisfactory results.

2. The ants that infest our houses live only in rotten wood, either in the decayed sills of the house or in rotten timbers and old fences near by. It is best to remove all such hiding places if possible.

3. **Remedy.**—Ants are very fond of sugar, and anything containing it will attract them. Sweeten a pan of water to a thin syrup, and then dip a large sponge into it, and wring it out. Place the sponge where the ants can get at it; it will soon be filled through and through with ants, then take it up carefully and plunge it into boiling water, and again set it by saturating it with the thin syrup. A few days' trial will, for a long time, exterminate the annoying pests.

4. A trap more simple but not so effectual is a plate covered with a thin layer of lard and placed where the ants can easily get at it. This trap is more to destroy the little yellow ant than the larger species.

HOW TO DESTROY ANTS.

Boiling water, kerosene, or a solution of fresh insect powder in water, poured into the hill, will destroy the inhabitants at once. Where the nests are outside of the house this is a sure remedy.

OTHER REMEDIES.

1. Cayenne pepper sprinkled in cupboards and storerooms will drive away ants and cockroaches. The pepper ought to be fresh and strong and very fine.

2. Black ants can be put to rout by washing shelves or floors whereon they congregate with hot water in which some ammonia has been dissolved.

3. Take five cents' worth of tartar emetic, mix it with an equal amount, in bulk, of soft or granulated sugar, put the mixture into dishes, keep it moist (quite moist), and set the dishes, one on each shelf where the ants appear, they will promptly take their departure. I do not know what becomes of them, but they are gone. I never find dead ones, either in the dishes or on the shelves. When not needed the dishes can dry out and be put away to be wet again for the next time.

4. You will find a most effectual remedy for the ant by mixing honey and insect powder and setting in shallow pan so that easy access may be had. The ants will come and partake in great numbers, never to return.

5. This is an effectual remedy for ants: In the center of a shallow dish put a very little Paris green, and on it a spoonful of honey—then pour in half a cupful of water. Set in their trail, and in a few days they will be gone. It is possible they will come again in a few weeks, but the second dose is effectual.

6. A sure way to keep the little common black ants out of food is to set the food on a board as large as desired, which is isolated by supporting the four corners in little tins of common insect powder. I drive a nail in each corner, letting it project say an inch, so as to form four legs, which I surround with insect powder either on the shelf itself or in little tin can covers which prevent the powder from getting brushed away. I never knew this plan to fail. A table or a cupboard may have its legs stand in dishes of powder. Borax, salt, kerosene, etc., are of no account in most cases. The kerosene soon evaporates and they will crawl right over the others. Pepper and camphor would be objectionable to have about. It's well enough to shoot powders into places like cracks where they come in, if you can find them and are willing to have the untidiness of it.

HOW TO GET RID OF RATS.

1. Common steel traps set in their holes or runways covered up with chaff or crushed dried leaves, will soon exterminate rats, or drive them from the premises.

2. To place the steel traps in pans of wheat-bran is a good device. After catching two or three rats in the same pan, leave out the trap a few nights, and then replace it.

3. Raw meat sprinkled with strychnine nailed to a small board, and placed as above, generally answers the purpose, unless the rats are very cunning, having been trapped and poisoned considerably.

HOW TO POISON RATS.

1 qt. warm water, 2 lbs. lard, 1 oz. phosphorus.

Mix and thicken with flour; to be spread on bread and covered with sugar.

N. B.—Most of these patent preparations, such as "Rough on Rats," etc., for the extermination of rats and mice, are of little benefit. If they could be used when first prepared, they would be much more effective; but they are often kept in stores for months and years, and thereby lose all their strength.

How to Get Rid of Rats and Mice.

A Sure Remedy.—It does not pay to try to raise rats and chicks in the same place; yet it is nearly impossible to keep the former down when farm buildings offer convenient hiding places. Various plans have been devised for dealing with this pest, with only partial success. A good method to get rid of a few rats is to slit a piece of fresh meat and fill it with powdered glass. Rats are very fond of wheat, and we have been quite successful with this method: Take 25 cents' worth of strychnine and dilute it with a cup of water (a quart bottle is a good article to use for this purpose). After the poison is dissolved add a few handfuls of wheat; set in a warm place, and when the wheat is swelled as much as possible scatter it in and around the rat-holes, or where the rats go. It is sure death to rats, cats, chicks or man. Be careful how you use it.

A SURE CURE FOR THE EXTERMINATION OF MICE.

1. The best and most careful trapper of mice will find great difficulty in capturing the shrewder and older ones. They simply will not go into a trap. The best method for capturing those is illustrated in the above cut. Take a small box and fill it with brick or stones, and place under it a figure 4, baited with cheese, meat, or other attractive food, and as the box comes down it will destroy the sharpest and shrewdest mouse. By this method it is not difficult to keep rid of mice in any house.

2. Fill a sewing thimble with any eatable, as bread crumbs, pressed down tightly. Place the thimble under the edge of a good-sized bowl, with the open end inward. The mouse will nibble at the bread and the thimble will gradually work down and the mouse will be caught. The bowl should be put upon a loose board. The mouse can then easily be dispatched. This may seem too simple to try, but is very effective.

YARD AND GARDEN.

How to Kill Worms on Rose Bushes.—Take a pail of water and stir in a tablespoonful of hellebore and sprinkle the bushes thoroughly. One application will generally be sufficient.

Flower Seeds.—Put away garden and flower seeds in paper sacks properly labeled, then keep them away from the mice.

How to Improve a Lawn.—Lawns can be kept green and thickest without the use of stable manure. City and village people who have a few square rods of grass usually imagine it necessary to keep the plot covered for weeks with highly-scented and ill-looking manure, when the fact is that one-half the money's worth of nitrate of soda and powdered phosphate of lime will answer better and create no nuisance. They furnish to the soil what is most needed, an alkali, phosphoric acid and nitrogen. Both of them are inodorous and show their effects immediately on their application.

Flower Beds.—Don't cut up your lawn with flower beds, for the effect will be sure to be displeasing. Leave your lawn in its restful, unbroken greenness and confine your flowers to the old-fashioned borders where they are always charming.

House Plants.—Saturate the earth around house plants every day with coffee left over from breakfast. It stimulates them. Plants that have a red or purple blossom will be rendered extremely brilliant in color by covering the earth in their pots with about half an inch of pulverized charcoal. A yellow flower will not be affected in any way by the use of charcoal.

A Nice Little Flower Garden.—Get your bed in a nice sunny place, well spaded and full of rich stuff, and I'll tell you six first-rate flowers. Right in the middle set a circle of woven wire as large around as you can afford ground—not more than two feet in diameter, or six feet, if you prefer. Plant sweet peas on both sides of it six inches deep and earth pressed down on top. If the diameter can be eight feet, plant in the middle of that a ricinus seed, or three so you will be sure of one plant; do not let more than one plant grow. This will fill all the space and stand two feet high. The woven wire must be four or five feet wide to train your peas to as they grow. Outside grow a circle of petunias. This flower is wonderfully improved of late. Select the new blue-flowered and the fancy sorts, which are magnificent in the latest strains. Outside plant a ring of nasturtiums. Better take the dwarf sorts, if you do not have abundant room. This is the finest annual in existence, sweet, floriferous, and elegant. Next plant a mixed ring, made up of patches of mignonette, dwarf convolvulus and verbenas. If that doesn't make you happy, nothing will.

SWEET PEAS.

Sweet Peas have become so universally popular that all who have the ground wish to grow their own sweet peas; and there is no reason why they should not grow them and have glorious success with them, too, if they will observe a few simple rules. First—Order your seeds from some reliable seedsmen, and not from the corner grocery, and then get them into the ground as early as possible in the spring. Select a sunny spot and run your rows from north to south, so that the morning sun can get at the roots. The soil should be moderately rich and heavy, and if you neglected in the fall to dig in a liberal dressing of manure, you must have especial care now that only that which is well rotted be used. Sow your seed about an inch apart and cover to a depth of not less than four inches. When they have peeped above the ground two inches or so, draw the earth up about them until only the tips are still showing, and later thin them out until they stand three inches apart.

Where there is plenty of ground, the rows should be single and not less than four feet apart, but where economy of space is a consideration the rows may be double and the seed sown in two lines, from six to twelve inches apart. The trellis for the plants to grow on should be six feet high. Wire netting is good, but no better than the cheaper bush supports of beech or birch branches.

Follow these directions, and when your sweet peas begin to bloom give them plenty of water and keep every blossom picked, and you will have sweet peas that will be a joy from June till September.

Don't expect sweet peas to thrive in soil too poor for any other culture, or in a sunless location. They need, as nearly as possible, a free clay loam, moderately rich and freely cultivated.

Don't sow too shallow. ' Plant the seeds not less than two inches deep, and, as the plants become established, bank the soil against them, repeating this two or three times throughout the season.

Don't over-feed. With a view to obtaining vigorous growth and profusion of bloom, bone, in some form, is the best fertilizer. Nitrate of soda will do for a "hurry-up" stimulant, should such be needed; but use it sparingly.

Don't gather the blooms grudgingly. The more you cut the longer the vine will continue to flower. Remember, when they go to seed, sweet peas cease flowering.

HOW TO DESTROY CABBAGE WORMS.

The cabbage worm has been very troublesome of late years, but is easily gotten rid of. Our plan is to go over the patch in the morning and sift a little fresh Persian insect powder over the heads while the dew is on. This will kill every worm it touches in less than five minutes and it is but a short job to treat five hundred heads if a common pepper-box, such as ground pepper comes in, is used to hold the powder. One shake on a calm morning before the breeze starts up is sufficient for a head, and it can be done almost at a walk. This operation should be repeated at least once a week as long as the millers are seen flying around. The insect powder is entirely harmless and is only poisonous to insect life.

Hot Water.—Hot water is also an excellent remedy. Apply at about 150 degrees Fahr. No injury to the cabbage will result.

HOW TO DESTROY CURRANT AND GOOSEBERRY WORMS.

Take a tablespoonful of hellebore and stir it into a pail of water, and apply to the bushes with a sprinkler. One or two applications will generally be sufficient. A little care in watching the bushes is necessary. The worms generally begin at the bottom, and are not noticed until the bush is nearly destroyed.

HOW TO DESTROY PLANT-LICE.

There is scarcely a tree, bush or herb that grows in our gardens or fields, that is not infested with some species of plant-lice. Their manner of living, and of reproduction, have attracted much interest. They both deposit their eggs and bring forth their young alive, a peculiarity which does not take place in any of our four-winged insects. Their multiplication is immense, and were it not for their numerous enemies, all our vegetable products would be consumed as fast as they grow.

Remedy. When the plant-lice get too numerous take a little flour of sulphur, and mix it with a little sawdust, and scatter it over the plants.

DARK BRAHMAS.

PRACTICAL RULES FOR KEEPING POULTRY.

1. A little glycerine applied occasionally to the combs and wattles will prevent injury by frosting.
2. A great source of contagion is the drinking troughs. Remember this if roup should make its appearance in your poultry-house.
3. In place of "tonics," drop a nail into the drinking trough and allow it to remain there. It will supply all the "tincture of iron" required.
4. If you feed whole corn, place it in the oven and parch it occasionally and feed smoking hot. The fowls appreciate it in the cold, frosty weather.
5. A little linseed or oil meal given once a week in the soft feed will promote laying. This will not come under the heading of "dosing the fowls with medicine."
6. Do not throw your table scraps into the swill barrel. Give them to the chickens.
7. One of the most important points in the keeping of ducks is to give them clean, dry quarters at night. They are very prone to leg weakness from cold, damp quarters.
8. Feed your fowls just what they will eat up clean. Fat hens or pullets are poor layers, and the latter are just what you don't want.
9. Fowls over three years old are not, as a rule, good

514   *Practical Rules for Keeping Poultry.*

for breeders. The males are unable to properly fertilize eggs for hatching, while the stock is usually weak. Four years is generally considered a "ripe old age" for a fowl.

10. Each hen, if properly kept, will lay from 200 to 250 eggs a year.

11. Liver and intestines are an excellent food to make hens lay.

12. Keep an abundant supply of lime where the hens can easily get at it if you desire your hens to lay well.

13. Always clean the nest well and put in fresh straw before the hen begins to set.

14. It is best in breeding to cross or mix the breeds more or less every year. It improves the flesh and general health of the fowls.

15. Pullets are better layers than old hens. Keep your stock young by disposing annually of the old broods.

16. Keep at least one rooster for every eight hens if you desire vigorous young chickens.

17. It is a good plan to change roosters every year.

18. Roosters are best at two years of age.

PARTRIDGE COCHINS.

DISEASES AND THEIR TREATMENTS.

In North America the climate is very good for all kinds of poultry. There are very few diseases but what readily yield to judicious treatment.

Most of the diseases to which fowls are subject are the results of neglect, exposure or bad diet.

HOW TO CURE THE CHICKEN CHOLERA.

Symptoms.—The symptoms of chicken cholera are greenish droppings, prostration, and intense thirst. It should not be mistaken for indigestion. Cholera kills quickly, and this is a sure indication.

Remedy.—The best remedy is to add a teaspoonful of carbolic acid to a quart of water and give no other water to drink. The remedy is not a sure cure, but is one of the best. When cholera puts in an appearance, everything on the place should be thoroughly cleaned and disinfected, the remedy mentioned above being also an excellent disinfectant.

ANOTHER GOOD RECIPE.

½ pound madder.
½ pound sulphur.
2 ounces antimony.
2 ounces saltpeter.
¼ pound cayenne pepper.

Mix a tablespoonful in feed for 30 chickens.

ASTHMA.

Symptoms.—The fowls labor for breath, opening the beak often and for quite a time, and sometimes drops of blood appearing on the beak.

Treatment.—Take the disease in hand as soon as discovered, keep the fowl warm, and give equal parts of sulphur and butter mixed in fresh lard.

FEVER.

Symptoms.—Restlessness, refusing to eat, drooping wings and excessive heat.

Treatment.—Mix a little castor oil with burnt butter and give a teaspoonful three times a day.

LOSS OF FEATHERS.

This disease, common to confined fowls, should not be confused with the natural process of moulting. In the diseased state no new feathers come to replace the old.

Treatment.—Keep warm, and feed hemp seed and corn. Add brown sugar to the water.

GAPES.

The Gapes is a very common ailment of poultry and domestic birds. More common among the young than the old.

Cause.—The disease is caused by the presence of little red worms, in the wind-pipe, about the size of a small cambric needle.

Symptoms.—Gaping for breath with beak wide open, yellow beak, tongue dry and feathers ruffled on the head and neck.

Treatment.—Give a pill each morning made of equal parts of scraped garlic and horse radish, with as much cayenne pepper as will outweigh a grain of wheat; mix with fresh butter.

If a good many are affected, put from five to ten drops of turpentine to a pint of meal.

Treatment must be given in the early stages of the disease, or all remedies will fail.

HOW TO DESTROY AND KEEP RID OF HEN'S LICE.

All fowls are more or less infested with lice. Fowls are sometimes so covered that the natural color of the feathers can not be distinguished. These loathsome vermin will not only cover the fowls, but will multiply and spread over the entire hen-house, barn, wood-shed or any other place frequented by the poultry.

Poultry cannot be fattened when covered with lice.

1. **Remedy.**—Whitewash the hen-house frequently, whitewash all the roosting poles, etc., or run them slowly through a fire of old straw or hay.

2. Close the hen-house up tightly and burn sulphur in it. The sulphur fumes will penetrate every crevice and destroy the vermin.

3. Flour of sulphur may be mixed with Indian meal and water, and be fed in the proportion of one pound of sulphur to two dozen fowls, every two days.

4. Applying grease of any kind by rubbing it among the feathers is certain death to the vermin.

5. Remove droppings daily and keep the house clean and you will not be troubled with these pests.

Practical Rules for Keeping Poultry.

BROWN LEGHORNS.

HOW TO PICKLE EGGS.

1. A good, cool place is necessary. The temperature must be kept above the freezing point.

2. Select a good kerosene barrel and take out the head and set fire to the inside and burn it until slightly charred, then smother out the fire by turning it bottom side up. Scrape off charred parts and soak in lime-water until the smell of kerosene is entirely removed.

3. To Make the Pickle.—Take one bushel of best fresh lime, one peck of rock-salt, and 60 gallons of clean water (use similar proportions for smaller quantities). Slake the lime as for making whitewash, add the rest of the water, and then the salt. Stir well two or three times the first day and then let it stand until well settled and cold.

4. Now dip off the clear fluid carefully and put it into the barrel until about one-half full.

5. Now put in the eggs, without breaking. When you have about a foot of eggs on the bottom of the barrel pour in some of the "milky" pickle made by stirring up the lime and water left. It is these light, fine particles of lime settling on the eggs and filling the pores that preserve the eggs.

6. Care should be taken not to put in too much or too little of the "milky" pickle, pour in enough to cover the

eggs nicely when settled. If not enough lime, the white of the egg will get watery, if too much it will stick on the outside like plaster, and be difficult to remove.

7. A faucet should be fitted into the barrel about six inches from the bottom, so that the pickle can be drawn off when necessary.

8. A common method for small quantities: Take a box or half barrel and first put in a layer of common salt, and then a layer of eggs, and so on, until the desired quantity is packed.

"POULTRY RAISERS' EGG FOOD POWDER."

(TO MAKE HENS LAY EGGS.)

Red pepper powdered, 2 ounces,
Allspice powdered, 4 ounces,
Ginger powdered, 6 ounces.

Mix them by sifting.

1 tablespoonful to be mixed with every pound of food, and fed 2 or 3 times a week.

Also feed chopped-up fresh meat.

FOR SCALY LEGS.

Apply a little kerosene oil once a week. Be careful not to get on too much, or it will blister and injure.

WHAT TO FEED.

1. Dry food is best for chickens.
2. Burying grain usually does away with idle hens.
3. Healthy fowls pick up their food quickly and relish it.
4. When it can be done, it pays to grind bone for poultry.
5. Fowls having a good range gather a good variety of food.
6. The morning meal should be warm and fed as early as possible.
7. With poultry, as with everything else, good feeding always pays.
8. Stale bread soaked in milk makes a good feed for young poultry.
9. Feeding soft feed exclusively is almost certain to induce disease.
10. The true secret of profitable breeds is in the food and care given them.
11. Cooked corn meal is much better than raw to feed to young poultry.
12. Care and cleanliness in feeding fowls will be richly repaid in better health and thrift.
13. Ducks will eat all sorts of coarse food, such as cabbage, chopped turnips, etc., and do well on it, and while they are voracious eaters, they can be fed very cheaply.
14. When turkeys have been kept growing from the start as they should, three weeks of good feeding is all that is necessary to put in a good condition for market.
15. Turnips, beets, carrots and the cabbage that has failed to head up properly can be used to a good advantage in feeding poultry during the winter. Better results can always be secured if the fowls can have something green during the winter, or something that will in an emergency take its place, and any one of these things can be used to a good advantage.

POULTRY POINTERS.

1. Hens will lay as well when not in company with males as with them, and the eggs will keep twice as long.
2. Be careful to lay in a good supply of dry road dust early in the season for use during the coming winter. Do not put it off until the last moment, but attend to it at the first opportunity.
3. To make poultry pay well, there are some things which must be understood. You must keep in view your

object in breeding, whether it be for eggs or for table; you must know how to breed and select the best birds suited for your purpose; you must keep your eyes wide open in order to sell your produce to the best advantage. Follow these principles steadily, and you will make poultry pay.

4. There is but one sure method of cleaning earth floors, and that is to remove the top soil to the depth of four inches and add clean earth in its place. This must be done every summer, fall and spring; the floor should be kept well covered with litter, leaves being best for that purpose. During the summer air-slacked lime should be applied once a week, thus destroying the germs of any disease that may be present. It will lessen the liability of loss.

5. A market report gives quotations on eggs that are described as "Western dirties." It is a commentary upon the habits of certain farmers that their careless methods have to be branded in the market reports.

6. If when an egg became dirty it was an impossibility to clean it the matter would be different, but all that is required is a little warm water and a little time.

7. It was also noteworthy that while fresh clean eggs were quoted by the dozen, and at a good price, yet the "Western dirties" were quoted by the case. The price was too low to bother with giving it for a single dozen. But such things have their bright side.

8. Dirty eggs make an increased market for clean eggs. If everyone sent his eggs to market in good condition there would be only one grade, and the price of that would be lower than it is now. So the man who employs careless methods, whether it be in the egg business or in the dairy business, helps along his neighbor who takes pains.

9. If you want to help along your neighbor send your eggs to market without washing, and your butter in such shape that it will deserve to be classed as axle grease.

10. Peas and beans are both good egg foods, and where there is a supply of either they should be boiled and fed to the fowls.

11. Sell some of the corn you were going to feed your chickens and buy oil meal with the money. It will be a profitable trade.

12. Fowls like a variety of food. Give them a cabbage head to pick at or some chopped turnips, beets or potatoes.

Practical Rules for Keeping Poultry.

13. Keep the ducks and geese well fed during the winter and they will begin to lay earlier in the spring for it.

14. No farmer expects his cattle or swine to do well if they run at large, and most farmers know that to allow this is a waste of feed, but a good many seem to forget that the same rule applies to fowls. They must be well kept or they will not pay for their keeping.

15. A good morning feed for a cold snap is corn parched in the oven of the kitchen stove until it is charred black on the outside. Feed this as warm as it can be held in the hand without burning. A crop full of this hot corn warms a chicken clear through.

16. Whatever other animals can bear, fowls must have a well drained location and a south exposure. A stone foundation put in a trench, not above the ground, will keep out rats. A double wall, with an air chamber, gives the warmest kind of building. It is less important whether plaster or ceiling be used inside than that the air chamber be small and that there shall be plenty of ventilation. Ventilating tubes can be closed during cold weather, but a sufficient number of tubes are needed to thoroughly change the air when thaws and dampness come.

17. The equivalent of five pecks of corn will keep a hen a year. If this year's rations are made up of two pecks of wheat, two pecks of oats and one peck of corn, together with what bugs and insects the hen can pick up about the farm, she will do her best. The man who feeds his chickens with a scoop shovel will not be boasting about the number of eggs he gets.

A COMPLETE

MEDICAL DICTIONARY.

Abdomen—The lower front part of the body.
Abnormal—Unhealthy, unnatural.
Abortion—A premature birth, or miscarriage.
Abrasion—Bruising and consequent rubbing off of the skin.
Abscess—A cavity containing pus.
Acetate—A salt prepared with acetic acid.
Acidity—Sourness.
Aconite—Aconitum Napellus; Monk's Hood.
Acrid—Irritating, biting.
Adipose—Fatty.
Adult—Person of full growth.
Albumen—Constituting the chief part of the white of eggs.
Aliment—Any kind of food.
Alimentary Canal—The entire passage through which food passes; the whole intestines from mouth to anus.
Alterative—Medicines which will gradually restore healthy action.
Alteratives change in some unexplained way the conditions and functions of organs.
Amenorrhea—Absence of menses.
Anesthetics—Medicines depriving of sensation and suffering.
Anemia—An impoverished state of blood. Bloodlessness.
Anodyne—A medicine which will allay pain.
Anodynes allay or diminish pain.
Antacids—Remedies for acidity of the stomach.
Antelmintics kill or expel worms.
Antidote—A medicine used to counteract poison.
Antiphlogistic—Remedy for Fever and Inflammation.
Antiperiodics obviate the return of a paroxysm in periodic diseases.
Antiscorbutic—A remedy for scurvy.
Antiseptics prevent, arrest or retard putrefaction.
Antisialagogue—Remedy for salivation.
Antispasmodics prevent or allay cramps.
Antisyphilitic—Remedy for venereal diseases.
Anus—Circular opening or outlet of the bowels.
Aperient—A gentle laxative or purgative.

Aperients gently open the bowels.
Aphtha—Thrush; infant's sore mouth.
Aqua—Water.
Aqua Ammonia—Water of ammonia.
Aromatic—Spicy and fragrant drugs, used to prevent griping of drastic purgatives.
Aromatics—Strong-smelling stimulants which dispel wind and allay pain.
Arsenic—A metal, commonly called ratsbane.
Astringents cause contraction of vital structures; used in diarrhea, whites, etc.
Auscultation—Act of listening to sounds in any part of the body.

Bacteria—Infusoria; microscopical insects, supposed to cause many diseases.
Balm—Aromatic and fragrant medicine, usually an ointment.
Balsam—Resinous substances, possessing healing properties.
Basilicon—An ointment containing wax, resin, etc.
Belladonna—Name of the plant, night shade.
Bergamot—Oil extracted from the citrus bergamia.
Benzoin—Balsamic resin from styrax benzoin.
Bile—A secretion from the liver.
Bilious—An undue amount of bile.
Bolus—A large pill.
Bronchia—Branches of the windpipe.
Bronchitis—Inflammation of the bronchial tubes, which lead into the lungs.
Butyric Acid—An acid obtained from butter.

Calamus—Sweet flag.
Calcareous Deposit—Stone or gravel found in the bladder, gall ducts, kidney, etc.
Calenduline—Mixture of calendula and cosmoline.
Callous—A hard bony substance or growth.
Capillaries—Hair-like vessels for conveying the blood from the arteries to the veins.
Capsicum—Cayenne pepper.
Carminatives—Warming stimulants (Aromatics).

Medical Dictionary. 523

Catarrh—Flow of mucus from the nose or other parts of the body.
Cathartic—A drug that increases the action of the bowels.
Cathartics freely open the bowels.
Catheter—Tube for emptying the bladder.
Caustic—A corroding or destroying substance, as nitrate of silver, potash, etc.
Cauterize—To burn a diseased or injured part.
Cellular—Composed of cells.
Cervix—Neck.
Cholagogues increase the secretion of bile.
Chronic—Of long standing.
Citric Acid—Acid made from lemons.
Cohosh—Black snake root. Squaw root.
Collapse—A sudden failing of the vital powers.
Coma—Stupor. Lethargy.
Condiment—That which gives relish to food.
Congestion—Over-fullness of blood-vessels.
Contagious—Disease that may be given to another by contact.
Constipation—Costiveness.
Contusion—A bruise.
Convalescence—Improvement in health.
Corrosive—Eating away.
Cuticle—The outer or first portion of the skin, which consists of three coats.

Datura Stramonium—Thornapple, jimson, etc.
Decoction—Preparation made by boiling.
Defecation—To go to stool.
Demulcent—Mucilaginous, as flax seed and gum arabic.
Demulcents sheathe and protect irritated surfaces.
Dentition—Act or process of cutting teeth.
Dentifrice—A preparation to cleanse the teeth.
Detergents—Cleansing medicines, as laxatives and purgatives.
Diagnosis—The art of discriminating disease.
Diaphoretics—Medicines which aid or produce perspiration.
Diaphoretics cause perspiration.
Diaphragm—Midriff.
Diarrhœa—Looseness of the bowels.
Dietetics—Relating to diet or food.
Diluent—A substance that dilutes or thins liquid.

Diluted—Reduced with water, as dilute alcohol, half alcohol and half water.
Diphtheria—A malignant membranous disease of the throat.
Discutient—A medicine which will scatter or drive away tumors.
Discutients dispel enlargements.
Disinfectants destroy infecting matter.
Diuretic—Causing increased discharge of urine.
Diuretics increase the secretion of urine.
Dorsal—Having reference to the back.
Douche—A dash or stream upon any part.
Drachm—60 grains, a teaspoonful.
Duodenum—The first part of the small intestines.
Dyspepsia—Difficult digestion.
Dysuria—Difficult or painful urination.

Ebullition—Boiling.
Ecbolics cause contraction of the womb.
Eclectic—The act of choosing, selecting.
Eclectic Physician—One who professes to be liberal in views and independent of medical schools.
Effervesce—To foam.
Effete—Worn out, waste matter.
Efflorescence—Redness of the general surface; eruption.
Electuary—Medicine prepared in the consistence of honey.
Elixir—A tincture prepared with more than one article.
Emetic—Medicines which produce emesis, vomiting.
Emetics are medicines which cause vomiting.
Emmenagogue—Remedy that promotes the menstrual discharge.
Emulsion—Mucilage from emollients.
Enceinte—Pregnant.
Enema—An injection into the rectum.
Ennui—Lassitude, dullness of spirit, disgust of condition, etc.
Enteritis—Inflammation of the intestines.
Epidermis—Outer skin.
Epilepsy—Convulsions, fits, with loss of sense for the time, and foaming at the mouth.
Epistaxis—Nose-bleed.
Ergot—Smut of rye. A poisonous fungous growth.

Eructation—Raising wind from the stomach, belching.
Eruption—Pimples or blotches on skin or pustules from small-pox.
Escharotic—That which will destroy the flesh.
Ether—A volatile fluid.
Eustachian Tube—A tube leading from behind the soft palate to the drum of the ear.
Evacuation—The act of discharging by stool.
Evaporation—Conversion of a liquid into vapor.
Exacerbation—Violent increase in disease.
Exanthemata—Rash or eruption on the skin, as in small-pox, scarlet fever, measles, etc.
Excoriation—A chafing or abrasion of the skin.
Excrement—The faeces, that which passes by stool.
Excrescence—An unnatural growth
Exhalent—Giving off fumes.
Expectorant—Tending to produce free discharges from the lungs or throat.
Expectorants increase the secretions from the air tubes.
Excision—The cutting out, or cutting off any part.
Extremity—Applied to the arms and legs.
Extirpation—The complete removal of a part.
Extract—To take out, as a tooth, to extract a ball or any foreign substance from a wound.
Extravasation—A collection of a fluid in a cavity, or under the skin, outside of its proper vessels.

Faeces—Discharge from the bowels.
Fallopian Tubes—Tubes from ovaries to uterus. Oviducts.
Farina—Meal or flour from vegetables.
Fauces—The upper part of the throat.
Febrile—Having reference to fever.
Febrifuge—Medicines to drive away fever, producing perspiration.
Febrifuges counteract fever—lower temperature.
Feces—Discharge from the bowels.
Felon—A deep abscess of the finger.
Femur—The thigh bone.
Femoral—Relating to the thigh.
Ferment—To effervesce, to work, as emptyings, beer, wine, cider, etc.

Fermentation—The process by which the above work of fermenting is carried on by nature or art.
Ferrum—Iron.
Ferri Limatura—Iron filings, very valuable in female debility and for males of weak habit of body.
Fetal—Pertaining to the fetus or child in the womb.
Fetus—Child in the womb after the fifth month.
Fibre—A very small thread-like substance of animal or vegetable matter.
Fibula—The smallest bone of the leg below the knee.
Filter—To strain through paper, made for that purpose.
Fistula—An ulcer having a sinuous external opening.
Flaccid—Flabby, soft, relaxed.
Flatulence—Gas in the stomach or bowels.
Flatus—Collection of wind or gas in the stomach or bowels.
Flooding—Uterine hemorrhage.
Fluor—An increased discharge, a flowing, flux.
Fluor Albus—White flow, leucorrhea, whites, etc.
Fluoric Acid—A fluid obtained from the fluor spar cut with sulphuric acid.
Flux—Diarrhea, or other excessive discharges.
Formula—Medical prescription.
Fumigate—To smoke a room, or any article needing to be cleansed.
Function—The particular action of an organ, as the functions of the stomach, liver, lungs, etc.
Fundament—The anus.
Fundus—Body.
Fungus—Spongy flesh in wounds, proud flesh, or a soft cancer.
Fusion—The act of melting by heat.

Galbanum—A resinous gum from a genus of plants.
Galipot—A glazed jar, used for putting up gummy extracts or ointments.
Gall—Bile.
Galla—The gall-nut, an excrescence found upon the oak.
Gall Bladder—A bag which receives the gall, or bile, through ducts, from the liver, delivering it to the stomach.
Gallic Acid—An acid from the nutgall.
Gall Stones—Hard, biliary concretions found in the gall bladder.

Medical Dictionary.

Galvanic—Having reference to galvanism.
Gamboge—A drastic purgative, unless combined with aromatics.
Ganglion—A knot, or lump on tendons, ligaments, or nerves.
Gangrene—The first stage of mortification.
Gaseous—Having the nature of gas.
Gastric—Of or belonging to the stomach.
Gastric Juice—Secretion of the stomach.
Gastritis—Inflammation of the stomach.
Gastrodynia—Pain in the stomach, sometimes with spasm.
Gelatine—Isinglass.
Gelatinous—Like jelly.
Genitals—Belonging to generation; the sexual organs.
Gentian—A European root, possessing tonic properties.
Genu—The knee.
Genuflexion—Act of bending the knee.
Genus—Family of plants, a group, all of a class or nature.
Germ—The vital principle, or life-spark.
Gestation—Period of growth of child in the womb.
Gleet—Chronic gonorrhea.
Globules—Small, round particles, having special reference to particles of the red part of the blood.
Glossa—The tongue.
Glossarist—A writer of glosses or comments.
Glossitis—Inflammation of the tongue.
Glottis—The opening of the windpipe, at the root of the tongue, larynx, covered by the epiglottis.
Gluten—Vegetable fibrine, existing in farinaceous grains.
Glutton—One who eats excessively.
Gonorrhea—An infectious discharge from the genital organs.
Gout—Painful inflammation of the joints, especially those of the toes, or of the fingers.
Granule—A small particle of healthy matter, not pus.
Granulation—Healing up of an ulcer, or wound, by filling up with healthy matter.
Gravel—Crystalline, sand-like particles in the urine.
Griping—Grinding pain in the stomach, or bowels.
Gustatory—Pertaining to taste.
Gutta Percha—Dried juice of a genus of trees (*Isonandra gutta*).

Guttural—Relating to the throat.
Gymnasium—A place for sportive exercise.
Gypsum—Sulphate of lime, more commonly called plaster of Paris.

Hectic—The fever caused by irritation.
Hema—Blood, prefixed to other words.
Hematemesis—Vomiting of blood.
Hematuria—Hemorrhage from the bladder, or urinary passages.
Hemoptysis—Hemorrhage from the lungs. Literally, spitting of blood.
Hemorrhoids—Piles. Tumors in and about the anus.
Hereditary—Transmitted from parents.
Hernia—Rupture, which permits a part of the bowels to protrude.
Herpes—Disease of the skin. Tetter.
Hiera Picra—A medicine containing aloes and canella.
Humeral—Pertaining to the arm.
Humerus—The single bone of the upper arm.
Humors—The fluids of the body, excluding the blood.
Hydragogues—Medicines which remove water from the system; used in dropsy.
Hydrargyrum—Metallic mercury, quicksilver.
Hydrastis—Golden seal, yellow root.
Hydrocyanic Acid—Prussic acid; nothing more poisonous.
Hydrofluoric Acid—Same as fluoric acid.
Hygeia—Health.
Hygiene—The art of preserving health.
Hypoglottis—Under part of the tongue.
Hysteria—A nervous affection, marked by alternate fits of laughing and crying, with a sensation of strangulation.
Hysteritis—Inflammation of the uterus.

Ichor—An acrid, biting, watery discharge from ulcers or wounds.
Icterus—Jaundice, a bilious disease, which shows yellowness of the eyes and skin.
Icterus Albus—Chlorosis, whites, etc.
Ignition—Set on fire, from state of being Ignis (fire).
Ileus—Colic in the small intestines.

Iliac—Situated near the flank.
Iliac Region—Sides of the abdomen between the ribs and the thighs.
Imbecile—One weak of mind.
Imbibe—To absorb; to drink.
Imbricate—To overlap, as tiles on a house.
Immobile—Immovable, as stiff joints
Imperforate—Without a natural opening.
Impervious—Closed against water.
Impotence—Sterility; inability to produce.
Impregnation—The act of reproducing.
Incision—The cutting in with instruments.
Incontinence—Inability to hold the natural excretions.
Incubation—The hatching of eggs; slow development of disease.
Indication—That which shows what ought to be done by physician.
Indigenous—Peculiar to a country, or to a small section of country; applied to a disease, plants, etc.
Indolent—Slow in progress; applied to ulcers and tumors, which are slow, with but little or no pain.
Induration—Hardening of any part of the system by disease.
Infectious—Communicable from one to another, as disease.
Infirmary—Place where medicines are distributed gratuitously to the poor.
Inflammation—Disease, attended with heat, redness, swelling, tenderness, and often with throbbing.
Inflatus—Collection of wind or gas, as in the stomach, bowels, etc.
Influenza—A disease affecting the nostrils, throat, etc.; of a catarrhal nature.
Infusion—Medicines prepared by steeping in water, without boiling.
Infusoria—Microscopical animals.
Inguinal—Belonging to the groin.
Ingredient—One article of a compound mixture.
Inhalation—Act of drawing in the breath.
Injection—Any preparation introduced into the rectum, or other cavity, by syringe.
Insanity—Derangement of the mind.
Introversion—State of being turned inward.
Inspiration—The act of drawing in the breath.

Inspissation—Thickening, by boiling, to make what is called the concentrated extracts.
Instinct—An involuntary action, as closing the eyelids, breathing, etc.; natural perception of animals.
Insomnia—Sleeplessness.
Integument—A covering, the skin.
Intercostal—Between the ribs.
Intermission—Time between paroxysms of fever, or other disease.
Intermittent Fever—Fever which comes on at regular periods.
Interosseous—Between the bones.
Interval—The time between paroxysms of periodical diseases, as ague, etc.
Intestines—Contents of the abdomen.
Inversio Uteri—Inversion of the uterus.
Inversion—Turning inside out.
Irreducible—Applied to hernia, and to joints which have been put out, and cannot be put back to their place.
Ischuria—Inability to pass the urine.
Issue—Sore, made as a counter-irritant, to draw irritation from a diseased part.
Itch—Scabies. A catching eruption of the skin, accompanied by severe itching.
Itis—An addition to a word, denoting inflammation, pleuritis, pleurisy, etc.
Ivory Black—Animal charcoal.

Jaundice—A disease caused by the inactivity of the liver, or ducts, leading from it.
Jesuits' Bark—First name of Peruvian bark, from its having been discovered by the Jesuit missionaries.
Jugular—Belonging to the throat.
Jujube—A fruit, growing in Southern Europe, something like a plum; used in coughs.

Kali—Potash.
Kelp—Ashes of sea-weed.

Labia—Lips.
Labia Pudendi—Lips or sides of the vulva.
Labial—Of or belonging to the lips.
Laboratory—A place of chemical experiments or operations.
Lancinating—Sharp, piercing, as lancinating pains.

Medical Dictionary. 527

Laryngeal—Of the larynx.
Laryngitis—Inflammation of the throat.
Larynx—The upper part of the throat.
Latent—Hidden, as latent heat. See the remarks connected with steam boiler explosion.
Lassitude—Weakness, a feeling of langnor.
Laxative—Remedy increasing action of the bowels.
Leptandrin—Active principle extracted from the *leptandria virginica*, black root, Culver's physic.
Leucorrhea—Fluor albus, whites, chlorosis, etc.
Ligature—A thread of silk or other substance, to tie arteries, etc.
Lingua—The tongue.
Lithontriptic — A medicine reported to dissolve gravel or stone in the bladder.
Lithotomy—The operation of cutting, to take out stone of the bladder.
Livid-Dark colored, black and blue.
Loins—Lower part of the back.
Lotion—A preparation to wash a sore.
Lubricate—To soften with oil, or to moisten with fluid.
Lumbago — Rheumatism of the loins.
Lute—A paste with which to close chemical retorts; the cassin, curd of milk, is used for that purpose.
Lymph—A thin, colorless fluid carried in small vein-like vessels, called lymphatics.

Mal—Bad; malpractice, bad practice, not according to science.
Malformation — Irregular, unnatural formation.
Malaria—Bad gases, causing disease, supposed to arise from decaying vegetable matter, also the disease itself.
Malignant—A disease of a very serious character.
Mamma—The female breast, which is composed of glands that secrete the milk.
Mastication—The act of chewing.
Masturbation — Excitement, by the hand, of the genital organs.
Maturity — Ripeness, having arrived at adult age, beyond further growth.
Materia — Matter, healthy substance.

Materia Medica—The science of medicine, and the medical combinations.
Maturation — The formation of pus. The act of maturing.
Meconium—The first passage of babes after birth.
Medicated—Having medicine in its composition.
Membrane—A thin, skin-like lining or covering.
Metritis — Inflammation of the womb.
Medicinal—Having medical properties.
Medullary—Like marrow, brainlike
Menstruation—Monthly flow.
Median—The middle.
Mellifluous — Flowing as with honey, sweet, delicious.
Menorrhagia—Profuse menstruation.
Micturition—Urinating, passing the urine.
Midwifery — Art of assisting at child-birth.
Miscible—Capable of being mixed.
Minimum — The smallest, the smallest dose, the opposite of maximum.
Morbid—Unhealthy.
Morbus—A disease; hence cholera morbus, a disease of the bowels.
Mucus—Fluid secreted by mucous membranes.
Muriatic—Having reference to sea salt.
Muriatic Acid — Acid prepared from common salt, often called hydrochloric acid.
Muscle—Bundles of fibres, producing motion in animals.
Muscular — Having reference to the muscles, strongly built.
Myrrh—A resinous gum.

Narcotic—Stupefying, producing sleep.
Narcotics allay pain and produce sleep.
Nasal—Of the nose.
Nausea—Sickness of the stomach.
Nauseant — That which produces nausea.
Navel—Center of the abdomen.
Necrosis—Death of a bone.
Nephritis — Inflammation of the kidneys.
Nervine—That which will allay, or soothe nervous excitement.
Nervous—Easily excited.
Neuralgia—Pain in nerves.
Nisus—Effort, attempt, to expel anything from body.

Medical Dictionary.

Nitrate — Nitric acid combined with alkalies or alkaline salts.
Nitre — Saltpeter.
Nocturnal — Occurring in the night.
Nosology — The classification of diseases.
Nostrum — A quack preparation, usually of the patent order.
Nudus — Nude, without clothing.
Nucleolus — A central granule or spot within a nucleus.
Nutrition — Nourishment.

Obesity — Corpulence, excess of fat, or flesh.
Obstetrics — The science of midwifery.
Ochre — An ore of iron.
Oculist — An eye doctor.
Oculus — The eye.
Œsophagus — The tube leading from the throat to the stomach.
Oleaginous — Oily.
Omentum — The caul, peritoneal covering of the intestines.
Ophthalmia — Disease of the eye, inflammation of the eye.
Ophthalmos — The eye.
Optic Nerve — The nerve which enters the back part of the eye.
Organic — Pertaining to produce by organs.
Organized — Furnished with life.
Orgasm — The closing excitement of sexual connection.
Orifice — An opening.
Os — Mouth as of the womb, or uterus.
Osseous — Bony.
Ossification — Formation of bone; from os, a bone.
Ostalgia — Pain in the bone.
Osteoma — Tumor of a bone.
Ostitis — Inflammation of a bone.
Otorrhea — Discharge from the ear.
Oviparous — Birds, or any animals that produce their young from eggs or by eggs.
Ovum — An egg.
Oxalic Acid — An acid found in sorrel, very poisonous.
Oxide — A combination of oxygen with a metal or other substance.
Oxygen — One of the elements contained in the air and water.
Ozena — Fetid ulcer in the nose, with very fetid discharge.
Ozone — Oxygen in the nascent state, or with its chemical activity otherwise intensified (dynamised).

Pabulum — Food; aliment.
Palliative — Affording relief only.
Palpitation — Unhealthy, or unnatural beating of the heart.
Panacea — Remedy for all diseases.
Paralysis — Loss of motion; numb palsy.
Paroxysm — An increased fit of disease, occurring at certain periods.
Parturients — (Ecbolics).
Parturition — Child-birth.
Partus — Labor; the young when brought forth.
Pathological — Morbid, diseased.
Pectoral — Pertaining to the breast.
Pediluvium — A foot-bath.
Pendulous — Hanging down.
Pepsin — A peculiar substance in the stomach, which aids digestion.
Peptic — Digestive; promoting digestion.
Percolation — The process of running, or drawing a liquid through some substance.
Pericardium — Sac containing the heart.
Pericarditis — Inflammation of the pericardium.
Perineal — Relating to the region of the perineum.
Periodicity — Returning at a certain time.
Periosteum — The membrane which covers all bones.
Peristaltic — The peculiar wormlike movement of the intestines.
Peritonitis — Inflammation of lining membrane of bowels.
Perturbation — Disturbance.
Perversion — An unhealthy change; a change from its proper or natural course.
Pessary — That which will support or hold up the womb in prolapsus.
Phagedenic — Eating and fast spreading, as an ulcer.
Pharmacy — The art of combining and preparing medicines.
Phlegm — Mucus from the bronchial tubes and throat.
Phlogistic — Tending to inflammation.
Phosphate — Phosphoric acid in combination with bases, as phosphate of iron, phosphate of lime, etc.
Phosphorus — An inflammable and luminous substance, prepared from bones.
Phthisis — A wasting; consumption.

Medical Dictionary.

Piles—Tumors at or in the anus; sometimes protruding.
Piperine—The active principle prepared from black pepper, considered valuable in ague.
Placebo—A remedy to gratify the patient.
Placenta—After-birth.
Plethora — Over-fullness; if healthy, causing obesity, corpulence.
Plethoric—Full of blood. Fleshy.
Pleura—The serous membrane covering the lungs, and folded upon the sides.
Pleuritis — Inflammation of the pleura; pleurisy.
Pneumonia—Inflammation of the lungs.
Podophyllin -The active principle made from the podophyllum peltatum, mandrake root.
Potassium—The basis of potash. It is a metal.
Potus—A drink; hence, potion, a medicated drink.
Predisposition—A tendency to a certain disease.
Pregnancy—The condition of being with child.
Prognosis — The art of knowing how a disease will terminate.
Prolapsus—A falling.
Prolapsus Uteri — Falling of the uterus.
Pruritis—A skin trouble causing intense itching.
Prussiate—A salt formed by a base with prussic acid.
Prussic Acid—Hydrocyanic acid; one of, or the most virulent poison in existence.
Psora—The itch.
Puberty—Full growth; mature age.
Pubes — The prominence of the lower front part of the body in females.
Pudendum—The organs of generation.
Puerperal—Belonging to or consequent on child-birth.
Pulmonitis—Inflammation of the lung or lungs.
Pulmonary—Relating to the lungs, as pulmonary balsam, pulmonic waters, etc.
Pupil—The dark circle in the eye.
Purgative—A cathartic.
Pus—Matter discharged by sores, abscesses, etc.
Pustule—A slight elevation, having pus.
Putrefaction — Decomposition by rotting.

Putrid—Rotten; decomposed.
Puerperal—Belonging to or consequent upon child-birth.
Pyæmia—Poisoning by absorption of pus.

Quassia—A bitter tonic; the chips of the wood are used.

Rachitis—Rickets, bending of the spine, and sometimes the long bones of the limbs; may be also connected with enlargement of the head, etc.
Radius—One of the bones of the forearm.
Radix—A root.
Ramus—A branch.
Ramification—The act of branching.
Rancidity—State of being rancid, stale; applied to oil, fat, butter, etc.
Rash—A redness of the skin in patches.
Ratsbane — Arsenious acid; arsenic.
Recession — Striking in of the blood, or disease going to the internal organs.
Rectum—The lower portion of the intestines.
Refrigerant—Cooling as of medicines or drink.
Regimen—Regulation of diet and habits.
Relapse — Recurrence of disease after an improved appearance.
Relaxation—Losing the healthy tone of any part, or the whole system.
Reproduction — Generation; procreation.
Respiration—The act of breathing, including both inspiration and expiration.
Retching—An effort to vomit.
Retention—Delay of the natural passage of the urine or feces.
Revulsion—The drawing away of disease, as by blisters, irritating plasters, etc.
Rheumatism — Inflammation of the fibrous tissues, mostly confined to the large joints.
Rochelle Salts—A chemical mixture of tartrate of potash and soda.
Rubefacients — Medicines which cause redness of the skin, as mustard, radish leaves, etc.
Rupture—Hernia; by some called a breach.

Saccharine—Having the properties of sugar.
Saliva—The secretion of the mouth, spittle.
Salt—A compound of an acid with a base.
Saltpeter—Nitrate of potash.
Salubrious—Favorable to health.
Sanative—Curative, healing.
Sanguineous—Bloody; sanguineous discharge, as bloody-flux.
Santonine—A powder obtained from worm-seed.
Sarcoma—A fleshy tumor, generally of a cancerous nature.
Scabies—The itch.
Scirrhus—A hard tumor, generally of a cancerous nature.
Scrofula—A constitutional tendency to disease of the glands, particularly of the neck.
Scrotum—The sac which encloses the testicles.
Sedative—Depressing, the opposite of stimulating.
Sedatives depress nervous power or lower circulation.
Sialogogues increase the flow of saliva.
Slough—Death of a part, allowing it to come out from the healthy part.
Snake Root—Common or Virginia snake-root; but black snake-root is the black cohosh.
Soporifics induce sleep.
Spasm—Cramp or convulsion.
Specific—A remedy having a uniform special action.
Sperm—Seminal fluid, now more often called the semen, seed.
Spine—The backbone; hence spine.
Stimulant—A medicine calculated to excite an increased and healthy action.
Stimulants temporarily excite the nervous or circulatory system.
Stitch—A spasmodic pain.
Stomatitis—Inflammation of the mouth.
Strangulation—The state of choking; also applied to hernia, which cannot be reduced.

Styptic—Having the power to stop bleeding.
Sudor—Sweat; hence, sudorific, inducing sweat.
Sudorifics—(Diaphoretics).
Sulphate—A chemical combination of a base with sulphuric acid.
Sulphuric Acid—Oil of vitriol.
Suppuration—The process of inflammation, by which pus is formed.
Symptom—A sign of a disease.
Syncope—Swooning; fainting.

Tonics gradually and permanently improve digestion and nutrition.
Tannic Acid—An acid obtained from oak bark; an astringent.
Tartaric Acid—An acid from cream of tartar, found in grapes.
Tenesmus—Difficulty and pain at stool, with a desire to go to stool often.
Therapeutics—Branch of medicine. Relating to a knowledge of treating diseases.
Thorax—The chest.
Tibia—The large bone of the lower leg, shinbone.
Tonic—A medicine which increases the strength of the system.
Tonsils—Glands on each side of the throat.
Trachea—The windpipe.
Translation—The act of transferring disease to some other part.
Triturate—To rub into a powder.
Tumor—A morbid enlargement of a part.

Ureter—Duct leading from the kidney to the bladder.
Urethra—Duct leading out from the bladder.
Uterus—The womb.

Vagina—The passage from the womb to the vulva.
Vermifuges kill and expel worms.
Virus—Contagious poison.
Vulva—External opening of the female genitals.

ALPHABETICAL INDEX.

A
	Page.
Accidents and emergencies	88
Advice to cooks	404
Advice to weary women	41
Ague	180
Ailing child	230
Air contamination	82
Airing the sleeping room	346
Air, pure	33
Alcohol, effects of	185
Almond Meal	264
Alopecia	180
Alum, medical qualities	116, 236
American Golden Rod	111
American Poplar	113
Amusements	318
Angel of the home	25
Animals we drink in water	83
Ants, how to destroy	505, 508
Apoplexy	163, 180
Appetite, loss of	180
Apple Butter	471
Apple Snow	382
Arrangement, gift of	28
Arrow Root	208
Art of breathing	38
Art of cooking	400
Art of happy living	27
As I grow old	56
Asthma	135, 136, 180
Asthma (see Lobelia)	120
Asthma (see Saltpetre)	124
Autumn Leaves	344

B
Bad Breath	169, 268
Baking Soda, medicinal	123
Bandages, different kinds	103
Barb Wire Cuts	96
Barber's Itch	180
Bath, Morning	62, 66
Baths, different kinds	67, 69, 70
Bathing	63
Bathing, rules for	68
Beautiful Form, to acquire	252
Beautiful Women	64
Beauty	250
Beauty Evanescent	253
Beauty in the Bath	64
Bed Bugs, how to get rid of	502
Bed Hammock for Sick	253

	Page.
Bed Room, care of	346
Bed Sores	180
Bed Wetting	242
Beef, how to pickle	409
Beef Tea	475
Be Good to Yourself	56
Beneath the Finger Nails	74
Benefit of Poultices	100
Bicycle Exercise	85
Bilious Attacks	131, 180
Biliousness (see Dandelion)	115
Bills of Fare	432
Black Elder, medicinal	114
Blackheads	255, 261
Blacking for Boots and Shoes	394
Bladder, catarrh of	120
Bladder, inflammation of (see Sassafras)	122
Bleeding, how to stop	88
Bleeding (see Alum)	116
Blues, cure for	51
Boils, cure for	104, 181
Boneset, medicinal	116
Books and Music	331
Borax, antiseptic, etc.	111
Borax, ruinous to kidneys	112
Borax, use in kitchen	346
Boston Brown Bread	479
Bottle Feeding	235
Bowels, disorder of (see Flaxseed)	118
Bowels, disorder of (see Lima)	120
Bowels, inflammation of	181, 228
Bowel Trouble	284
Brass, how to keep clean	368, 389
Bread	434
Breakfast Cakes	436
Breathing, art of	38
Breathing, deep	38
Breathing, systematic	39
Bright's Disease	148
Broken Bones	96
Bronchitis	181
Bruises and Sprains	104, 106, 181, 197
Builders' Rules	378
Bunions, how to cure	290
Burdock	114
Burns	94, 95
Burns (see Black Elder)	114
Burns (see Glycerine)	113
Burns (see Kerosene)	119
Business Men	62, 67

531

Alphabetical Index.

	Page.
Buttermilk	475
Buzzing in Ears	181

C

	Page.
Cabbage Worms, how to destroy	511
Cake-baking Rules	437
Cakes, how to make	438
Camphor, medicinal	114
Canaries, disease and cure	382
Canaries, how to raise	382
Cancers	157, 181
Cancer (see Red Clover)	110
Candies, how to make	486
Candies, homemade best	486
Canker of Mouth	181
Canned Fruits, caution for	467
Canning Fruits	467
Carbuncles	106, 233
Carpet Cleaning Mixture	377
Carpet Bugs, how to exterminate	498
Carpets, how to clean	376, 377
Carpet Sponging	376
Car Sickness	361
Catarrh Cure	141, 181
Catnip	115
Catsup	429
Cayenne Pepper, Condiment	115
Cayenne Pepper, Medicine	115
Chapped Hands	269, 271
Charcoal	357
Charity	52
Cheerfulness and Health	238, 254, 331
Cheerfulness, crowning grace	331
Chicken Broth	476
Chicken Cholera	515
Chicken Pox	181, 241
Chilblains, how to cure	289
Children, diseases of	229
Children, healthy, vigorous and beautiful	227
Children, training	331
Chill and Fever (see Boneset)	116
Chinese Doctors	177
Choking	94
Cholera Morbus	164
Cholera of Children (see Peppermint)	122
Chorea	181
Cigarette Smoking	189, 190
Cinnamon	115
Cleanliness	60, 81
Clothes, how to take measure for	385, 386
Clothes Moths, how to destroy	499
Clover Tea	111
Coal Gas Suffocation	94
Coffee	46, 433

	Page.
Coffee Cake	435, 441
Cold Air	36
Cold Cream	264
Cold Dinners	485
Cold Feet	290
Cold, how to cure	141
Cold in Chest	181
Cold in the Head	145, 181
Colds and Fever	36
Colds (see Camphor)	114
Colds (see Catnip)	115
Colds (see Eggs)	112
Colds (see Flaxseed)	118
Colds (see Garlic)	114
Colds (see Glycerine)	113
Colds (see Ginger)	117
Colds (see Horehound)	111
Colds (see Lemon Juice)	108
Colds (see Lobelia)	120
Cold Water, how to use	175
Colic	181, 196, 234
Colic in Adults	125, 126
Colic in Children	126, 182
Colic (see Camphor)	114
Colic (see Cinnamon)	115
Colic (see Ginger)	116
Colic (see Magnesia)	120
Colic (see Olive Oil)	119
Colic (see Peppermint)	122
Complexion, hints on	256, 259
Conditions of Health	46
Condition of Many Wells	85
Constipation	132, 152, 181, 183, 196, 238
Constipation (see Black Elder)	114
Constipation (see Dandelion)	115
Constipation (see Rhubarb)	120
Constipation (see Senna)	122
Consumption	181
Consumption (see Wild Cherry)	123
Contagious Diseases	74, 75
Convulsions	92, 181, 213
Cookies, all kinds	450
Cooking, art of	401
Cooks, advice to	404
Cooks, hints for	401
Copper, how to shine	368
Cotton Fabrics, colors "set"	495
Corn Bread	435, 436
Corn Cure	289
Corn, new ways of preparing	427
Cosmetics	254, 258, 271, 272
Costiveness	181
Coughs and Colds	142, 181, 233
Coughs and Colds (see Dandelion)	115
Coughs and Colds (see Eggs)	112
Coughs and Colds (see Gum Arabic)	111

Alphabetical Index. 533

	Page.
Coughs and Colds (see Goose Grease)	122
Coughs and Colds (see Horehound)	111
Coughs and Colds (see Pennyroyal)	121
Coughs and Colds (see Sage)	124
Coughs and Colds (see Snakeroot)	122
Coughs and Colds (see Wild Cherry)	123
Cough Syrup	141
Cracked Wheat	477
Crackers	480
Cramps in Legs	126, 193
Croup	181, 233, 235
Croup (see Alum)	116
Croup (see Lime)	120
Crullers	465
Curative properties of Salt	108
Cure for Blues	51
Currant Worms, how to destroy	512
Cystitis	182

D

	Page.
Dandelion	115
Dandruff	281, 285
Dandruff (see Borax)	111
Dangers of Over-feeding	215
Deafness	182
Death Gas in a Well	96
Decorating with Natural Objects	343
Decorations, home	327
Decorations, wall	338
Deep Breathing	28
Delineator, how to make	334
Delirium Tremens (see Red Pepper)	124
Dentrifice (see Borax)	111
Depilatories	271
Desserts	465
Developing Healthy Children	224
Diabetes	147
Diarrhea	134, 182, 244
Diarrhea (see Baking Soda)	123
Diarrhea (see Blackberry)	114
Diarrhea (see Camphor)	114
Diarrhea (see Eggs)	112
Diarrhea (see Ginger)	117
Diarrhea (see Oak Bark)	121
Diarrhea, sure cure	135
Digestion, time required for	44
Dining Room, the	349
Diphtheria	182, 228, 240
Diphtheria (see Lime)	120
Disease Germs in Drinking Water	84

	Page.
Diseases, kinds, descriptions	74
Diseases of Infants	182, 229
Disinfection	79, 82
Dislocation	96
Distinguished Guests	324
Diuretic (see Gum Arabic)	111
Diuretic (see Woodsage)	110
Doilies	350
Dogwood	117
Doughnuts	452
Drains and Sinks	81
Drains, how to purify	374
Dress of Ladies	274
Drink, best	45
Dropsy	182
Dropsy (see Horseradish)	118
Dropsy (see Juniper)	118
Dropsy (see Lemon Juice)	118
Drowning Person, how to treat	97
Dyeing Cloth, Silk, etc.	388
Dysentery (see Blackberry)	114
Dysentery (see Bloody Flux)	182
Dysentery (see Saltpetre)	124
Dysentery (see Sassafras)	122
Dysentery (see Slippery Elm)	110
Dyspepsia	108
Dyspepsia, how to cure	149, 160, 166, 182
Dyspepsia (see American Poplar)	113
Dyspepsia (see Lime)	120
Dyspepsia (see Magnesia)	120
Dyspepsia (see Mustard)	120
Dyspeptics, pie for	482

E

	Page.
Earache	160, 182
Economics of Health	46
Eczema	157, 182
Effects of Wearing Tight Shoes	221
Egg Dishes, new	430
Eggs as Medicine	112
Eggs, boiled, poached	461
Eggs, how to pickle	517
Egg Lemonade	474
Emergencies	83, 91
Emollients	264
Engravings, how to enlarge	384
Epilepsy	182
Epistaxis	182
Erysipelas	157, 182
Etiquette, rules	293, 296
Etiquette, in speech	295
Etiquette of Dress and Habits	306
Etiquette on the Street	301
Etiquette of Calls	302
Evils of Over-eating	40

Alphabetical Index.

Eyebrows and Lashes, beautiful 352
Eyes, saving the 159
Eyes, sore, how to doctor.160, 182
Eye Water 160

F

Face Ache or Neuralgia..... 182
Fainting 92
Family Recipes 351
Feeding the Sick 206
Feeding the Unfortunate Poor 52
Felon 105, 106
Ferns 344
Fever 183
Fever (see Boneset) 116
Fever (see Oak Bark) 121
Fever and Ague (see Dogwood) 117
Fever and Ague (see Willow) 123
Filters, homemade 83
Finger Nails 74, 269, 272
Fish, how to cook 415
Flannels, shrinking 496
Flannels, washing of 493
Flatulence 183
Flax Seed Lemonade 47
Flaxseed, medicinal 119
Fleas, how to destroy 497
Flies, how to destroy 504
Floors, hardwood, care of 372
Floor, how to stain 372
Flowers, how to keep fresh.. 383
Flowers and Flower Seeds.. 509
Fly Spots, to remove 375
Food, well cooked 349
Footwear, pointers on 292
Foreign Bodies in Ear, Nose, Throat 93
Freckles 258, 261
Freckles (see Borax) 111
Freckles (see Lemon Juice).. 118
Fritters 435
Frost Bites 162
Frosted Windows, to prevent 356
Frosting, all kinds of 447
Fruit Ice 462
Fruit Jars 352
Fruits, health in 71
Furniture 339, 340
Furniture Polish 370, 371

G

Gall Stones 183
Gapes 516
Garlic, medicinal 114
Gas in Well 99
Giddiness 183

Gilt Frames, how to clean....
Ginger Bread
Ginger Snaps
Gladstone
Glass, to clean
Glass Stoppers, how to remove
Glue, how to make 351,
Golden Rules for the Kitchen
Good Behavior, hints on .....
Goose Grease
Graham Bread
Graham Gems 485,
Grahams 478, 480,
Grasses
Gravel
Gravel (see Saltpetre).......
Grease Spots 362, 366,
Griddle Cakes
Grippe, how to cure
Gruels 476,
Gum Arabic
Gymnasium director's advice

H

Hair Brushes
Hair, care of 259,
Hair Dressings
Hair Dyeing
Hair Falling Out 279,
Hairs, gray
Hair Oils and Tonics, 281, 284, 285
Hair, structure of
Hair, style of wearing
Hams, how to pickle
Hands, care of
Happy, how to manage to be.
Happy Living, art of
Happiness, length of days ...
Hay Fever
Headaches, cause and cure, 131, 133
Headaches (see Golden Rod)..
Health 29,
Health, conditions of
Health, Economics of
Health in Vegetables and Fruits
Health, occupations
Health Rules
Healthy Homes
Heartburn
Heartburn (see Baking Soda).
Heartburn (see Lime)
Heartburn (see Magnesia) ...
Heart Disease
Hectic Fever
Hiccough 133,
Hides, how to tan

Alphabetical Index. 535

	Page.
Gilt Frames, how to clean	374
Ginger Bread	451
Ginger Snaps	451
Gladstone	69
Glass, to clean	377
Glass Stoppers, how to remove	375
Glue, how to make	391, 395
Golden Rules for the Kitchen	403
Good Behavior, hints on	292
Goose Grease	122
Graham Bread	434
Graham Gems	435, 436
Grahams	479, 480, 451
Grasses	344
Gravel	148
Gravel (see Saltpetre)	134
Grease Spots	265, 366, 495
Griddle Cakes	436
Grippe, how to cure	161
Gruels	475, 476
Gum Arabic	111
Gymnasium director's advice	248

H

	Page.
Hair Brushes	282
Hair, care of	280, 282
Hair Dressings	278
Hair Dyeing	283
Hair Falling Out	279, 287
Hairs, gray	282
Hair,	285
Hair, structure of	278
Hair, style of wearing	278
Hams, how to pickle	400
Hands, care of	208
Happy, how to manage to be	239
Happy Living, art of	27
Happiness, length of days	68
Hay Fever	123
Headaches, cause and cure, 133	162
Headaches (see Golden Rod)	111
Health	29, 87
Health, conditions of	46
Health, Economics of	45
Health in Vegetables and Fruits	71
Health, occupations	47
Health Rules	78
Healthy Houses	82
Heartburn	195
Heartburn (see Baking Soda)	132
Heartburn (see Lime)	120
Heartburn (see Magnesia)	190
Heart Disease	183
Hectic Fever	182
High	122, 262
Hides, how to tan	370

	Page.
Hints for All	44
Hints for the Cook	401
Hints on Seasoning	402
Hints and Helps for the Sick Room	201
Hoarseness	72, 143, 183
Hoarseness (see Eggs)	112
Hoarseness (see Gum Arabic)	111
Hoarseness (see Goose Grease)	122
Hoarseness (see Horse Radish)	118
Home	22
Home Adornments	337
Home Atmosphere	28
Home Made Mattresses	348
Home Nursing	204
Home Remedies and How to Use Them	107
Home Remedies and Home Treatment for all Diseases	125
Home Remedies and Home Treatment for Diseases of Children	229
Homeopathic Medicines	179
Homeopathic Remedies	180
Hominy	479
Hooping Cough	183, 242
Hops, medicinal	117
Horse Radish, medicinal	118
Hot Milk	476
Hot Water	367
Hot Water, how to use as a medicine	173
Hot Water, how to apply in diseases	174
Hot Water, what it will do	175
Household Measures and Weights	354
Household Hints	356
House Insects	497
Housekeeper, the	328
House Plants	509
Housewife, a model	329
How Ladies Should Dress	274
How to Amuse Children	319
How to Break a String	373
How to Carve Ducks, Turkeys, etc.	413
How to Cure Earache	160
How to Cure the Grip	161
How to Cure Nightmare	126
How to Cure Snakebite	97
How to Check Vomiting	129
How to Destroy Microbes	78
How to Disinfect a Room	79
How to Develop the Chest	260
How to Eat Oranges	355
How to Enlarge Embroidery, Engravings, etc.	384
How to Gather and Prepare Medicinal Plants and Barks	113

	Page.
How to Keep a Baby Well	221
How to Keep Well	37
How to Make Children Healthy, Vigorous and Beautiful	227
How to Make a Hole in Glass	374
How to Mix Paints	389
How to Tell Contagious Diseases	75
How to Treat a Drowning Person	97
How to Vaccinate	158
Hydrophobia	98
Hygiene of the Bed Room	346
Hysteria	183

I

	Page.
Ice Cream	465
Impure Blood	183
Incontinence of Urine	147
Indigestion (see Wild Cherry)	123
Infants, care and feeding	210, 213
Infants, how to preserve Health and Life	216, 229
Influenza	183
Ingrowing Nails	291
Inks, different kinds	392
Ink Stains	365, 397
Ink Stains (see Household Hints)	356
Ink Stains (see Lemon Juice)	118
Invitations, how to write	312
Iron, to polish	366
Iron, to prevent rust on	379
Itch, how to cure	165, 183
Itch (see Sulphur)	123

J

	Page.
Jams	471
Jaundice	151, 183
Jellies	469
Jelly Water	474
Johnny Cake	436
Juniper Berry, medicinal	118

K

	Page.
Kalsomine, how to prepare	375
Kerosene Oil	119, 236
Kerosene Stains in Carpets	376
Kidney Affections (see Parsley)	110
Kidney Affections (see Flaxseed)	118
Kidney Troubles	183, 195
Kidney Weakness (see Tansy)	110
Kitchen Utensils, care of	351, 367
Knives, to clean	392

Alphabetical Index.

L

	Page
Lamp Chimneys, how to toughen	359
Lamps, how to care for	358
Lard and Salt	233
Late Rising	81
Laughter, a great tonic	50
Laundry, in the	491
Laureline	273
Lawn, how to improve	509
Laxative, a palatable	167
Laxative (see Magnesia)	120
Laxative (see Mandrake)	121
Laxative (see Mustard)	120
Laxative (see Olive Oil)	119
Laxative (see Rhubarb)	120
Laxative (see Sulphur)	122
Lead Colic	183
Leather, how to improve	396
Lemonade	474
Lemon for Felons	105
Lemon Juice	113, 272
Leucorrhoea	184
Lice, how to destroy	516
Lime, medicinal	120
Liniments, how to make	169
Little Mischief	231
Liver Complaint (see Mandrake)	121
Liver Enlargement	183
Liver Inactive	183
Liver, inflammation of (see Dandelion)	115
Lobelia, medicinal	120
Lobster Cutlets	417
Lockjaw (see Lobelia)	120
Lumbago	184
Lungs, bleeding (see Oak Bark)	121
Lung Fever	137
Lungs, how to ascertain state of	138
Lungs, inflammation of	184
Lung Strengthener	33

M

	Page
Magnesia	120
Malaria	140
Malaria and Water	87
Mandrake	121
Marble, how to clean	397
Marmalade	471
Massage	192
Matting, Straw, how to clean	376
Measles	184, 241
Measles (see Rhubarb)	120
Measles (see Snakeroot)	122
Meats, all kinds	404
Medical Dictionary	522
Medicine, history of	176
Medicines, homeopathic dose	179

	Page
Medicine, how much is a dose	178, 179
Medicine, revolution in practice	177
Method a Servant	331
Mice, how to get rid of	508
Microbes or Bacteria	77, 78
Microscope, revelations of	76
Mistress, the	340
Mistress, rules for	332
Moles	270
Mosquitoes	504
Moth, how to destroy	500, 502
Moth, to keep from furs	501
Mother	26
Mucilage, how to make	395, 396
Muffins	436, 479
Mumps	184, 243
Mush, different kinds of	477, 478

N

	Page
Napkins	350
Nausea (see Peach Tree Bark)	121
Nauseous Remedies	232
Neckties, how to clean	387
Nervousness	156
Nervousness (see Wild Cherry)	123
Nervous Children	232
Nervous Debility	184
Nettle Rash	184
Neuralgia	129, 182, 183
Neuralgia (see Kerosene Oil)	119
Nickel Plate, to polish	369, 379
Night Cough, to prevent	145
Nightmare, how to cure	126
Night Sweats	164
Night Sweats (see Sage)	124
Nose Bleeding	90

O

	Page
Oak Bark	121
Oat Meal Tea	474
Oat Meal Snaps	480
Obesity	184
Occupations	47
Ointments, how to make	168
Olive Oil	119
Omelets	418
Onions, best nervine	72
Onions, medicinal qualities	109
Onions, roasted	428
Only a Sprain	104
Ophthalmia (see Cayenne Pepper)	115
Ophthalmia	184
Opiates and Nervousness	156
Oranges, how to eat	365

Alphabetical Index.

Page (left column, partially cut off)

licine, how much is a
se 178, 179
licine, revolution in prac-
ce 177
hod a Servant 331
e, how to get rid of 508
robes or Bacteria 77, 78
roscope, revelations of.... 76
tress, the 340
tress, rules for 332
s 270
quitoes 504
h, how to destroy 500, 502
h, to keep from furs ... 501
her 26
llage, how to make ...395, 396
ins 436, 479
ps 184, 243
h, different kinds of ..477, 478

N

tins 350
es (see Peach Tree
rk) 121
cous Remedies 232
ties, how to clean 387
ousness 156
ousness (see Wild Cher-
.... 123
ous Children 232
ous Debility 184
e Rash 184
algia 129, 182, 183
algia (see Kerosene Oil) 119
al Plate, to polish .. 369, 379
t Cough, to prevent 145
mare, how to cure 126
Sweats 164
Sweats (see Sage) 124
Bleeding 90

O

Bark 121
leal Tea 474
leal Snaps 480
ty 184
ations 47
ents, how to make...... 168
Oil 119
ts 418
a, best nervine 72
s, medicinal qualities.. 109
s, roasted 428
a Sprain 104
almia (see Cayenne
er) 115
almia 184
s and Nervousness ... 156
es, how to eat 355

Page (middle column)

Orange Whey 474
Orris Root 496
Over-eating, evils of......... 40
Oysters 416, 426, 482

P

Paints, how to mix 389
Palpitation of Heart (see
  Wild Cherry) 123
Palsy (see Horseradish)... 118
Paralysis 184
Parsley 110
Parsley after Onions 109
Patterns, how to take meas-
  ures for 395
Peach Tree Bark 121
Pennyroyal, medicinal 121
Peppermint, medicinal ... 122
Perspiration (see Pennyroyal) 121
Perspiration (see Snakeroot), 122
Physical Culture 254
Pickles 430, 482
Pies 453, 482
Pie Plant Baked 482
Piles, how to cure 164, 184
Pimples 202, 288
Pimples (see Alum) 116
Plant Lice, how to destroy..512
Plaster, to fill cracks in.... 378
Pleurisy 135, 184, 233
Pneumonia 137, 233
Poisoning (see Mustard) ... 120
Poisoning 81
Politeness 309
Porridge 475
Potatoes 422
Potato Dishes 423
Pot-Pourri of Roses........ 341
Poultices, benefit of 100
Poultice, wood sage 110
Poultice, slippery elm 110
Poultice, hops 117
Poultices, different kinds .. 102
Poultices, how to make 101
Poultry, diseases and treat-
  ments 514
Poultry, how to cook all
  kinds 412
Poultry Pointers 519
Poultry, rules for keeping..513
Poultry, what to feed 519
Practical Health Rules ... 73
Practical Rules for Bathing.. 68
Preserves 472
Preserving the Figure 247
Prurigo 184
Puddings 455, 463, 478, 481
Pudding Sauces 464
Pure Air 33
Purgative (see Senna) 122

Q

Quinsy 163, 184
Quotation Hunt 324

R

Rash 184
Rats, how to get rid of 507
Razor, how to sharpen 386
Reading the Paper 398
Red Clover, good for cancer.110
Red Pepper, medicinal ... 124
Refrigerators 33
Remittent Fever 184
Rest, wisdom and beauty in.. 49
Retention of Urine 184
Rheumatic Fever 183
Rheumatism 155, 184
Rheumatism (see Turpentine) 113
Rheumatism (see American
  Poplar) 113
Rheumatism (see Black El-
  der) 114
Rheumatism (see Camphor).. 114
Rheumatism (see Horserad-
  ish) 113
Rheumatism (see Lemon
  Juice) 118
Rheumatism (see Kerosene
  Oil) 119
Rheumatism (see Snakeroot). 122
Rheumatism (see Saltpetre).. 124
Rhubarb, medicinal 120
Ribbons, how to clean 387
Rice, boiled 81
Rice Dishes 421, 478, 479
Rice Pudding 459, 479
Rickets 184
Ring Games 321
Ringworm 184
Round Shoulders, cure 249
Rust, to remove from steel .. 389
Rustic Flower Stand....... 342
Rusty Nail or Wire, injury
  from 162

S

Sage, medicinal 124
Salads 430
Salivation 185
Salmon, baked................ 417
Salmon, canned 415
Salt, uses in kitchen 357
Salt as a Nervine 72
Salt, curative properties... 108
Salt for Toothache 168
Saltpetre, medicinal 124
Salves, healing, how to make 171
Sanitation 81
Sassafras 122
Sauerkraut 428

Alphabetical Index.

	Page.
Sausages	410
Scarlatina	185
Scarlet Fever	183, 233, 238, 239
Scarlet Fever (see Snakeroot)	122
Sciatica	185
Sciatica (see Kerosene Oil)	119
Scrofula (see Burdock)	114
Scrofula (see Juniper)	118
Scrofula (see Oak Bark)	121
Scurvy, remedy for	71
Sea Sickness (see Red Pepper)	124
Seasoning, hints on	402
Senna	122
Servant Question	334
Servant, rules for	333
Sewing Box	342
Shaving, hints on	286
Shirt Bosoms, how to polish	492
Sick Headache	131, 134
Silk, how to clean	387
Silk, how to wash	387, 495
Silver, how to shine	368
Silverware	352
Sinks, how to purify	353, 374
Skin Diseases (see Burdock)	114
Skin Diseases (see Juniper)	118
Skin Diseases (see Lime)	120
Skin Diseases (see Oak Bark)	121
Skin Diseases (see Baking Soda)	123
Skin Diseases (see Saltpetre)	124
Skin Troubles	257
Sleep	53
Sleep, need of	54
Sleeping Rooms	54, 346
Sleep, how to induce	55
Sleeplessness	127, 185
Sleeplessness (see Hops)	117
Slippery Elm	110
Small Pox	158
Snake Bite, how to cure	97
Snake Root	122
Soap, how to make	492
Social Duties	306
Soda, washing	357
Sore Throat, how to cure	147, 185
Sore Throat, remedy for	146
Sore Throat (see Salt)	108
Sore Throat (see Goose Grease)	122
Sore Throat (see Snake-root)	122
Sore Throat (see Saltpetre)	124
Soup Making	405, 424, 425
Soups for the Sick	476
Sprains	91, 104, 105
Sprains (see Kerosene Oil)	119
Sprains (see Spruce Beer)	361
Stains, removing all kinds	362, 363
Starch, improved	495
Statuary, how to clean	397
Steel, to prevent rust on	379
Steel, to remove rust from	368, 369
Stewed Chicken	419
Stimulant (see Mandrake)	12?
Stings, Insect, how to cure	185, 50?
Stomach, acidity of (see Magnesia)	12?
Stomach, disorder of	170
Stomach or Bowels, pain in, (see Sweet Flag)	12?
Stomach, sour (see Baking Soda)	12?
Stomach's Plea	15?
Stoves, how to clean	350
Stoves, how to keep from rusting	350
Strangulation	9?
String, how to break	87?
Successful Life	2?
Sulphur	12?
Summer Complaint	24?
Sunburn	26?
Sunlight and Health	2?
Sunstroke	94, 18?
Superfluous Hair	27?
Sweet Flag	12?
Sweet Little Woman of Mine	2?
Sweet Peas	51?
Sweet Potato Dishes	42?

T

Table Linen, how laundered	49?
Table Manners	30?
Take Life as it Comes	25?
Tan, how to remove	258, 26?
Tapioca Milk	47?
Tarts	45?
Tea	4?
Tea, how made	43?
Tea Stains, to remove	36?
Teeth, cleaning the	26?
Teeth, care of	265, 26?
Teeth, facts about	26?
Teething, difficult	182, 226, 24?
Tidyness	60, 6?
Time Required for Digestion	4?
Tin, how to shine	368, 36?
Tinware	35?
Toasts	48?
Toasts, different kinds	48?
Toast Water	47?
Toilet Hints	26?
Tomatoes	428, 429, 48?
Tongue, coated	18?
Tonics (see American Poplar)	11?
Tonics (see Boneset)	11?
Tonics (see Horehound)	11?
Tonics (see Mandrake)	1?
Tonics (see Peach Tree Bark)	1?

Alphabetical Index

	Page.
Toothache	185
Toothache (see Cinnamon)	115
Toothache (see Salt)	108
Toothpicks	207
Tooth Powder	265, 268
Tuberculosis	185
Turkey, roasted	410
Turpentine, medicinal qualities	112
Turpentine, cleansing properties	495
Typhoid Fever	140
Typhoid Fever, how to nurse	139
Typhus Fever	185

U

Ulcers (see Oak Bark)	121
Urinary Difficulties	185

V

Vaccination	158
Varnish, how to remove old	374
Vegetable Diet	42
Vegetable Dishes	426
Vegetables, health in	71
Vegetable Soups	424
Ventilation	34, 36
Vermifuge	237
Vinegar, how to make	380
Vomiting, how to check	128, 185
Vomiting (see Peach Tree Bark)	121

W

	Page.
Waffles	436
Warning to Mothers	215
Warts, how to remove	106, 155, 270
Water Brash (see Baking Soda)	123
Water, to purify	367
Water, hot and cold, how to use	173, 175
Weary Women, advice to	41
Whitewash, how to make	374, 375
Whitlow	185
Whooping Cough	185, 242
Whooping Cough (see Horehound)	111
Whooping Cough (see Garlic)	114
Why Don't You Laugh	51
Why People Die Before Their Time	57
Wild Cherry	123
Willow, medicinal	123
Wisdom and Beauty in Rest	49
Woman	25
Woman's Influence	60
Wood, how to polish	374
Woodsage	110
Worms	185, 237
Wounds	90, 91, 182

Y

Yard and Garden	509

Z

Zinc, how to polish	379

CPSIA information can be obtained
at www.ICGtesting.com
Printed in the USA
BVHW060256231121
622231BV00009B/253